VISUAL CODING AND ADAPTABILITY

Edited by

CHARLES S. HARRIS
BELL LABORATORIES, MURRAY HILL, NEW JERSEY

LAWRENCE ERLBAUM ASSOCIATES, PUBLISHERS
Hillsdale, New Jersey   1980

OPTOMETRY

6419-8807 ✓

Lawrence Erlbaum Associates, Inc., Publishers
365 Broadway
Hillsdale, New Jersey 07642

Library of Congress Cataloging in Publication Data

Main entry under title:

Visual coding and adaptability.

Includes bibliographical references and indexes.
1. Vision. 2. Visual perception.
I. Harris, Charles S.
BF241.V56   152.1'42   79-26604
ISBN 0-89859-016-7

Printed in the United States of America

Contents

Preface

This book is the first integrated presentation of two of the most active areas in present-day visual research. Its inspiration and nucleus were provided by two Optical Society of America symposia, one on the coding of spatial information in the visual system and the other on adaptability of the visual system. Although the two topics might seem, at first sight, only distantly related, they are actually extensively intertwined in contemporary research. Some investigators focus on mechanisms of visual analysis but rely on experimental modification of perception to reveal the nature of the coding; others focus on perceptual modification but look at analytic elements for indications about what it is that gets modified. Likewise, most of the chapters in this book combine, in varying proportions, both themes. Adult human perception is the primary concern, but illuminating data from animal, infant, and neurophysiological studies are also discussed.

In considering visual coding—the spatial analysis and transformation of incoming stimuli—the emphasis is on recently developed concepts of representation in terms of elementary features (such as oriented line segments), or spatial-frequency components (repeated patterns of light and dark). Detailed treatment of spatial-frequency or Fourier analysis has generally been confined to technical papers, often heavily mathematical. Here this fruitful approach is made accessible even to those with little mathematical background. (Indeed, Weisstein's tutorial, "The Joy of Fourier Analysis," provides an entertaining introduction to the basic concepts of spatial-frequency analysis as they are being applied in visual science.)

The research covered in the book runs from very simple tasks and stimuli (detecting spots of light or striped gratings), in Teller's, Graham's, and Robson's chapters, to complex perceptions of faces and objects, in Julesz's and in Weisstein & Harris's. Links between psychophysical data and physiological mechanisms are examined by Teller and by Robson; Julesz and Weisstein & Harris point to links with cognitive psychology as well.

The gamut of perceptual modifications discussed is also wide, encompassing short-, medium-, and long-term changes in perception that result from exposure to unusual visual inputs. Mitchell deals with alterations in physiology and perception that occur early in life as a consequence of atypical visual stimulation (for example, astigmatic blurring of lines in a certain orientation); such alterations may persist into adulthood. Chapters by Held and by Harris deal with changes in adults' perceptions—nonvisual as well as visual—that result from other forms of atypical stimulation (produced by wearing distorting goggles or by staring at colored contours); these changes can also be surprisingly long-lasting after just a few minutes' exposure. Hein relates the conditions for spatial adaptation in the adult to those for the initial establishment of visually guided behavior in the infant animal.

As editor, I have attempted to foster throughout an informal, lively, and lucid style. I have also encouraged the authors to offer a more personal account than is usual in scientific publications, presenting explicitly the underlying assumptions and motivations that so often remain unstated. Although the authors focus on their own research, their varied viewpoints contribute to a broad and timely survey that can stand alone or serve as a foundation for further reading and research. I hope that the result is a book that will be readable and comprehensible for students, yet illuminating and thought-provoking for specialists in many fields, including the psychology and physiology of sensation and perception, ophthalmology and optometry, computer graphics and simulation, and visual communication (transmission, display, and recognition).

ACKNOWLEDGMENTS

My thanks go first of all to the chapter authors for their continuing cooperation and for the time and effort they have devoted to perfecting their contributions. Special thanks are due to Naomi Weisstein and Norma Graham, for providing assistance with chapters other than their own, and to Francine Frome, for her invaluable advice and encouragement.

Credit should be given to Lorrin Riggs, John Lott Brown, Robert Boynton, and Richard Blackwell for organizing the symposia that gave rise to this book, and to Richard Held and Donald H. Kelly for chairing the sessions. The six original talks have been updated and expanded, and four chapters have been added (by Held, Teller, Weisstein, and Weisstein & Harris). A number of helpful suggestions were made by participants in a summer seminar at Bell Laboratories—especially Jean Benisch, Sherryl Berggren, and Barry J. Schwartz.

The generously shared expertise of Lee McMahon, Brian Kernighan, Greg Chesson, Ken Thompson, Dennis Ritchie, and the late Joseph F. Ossanna made it possible to edit and format the text for a Graphic Systems phototypesetter driven by a PDP* 11/70, under the UNIX** operating system.

I want to express my deep appreciation to my family (Judy, Nomi, and Elaine) and to the staff of Lawrence Erlbaum Associates (in particular, Larry Erlbaum) for their indispensable help and patience. I owe a special debt of gratitude to my wife, Judy, for her expert assistance with many phases of the creation of this book.

Charles S. Harris

---

*Trademark of Digital Equipment Corporation.
**Trademark of Bell Laboratories.

The Influence of Early Visual Experience on Visual Perception

Donald E. Mitchell

Dalhousie University

THE NATURE-NURTURE CONTROVERSY IN VISUAL PERCEPTION

The extent to which our ability to perceive the world depends upon visual experiences at an early age has been a controversial issue for centuries. It is an offshoot of the old philosophical debate over how our minds obtained knowledge and ideas. On the one hand, there were the nativists who held that man was born with some knowledge of the world. On the other, there were the empiricists who claimed that all knowledge was derived from sensory experience; to them the infant mind was, as Walls (1951) put it, "a tabula rasa, a blank plate of wax upon which the moving finger of experience wrote the entire eventual content of consciousness and memory." Since much knowledge is acquired through our senses, the question naturally arose as to whether our ability to perceive the world was innate or acquired through experience (for reviews of this debate see Boring, 1942; Walls, 1951; Hochberg, 1962; McCleary, 1970).

New Evidence

Over the years, a number of different experimental approaches have been utilized in an attempt to find out about the origin of our perceptual abilities (Epstein, 1964; Held & Hein, 1967). Data from three different sources have often been cited as relevant: (a) the perceptual abilities of newborn animals and humans, (b) the perceptual abilities of animals and humans totally or selectively deprived of visual input early in life, and (c) the adaptability of the adult an-

1

imal or human to optically distorted visual input. Until recently, data from these sources have not provided an unambiguous resolution of the nature-nurture controversy. For example, even if the adult visual system can adapt to distorted visual input, that does not necessarily imply, as Helmholtz (1925) originally suggested, that the properties of the infant visual system were initially molded by visual experience.

During the last decade, however, a detailed and unequivocal answer to the nature-nurture debate has at last begun to emerge. Recordings of the electrical activity of single neurons in the visual cortex of the cat have clearly demonstrated that their properties are profoundly and permanently influenced by the nature of the cat's visual experience during its first few months of life.

MODIFICATION OF VISUAL NEUROPHYSIOLOGY IN THE CAT

Most cells in the adult cat's visual cortex respond only to quite complex visual stimuli, usually straight (linear) contours such as edges or bars of light with certain precise orientations, moving across the retina through the receptive field of the cell (Hubel & Wiesel, 1962). The orientation of the contour that best activates each cell varies from one neuron to the next, but all orientations are represented approximately equally. The majority of cells respond to identical stimuli imaged in either eye (Hubel & Wiesel, 1962), although there is some variation from cell to cell in what locations in the two eyes give the optimal response to two simultaneous contours (Barlow, Blakemore, & Pettigrew, 1967; Nikara, Bishop, & Pettigrew, 1968). In other words, each cell responds best to binocular contours with a certain horizontal disparity, which has led to the suggestion that such cells may provide the neural basis for stereoscopic vision (Pettigrew, 1972a).

Within the last several years all three of these important properties of cortical neurons—their orientational specificity, binocularity, and disparity specificity—have been shown to be influenced by the animal's early visual experience.

Modification of Binocularity

The first clear demonstration of the powerful effect that early visual experience exerts on the cat's visual cortex was provided by Wiesel and Hubel (1963). They found that the number of neurons that could be activated through either eye was drastically reduced in cats that had had one eye sewn shut for periods of one to four months, starting at the time of normal eye-opening. In these animals nearly all cells could be activated only through the eye that had been open when the animals were young; hardly any could be driven by the eye that had been sewn closed.

More recently, Hubel and Wiesel (1970) have shown that there is a rather short but well-defined period of susceptibility (a *critical period*) for producing this effect. They sutured the lids of the right eye shut in a number of kittens for periods of a few days or weeks early in the animal's life. The kittens were allowed normal binocular vision before the period of monocular deprivation. Immediately after the period of eye closure Hubel and Wiesel recorded from cells in the visual cortex of the left cerebral hemisphere. They found that the proportion of cells that could be influenced through either eye depended on how old the cat was when its right eye was closed. Monocular deprivation imposed before 19 days of age, or after the age of three months, did not significantly reduce the degree of binocularity. However monocular closure for as little as six days during the fourth week of life resulted in a dramatic shift in ocular dominance—as much of a change as that following a full three months of deprivation!

Figure 1 depicts the results of monocular deprivation at various ages. The results are shown in the form of histograms which indicate the number of cells that belong to each of seven ocular dominance groups. Cells in groups 1 and 7 can be influenced only by visual stimuli presented to one eye or the other. Neurons in group 1 can be influenced only through the eye that is contralateral to the recording electrode (the right eye), while those in group 7 respond only to stimuli imaged in the ipsilateral eye (the left). Cells in groups 2 and 3 respond more strongly when stimulated through the contralateral eye while those in groups 5 and 6 are more strongly influenced through the ipsilateral eye. Those in group 4 respond equally to stimulation through either eye.

Clearly, monocular deprivation has an effect in the cat only when imposed during a brief period which begins during the fourth week and ends at the age of three months. As can be seen from Fig. 1, monocular deprivation for only six days in the fourth week can nearly eliminate all binocular neurons. Only one cell out of 37 could be influenced at all through the deprived eye. Similar effects of monocular deprivation are also found in the monkey (Baker, Grigg, & von Noorden, 1974). Although some behavioral evidence suggests that the monkey's period of susceptibility is similar to the cat's (von Noorden, Dowling, & Ferguson, 1970), physiological recording indicates that it extends to 18 months of age (Wiesel, 1975).

The binocularity of cortical cells can be influenced by a number of other experimental maneuvers that disrupt binocular vision early in life. One such procedure is to cover one eye one day, the other the next, and so on. Both eyes receive equal visual exposure, but never simultaneously. When simultaneous binocular vision was prevented in this way, Hubel and Wiesel (1965) found that nearly all cells were monocularly driven, with about the same number driven by each eye.

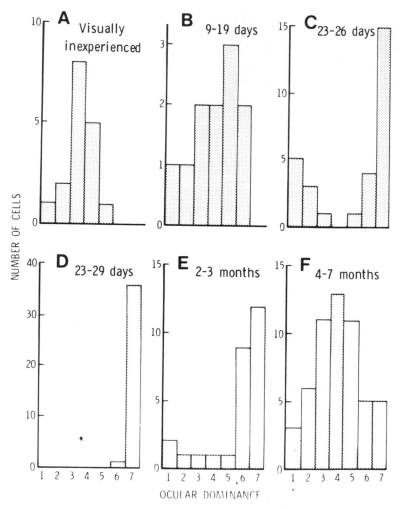

FIG. 1. Critical period for susceptibility to the effect of monocular deprivation. The histograms show the number of cells with various degrees of ocular dominance. All cells were in the left hemispheres of kittens that had their right eyes closed. The upper left histogram gives results for two young (8 and 16 days old) visually inexperienced kittens, while the other histograms (B through F) show the distributions of ocular dominance in cats that had been monocularly deprived during the periods indicated. Group 1 cells were activated only by the right eye; group 2 cells showed a markedly stronger response for the right eye than for the left, while group 3 cells showed only slight right-eye dominance. Group 4 cells were influenced equally by the two eyes. In group 5, the left eye dominated slightly and in group 6 markedly. Group 7 cells could be influenced only by the left eye. (Redrawn from Hubel & Wiesel, 1963, 1970.)

4

A similar result is found if binocular vision is simultaneous but discordant. Such discordance can be imposed in two ways. If a single extraocular eye muscle is cut, one eye will point in a different direction from the other, thereby producing an artificial strabismus (Hubel & Wiesel, 1965). Or very different inputs can be assured by making the kittens wear goggles containing different stimulus patterns for the two eyes (Hirsch & Spinelli, 1970, 1971). Both rearing procedures result in a scarcity of binocular neurons.

Modification of Orientational Specificity

Probably the evidence for modification of the visual cortex that attracted the most attention was provided by the experiments of Hirsch and Spinelli (1970, 1971) and of Blakemore and Cooper (1970) which demonstrated that the orientational selectivity of cortical cells can also be affected by an animal's early visual experience.

Rearing with goggles. Hirsch and Spinelli (1970) fitted young kittens with goggles that presented different visual patterns to the two eyes. One eye saw three vertical stripes, while the other saw three stripes that were horizontal. The goggles were worn for a few hours each day and the rest of the time the kittens were kept in the dark. After the kittens had been reared in this way for between one and three months (they were then between ten and twelve weeks of age), the receptive fields of single neurons in the visual cortex were mapped.

The finding was that not only were most neurons with elongated fields driven by only one eye, but they responded best to contours with orientations that closely matched the orientation of the stripes to which the eye had been previously exposed. (Hirsch and Spinelli also noted a higher than normal proportion of neurons with receptive fields that were not selective for orientation.) Exposure of one eye to vertical contours in early life had so modified the cortex that only vertical or nearly vertical contours could elicit a vigorous response from orientationally selective neurons through that eye.

Rearing in a striped cylinder. An even more clear-cut result was reported by Blakemore and Cooper (1970). They restricted the visual input of two young kittens to stripes of just one orientation, seen with both eyes. The kittens stood on a glass plate mounted halfway up a tall cylinder; on the inside wall were painted stripes of various widths but a single orientation. For one kitten the stripes were vertical, while for the other they were horizontal. The kittens wore a cardboard ruff around their necks, similar to those employed by Hein and Held (1967), to prevent the kittens from seeing their own bodies. Figure 2 shows a photograph of a kitten reared in a similar manner in my labora-

FIG. 2. Photograph of a kitten in a cylinder similar to that used by Blakemore and Cooper (1970) to restrict visual input to contours of a single orientation (in this case vertical).

tory. The two animals spent a few hours each day in the cylinder until they were 5½ months of age; when they were not in the cylinder they were kept in a totally dark room.

When Blakemore and Cooper recorded from the kittens' visual cortices, they found that most neurons responded best to contours having an orientation similar to that of the stripes to which each kitten had been exposed. This can be seen in Fig. 3 which shows the distribution of preferred orientations for a sample of neurons recorded in these two cats. Each line shows the orientation of the contour that is optimal for a particular cell. In contrast to normal cats, where all orientations are about equally represented, neurons from these two kittens show a distinct bias for contours having orientations similar to those of the stripes in their early visual environment. In neither cat were there any

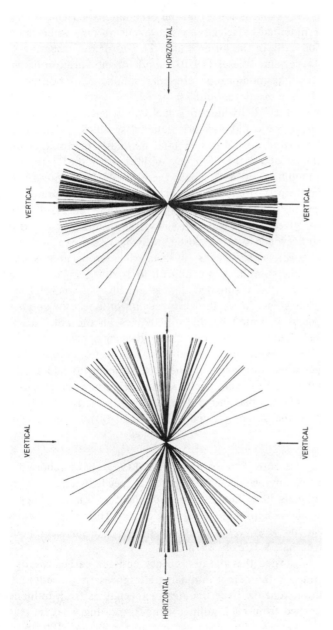

FIG. 3. Optimum contour orientation for neurons in a cat with early exposure only to horizontal stripes (left), or only vertical stripes (right). Each line represents the preferred orientation of one neuron. (From Blakemore & Cooper, 1970.)

7

neurons with preferred orientations within 20° of the orientation perpendicular to that of the stripes they saw early in their lives.

Blakemore (1973, 1974a) has shown that the orientational specificity of cortical neurons can be modified by selective visual exposure only when imposed within a critical period early in the kitten's life. This turns out to be the same critical period that Hubel and Wiesel (1970) found for modification of ocular dominance. Moreover, like modification of ocular dominance, modification of orientational specificity can occur very quickly.

During the summer of 1972, Blakemore and I conducted an experiment to find out just how quickly we could alter orientational specificity (Blakemore & Mitchell, 1973). We reared six kittens in total darkness, except that on or symmetrically distributed about the 28th day of life, when the cortex is extremely sensitive to modification, we exposed them briefly (1, 3, 6, 18, 27, or 33 hours) to vertical stripes. Figure 4 shows the results of recordings made when the kittens were six weeks old. As in Fig. 3, each line represents the optimal orientation for a given cell. Figure 4A shows the results obtained from a kitten raised with both eyelids sutured closed, with no visual exposure at all, until the recording session at six weeks of age. All neurons in this animal responded poorly to visual stimuli. It was difficult to establish any orientational specificity, since each neuron responded almost equally (but poorly) to all orientations. Most cells showed only the slightest hint of a bias for one particular orientation which is indicated by the dotted lines on the polar diagram. All cells in this animal would also respond to small moving spots.

However, as Fig. 4B shows, in a kitten that was given just one hour of exposure to vertical stripes after four weeks in the dark, all neurons had a definite orientational preference. Moreover, the one-hour exposure to stripes was sufficient to produce a marked bias in the distribution of preferred orientations. Additional exposure to the stripes yielded only a small further refinement in orientational selectivity.

Discrepant findings. Recently Stryker and Sherk (1975) have reported that they were unable to find any bias in the orientational specificity of cortical neurons after rearing animals in cylinders similar to those of Fig. 2. They did, however, observe a bias when they used goggles like Hirsch and Spinelli's (1970) to insure that the only visual input was stripes of a single orientation (Stryker, Sherk, Leventhal, & Hirsch, 1978).

Stryker and Sherk suggested that the discrepancy between earlier results and their own may be due to three precautionary differences in procedure they adopted. In order to prevent the experimenter's expectations from influencing the results, they recorded from each animal without knowing what its rearing history was. They advanced the electrode in large steps of 100 microns between each recording site so as to provide a more extensive sample of cortical cells. Finally, they had a computer plot all receptive fields to provide a greater degree of objectivity than is possible when plotting by hand. Important

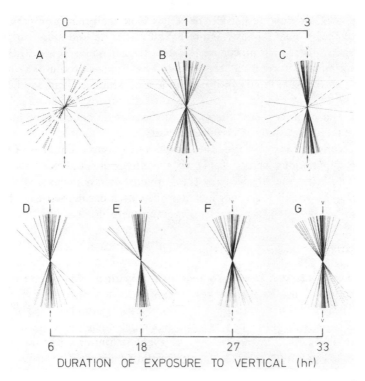

FIG. 4. Polar histograms showing the optimum orientations of about 40 neurons recorded in each of six kittens (B to G) who had been exposed to vertical stripes for 1, 3, 6, 18, 27, and 33 hours on or around the 28th day of life. The polar histogram drawn with dashed lines (A) shows the vague orientation preference of a number of neurons recorded from a kitten that had had both eyes sutured shut throughout its life. (Reproduced from Blakemore & Mitchell, 1973.)

as these procedural modifications were, it is nevertheless unlikely that they actually account for the discrepancy with the earlier results and later replications (Freeman & Pettigrew, 1973; Mize & Murphy, 1973; Flood & Coleman, 1979; Gordon, Presson, Packwood, & Scheer, 1979). Impressive orientational biases *have* been found in cats that we reared in much the same way as Blakemore and Cooper (1970) and then sent for receptive-field analysis to Jack Pettigrew, who employed precautions much like Stryker and Sherk's. The results from one of these cats are shown in Fig. 9.

Basically, the current disagreements boil down to two points. The first concerns the reliability of two different rearing procedures. All groups agree that a bias in the orientational specificity of neurons can be observed when goggles insure that visual input indeed consists of contours of only one orientation. Although using a striped cylinder instead of goggles may also restrict input, an animal in a cylinder is much more likely to receive unplanned stimulation by tilting its head, or lying on its side, or simply looking at the rims at the top and bottom of the cylinder. Thus it is not too surprising to find more variability in results when this rearing procedure is used. In fact Blakemore (1977) reports that of six animals recently reared in cylinders, four showed a bias consistent with their early visual input, one showed no bias whatever, and one had a bias in the opposite direction.

The second point concerns the origin of the shift in orientational specificity. A bias in the distribution of preferred orientations could arise in either of two ways as a consequence of rearing in contours of a single orientation. Cells with preferred orientations perpendicular to the environmental one could either change their orientational specificity (recruitment) or else they could simply die (atrophy). As yet there is insufficient evidence to decide between these hypotheses.

Modification of Binocular Disparity

The responses of cortical cells to binocular disparity, like their responses to orientation, have also been shown to depend on the animal's early visual input. Shlaer (1971) had kittens wear vertical prisms during the first four months of life. The prism in front of one eye was base up and the one for the other eye was base down, thereby displacing one eye's image upward and the other downward. The result was a substantial vertical disparity (up to 2°) between the two retinal images. When Shlaer later tested the responses of cortical cells, he found that the distribution of vertical disparities required for optimal excitation was shifted, compared to a normally raised cat's distribution. The shift was in the same direction as the vertical disparity induced by the prisms worn early in life.

Production of Novel Properties

If the major properties of cortical neurons can be so strongly influenced by early visual input, would it be possible to produce neurons with completely novel properties by imposing suitably novel visual inputs early in life? Some recent evidence suggests that this can in fact be done under certain conditions.

Cynader, Berman, and Hein (1973) raised kittens in a stroboscopically illuminated environment. The pulses of light were so brief that the kittens never experienced an optical image moving on their retinas. In marked contrast to neurons in normal cats, more than half of the neurons in these strobe-reared animals responded to diffuse stroboscopic illumination of the whole visual field; there were even some neurons (21%) for which this was the optimal stimulus.

A yet more amazing result has been reported by Pettigrew and Freeman (1973), who reared two kittens in an environment resembling a small planetarium. The visual environment was devoid of straight lines or edges and consisted solely of small spots of light. Most neurons in these animals were later found to respond best to small spots of light moving within an irregularly shaped region of the retina that was much larger than the diameter of the spot that best excited the cell. The optimal stimuli for neurons in the normal cortex, linear contours such as edges or bars of light, proved to be quite ineffective as stimuli for these cells. A similar result was produced when Van Sluyters and Blakemore (1973) limited the visual environment of young kittens to patterns of randomly distributed dots.

Cortical Cells in the Newborn

These experiments imply that some neurons with properties unlike those normally found can be produced by imposing very abnormal visual input early in life. This suggests that any genetic predisposition for processing of linear contours may not be strong enough to keep neuronal connections from changing to match more closely prominent features of early visual inputs.

Although Hubel and Wiesel (1963) originally reported that some cortical neurons in newborn, visually inexperienced kittens were similar to those found in the adult cortex, more recently this has been questioned. Several investigators have reported that the proportion of cells with orientational specificity comparable to that observed in the adult is quite low (Barlow & Pettigrew, 1971; Pettigrew, 1974; Blakemore & Van Sluyters, 1975; Buisseret & Imbert, 1975), although Sherk and Stryker (1976) report a very high proportion (90 of 98 cells). All groups agree that the responses of cells in the newborn are weaker and habituate more rapidly than in the adult. In addition, neurons in newborn kittens respond to an extremely broad range of binocular disparities (Pettigrew, 1972b, 1974).

Thus, there are very clear differences between a newborn's neurons and those in the adult. Nevertheless, in some respects they are similar. For example, the ocular dominance distribution of neurons in the newborn's cortex is virtually identical to that seen in the adult. Certainly the receptive fields of cortical cells occupy approximately the same positions on the retina at birth as they do later in life. There is also evidence that selectivity for specific directions of motion may be present at birth in some cortical neurons (Barlow & Pettigrew, 1971).

The indications that the responses of a newborn kitten's cortical neurons are partially unspecified is consistent with the fact that the number of synaptic connections per neuron at birth is only 1.5% of the number found in the adult (Cragg, 1972). In fact, there is a dramatic rise in the number of synapses per neuron in the kitten's visual cortex between the 7th and 36th days of life—just the period when the kitten cortex is so susceptible to environmental modification.

The somewhat cloudy picture that one obtains from the many reports on cortical cells in the newborn kitten arises in part because of a corresponding cloudiness in the optics of the kitten eye. For the first few weeks of life the kitten's lens is surrounded by a membrane that doesn't disappear completely until the fourth week. In the monkey, however, there is no such impediment to sharp images early in life, so the state of cortical neurons can be examined without contamination. Present evidence suggests that the visual response characteristics of cells in the newborn monkey's visual cortex are more selective than in the newborn kitten (Wiesel & Hubel, 1974), although even such a fundamental organization as ocular dominance columns in the cortex is not completed until six weeks after birth (Rakic, 1976).

Permanence of the Effects of Early Visual Exposure

There is good evidence that many of the effects of early selective visual exposure are permanent. The most dramatic consequences of early monocular deprivation or selective pattern deprivation remain virtually unaffected by as much as five years of normal visual input, if the normal input starts after the age of four months (Hubel & Wiesel, 1970; Pettigrew, Olsen, & Hirsch, 1973).

Both the empiricist and the nativist viewpoints in the old nature-nurture controversy receive some support from these varied animal studies. Many properties of cortical cells, such as their topographic organization and binocularity, are genetically specified. Nevertheless experience is necessary since only after exposure to visual stimulation do these cells acquire their final highly specific properties. In the absence of any visual input this specificity either is not maintained or fails to develop (Blakemore & Van Sluyters, 1975; Buisseret & Imbert, 1976; Frégnac & Imbert, 1978).

INFLUENCE OF EARLY VISUAL EXPERIENCE
ON PERCEPTION IN THE CAT

The evidence that early visual input permanently influences the physiological responses of cortical neurons suggested to me that *perceptual* capabilities might be influenced similarly. For example, a cat reared in an environment containing only vertical stripes might not see horizontal contours as well as vertical contours later in life.

Several years ago, Darwin Muir and I began to measure the perceptual capacities of adult cats that had been reared in an environment containing contours with only one orientation (Muir & Mitchell, 1973, 1975; Muir, 1974). As kittens, most of the cats had been exposed to light for several hours each day while inside a cylinder like the one shown in Fig. 2. Some kittens viewed the inside of a cylinder that had only vertical stripes; for others, the stripes were horizontal. The kittens wore a cardboard ruff around their necks in order to prevent them from seeing their own bodies and were free to move about within the cylinder. When not in the cylinder they were kept in a totally dark room. A third group of kittens were reared in a slightly different fashion, with diagonal stripes inside the cylinder (Fig. 5). Before being removed from the dark, they were firmly wrapped in cloth and restrained within a box. The box was then positioned so that it permitted the kitten's head to be inserted through an opening in the cylinder as illustrated in Fig. 5. This procedure was designed to reduce the extent of head and body rotations, so that the stripes would remain diagonal on the kitten's retinas. The cycle of four hours in the cylinder and twenty hours in darkness was continued for four to six months for all animals, after which they were placed in a normally illuminated environment.

When brought into light, all cats shared the dramatic deficits described by Blakemore and Cooper (1970). At first they appeared blind. They would not respond at all to visual stimuli and repeatedly bumped into objects. Although optokinetic nystagmus (the unconscious eye movements that occur when looking at a slowly moving repetitive pattern of stripes) could be elicited by both

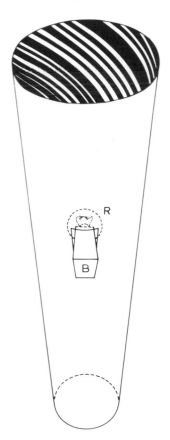

FIG. 5. Apparatus used to restrict the visual input of one kitten, OL-1, to stripes tilted obliquely to the left.

horizontal and vertical moving stripes, we found that visual placing responses, tracking of slowly moving objects, and startle responses to sudden visual presentations were all absent.

Most deficits disappeared with about 16 to 20 hours of opportunity to move about in a normal visual environment. However, one response remained deficient for several weeks: When a rod was slowly moved in front of the cats they would follow it or strike at it only if it was held in a certain orientation— the same orientation as the stripes they had viewed early in life. When the rod was rotated 90° from that familiar orientation, the animals stopped responding to it or struck at it only in a very hesitant fashion. Some cats developed certain strategies in this situation so that the retinal image took on the preferred orientation. Many of the cats would look toward the end of the rod or else rotate their heads through 90° when the rod was held perpendicular to the orientation of the stripes they saw early in life. Eventually, however, even these deficits disappeared.

Measuring the Perceptual Deficit

After the animals had been in normal visual surroundings for a few months we measured their ability to see stripes with different orientations, using operant techniques developed by Berkley (1970). The apparatus employed for these measurements is illustrated in Fig. 6. Basically, the animal's task was to

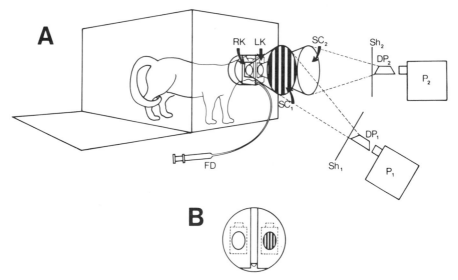

FIG. 6. A. The apparatus employed for testing the ability of the cat to resolve gratings of different orientations. See text for details. B. The discriminative stimuli as seen by the cat. (From Muir & Mitchell, 1975.)

choose between a striped and a blank field which had the same average luminance. The striped field was a square-wave grating consisting of black and white stripes of equal width. The cat was placed in a box with a short cylindrical tube at one end. When the cat placed its head into the tube it could look through transparent plates, RK and LK, at the two stimulus fields. The stimuli were projected onto two screens, SC_1 and SC_2, situated 30 centimeters behind the transparent plates. Dove prisms, DP_1 and DP_2, in front of the projectors, P_1 and P_2, were used to change the orientation of the projected stripes. Shutters, Sh_1 and Sh_2, were used to time the stimulus presentations. The side on which the striped grating was projected was changed randomly from trial to trial.

The cat was trained to press its nose against the transparent plate through which the stripes were visible, by rewarding it with beef baby food every time it pressed the correct plate. If it chose the side without stripes, the next trial was delayed. Typically, each day 80 trials were given with stripes with a particular spacing but with two different orientations. After we judged that the cat was performing about equally well on a number of successive days we decreased the width of the lines and the distance between them, thereby increasing the spatial frequency of the grating (the number of dark or light stripes per degree of visual angle). This process was continued with finer and finer gratings until the cat's performance fell to chance.

A comparison of Figs. 7 and 8 reveals the effects of selective visual experience on perception. Figure 7 shows the performance of a normal cat on this task. The open and closed circles and squares show the proportion of correct responses to gratings of four different orientations. Clearly orientation had no

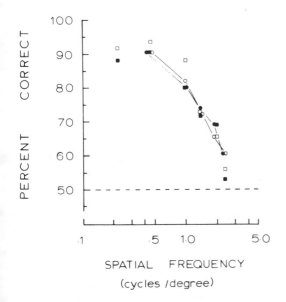

FIG. 7. The percentage of correct responses made by a normally reared cat when choosing between stripes and a blank field with the same average luminance. Results are shown for four stripe orientations: vertical (o), horizontal (●), 45° (□), and 135° (■).

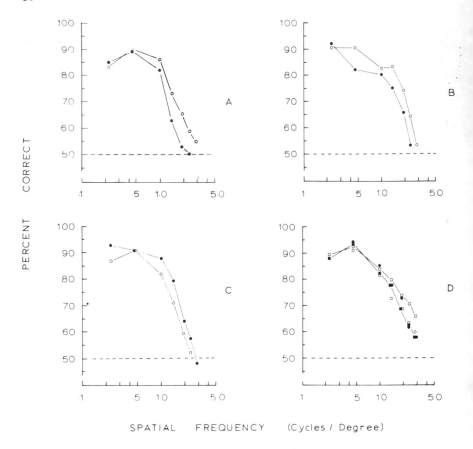

SPATIAL   FREQUENCY   (Cycles / Degree)

FIG. 8. Performance of four selectively deprived cats when choosing between stripes and a blank field with the same average luminance. Orientation of test stripes: vertical (O), horizontal (●), 45° (□), and 135° (■). A. Results for a cat (V20) that saw only vertical stripes from age three weeks to five weeks. B and C. Results for two cats (V2 and H1) reared in vertical and horizontal stripes respectively from three weeks to five months of age. D. Results for a cat (OL-1 of Fig. 5) that saw only diagonal stripes oriented at 135° from day 45 to day 110.

systematic effect on visibility since the percentage of correct responses to gratings of different spatial frequencies was about the same for all four orientations. Figure 8 shows the results obtained from four selectively exposed cats: two exposed only to vertical stripes, one to horizontal, and the last to diagonal stripes tilted 45° counterclockwise (135°). In contrast to the normal cats, such animals did not perform equally well for all test orientations. In all cases they did best when the gratings had the same orientation as the stripes of their early visual environment. Performance with this favored orientation was nearly as good as that of the normal cat. However, performance with gratings perpendicular to the favored orientation was considerably worse.

To obtain a quantitative estimate of the deficit, we can consider the spatial frequency at which the animal's performance fell to chance. Estimates of visual acuity obtained in this manner for the four selectively deprived cats represented in Fig. 8 are given in Table 1. (Actually we obtained the estimates in a somewhat more complicated manner using signal detection theory.)

The deficit for gratings at right angles to stripes in the animal's early visual environment can be quite large. In one case (cat OL-1, Fig. 8D) the visual acuity for oblique gratings at 45° was reduced by nearly a factor of two (0.8 octaves) from that for gratings at 135°. These results complement those obtained by Hirsch (1972). His selectively deprived cats showed a deficit in their ability to discriminate the orientation of lines perpendicular to the contours they saw early in life. (I should mention that the particular behavioral technique we used yielded estimates of visual acuity that are slightly lower than those obtained with other methods [Berkley & Watkins, 1973; Campbell, Maffei, & Piccolino, 1973]. Since we were concerned only with finding a difference between acuities for gratings of different orientations, we did not at that time try to find techniques and conditions that would optimize visual acuity. Subsequently we have developed a behavioral technique for quickly measuring the perceptual capabilities of kittens which yields acuities that are considerably better than these [Mitchell, Giffin, & Timney, 1977].)

Clearly these results indicate that selectively deprived cats see contours that they were exposed to early in life better than contours of other orientations. Such results supplement those from studies of cortical neurons by demonstrating that the early visual input affects the adult animal's perceptual abilities.

Table 1

Estimates of the visual acuity for gratings of different orientations measured in four selectively deprived cats. Also listed are the deficits, expressed in octaves, in the acuities for gratings perpendicular to the stripes that were present in the animal's early visual environment.

Cat	Acuity (cycles/degree)				Deficit (octaves)
	Grating Orientation				
	0°	45°	90°	135°	
V_{20}	1.7		3.0		0.87
V_{20}	2.3*		4.0*		0.85*
V_2	2.5		3.2		0.44
H_1	2.75		2.35		
OL−1		3.7		5.8	0.7

*Values obtained on a second replication when the animal was punished (with weak electric shock applied to the feet) for incorrect responses.

As with the physiological deficits, there is strong evidence that the perceptual deficits that follow early selective visual deprivation are permanent. We have repeatedly tested these cats for more than four years and have observed no sign of improvement in their performance with gratings perpendicular to the stripes they saw as kittens.

Relation of Perceptual to Physiological Deficits

Do the perceptual difficulties of these cats result from changes induced in visual cortical neurons by their abnormal early visual experience? Darwin Muir and I were convinced that they do, and we now have empirical support for our convictions. When Jack Pettigrew visited Halifax late in 1972 he mentioned that early selective visual exposure has such a striking effect on cortical neurons that he thought he could deduce what sort of early visual experience an animal had had simply by recording from 50 or so cortical neurons. We were very impressed with Pettigrew's claim and suggested that we could put it to the test by sending him one of our cats without letting him know about its early visual experience. He agreed, so we shipped cat OL-1 (Fig. 8) by air express to California. Although the cat was lost for a while in a snowstorm, it eventually reached Berkeley. Five days later, Pettigrew phoned us and guessed correctly that OL-1 had seen contours tipped obliquely to the left early in its life. Figure 9 shows a tally of the preferred orientations of 49 units recorded from the visual cortex of this animal (Blasdel, Mitchell, Muir, & Pettigrew, 1977). There is a pronounced clustering of units around 135°, which is the orientation of the stripes inside the cylinder in which the cat had been reared. We were so impressed by this performance of the physiologists that we agreed to send them four more animals. They were equally successful at guessing the early visual environment of these cats as the first one we sent (Blasdel, Mitchell, Muir, & Pettigrew, 1977).

There is yet stronger evidence linking the perceptual deficits in selectively deprived cats to anomalies in cortical neurons: The period of susceptibility of the visual cortex to environmental modification is identical to that for producing a permanent perceptual deficit. This critical period begins during the fourth week of a kitten's life and ends at three months for both physiological (Blakemore, 1974a) and behavioral modifications (Muir, 1974).

Other studies have shown that, like selective exposure to contours of a single orientation, early total monocular deprivation also leads to deficits in performance on visual tasks in both cats (Ganz & Fitch, 1968; Dews & Wiesel, 1970; Giffin & Mitchell, 1978) and monkeys (von Noorden, 1973; von Noorden, Dowling, & Ferguson, 1970). Animals that had one eye kept closed throughout early life have normal vision in the eye that received normal visual input, but much poorer vision in the eye that was closed. Again, the perceptual shortcoming parallels the scarcity of cortical neurons activated by the eye that was closed.

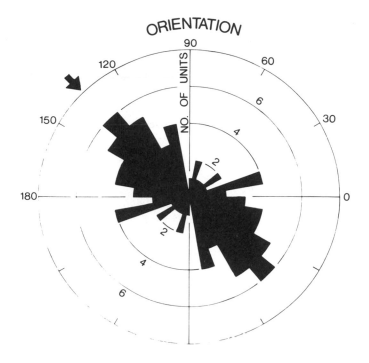

FIG. 9. Polar histogram showing the optimum orientations of 49 neurons recorded from a cat (OL-1) reared in stripes oriented at 135° from day 45 to the 110th day of life.

MODIFICATION OF VISION IN HUMAN BEINGS: ACUITY

The studies discussed above show that in cats and monkeys both the properties of cortical neurons and the animal's perceptual capabilities are strongly influenced by the nature of the early visual input. This naturally prompts the question: Are neural connections in the human visual cortex, and hence our own perceptual abilities, also molded by early visual input? A number of experiments conducted over the last few years provide strong evidence that the properties of neurons in the human visual cortex are indeed permanently influenced by early visual experience.

In animals, the key to revealing the profound and permanent influence of early visual inputs was the use of a very abnormal visual environment. Of course, we cannot alter and restrict a human baby's visual environment in the same drastic way. Nevertheless, there are some clinical conditions that arise naturally and that, to some degree, mimic the unusual visual inputs used in experiments on cats. This thought first occurred to me several years ago during the course of an experiment on human visual acuity.

Initial Findings

In 1966 while I was a graduate student at the University of California at Berkeley, I conducted an experiment with Ralph Freeman and Gerald Westheimer on the effect of orientation on visual acuity. It had been known for nearly 40 years that diagonal lines are harder to see than either vertical or horizontal lines. However, at the time of our experiment it was not known for certain whether the lower acuity for oblique contours was merely the result of some optical property of the eyes, or instead reflected an interesting neural characteristic of the visual system (Emsley, 1925; Taylor, 1963).

In order to find out whether the poorer visibility of diagonals stems from optical or neural limitations, we decided to try using a technique that, in effect, bypasses the eye's optics. We produced a grating of interference fringes directly on the retina, the result of interference between light waves from two coherent point sources imaged in the plane of the pupil. Essentially, since the grating consisted of light and dark stripes formed by interference occurring within the eye itself, both the spacing and contrast were unaffected by the focussing mechanism of the eye (Le Grand, 1937; Westheimer, 1960; Campbell & Green, 1965; Campbell, Kulikowski, & Levinson, 1966). Using this testing technique we found that for all our normal subjects oblique interference fringes were less visible than vertical or horizontal fringes—the same finding as with ordinary lines imaged by the eye's optics. Since our stimuli could not have been affected by the optics of the eye, we could confidently conclude that the orientational variations in acuity must be of neural origin (Mitchell, Freeman, & Westheimer, 1967).

Ralph Freeman and I both served as subjects in this study. We were amazed to find that our data were very different from all the other subjects'. I was surprisingly bad at seeing horizontal interference fringes (almost as bad as at seeing oblique ones), while Ralph had some difficulty seeing vertical fringes. Of course, we already knew that our eyes are not strictly normal, since we both have astigmatism: Ralph's is the type that blurs vertical contours; mine blurs horizontal ones. But our measurement technique was specifically chosen to *eliminate* any such effects of the eye's optics. The horizontal interference fringes were just as sharp and had just the same contrast on my retina as the vertical ones. Nevertheless, I saw the horizontal fringes less well than the vertical ones.

Why was my acuity for horizontal interference fringes so poor? A clue was provided by the fact that the variations in acuity measured by this method, unaffected by the eye's optics, followed the same pattern as found with ordinary viewing without glasses, when of course my eye is optically uncorrected. Assuming that the astigmatism was present early in my life, then it seemed possible to me that my visual system had been permanently modified by the early abnormal visual experience resulting from the uncorrected astigmatism.

The notion that the visual system might be molded by its early visual input was a radical one then, but unfortunately we were unable to pursue the idea any further at that time. When the papers on kittens by Hirsch and Spinelli and by Blakemore and Cooper appeared four years later, I realized how important our earlier observations were. If they could be verified with other astigmats they would constitute strong evidence for early environmental modification of the *human* visual system. The later experiments that I will now describe have fully confirmed our earlier observations.

The Nature of Astigmatism

Astigmatism is an optical defect in which the cornea, instead of being spherical, is less curved in one direction than in others. The toroidal shape brings contours with one orientation into clearer focus than others. The meridians of maximum and minimum curvature (which are referred to as the axes of the astigmatism) are at right angles to one another. In most cases of astigmatism, for unknown reasons, the axes are close to vertical and horizontal. An astigmatic optical system does not form an image of a point as a point, but rather as two focal lines parallel to the meridians of maximum and minimum curvature. This is illustrated in Fig. 10 which shows what happens to light from a distant point source after it passes through an astigmatic optical system like that of the eye. After refraction, wave fronts parallel to the vertical meridian V-V′ converge to an axial focus at F_V and form there a horizontal focal line. Similarly, wave fronts parallel to the horizontal meridian H-H′ converge to form a verti-

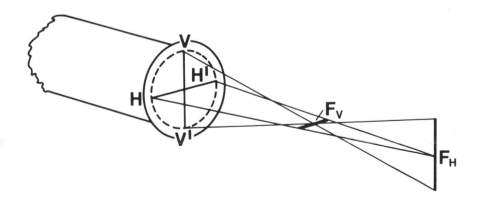

FIG. 10. Image formation by an astigmatic optical system with positive power in both principal meridians which in this case are vertical and horizontal. (From Mitchell, Freeman, Millodot, & Haegerstrom, 1973.)

cal focal line at F_H. Distant linear contours that are horizontal will be imaged sharply at F_V while distant vertical contours will be imaged at F_H.

In general, contours parallel to the focal line that lies closest to the retina will be seen more clearly than contours of other orientations. Since in most cases of astigmatism the axes are vertical and horizontal, most astigmatic subjects see contours of one of these two orientations as clearest while contours of the perpendicular orientation appear blurred. The photographs in Fig. 11 mim-

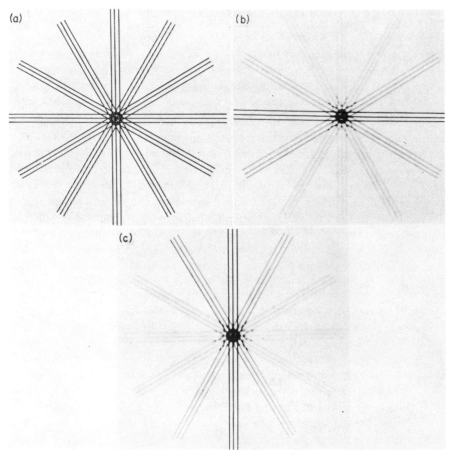

FIG. 11. Photographs that mimic the appearance of objects to an astigmat. (a) the object consisting of a clockface of lines of different orientations as seen by an eye free of any refractive error. In (b) and (c) are shown the appearance of this object to an astigmatic eye that was emmetropic in either the vertical and horizontal meridians respectively. Lines parallel to the emmetropic meridian are blurred, however contours parallel to the most defocussed meridian are sharp. (From Mitchell, Freeman, Millodot, & Haegerstrom, 1973.)

ic the appearance of lines with different orientations to subjects with astigmatism in which the axes are vertical and horizontal. When the horizontal focal line is focussed on the retina, contours of this orientation are seen clearly, but vertical ones are blurred (Fig. 11B). The reverse is true in cases where the vertical focal line is coincident with the retina (Fig. 11C). Note that in both cases oblique contours are blurred.

Astigmats' Early Visual Inputs

A person born with astigmatism receives early visual inputs reminiscent of those imposed on the kittens in Blakemore and Cooper's (1970) study; some of their kittens saw no horizontal contours, some astigmatic humans see only blurred ones. In fact, Freeman and Pettigrew (1973) have demonstrated in a number of kittens who were reared wearing cylindrical lenses, thus artificially creating astigmatism, that such partial selective deprivation can modify the distribution of preferred orientations of cortical neurons. Now, if neural connections in the human visual system are also influenced by early visual experience, then the astigmat's visual system may not develop equally in its capacity to deal with contours of different orientations because of the unequal sharpness of the early visual input.

If the human's visual system, like the cat's, is permanently altered by abnormal early inputs, then adult astigmats might show large differences in their ability to see contours of different orientations even after their eyes' optical error is fully corrected by glasses. Of course, this argument presupposes that the astigmatism is present at or near birth and remains uncorrected for a sufficiently long time. In fact, clinical data on this point are not strong but certainly in cases of high astigmatism there is good evidence that the condition is present shortly after birth and remains relatively unchanged throughout life (Hirsch, 1963; Duke-Elder, 1969).

Throughout this discussion of the nature of astigmatism the effects of changes of accommodation have been ignored. Clearly in many cases of astigmatism, particularly those where one or both focal lines lie behind the retina when the eye is in its unaccommodated state, contours parallel to either focal line could be imaged sharply by altering the state of accommodation of the eye. While this may occur on many occasions, recent measurements of accommodative responses show that most adult astigmats do not usually freely change their accommodation in this way. On the contrary, these measurements show that they usually preferentially accommodate for contours of one particular orientation, usually those parallel to the focal line that lies closest to the retina (Mitchell, Freeman, Millodot, & Haegerstrom, 1973; Freeman, 1975). As a result, contours of this orientation are seen clearer more frequently than all others. Thus, if this also happens *early* in life, the visual input of even these astigmats would be abnormal.

Deficits in Acuity

To find out whether the human visual system is modified by its early input, I collaborated with Michel Millodot and again with Ralph Freeman at the optometry schools at the Université de Montréal and the University of California at Berkeley, respectively. Through the optometry clinics at these schools and through the help of a local optometrist, Dr. Ralph Rosere in Halifax, we found a large number of astigmats and carefully measured their ability to see gratings of different orientations after full and careful correction of their optical deficits (Freeman, Mitchell, & Millodot, 1972; Mitchell, Freeman, Millodot, & Haegerstrom, 1973). Their results were compared with similar data obtained from a smaller sample of subjects with normal vision.

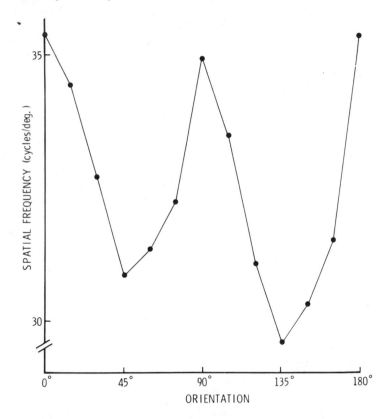

FIG. 12. Orientation differences in grating acuity for a typical normal (emmetropic) subject. The gratings had a sinusoidal luminance profile, a contrast of 0.6, and a mean luminance of 170 candelas/meter^2. The subject adjusted the spatial frequency of the gratings starting from a frequency beyond which they could be resolved until they were just visible. Each point represents the mean of six settings.

There is a general consensus that normal (emmetropic) subjects show nearly equal acuity for vertical and horizontal gratings (Emsley, 1925; Higgins & Stultz, 1948, 1950; Leibowitz, 1953; Campbell, Kulikowski, & Levinson, 1966). To obtain an estimate of the range of differences in acuity for vertical and horizontal gratings in the population, we took measurements on ten normal subjects. Confirming the earlier studies, we found that the acuities for vertical and horizontal gratings were invariably nearly equal but the ability to resolve oblique gratings was always less. Figure 12 shows cutoff spatial frequencies (the maximum number of cycles of the grating per degree of visual angle that can be resolved) in a typical normal subject. The conditions of the experiment are given in the figure legend. The figure shows that the bars of the grating had to be farther apart to be seen as separate when oblique than when horizontal (0°) or vertical (90°). While the acuities for horizontal and vertical gratings were almost equal, there was a decrement in acuity of about 5 cycles/degree for oblique gratings.

The results for astigmatic subjects were in striking contrast to those for normal subjects. Whereas normal subjects were equally good at seeing vertical and horizontal lines, many astigmatic subjects showed large differences between their acuities for vertical and horizontal gratings, even after the optical abnormality of their eyes was fully corrected by appropriate lenses. Figure 13 shows results from three astigmats who were substantially worse at seeing vertical gratings. The filled and open circles represent data from the right and left eye respectively. The schematic drawings of eyeballs portray for each subject the locations of the two focal lines when the eye is not optically corrected and is accommodated for infinity. In these three subjects, the horizontal focal line lies closest to the retina and so without glasses these subjects see horizontal contours clearly while vertical ones appear blurred. Thus the lower acuity for vertical contours when these subjects' optical error is fully corrected matches their lower acuity for verticals when their vision is uncorrected.

Typical results for two subjects who performed more poorly with horizontal gratings are shown in Fig. 14. Again, the difference in acuity for vertical and horizontal gratings measured with the optics fully corrected matches the difference in clarity of these two orientations when seen with the naked eye.

For some astigmats, the difference in the acuities for vertical and horizontal gratings was huge: Lines of one orientation had to be *twice* as far apart as lines of another orientation in order to be equally visible. (See, for example, A.C. and H.F. in Fig. 13 and R.B. in Fig. 14.) This is a difference of one octave, a factor of two in spatial frequency.

More recently, we have confirmed these findings with a somewhat different kind of measurement. In Figs. 13 and 14 we showed how closely lines could be spaced and still be resolvable, when light-dark contrast remained constant. We get similar results if we ask instead how low contrast can be and still permit visual resolution of gratings with a given spacing. Figure 15 shows the results

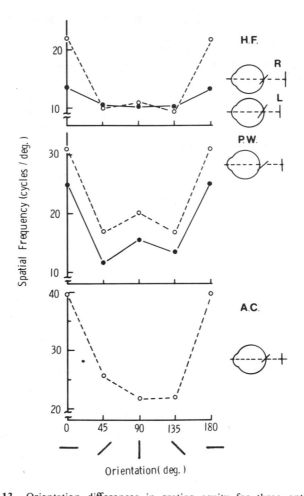

FIG. 13. Orientation differences in grating acuity for three optically corrected astigmats. Open and closed circles plot the mean of five measurements made with the left and right eyes, respectively. The measurements for H.F. and P.W. were made with gratings having a sinusoidal luminance profile (sinusoidal gratings), at a luminance of 10 candelas/meter^2 and a contrast of 0.7, while those for A.C. were made with gratings having a rectilinear luminance profile (square-wave gratings) at a luminance of 50 candelas/meter^2. An eye is drawn adjacent to each curve to show the dispositions of the two focal lines with respect to the retina when the eye is optically uncorrected and unaccommodated. Note that for all subjects vertical contours are most defocussed under these conditions. The refractive errors were: H.F. R. +4.00 sph, cyl −4.25 axis 17°; L. +2.75 sph, cyl −4.25 axis 2°. P.W. R. +5.25 sph, cyl −4.00 axis 5°; L. +5.75 sph, cyl −4.75 axis 18°. A.C. L. +4.50 sph, cyl −5.00 axis 180°. By way of comparison, the mean acuity of *normal* subjects for horizontal and vertical gratings with these stimuli were 43 cycles/degree and 31.3 cycles/degree for the square wave and sinusoidal gratings, respectively. (From Mitchell, Freeman, Millodot, & Haegerstrom, 1973.)

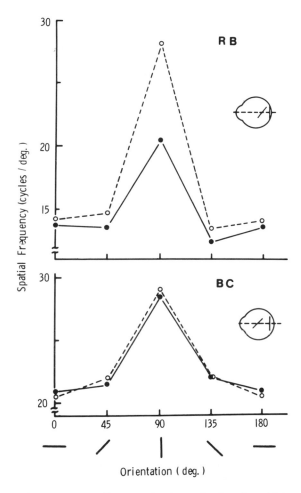

FIG. 14. Orientational differences in the acuity for sinusoidal gratings measured on two optically corrected astigmats who showed a marked reduction in acuity for horizontal gratings. Open and closed circles plot the mean of five measurements made with the left and right eyes respectively. Note that for both subjects horizontal contours are the most defocussed when the eye is uncorrected. The refractive errors were: R.B. R. −0.25 sph, cyl −3.50 axis 177°; L. −0.50 sph, cyl −4.00 axis 7°. B.C. R. −2.00 sph, cyl −4.25 axis 2°; L. −1.00 sph, cyl −4.50 axis 2°. (From Mitchell, Freeman, Millodot, & Haegerstrom, 1973.)

of such measurements made on myself and one other astigmat for gratings of several different spatial frequencies (Mitchell & Wilkinson, 1974). Even with spatial frequencies as low as 1.17 cycles/degree, horizontal gratings were harder to see than vertical ones: The modulation sensitivity (the reciprocal of the threshold contrast) for horizontal gratings was lower than that for vertical.

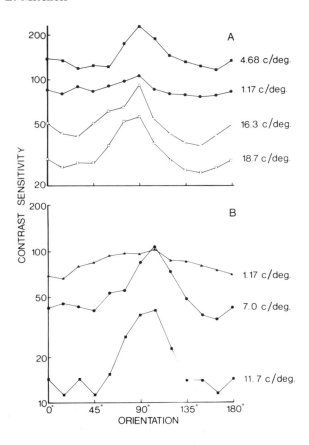

FIG. 15. Orientation differences in the modulation sensitivities (the reciprocal of the threshold contrast) for sinusoidal gratings measured on two fully corrected astigmats. The gratings had a luminance of 170 candelas/meter^2 and were viewed through 3 millimeter artificial pupils. A. Results obtained from the right eye of D.E.M. on gratings having the spatial frequencies indicated. B. The results of similar measurements made on the left eye of A.M. (From Mitchell & Wilkinson, 1974.)

These differences in modulation sensitivity became progressively greater with increasing spatial frequency.

Orientational variations in acuity exist not only in the central fovea but in the peripheral retina as well. This can be seen from Fig. 16 which shows the results of measurements of my acuity for horizontal, vertical and oblique gratings at a number of different retinal locations in my right eye. The reduced acuity for horizontal and oblique gratings persisted even 16° from the fovea.

After our first extensive study (Mitchell, Freeman, Millodot, & Haegerstrom, 1973) was completed, we carefully searched the literature to see wheth-

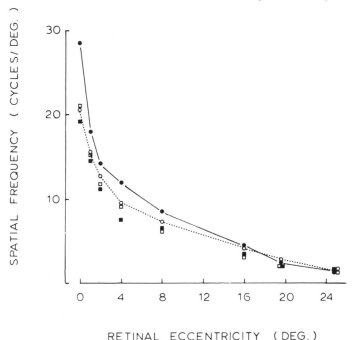

FIG. 16. The change with eccentricity from the fovea of the acuity for vertical (O), horizontal (●), 45° oblique (□), and 135° oblique (■) gratings. Appropriate lenses were added to offset changes in the refractive state due to spherical aberration at each retinal location. The gratings filled a circular field subtending 2.5°, had a luminance of 3 candelas/meter² and were flashed on and off at a frequency of 1 Hertz.

er anyone else had reported striking differences in acuity for different orientations in optically corrected astigmats. Although it is often mentioned that astigmats show reduced acuity when tested by normal clinical methods (Duke-Elder & Abrams, 1970), we could find only one report of orientational differences in acuity. Nearly 90 years ago Georges Martin, an ophthalmologist from Bordeaux, demonstrated that many astigmats, even after careful correction of their optical error, still showed differences in their ability to resolve contours of different orientations (Martin, 1890a, 1890b). In many cases, the astigmats had trouble seeing contours that were habitually seen blurred, even after full optical correction of the astigmatism. Martin coined the term "meridional amblyopia" for this condition.

Proof that the Deficits are Neural

In our studies, we took great pains to choose lenses that compensated exactly for each subject's optical abnormality. Thus, we had little doubt that their vast differences in acuity for different orientations were of neural origin, rather than stemming from any miniscule optical defects that may have remained. Nevertheless, we wanted to be certain that we had completely eliminated any trivial optical explanation for our findings.

There are several lines of evidence that conclusively rule out an optical explanation. The most straightforward is that the differences in acuity for different orientations persisted even when the test stimuli were interference fringes on the retina, unaffected by the eye's optics (Mitchell, Freeman, & Westheimer, 1967). As an example, Fig. 17 shows measurements made on my astigmatic right eye using two different kinds of stimuli: interference fringes formed directly on the retina (filled circles) and external gratings viewed through corrective lenses plus a 3 millimeter artificial pupil to further minimize any uncorrected optical error (open circles). In both cases, 21 cycles/degree gratings were used, adjusted for the same retinal illuminance, about 600 trolands. Although the measurements with interference fringes were made two years earlier than those with the more conventional method, the general shapes of the resulting curves are very similar. They both show less sensitivity for horizontal gratings than for vertical ones, and the reduction in sensitivity

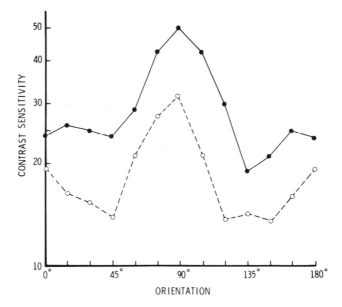

FIG. 17. Orientation differences in the modulation sensitivities for sinusoidal interference fringes (●) generated by a helium-neon gas laser and for sinusoidal gratings generated on the face of an oscilloscope (○) measured on my right eye. The gratings had a spatial frequency of 21 cycles/degree and a retinal illuminance of 600 trolands in both cases. (From Mitchell & Wilkinson, 1974.)

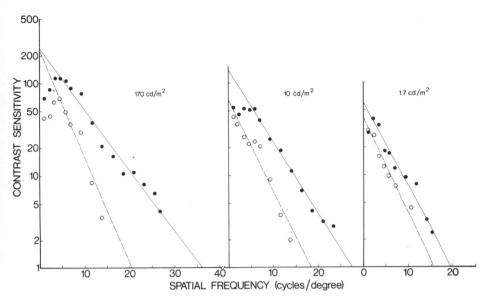

FIG. 18. Modulation sensitivity for sinusoidal gratings as a function of the spatial frequency for two orientations, 75° (●) and 165° (○), measured on the right eye of the fully corrected astigmat A.M. at three different luminance levels. Straight lines have been fitted by eye through the data for spatial frequencies of 5 cycles/degree and above. (From Mitchell & Wilkinson, 1974.)

is, if anything, more pronounced for the upper curve, which was obtained with a method that rules out effects of the eye's optics.

The same comparison has been made on many other astigmats, with the same outcome. Thus, the orientational differences in acuity must be of neural origin. Also the finding that sensitivity is greater for interference fringes than for a grating image formed by the eye's optics is in agreement with findings by Campbell and Green (1965) in normal subjects.

Further evidence for a neural rather than optical origin for the orientational differences can be found by comparing Figs. 18 and 19. Both figures present modulation transfer functions that tell how sensitive the observer is to gratings with different spatial frequencies. When the modulation sensitivity is plotted on a logarithmic scale, as in these figures, the data can be fitted satisfactorily by straight lines for spatial frequencies higher than about 5 cycles/degree. The farther to the right these lines hit the x-axis, the better the person's acuity. Figure 18 shows data taken from an astigmatic subject at three different overall intensities, 170, 10 and 1.7 candelas/meter^2 (Mitchell & Wilkinson, 1974). This subject's best acuity was for gratings oriented at 75° (filled circles in Fig. 18); his worst acuity was for 165° (open circles). At the highest

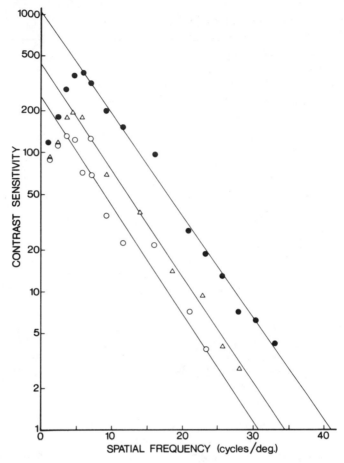

FIG. 19. Effect of optical defocus on modulation sensitivity. Filled circles show results with the eye in focus while the open triangles and open circles show the effects of placing the gratings 0.75 diopters and 1.00 diopters out of focus respectively. The gratings had a mean luminance of 170 candelas/meter^2.

luminance level, he exhibited an orientational deficit almost as large as the largest reported so far (Mitchell, Freeman, Millodot, & Haegerstrom, 1973). His two lines intersect the x-axis nearly an octave apart, 20 versus 36.5 cycles/degree.

The difference between Fig. 18 and Fig. 19 provides the evidence against an optical explanation of the orientational differences that are shown in Fig. 18. Figure 19 presents data from a normal subject whose focussing mechanism was paralyzed by homatropine while measurements were taken with a focussed image (filled circles) or with a blurred image that was defocussed by 0.75 diopters (open triangles) or 1.00 diopters (open circles). It is clear that these lines are parallel, rather than divergent as in Fig. 18. In other words, as Campbell, Kulikowski, and Levinson (1966) reported, optical blur due to small focussing errors results in an equal reduction in contrast sensitivity for all spatial frequencies beyond about 5 cycles/degree. Thus the different results for gratings at 105° and at 75° in Fig. 18 must be due to neural rather than optical factors; if the deficit were optical, the Fig. 18 lines would be parallel like those in Fig. 19.

It is worth mentioning that the same reasoning applies to the deficit that normal observers show for oblique contours. Figure 20 presents data from a normal subject viewing horizontal or vertical gratings (circles) or gratings tilted 45° right or left (triangles). As in Fig. 18, the lines through the triangles differ in slope from the line through the circles. They are not parallel, as they would be if optical blurring were to blame for the reduced visibility of obliques.

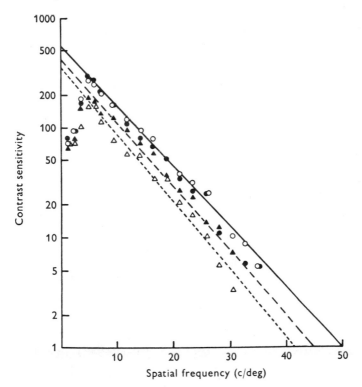

FIG. 20. Modulation sensitivity as a function of the spatial frequency for sinusoidal gratings of four orientations: vertical (O), horizontal (●), 45° (△), and 135° (▲) measured on the normal subject of Fig. 12. Straight lines have been drawn by eye through the data for spatial frequencies of 5 cycles/degree and above. The gratings had a mean luminance of 170 candelas/meter^2. (From Mitchell & Wilkinson , 1974.)

In fact, a single equation provides a good fit for all of the data in Figs. 18 and 20 (above 5 cycles/degree), which indicates that the orientational differences in visibility experienced by astigmats is an exaggerated version of that observed in normal people. Campbell, Kulikowski, and Levinson (1966) give the equation as: $S(f) = A^{-akf}$, where $S(f)$ is the modulation sensitivity, A is a constant that depends on intensity and state of focus, a is the slope of the data line for the most-visible orientation, f is spatial frequency, and k is a coefficient that depends on orientation of the grating. Variations in acuity for different orientations is reflected in variation in the size of k, which means a variation in slope of the data line in semilogarithmic graphs like these. Although the extent of orientational difference, and hence of the change in k, can be greater in astigmatic than in normal subjects, the same equation holds for both.

The Role of Early Visual Experience

What is the origin of the astigmats' large deficits in visual acuity for certain orientations? Two kinds of evidence suggest that it is their abnormal visual experience early in childhood. First, when an astigmat's optical defect is completely corrected by suitable lenses, the orientation that he has most trouble seeing is the same as the one that he sees most blurred with his naked eye. Second, the size of the difference between astigmats' best and worst orientations, viewed through corrective lenses, correlates well with the amount of their astigmatism. People with high astigmatism tend to show a greater acuity deficit than those with small or moderate optical errors. The close correspondence between vision with and without corrective lenses strongly suggests a causal relation, and obviously it was vision without glasses that came first.

Figures 13 and 14 provide a good picture of the agreement on best and worst orientations, with and without corrective lenses. We have found similar agreement for all astigmatic subjects, given certain assumptions about the focussing strategies astigmats use (Mitchell, Freeman, Millodot, & Haegerstrom, 1973). Just how precise the agreement can be is illustrated in Fig. 21. The data are from the left eye (filled circles) and right eye (open circles) of the same subject as in Fig. 18. What is plotted, for various orientations, is the cutoff spatial frequency, indicating how fine a grating the subject can see through corrective lenses. The arrows indicate the orientations that this subject sees most clearly or most blurred with his naked eye. The close agreement between the arrows and the peaks and troughs of the corresponding curves shows the close match between the subject's corrected and uncorrected vision. The match suggests that uncorrected blurred vision early in life was the cause of the adult's deficit. The fact that orientational differences for corrected and uncorrected vision agree in the adult also bears out the claim that high astigmatism remains relatively unchanged throughout life (Hirsch, 1963; Duke-Elder, 1969).

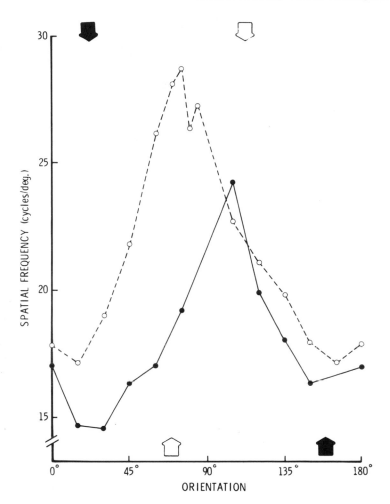

FIG. 21. Grating acuity (cutoff spatial frequency) as a function of orientation measured on the optically corrected right (○) and left eye (●) of the astigmat A.M. The upper set of filled and open arrows indicate the orientations of distant contours that are respectively most and least defocussed when the left eye is uncorrected. The lower set of arrows depict the corresponding orientations for the right eye. The gratings were sinusoidal, had a contrast of 0.6, and a mean luminance of 170 candelas/meter^2.

Additional corroboration of the agreement between corrected and uncorrected vision can be obtained from those rare astigmats whose optical axes are oblique. Only 5% of astigmats have oblique axes, making the retinal image of certain oblique contours sharper than that of verticals or horizontals. Whereas normal subjects never see obliques better than verticals and horizontals,

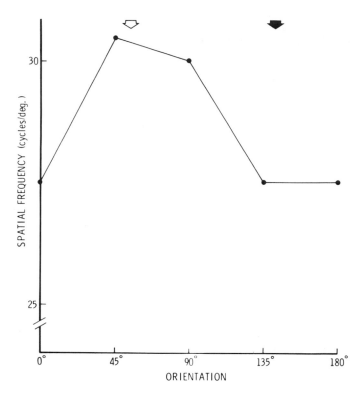

FIG. 22. Orientation differences in grating acuity for a subject with oblique-axis astigmatism. The gratings were sinusoidal, had a contrast of 0.7 and a mean luminance of 10 candelas/meter². The arrow shows the orientation of distant contours that are most defocussed when the eye is uncorrected. The refractive error was cyl −2.75 axis 37°. (Redrawn from Mitchell, Freeman, Millodot, & Haegerstrom, 1973.)

oblique-axis astigmats do. Figure 22 shows the cutoff spatial frequencies for various orientations in a subject with optically corrected oblique-axis astigmatism. The arrows indicate the orientations that this subject sees most clearly and most blurred with his naked eye. Again the relative visibilities for different orientations are the same for corrected and uncorrected vision, although the pattern differs from that for most astigmatic or normal subjects.

There is not only agreement on which orientation an astigmat sees most poorly with and without corrective lenses, but also a correspondence between the degree of difficulty with which contours of that orientation are seen with and without correction. If the astigmat's neural deficit is the result of having habitually seen contours of one orientation more blurred than all others, then we would expect the severity of the neural deficit to be related to the extent to which contours of that orientation were blurred by the astigmatic optics. We did find such a relationship (Mitchell, Freeman, Millodot, & Haegerstrom,

1973). However, although the correlation between the depth of the optical and neural deficits was highly significant, it was not overwhelmingly large, only about 0.5. This means that some subjects with severe astigmatism demonstrated rather small differences in acuity for different grating orientations, variations which were comparable to those found in normal eyes. How can this be, if optical blurring causes neural deficits? One possible answer that has been raised already, is that in many cases of astigmatism, contours of any orientation can sometimes be imaged sharply, if the person changes either his viewing distance or the state of accommodation of his eyes. By employing these strategies some astigmats may have given themselves exposure to sharp contours in all orientations, enough to maintain approximately equal acuity in all meridians.

Electrophysiological Evidence

The psychophysical data we have been discussing strongly suggest that abnormal early visual experience can produce a neural deficit in the human visual system. A recently developed technique provides more direct information about the neural modification. Campbell and Maffei (1970) have been able to record a visual evoked potential from the occipital region of the head in response to a grating that is shifted side to side by half a cycle (so that the bright bars of the grating exchange places with the dark bars) several times a

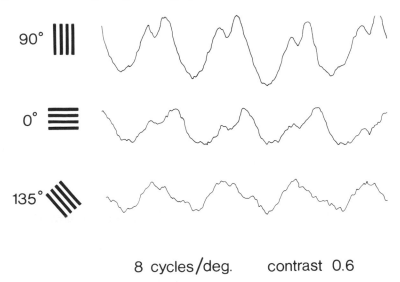

8 cycles/deg.   contrast 0.6

FIG. 23. Evoked cortical potentials recorded from my scalp in response to gratings alternated in phase at 8 Hertz. Responses were obtained with square wave gratings of 8 cycles/degree with a contrast of 0.6 at three orientations, namely, vertical, horizontal and 135°. The responses shown represent the sum of 256 repetitions. The data were kindly recorded by Dr. Mark Berkley at Florida State University, Tallahassee.

second. The same procedure has been tried on astigmats. While wearing corrective lenses, astigmats who show reduced acuity for a certain orientation also show diminished evoked potentials to gratings of this orientation (Freeman & Thibos, 1973, 1975; Fiorentini & Maffei, 1973). Figure 23 shows the potentials evoked by gratings of different orientations presented to my right eye. The data were kindly recorded by Dr. Mark Berkley at Florida State University in the standard manner described by Campbell and Maffei (1970). Clearly, the amplitude of the evoked response was much greater when the grating was vertical than when it was either horizontal or oblique. This agrees well with my reduced acuity for horizontal and oblique gratings (Fig. 15).

Electrical recordings like these complement the psychophysical evidence that abnormal early visual input can produce neural deficits. Moreover, such recordings narrow down the possible sites of the neural deficits: The deficit must reside at or prior to the place in the nervous system where the evoked response originates.

Effects of Environmental Asymmetries

As mentioned above in connection with Fig. 12, people with "normal" vision typically see vertical and horizontal contours somewhat better than oblique ones. This "oblique effect" is a rather small one compared to the large meridional variations in acuity found in astigmats. Nevertheless, the similarity between data from astigmats (Fig. 18) and normal observers (Fig. 20) suggests that the variation in acuity for astigmatic subjects is simply an exaggeration of the smaller variation observed in normal subjects. This in turn raises the interesting possibility that the oblique effect observed in normal subjects may, like the deficits seen in many astigmats, arise as a consequence of some asymmetry in their early visual inputs.

For the astigmatic subject the asymmetry in visual stimulation is produced by the eye's optics. Could it be that normal observers have been affected by some asymmetry in the external environment? For example, could the reduced acuity for oblique contours result from being reared in urbanized cultures in which vertical and horizontal contours are much more prevalent than oblique ones?

Annis and Frost (1973) have offered data that seemed to show a relation between the oblique effect in normal subjects and the scarcity of oblique contours in their surroundings. They compared orientational variations in acuity of 20 students from Queen's University in Kingston, Ontario, with those observed in 16 Cree Indians from James Bay, Quebec. The students had all been raised in typical North American buildings while the Cree Indians were among the last to be raised in traditional housing consisting of a cook tent or *meechwop* in summer and a winter lodge (*matoocan*) during the rest of the year. Both the insides and outsides of these structures are rich in contours of all orientations with no obvious preponderance of vertical and horizontal. In addition, the natural environment of the Cree Indians provided a far more heterogeneous array of contour orientations than existed in the students' urbanized environment.

The measures of acuity showed a reduction for oblique gratings relative to vertical or horizontal ones for the students but no such reduction for the Cree Indians.

Data from a different kind of experiment, on infants, fit in well with Annis and Frost's conclusion that the oblique effect is due to environmental asymmetries. Infants generally prefer to look at patterned surfaces rather than uniform ones, so one can assess acuity by seeing how fine stripes can be and still attract the infant's gaze more than a homogeneous area. Using a refined version of this technique, Teller, Morse, Borton and Regal (1974) found no sign of any oblique effect in infants up to six months of age. The implication seemed to be that the oblique effect develops later, presumably because of prolonged exposure to environmental asymmetries.

More recent findings, however, may point to a genetic rather than environmental origin for the oblique effect. First, it now appears that the magnitude of the oblique effect is quite variable from person to person within an urbanized population, even though all of them presumably had similar early inputs. Quite a large proportion of the population do not exhibit it at all and some even have it in reverse, with acuity for oblique contours better than for either vertical or horizontal ones (Timney & Muir, 1976). Furthermore, Timney and Muir report that the effect may be smaller on average in Chinese than in Caucasians, implying some genetic determination of the phenomenon. Finally, there is some suggestion that the oblique effect may in fact be present shortly after birth: Infants as young as six weeks of age show a clear predisposition to look at fine vertical and horizontal gratings rather than equally fine oblique ones presented simultaneously (Leehey, Moskowitz-Cook, Brill, & Held, 1975). Therefore, the evidence to date concerning the origin of the oblique effect must be regarded as equivocal.

MODIFICATION OF VISION IN HUMAN BEINGS: BINOCULARITY

In the cat, three properties of cortical neurons have been shown to be modified by the animal's early visual experience: orientational selectivity, binocularity and disparity specificity. By investigating human astigmats we have obtained the evidence discussed above that early visual inputs can affect orientational selectivity in human beings as well as in cats.

Stereoblindness

By studying other clinical conditions, we have gone on to find evidence that the binocularity of human cortical neurons may also be influenced by early visual exposure. If cats or monkeys are deprived of concordant binocular input early in life, they end up with few binocular neurons. Since binocular neurons are thought to provide the basis for stereoscopic vision, a scarcity of binocular neurons should impair or eliminate stereopsis. Thus, absence of stereopsis may serve as an indicator of absence of binocular neurons.

From 2% (Julesz, 1971, p. 187) to 4% (Richards, 1970) of the human population lack stereopsis. In many cases, stereoblindness is associated with a strabismus (one eye points in a different direction from the other) or anisometropia (unequal refractive errors in the two eyes) or some other condition which could have produced discordance between the images in the person's two eyes early in life. By analogy with animal experiments, we might suppose that the adult's stereoblindness results from a loss of binocular neurons, and that the loss was caused by abnormal early visual input.

Transfer of Tilt Aftereffects

Movshon, Chambers and Blakemore in England, and Colin Ware and I in Halifax, have provided psychophysical evidence that stereoblind humans do indeed suffer from a loss of binocular neurons (Movshon, Chambers, & Blakemore, 1972; Mitchell & Ware, 1974; Ware & Mitchell, 1974). Our experiments made use of the tilt aftereffect, the change in perceived orientation of lines after prolonged viewing of other lines with a slightly different orientation. For example, inspection of a grating rotated 10° clockwise from vertical will cause a subsequently viewed vertical test grating to appear somewhat rotated counterclockwise. In normal subjects the illusory counterclockwise rotation is seen even if the tilted adapting grating is presented to one eye and the vertical test grating to the other eye. However, the amount of apparent rotation is greater when adapting and test stimuli go to the same eye; transfer from one eye to the other is thus only partial. These and other visual aftereffects are also strongest when adapting and test orientations are similar. Hence, it has been argued that they depend on orientation-specific neurons (Blakemore & Sutton, 1969; Blakemore & Campbell, 1969; Coltheart, 1971).

Transfer of the aftereffect from one eye to the other suggests that the effect depends on binocular neurons that receive input from both eyes. If so, the extent of transfer could be used to indicate the proportion of pertinent neurons that are binocular in both normal and stereoblind subjects.

For each of our subjects, we measured the change in apparent orientation of a vertical test grating following several minutes' inspection of a grating tilted 10° from vertical. Typical results from six subjects who have various degrees of stereoscopic vision are shown in Fig. 24. The filled bars indicate the size of the aftereffect in the eye that viewed the tilted adapting stripes while the open bars show the magnitude of the aftereffect when the vertical test grating was seen by the other, unadapted eye. Subjects with normal stereoscopic vision (Fig. 24A) show partial transfer to the unadapted eye (about 70% in the case of D.R.). The two subjects represented in Fig. 24B have extremely poor stereopsis (stereoacuities of 200 seconds of arc or worse), and showed only a small amount of eye to eye transfer. Finally, Fig. 24C gives results for two subjects who totally lack stereopsis; one has a right divergent strabismus (R.H.) while the other has no history of strabismus but is highly astigmatic in both eyes. Neither these two subjects nor the other two stereoblind individuals we tested showed any significant transfer of the tilt aftereffect to the unadapted eye.

Transfer of Other Aftereffects

We also checked on eye to eye transfer of two other aftereffects, namely the motion aftereffect (Addams, 1834) and the threshold elevation effect—the increased difficulty in seeing a low contrast grating after inspecting a high contrast grating (Gilinsky, 1968; Blakemore & Campbell, 1969). Unlike normal subjects, neither of two stereoblind individuals showed any transfer of either aftereffect (Ware & Mitchell, 1974).

The agreement between the amount of interocular transfer and the extent of stereoscopic vision strongly suggests that stereoblind individuals possess few binocular cortical neurons. We may further surmise that the scarcity of binocular neurons resulted from disagreement, early in life, between the inputs to the two eyes.

THE HUMAN "CRITICAL PERIOD"

Our findings of perceptual deficits in people with astigmatism or strabismus provide a persuasive parallel to the studies of cats and monkeys. It seems clear that the properties of neurons in the human brain, like those in cats and monkeys, can be influenced by the nature of visual stimulation.

In both cats and monkeys, visual input can exert an influence on the visual system only during a limited "critical period" early in life. In the cat the sensitive period is quite short, lasting only until the end of the third month of age

(Hubel & Wiesel, 1970; Blakemore, 1973). Is there a similar limited critical period for human beings? Evidence from clinical sources suggests that there is, but in humans the period of susceptibility may last considerably longer than in cats and monkeys. The relevant evidence comes from humans with amblyopia associated with various ocular abnormalities including unilateral refractive errors or cataract, and astigmatism.

Amblyopia is impaired vision in one eye without any discernible pathological cause. It is thought to develop in infancy whenever there is discordant visual input to the two eyes early in life, such as may arise through strabismus, unilateral media opacities or refractive errors, cataracts (present at birth or resulting from injury), or ptosis (drooping of the eyelid over the pupil). It is well known that if such visual obstructions are present from birth or occur very early in life, then irreversible impairment of vision will result and persist even if normal visual input is restored later in life.

How long does the period of susceptibility last in humans? Juler (1921) reported on 22 people who suffered from cataracts as a result of injuries and who had been successfully operated on later in life. He found that if the injury occurred before six years of age, there was an irreversible visual deficit, but if the injury occurred after the age of seven years, vision was usually normal. In 1903, Worth presented the results of his observations on 985 children with strabismic amblyopia whom he had treated over a period of ten years (summarized by Flom, 1970). His results indicated that the severity of the amblyopia depended not only on the age when the strabismus first appeared but also on the age when treatment of the condition began. When, for example, the onset of the strabismus occurred before the child had reached the age of three, the resulting amblyopia was irreversible if treatment was delayed for a year but, if it was begun immediately, then most patients achieved normal vision. If strabismus set in before the age of two, a severe and permanent amblyopia resulted.

Alerted by the results of monocular deprivation in cats and monkeys, von Noorden (1973) has attempted to define the human period of susceptibility to the effects of depriving one eye of visual input, relying on a number of cases of cataracts or closure of the lids of one eye. To date, his results indicate that serious impairment can occur even if the monocular deprivation begins as late as four years of age. In one case, as little as four weeks of monocular deprivation at the age of two months caused irreversible amblyopia. Although the end of the period of susceptibility is poorly defined, these clinical observations suggest that it lasts at least until five years of age.

We have examined too few astigmatic subjects so far to be able to tell how long the critical period for the effects of astigmatism lasts. However, there are some indications that it lasts beyond the age of three. Most of our subjects received their first corrective glasses after the age of six or so when reading difficulties at school first brought attention to their condition. However, one subject with a large amount of astigmatism obtained glasses early, at the age of

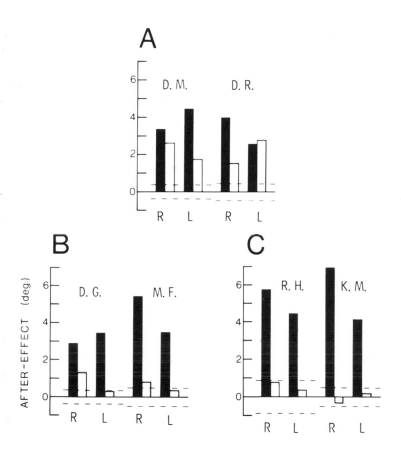

FIG. 24. Histograms showing the magnitude of the tilt aftereffect in subjects with varying degrees of stereopsis. Filled and open bars show the size of the aftereffect in the adapted and unadapted eye respectively. Below each pair of histograms is shown the eye in which the aftereffect was measured. The horizontal dashed lines show the 95% confidence limits for significant deviation from the preadapted settings. A. The results for two normal subjects with good stereopsis. B. The results for two subjects with extremely poor stereopsis (stereoacuities of 200 seconds of arc or worse). C. Two stereoblind observers (R.H. and K.M.) show no transfer whatsoever. While R.H. had a right divergent strabismus, the other stereoblind subject (K.M.) had no history of a strabismus. She was however highly astigmatic in both eyes. Adapting and test gratings 7.5 cycles/degree, contrast 0.6, mean luminance 3 candelas/meter^2. The data shows the average aftereffect that was obtained following adaptation to gratings tilted 10° clockwise and 10° counterclockwise from vertical. The test grating was vertical. (From Mitchell & Ware, 1974.)

three, and he did not show any neural deficit in visual acuity; apparently the optical correction had occurred within the critical period.

Recently, I have found a pair of 22-year-old identical twins who have very similar astigmatic conditions. One girl first wore corrective lenses at the age of five, while the other did not start until she was seven. Although the girl who received glasses at five showed a normal pattern of visual acuity, the girl who began wearing glasses later showed a small but significant neural deficit for horizontal stripes. From this comparison it appears that the human visual system is susceptible to environmental modification until somewhere between the ages of five and seven. Obviously, we will need many more cases like these before we can specify the exact period of susceptibility.

From the available evidence, it is already apparent that astigmatism is usually corrected too late to insure normal vision for all orientations of contour. The condition is rarely detected before the child has reached the age of seven or eight, by which time the neural deficit is permanent. Early screening of children for astigmatism, much earlier than the age at which it is presently conducted, is clearly called for.

Late in 1978, two independent groups using quite different techniques reported finding a very high incidence (greater than 50%) of clinically significant astigmatism (1 diopter or more) in infants during the first six months of life (Howland, Atkinson, Braddick, & French, 1978; Mohindra, Held, Gwiazda, & Brill, 1978). Thereafter there was a steady decline in the astigmatism, reaching adult proportions by the third year. As a consequence of this high incidence of astigmatism it might be thought that a correspondingly high proportion of infants could potentially develop meridional amblyopia. However, using the preferential looking technique (Teller, Morse, Borton, & Regal, 1974), Held's group have been unable to detect any meridional amblyopia in highly astigmatic infants before the end of the third year of life, which suggests that the critical period for the development of this condition does not even begin until sometime after two years of age (Mohindra, Held, Gwiazda, & Brill, 1978). This is certainly much later in life than the age at which amblyopia resulting from various binocular imbalances can arise (von Noorden, 1973).

FUNCTIONAL SIGNIFICANCE OF ENVIRONMENTAL MODIFICATION OF THE VISUAL CORTEX

The perceptual deficits that follow early selected visual deprivation can be quite severe. For example, even very short periods of monocular deprivation can produce a profound reduction in the visual acuity of the deprived eye in monkeys and humans (von Noorden, 1973). The potential for such severe deficits following accidental early visual deprivation is, however, the price that is paid for having a visual cortex that is subject to environmental modification. Since the price we pay for this property of neonatal cortical cells can be so high, we would expect the benefits that are bestowed by this early adaptive plasticity to be correspondingly great.

One benefit that follows is that the properties of cortical cells become matched to common features in the visual world. If complex objects in the visual world were indeed detected by specialized cortical neurons, as is implied by the term "detector" often applied to such neurons, then it would be of obvious benefit to match the properties of these neurons to the most frequently encountered features of the animal's visual environment in order to increase the ability of the visual system to process this environment. When looked at from this perspective the effects of selective visual deprivation might not always be deleterious. A cat reared in vertical stripes might be able to see vertical contours better than a normal cat since a much larger proportion of cortical neurons are tuned to vertical contours in such an animal than in normal cats. In a world composed of mainly vertical contours such an animal might therefore be able to perform better than a "normal" animal. At present we have no evidence from either cats or humans that selective visual exposure of this sort does lead to "superacuity" for features that were present early in life. Most human astigmats that I have seen in fact show only normal or, more frequently, slightly subnormal acuity for contours that were habitually focussed early in life. It should, however, be borne in mind that for the normal eye visibility of grating patterns is about as good as the optics of the eye permit (Campbell & Green, 1965). Thus in order to test for superacuity we would have to use a measure of acuity (for example, vernier acuity) that is not limited by the eye's optics.

The major difficulty with the idea that environmentally induced changes in neural circuitry are necessary in order to match the properties of "feature detectors" to the animal's visual world is the finding that modifiable cortical cells may be limited to animals with frontal eyes. Neurons in the visual cortex of the rabbit, an animal with lateral eyes, are not so susceptible to environmental modification (Mize & Murphy, 1973; Van Sluyters & Stewart, 1974).

If adaptive plasticity is found only in animals with frontal eyes perhaps its major function is to insure that binocular neurons become tuned to very similar features in the two eyes as a necessary prerequisite for stereopsis. This proposal, first suggested by Blakemore (1974b), provides a ready explanation for why the rabbit visual cortex is not subject to modification, since animals with lateral eyes are unlikely to possess stereopsis. For binocular neurons to serve any useful function, whether for stereopsis or for fusion of the two images, it would obviously be beneficial if they could adjust to any imbalance between the positions or orientations of the two eyes that might arise during periods of rapid growth early in the animal's life. Indeed, this may help to explain why the period of susceptibility is so much longer in humans than in the cat or monkey since the human head continues to grow over a much longer period of time.

CONCLUSION

In conclusion, I would like to reiterate a point made by Hirsch and Spinelli (1971). They argued that studies of the perceptual deficits in cats following "environmental surgery" (Hirsch, 1972) that removes all but one class of feature-detecting neurons should permit us to understand the role such neurons play in normal vision. In the same way, detailed knowledge of the perceptual deficits in humans with abnormal early visual inputs may help to clarify the connection between the properties of cortical neurons and visual perception. Thus, just as studies of people with defective color vision have enhanced our understanding of normal color vision, so studies of people born with certain visual impediments may help us understand the processes underlying normal form perception.

ACKNOWLEDGMENTS

This work has been generously supported by grants from the National Research Council of Canada (APA 7660), the Medical Research Council of Canada (MA 5027) and the Defence Research Board (Grant Number 9401-58).

REFERENCES

Addams, R. An account of a peculiar optical phenomenon seen after having looked at a moving body. *Philosophical Magazine,* 1834, *5,* 373-374.

Annis, R. C., & Frost, B. Human visual ecology and orientation anisotropies in acuity. *Science,* 1973, *182,* 729-731.

Baker, F. H., Grigg, P., & von Noorden, G. K. Effects of visual deprivation and strabismus on the response of neurons in the visual cortex of the monkey, including studies on the striate and prestriate cortex in the normal animal. *Brain Research,* 1974, *66,* 185-208.

Barlow, H. B., Blakemore, C., & Pettigrew, J. D. The neural mechanism of binocular depth discrimination. *Journal of Physiology,* 1967, *193,* 327-342.

Barlow, H. B., & Pettigrew, J. D. Lack of specificity of neurons in the visual cortex of young kittens. *Journal of Physiology,* 1971, *218,* 98-100P.

Berkley, M. A. Visual discriminations in the cat. In W. C. Stebbins (Ed.), *Animal psychophysics: The design and conduct of sensory experiments.* New York: Appleton-Century-Crofts, 1970.

Berkley, M., & Watkins, D. W. Grating resolution and refraction in the cat estimated from evoked cerebral potentials. *Vision Research,* 1973, *13,* 403-415.

Blakemore, C. Environmental constraints on development in the visual system. In R. A. Hinde & J. S. Hinde (Eds.), *Constraints on learning: Limitations and predispositions.* London: Academic Press, 1973.

Blakemore, C. Developmental factors in the formation of feature extracting neurons. In F. O. Schmitt & F. G. Worden (Eds.), *The neurosciences, third study program.* Cambridge, Massachusetts: MIT Press, 1974a.

Blakemore, C. Development of functional connexions in the mammalian visual system. *British Medical Bulletin,* 1974b, *30,* 152-157.

Blakemore, C. Genetic instructions and developmental plasticity in the kitten's visual cortex. *Philosophical Transactions of the Royal Society B,* 1977, *278,* 425-434.

Blakemore, C., & Campbell, F. W. On the existence of neurons in the human visual system selectively sensitive to the orientation and size of retinal images. *Journal of Physiology,* 1969, *203,* 237-260.

Blakemore, C., & Cooper, G. F. Development of the brain depends on the visual environment. *Nature,* 1970, *228,* 477-478.

Blakemore, C., & Mitchell, D. E. Environmental modification of the visual cortex and the neural basis of learning and memory. *Nature,* 1973, *241,* 467-468.

Blakemore, C., & Sutton, P. Size adaptation: A new aftereffect. *Science,* 1969, *166,* 245-247.

Blakemore, C., & Van Sluyters, R. C. Innate and environmental factors in the development of the kitten's visual cortex. *Journal of Physiology,* 1975, *245,* 663-716.

Blasdel, G. G., Mitchell, D. E., Muir, D. W., & Pettigrew, J. D. A physiological and behavioural study in cats of the effect of early visual experience with contours of a single orientation. *Journal of Physiology,* 1977, *265,* 615-636.

Boring, E. G. *Sensation and perception in the history of experimental psychology.* New York: Appleton-Century-Crofts, 1942.

Buisseret, P., & Imbert, M. Visual cortical cells: Their developmental properties in normal and dark reared kittens. *Journal of Physiology,* 1976, *255,* 511-525.

Campbell, F. W., & Green, D. G. Optical and retinal factors affecting visual resolution. *Journal of Physiology,* 1965, *181,* 576-593.

Campbell, F. W., Kulikowski, J. J., & Levinson, J. The effect of orientation on the visual resolution of gratings. *Journal of Physiology,* 1966, *187,* 427-436.

Campbell, F. W., & Maffei, L. Electrophysiological evidence for the existence of orientation and size detectors in the human visual system. *Journal of Physiology,* 1970, *207,* 635-652.

Campbell, F. W., Maffei, L., & Piccolino, M. The contrast sensitivity of the cat. *Journal of Physiology,* 1973, *229,* 719-731.

Coltheart, M. Visual feature-analyzers and aftereffects of tilt and curvature. *Psychological Review,* 1971, *78,* 114-121.

Cragg, B. G. The development of synapses in cat visual cortex. *Investigative Ophthalmology,* 1972, *11,* 377-385.

Cynader, M., Berman, N., & Hein, A. Cats reared in stroboscopic illumination: Effects on receptive fields in visual cortex. *Proceedings of the National Academy of Science,* 1973, *70,* 1353-1354.

Dews, P. B., & Wiesel, T. N. Consequences of monocular deprivation on visual behaviour in kittens. *Journal of Physiology,* 1970, *206,* 437-455.

Duke-Elder, W. S. *The practice of refraction.* St. Louis: Mosby, 1969.

Duke-Elder, W. S., & Abrams, D. Ophthalmic optics and refraction. In W. S. Duke-Elder (Ed.), *System of ophthalmology* (Vol. 5). London: Henry Kimpton, 1970.

Emsley, H. H. Irregular astigmatism of the eye: Effect of correcting lenses. *Transactions of the Optical Society,* 1925, *27,* 28-41.

Epstein, W. Experimental investigations of the genesis of visual space perception. *Psychological Bulletin,* 1964, *61,* 115-128.

Fiorentini, A., & Maffei, L. Evoked potentials in astigmatic subjects. *Vision Research,* 1973, *13,* 1781-1783.

Flom, M. C. Early experience in the development of visual coordination, In F. A. Young & D. B. Lindsley (Eds.), *Early experience and visual information processing in perceptual and reading disorders.* Washington: National Academy of Science, 1970.

Flood, D. G., & Coleman, P. D. Demonstration of orientation columns with [^{14}C] 2-deoxyglucose in a cat reared in a striped environment. *Brain Research*, 1979, *173*, 538-542.

Freeman, R. D., Asymmetries in human accommodation and visual experience. *Vision Research*, 1975, *15*, 483-492.

Freeman, R. D., Mitchell, D. E., & Millodot, M. A neural effect of partial visual deprivation in humans. *Science*, 1972, *75*, 1384-1386.

Freeman, R. D., & Pettigrew, J. D. Alteration of visual cortex from environmental asymmetries. *Nature*, 1973, *246*, 359-360.

Freeman, R. D., & Thibos, L. N. Electrophysiological evidence that abnormal visual experience can modify the human brain. *Science*, 1973, *180*, 876-878.

Freeman, R. D., & Thibos, L. N. Visual evoked responses in humans with abnormal visual experience. *Journal of Physiology*, 1975, *247*, 711-724.

Frégnac, Y., & Imbert, M. Early development of visual cortical cells in normal and dark-reared kittens: Relationship between orientational selectivity and ocular dominance. *Journal of Physiology*, 1978, *278*, 27-44.

Ganz, L., & Fitch, M. The effect of visual deprivation on perceptual behaviour. *Experimental Neurology*, 1968, *22*, 638-660.

Giffin, F., & Mitchell, D. E. The rate of recovery of vision after early monocular deprivation in kittens. *Journal of Physiology*, 1978, *274*, 511-537.

Gilinsky, A. Orientation-specific effects of patterns of adapting light on visual acuity. *Journal of the Optical Society of America*, 1968, *58*, 13-18.

Gordon, B., Presson, J., Packwood, J., & Scheer, R. Alteration of cortical orientation selectivity: Importance of asymmetric input. *Science*, 1979, *204*, 1109-1111.

Hein, A., & Held, R. Dissociation of the visual placing response into elicited and guided components. *Science*, 1967, *158*, 390-391.

Held, R., & Hein, A. On the modifiability of form perception. In W. Wathen-Dunn (Ed.), *Models for the perception of speech and visual form*. Cambridge, Massachusetts: MIT Press, 1967.

Helmholtz, H. von. *Treatise on physiological optics*, Vol. 3 (translated from the third German edition, J. P. C. Southall, Ed.). Menasha, Wisconsin: Optical Society of America, 1925.

Higgins, G. C., & Stultz, K. Visual acuity as measured with various orientations of a parallel line test target. *Journal of the Optical Society of America*, 1948, *38*, 766-768.

Higgins, G. C., & Stultz, K. Variation of visual acuity with various test object orientations and viewing conditions. *Journal of the Optical Society of America*, 1950, *40*, 135-137.

Hirsch, H. V. B. Visual perception in cats after environmental surgery. *Experimental Brain Research*, 1972, *15*, 405-423.

Hirsch, H. V. B., & Spinelli, D. N. Visual experience modifies distribution of horizontally and vertically oriented receptive fields in cats. *Science*, 1970, *168*, 869-871.

Hirsch, H. V. B., & Spinelli, D. N. Modification of the distribution of receptive field orientation in cats by selective visual exposure during development. *Experimental Brain Research*, 1971, *13*, 509-527.

Hirsch, M. The refraction of children. In M. Hirsch & R. Wicks (Eds.), *Vision of children*. Philadelphia: Chilton, 1963, Pp. 145-172.

Hochberg, J. Nativism and empiricism in perception. In L. Postman (Ed.), *Psychology in the making*. New York: Knopf, 1962, Pp. 255-330.

Howland, H. C., Atkinson, J., Braddick, O., & French, J. Infant astigmatism measured by photorefraction. *Science*, 1978, *202*, 331-333.

Hubel, D. H., & Wiesel, T. N. Receptive fields, binocular interaction and functional architecture in the cat's visual cortex. *Journal of Physiology*, 1962, *160*, 106-154.

Hubel, D. H., & Wiesel, T. N. Receptive fields of cells in striate cortex of very young, visually inexperienced kittens. *Journal of Neurophysiology*, 1963, *26*, 994-1002.

Hubel, D. H., & Wiesel, T. N. Binocular interaction in striate cortex of kittens reared with artificial squint. *Journal of Neurophysiology*, 1965, *28*, 1041-1059.

Hubel, D. H., & Wiesel, T. N. The period of susceptibility to the physiological effects of unilateral eye closure in kittens. *Journal of Physiology*, 1970, *206*, 419-436.

Juler, F. Amblyopia from disuse. Visual acuity after traumatic cataract in children. *Transactions of the Ophthalmological Society of the United Kingdom*, 1921, *41*, 129-139.

Julesz, B. *Foundations of cyclopean perception*. Chicago: University of Chicago Press, 1971

Leehey, S. C., Moskowitz-Cook, A., Brill, S., & Held, R. Orientational anisotropy in infant vision. *Science*, 1975, *190*, 900-902.

Le Grand, Y. La formation des images rétiniennes. Sur un mode de vision éliminant les défauts optiques de l'oeil. 2e Réunion de l'Institute d'Optique, Paris, 1937.

Leibowitz, H. Some observations and theory on the variation of visual acuity with the orientation of the test object. *Journal of the Optical Society of America*, 1953, *43*, 902-905.

Martin, G. Amblyopie astigmatique. Condition du développement parfait de la vision. *Bulletin de la Société Francaise d'Ophtalmologie*, 1890a, *8*, 217-227.

Martin, G. Théorie et clinique de l'amblyopie astigmatique. *Annales d'oculistique*, 1890b, *104*, 101-138.

McCleary, R. A. *Genetic and experiential factors in perception*. Glenview, Illinois: Scott, Foresman, 1970.

Mitchell, D. E., Freeman, R. D., Millodot, M., & Haegerstrom, G. Meridional amblyopia: Evidence for modification of the human visual system by early visual experience. *Vision Research*, 1973, *13*, 535-558.

Mitchell, D. E., Freeman, R. D., & Westheimer, G. Effect of orientation on the modulation sensitivity for interference fringes on the retina. *Journal of the Optical Society of America*, 1967, *57*, 246-249.

Mitchell, D. E., Giffin, F., & Timney, B. A behavioural technique for the rapid assessment of the visual capabilities of kittens. *Perception*, 1977, *6*, 181-193.

Mitchell, D. E., & Ware, C. Interocular transfer of a visual after-effect in normal and stereoblind humans. *Journal of Physiology*, 1974, *236*, 707-721.

Mitchell, D. E., & Wilkinson, F. The effect of early astigmatism on the visual resolution of gratings. *Journal of Physiology*, 1974, *243*, 739-756.

Mize, R. R., & Murphy, E. H. Selective visual experience fails to modify receptive field properties of rabbit striate cortex neurons. *Science*, 1973, *180*, 320-323.

Mohindra, I., Held, R., Gwiazda, J., & Brill, S. Astigmatism in infants. *Science*, 1978, *202*, 329-331.

Movshon, J. A., Chambers, B. E. I., & Blakemore, C. Interocular transfer in normal humans and those who lack stereopsis. *Perception*, 1972, *1*, 483-490.

Muir, D. W. Visual acuity deficits in cats following early selective visual deprivation. Unpublished Ph.D. thesis. Dalhousie University, 1974.

Muir, D. W., & Mitchell, D. E. Visual resolution and experience: Acuity deficits in cats following early selective visual deprivation. *Science*, 1973, *180*, 420-422.

Muir, D. W., & Mitchell, D. E. Behavioral deficits in cats following early selected visual exposure to contours of a single orientation. *Brain Research*, 1975, *85*, 459-477.

Nikara, T., Bishop, P. O., & Pettigrew, J. D. Analysis of retinal correspondence by studying receptive fields of binocular single units in cat striate cortex. *Experimental Brain Research*, 1968, *6*, 353-372.

Pettigrew, J. D. The neurophysiology of binocular vision. *Scientific American*, 1972a, *227*, 84-95.

50 Donald E. Mitchell

Pettigrew, J. D. The importance of early visual experience for neurons of the developing geniculo-striate system. *Investigative Ophthalmology*, 1972b, *11*, 386-394.

Pettigrew, J. D. The effect of visual experience on the development of stimulus specificity by kitten cortical neurones. *Journal of Physiology*, 1974, *237*, 49-74.

Pettigrew, J. D., & Freeman, R. D. Visual experience without lines: Effects on developing cortical neurons. *Science*, 1973, *182*, 599-601.

Pettigrew, J. D., Olsen, C., & Hirsch, H. V. B. Cortical effect of selective visual experience: Degeneration or reorganization? *Brain Research*, 1973, *51*, 345-351.

Rakic, P. Prenatal genesis of connections subserving ocular dominance in rhesus monkey. *Nature*, 1976, *261*, 467-471.

Richards, W. Stereopsis and stereoblindness. *Experimental Brain Research*, 1970, *10*, 380-388.

Sherk, H., & Stryker, M. P. Quantitative study of cortical orientation selectivity in visually inexperienced kittens. *Journal of Neurophysiology*, 1976, *39*, 63-70.

Shlaer, S. Shift in binocular disparity causes compensatory change in the cortical structure of kittens. *Science*, 1971, *173*, 638-641.

Stryker, M. P., & Sherk, H. Modification of cortical orientation selectivity in the cat by restricted visual experience: A reexamination. *Science*, 1975, *190*, 904-906.

Stryker, M. P., Sherk, H., Leventhal, A. G., & Hirsch, H. V. B. Physiological consequences for the cat's visual cortex of effectively restricting early visual experience with oriented contours. *Journal of Neurophysiology*, 1978, *41*, 896-909.

Taylor, M. M. Visual discrimination and orientation. *Journal of the Optical Society of America*, 1963, *53*, 763-765.

Teller, D. Y., Morse, R., Borton, R., & Regal, D. Visual acuity for vertical and diagonal gratings in human infants. *Vision Research*, 1974, *14*, 1433-1439.

Timney, B. N., & Muir, D. W. Orientation anisotropy: Incidence and magnitude in Caucasian and Oriental subjects. *Science*, 1976, *193*, 699-701.

Van Sluyters, R. C., & Blakemore, C. Experimental creation of unusual neuronal properties in visual cortex of kittens. *Nature*, 1973, *246*, 506-508.

Van Sluyters, R. C., & Stewart, D. L. Binocular neurons of the rabbit's visual cortex: Effects of monocular sensory deprivation. *Experimental Brain Research*, 1974, *19*, 196-204.

von Noorden, G. K. Experimental amblyopia in monkeys. Further behavioural observation and clinical correlations. *Investigative Ophthalmology*, 1973, *12*, 721-726.

von Noorden, G. K., Dowling, J. E., & Ferguson, D. C. Experimental amblyopia in monkeys. I. Behavioural studies of stimulus deprivation amblyopia. *American Medical Association Archives of Ophthalmology*, 1970, *84*, 206-214.

Walls, G. L. The problem of visual direction Part I. The history to 1900. *American Journal of Optometry & Archives of the American Academy of Optometry*, 1951, *28*, 55-83.

Ware, C., & Mitchell, D. E. On interocular transfer of various visual after-effects in normal and stereoblind observers. *Vision Research*, 1974, *14*, 731-734.

Westheimer, G. Modulation thresholds for sinusoidal light distributions on the retina. *Journal of Physiology*, 1960, *152*, 67-74.

Wiesel, T. N. Monkey visual cortex. II. Modifications induced by visual deprivation. Friedenwald Lecture presented at Association for Research in Vision and Ophthalmology, Sarasota, May 1975.

Wiesel, T. N., & Hubel, D. H. Single-cell responses in striate cortex of kittens deprived of vision in one eye. *Journal of Neurophysiology*, 1963, *26*, 1003-1017.

Wiesel, T. N., & Hubel, D. H. Ordered arrangement of orientation columns in monkeys lacking visual experience. *Journal of Comparative Neurology*, 1974, *158*, 307-318.

Worth, C. A. *Squint: Its causes, pathology and treatment.* Philadelphia: Blakiston, 1903.

The Development
of Visually Guided Behavior

Alan Hein

Massachusetts Institute of Technology

A thoughtful person, relaxing on a hillside and gazing at the rich panorama spread beneath him, may ask many questions about why the visual world appears as it does. He may notice that there is an infinitude of dimensions of variation between parts of the landscape shapes, sizes, colors, textures, brightnesses, distances, etc. He may also discover that he can apply a multiplicity of descriptions to the scene, using alternative categories and subcategories to capture what he experiences. Whatever description he chooses, though, admits the same inexhaustible question What are the *sources* of the perceived characteristics of the visual world?

Even if it were possible for the contemplative observer somehow to ascertain what structures and processes engender the visual characteristics of the scene, he would still have only a very partial understanding of vision. The limits of his understanding become clear the instant he stands up and begins to walk about. If he continues to think while walking, he may begin to wonder what relates the *appearance* of the world to the *actions* he must perform to move himself with respect to it. As he goes about translating perception into other forms of action, such as reaching out and moving objects, he may raise general questions about the *functional significance of vision*.

The way in which movement is coordinated with vision has been analyzed experimentally by using two general methods. One employs human adults for whom the normal relations between visual stimulation and movement are rearranged by an optical device such as a prism or mirror. The second method depends on selective deprivation during development, necessarily using infrahuman animals as subjects.

STUDIES WITH HUMANS:
IMPORTANCE OF MOVEMENT-PRODUCED VISUAL FEEDBACK

In a series of optical rearrangement studies, Richard Held and several co-workers attempted to clarify the role that movement-produced changes in visual stimulation play in the adjustment of coordination. I shall describe a representative set of experiments.

Arm Movements

To measure visually guided reaching, Held and I asked subjects to mark the apparent locations of four target points reflected in a mirror (Held & Hein, 1958). The subjects could not see their hands or the marks they made. This technique thus provides a measure of visually guided reaching without the complications introduced by error information. The subjects marked the targets before, and again after, opportunity to view the hand through prisms that displaced the scene to one side. If visual input while viewing the hand through prisms can be used to adjust one's movements to visual displacement, the subjects should change the way their marks locate the target points, in a direction opposite to the prismatic displacement.

We examined three conditions of viewing the hand. In the first, the hand was stationary. In both of the other conditions, hand and arm were strapped to a lever and the hand oscillated from side to side around a fulcrum at the elbow. In one case, the subject's relaxed arm was moved by a force applied by the experimenter to the opposite end of the lever. In the other, the subject actively produced the movements.

Only in the third condition, when the subject viewed the self-produced movements of his hand, was there any compensation for prismatic displacement of vision, as revealed by the postexposure test. There was no compensation if the subject looked through prisms at his hand while it was stationary or while it was moved by an external force.

Whole-Body Movement

In a study reported by Held and Bossom (1961), subjects wore sideways-displacing prisms while they either walked on a footpath or were seated in a wheelchair pushed over the same path. The test of coordination required the subject to orient head and torso to a luminous vertical line in an otherwise dark room.

No difference between pre- and post-exposure coordination was found if the subject had been transported in a wheel chair while wearing prisms. However, substantial adjustment to the displacement was observed after the subject had been walking while wearing prisms.

A further prerequisite for compensation was shown by another wheelchair experiment, in which the prism-wearing subjects wheeled themselves (Held & Mikaelian, 1964). Even though the subjects actively manipulated the wheels to move forward and to avoid obstacles, they showed no compensation for the prismatic displacement. Evidently the mechanism that utilizes visual feedback does not make effective use of feedback from *all* self-produced movements. We would speculate that only movements that an organism normally uses for locomotion are effective. (Incidentally, this finding also answers the objection that a passively wheeled subject fails to adapt only because he is not paying enough attention to the visual feedback, or because he is not motivated to make any decisions based on it.)

Degraded Coordination

Self-produced movement can *impair* coordination if the resulting visual feedback is related to the movements *unsystematically* rather than systematically. Cohen and Held (1960) used the same procedure as Held and Hein (1958), but instead of viewing the hand through a prism with a fixed displacement, Cohen and Held's subjects looked through a variable prism that produced a continually changing displacement, oscillating between 22° rightward and 22° leftward every minute. To a large extent, therefore, the changes in position of the image of the hand were independent of the motions of the hand itself.

The outcome, for subjects who actively moved their hands, was a degradation of performance. On the subsequent test of marking the locations of targets seen in a mirror, their responses showed a greatly increased scatter along the right-left dimension. (Subjects for whom the prism was oriented to produce varying displacements along a vertical axis showed increased scatter along that dimension instead.) As in the Held and Hein study, subjects who viewed the hand while it was moved by an external force showed no change in coordination.

It seems that the visual-motor system reacts to visual information provided by self-produced movements regardless of whether that information bears a systematic or an unsystematic relation to the movements. When the relation is unsystematic, visual-motor coordination suffers.

Full Compensation

Other studies indicated that when subjects underwent repeated exposure periods with visual feedback from self-produced movement, the level of adaptation to prismatic displacement approached 100% (Hein, 1972; Hein & Held, 1958; Held & Bossom, 1961). Eventually behavior was adapted perfectly to the rearranged optical input.

For us this finding had special significance: If full and exact compensation for the prismatic displacement can occur with no information beyond that from the correlation of active body movement with visual feedback, then such motor-visual feedback might provide a sufficient source of information for the original development of visually coordinated behavior in the newborn.

STUDIES WITH KITTENS:
DEVELOPMENT OF VISUALLY GUIDED BEHAVIOR

Our supposition that our work with prism-wearing adults might be relevant to the initial development of visual-motor coordination was strengthened by studies that Austin Riesen and his colleagues at the University of Chicago reported (Riesen, 1961). They had reared kittens in three conditions of visual deprivation. Some grew up in total darkness. Others were reared with exposure only to diffused light. Still others were allowed to view a visually patterned environment, but only while held in an apparatus that prevented locomotion. Rearing in the dark was found to interfere substantially with the kittens' form and motion discrimination. Moreover, animals that had been raised in diffused light were no better than dark-reared animals in learning these visual discriminations. Especially interesting to us was the report that even animals which had received patterned light stimulation, but only while standing in stocks that permitted them to remain comfortable and alert but prevented them from locomoting, were also markedly deficient in learning the discriminations.

Visual or Visual-Motor Deprivation?

At first it appeared that Riesen's findings might be attributed to insufficient visual stimulation. That is, an animal reared in the dark, in diffused light, or in patterned light with no opportunity to locomote, might have received a reduced amount and degree of variation in visual stimulation. Input to the visual system might have been below some threshold for organizing the visual nervous system so as to permit development of sensory-sensory linkages needed for pattern and motion discrimination. We suggested an alternate explanation: Instead of mere amount and variety of visual stimulation, we proposed that the crucial deprivation was the absence of *movement-produced changes* in visual stimulation.

In one experiment designed to decide between the sensory-sensory and motor-visual explanations, we reared kittens in the dark until they were about eight weeks of age (Held & Hein, 1963). Then they received daily visual exposure in an apparatus that is now called the kitten carousel (Fig. 1). Each kitten was assigned to one or the other end of a pivoted arm. At one end, a harness and neck yoke connected the animal to the arm as it walked about, but otherwise its movements were relatively free. Thus this kitten received visual feedback systematically associated with its locomotory movements. Another

FIG. 1. The "kitten carousel." (From Hein & Held, 1962.)

kitten from the same litter rode in a gondola at the opposite end of the beam. Whenever the animal that was free to locomote moved, a pulley and gear arrangement moved the gondola and the kitten within it in a very similar way. As the gondola moved, there were changes in visual input to the transported kitten. Self-produced movements of the gondola animal (e.g., turning the head) also produced changes in visual stimulation, but the relation between visual changes and the kitten's movement was perturbed by movements of the gondola.

The result was that visual stimulation varied systematically with self-produced movement for the locomoting animal and varied unsystematically with self-produced movement for the transported animal. (In previous reports, we have sometimes said that the kitten in the gondola was passive, thereby giving some readers the mistaken impression that the transported kittens were totally inactive, perhaps even dozing. In fact, they appeared alert, and could be seen to move their legs, bodies, heads, and eyes, of course without systematic relation to visual feedback.)

The sheer amount of visual stimulation and the extent of its variation from moment to moment were similar for the two groups of kittens (freely locomoting vs. transported in the gondola). Nevertheless, subsequent testing revealed that only the animals that had been locomoting developed the capacity to guide their bodies through space. These kittens could avoid obstacles (Fig. 2), they walked to the shallow rather than the deep side of a visual cliff (Fig. 3), and they performed visual placing responses (extending their forelimbs when brought down toward a surface). Acquisition of these capacities required an average of 30 hours of exposure.

The kittens transported in the gondola during the same time showed none of these visually controlled behaviors. In further studies, we tested kittens after hundreds of hours of exposure in the gondola. They too showed no evidence of visually controlled behavior.

We interpreted these results as implying that systematic movement-produced change in visual stimulation plays an important role in the acquisition of visually guided behavior, and that visual stimulation alone is insufficient for such development. Incidentally, during the first few months of life, the deficits that result from transport in the gondola are reversible. When the experiment was terminated and the animals were released to run about freely in a normally illuminated laboratory room, they all showed visually coordinated behavior when observed two days later.

Acquisition or Recovery of Visually Coordinated Behavior?

Let us consider the possibility that kittens are born with full potential for visually guided behavior and that display of these capacities awaits only their maturation. The period of maximum plasticity of the visual nervous system begins

FIG. 2. The obstacle course.

FIG. 3. The visual cliff. (Courtesy of Dr. Richard D. Walk.)

when the animal is about four weeks of age. Thus it is possible that dark rearing for eight weeks degrades innate capacities for visual control of movement. If this were true, then subsequent opportunity to move in light might support recovery of the capacities lost while the animals were in darkness. This view of the consequence of exposure in light contrasts with the one we have proposed: that movement in light is necessary for the initial acquisition of visually guided behavior.

We considered these alternatives in an experiment in which kittens were kept in total darkness only until they were four weeks old. They were then placed daily in the gondola apparatus for three hours of exposure in light. As in the previous study, all eight kittens that locomoted developed visual-motor coordination while the eight that were carried in the gondola did not. This result renders implausible the assertion that visually guided behavior is innate, and indicates that movement in light is indeed important for the initial acquisition of guided behavior.

Separate Exposure for Each Eye

There is an alternative explanation for why kittens transported in a gondola fail to show visual placing responses and visual cliff discrimination. Perhaps being transported in a gondola is a frustrating or unpleasant experience that leads to a generalized inhibition of movement in response to visual stimulation. We found evidence against this explanation when we exposed each of a kitten's eyes under different conditions (Hein, Held, & Gower, 1970). For 1½ hours daily, a group of dark-reared kittens locomoted freely in the carousel with one eye covered. For an additional 1½ hours each day, the kittens were carried in the gondola, with the opposite eye covered. Thus, each day, the kitten received through one eye visual feedback that varied systematically with its locomotion and through its other eye received visual input that was not systematically related to its self-produced movements.

After many days of alternating monocular exposure under these two conditions, the kittens were tested. When using the eye that had been uncovered only during transport in the gondola, none of the kittens showed a visually triggered placing response and none discriminated between the shallow and deep sides of the visual cliff. However, when using the eye that had been open during locomotion, these same kittens showed both visually triggered extension and a preference for the shallow side of a visual cliff.

In other words, the kittens were quite capable of carrying out visually controlled movements, provided the proper eye was open. Their experience in the gondola had *not* produced a generalized inhibition of responses to visual stimuli. Thus, the absence of visually coordinated behavior in an animal that has been exposed only in the gondola cannot be attributed to some general deficit in responsiveness to visual stimuli.

Transport in Light: Helpful, Harmful or Neutral?

One principal question remained unanswered by these experiments. Does exposure to patterned light while being transported in a gondola have consequences different from those of being reared in the dark? A period of being transported in a gondola might either facilitate, impede, or have no effect on the subsequent development of visually coordinated behavior.

To examine these alternatives, we raised another group of kittens in the dark until they were eight weeks old, and then placed them in the gondola for three hours a day of transport while exposed to patterned light (Hein, Held, & Gower, 1970). We repeated this procedure for 11 days, giving each kitten 33 hours of transport with patterned light. At the end of this period, the animals were permitted to locomote at the opposite end of the beam for three hours a day. After each daily period of locomotion, we tested the animals for visually triggered extension of the forelimbs—the visual placing response. When visual placing was displayed, we observed the kitten's performance on a visual cliff.

All of the kittens in this experiment ultimately displayed the visual placing response and all avoided the deep side of the visual cliff. However, after their experience in the gondola, it took them an average of 41 hours of locomoting freely to develop these capacities—much longer than the locomoting kittens in the previous experiment needed to develop the same skills. Those kittens, with *no* prior exposure to light, acquired the behaviors with an average of only 30 hours of locomoting.

Thus, it is clear that being transported in the gondola, while exposed to patterned light, actually *impeded* later development: Acquisition of visually controlled behavior was delayed when the animals later were allowed to locomote. Remember that the animal in the gondola is not immobilized. It is free to move its head around and can move its feet along the floor of the gondola. However, its movements are not systematically associated with the major changes in visual input, which are controlled by the locomoting kitten at the other end of the beam.

The implication is that perturbing the visual feedback from self-produced movement has a disruptive effect on development. There seems to be a parallel with the experiments on humans exposed to varying prismatic displacements. There, too, when visual changes were coupled unsystematically with self-produced movements, visual-motor performance suffered.

SEPARABLE COMPONENTS
OF VISUALLY COORDINATED BEHAVIOR

The results of the study reported above in which each eye was exposed independently had another important implication for us: It showed us that control of visually coordinated behavior may be acquired independently by each eye. The eye exposed without systematic visual feedback from self-produced movement was unable to mediate visual-motor coordination, at the same time that such responses were controlled efficiently by the other eye.

This suggested to us a model of visual-motor coordination consisting of a number of components. Acquisition of each component makes its own special demands for exposure to appropriate motor-visual feedback. By providing some kinds of feedback while withholding others, we might be able to demonstrate independence in the development of various components, and we might be able to specify what exposure conditions are essential for each component. This line of thinking encouraged us to search for other components of visual motor coordination that might be independently acquired.

Walking and Reaching

One aspect of visually coordinated behavior that especially interested us was the ability to reach out accurately enough to touch a visual target. Kittens are deservedly renowned for the accuracy and precise timing of their movements, directed toward either stationary or moving objects. It seemed to us that precise visual guidance of reaching or striking might constitute a component of visually coordinated behavior with unique exposure requirements.

The kind of exposure that permits use of the limb in locomoting with respect to the visual surroundings might not be adequate for developing the capacity to use that same limb in reaching for targets. In particular, we suggested that if an animal was free to walk about in light but could not view its limbs as it moved, it would acquire the capacity to locomote with respect to visual objects but be unable to guide the forelimbs to a small target (Hein & Held, 1967).

To test this idea we used the simple accessory shown in Fig. 4. Kittens were kept in the dark from birth until they were four weeks of age. Then they were permitted to move about in light for six hours daily but only while wearing a lightweight opaque collar. The collar did not impede walking and running but did keep the animals from seeing their forelimbs. We examined the behavior of these kittens after they had had 12 days of exposure in light. The collars were removed before testing.

When the kittens were placed at various locations in an obstacle course, they walked about readily without colliding with objects. This behavior indicated that the kittens could use their forelimbs (together with their hindlimbs) to move themselves competently with respect to seen objects. They were also able to use their forelimbs to descend from a raised platform to the shallow rather than the deep side of a visual cliff.

In contrast to their well coordinated locomotion, the kittens' behavior was very different when they were confronted with a ping-pong ball swinging at the end of a string. They looked at the ball and refixated on it as it swung across the visual field. Striking movements of the forelimb were elicited. However, the movements were not *directed* toward the object. The kitten might be looking at the ball swinging overhead, moving its head appropriately right and left as the ball passed, while nevertheless making striking movements toward an area close to the ground and unrelated to the momentary position of the ball. The fact that the kitten directed its gaze toward the swinging ball indicated to us that the animal could *see* the ball. And the kitten was able to execute accurate striking movements if the ball produced a sound (when dragged along the floor, for example). This observation revealed that the animal had good control of its limb movements. Thus, the deficiency when the ball was swinging soundlessly seemed to us a failure to *integrate* limb movements with visual information.

Components of Reaching

We tried a further test of guided reaching on the kittens that had locomoted without a chance to see their limbs. When a normally reared kitten is lowered slowly toward a broad horizontal surface, it will extend its forelimbs at the proper moment to prevent bumping its head. The precise timing implies that the animal is responding to the distance of the surface. We used the apparatus illustrated in Fig. 5 to show that, in the normal animal, this placing response is

FIG. 4. Kitten with an opaque collar that keeps it from seeing its limbs. (From Hein & Held, 1967.)

also accurately guided to a particular left-right location of the surface (Hein & Held, 1967). An animal that is carried down toward such a surface, interrupted with cutouts to form a series of prongs, may have to move its paw to the right or left to make contact with a prong and avoid going into the empty space between them. Rather precise visual guidance of the limb is called for, more than just visually triggered extension in the general direction of the surface.

Normally reared kittens were found to strike the prongs on 95% of their reaches, even when brought down at random locations. Quite a different picture emerged when we tested the kittens that had locomoted in light only while wearing collars that kept them from seeing their limbs. Although they did extend their paws as they neared the apparatus, they hit a prong on only half the trials. On the other half, their paws passed right through an open space. With regard to left-right positioning, then, their level of performance was at chance.

These observations demonstrate that visually controlled forelimb extension in the kitten consists of two components: a triggered component and a visually guided one. The triggered component develops without any sight of the forelimbs, but the guided component seems to require prolonged viewing of the limbs. A series of studies by Held and Bauer (1967; Bauer & Held, 1975) indicates that infant monkeys, too, need to observe their moving hands in order to develop visually guided reaching.

The deficits in guided reaching that we have described are not permanent. When these animals were subsequently permitted to view their limbs for a few hours, they all acquired the ability to reach out accurately toward small visual targets. In fact, they became indistinguishable from normally reared animals.

Eye-Specific Reaching

We noted earlier that an eye exposed during active locomotion is able to mediate guided locomotion while the other eye, exposed only during transport in a gondola, cannot. Having found that the visual placing response has two components (triggered and guided) that may be acquired independently, we wondered whether visually guided reaching might itself be separable into subcomponents specific to each eye (Hein & Diamond, 1971a).

After being reared in the dark until they were four weeks old, a group of kittens were brought into light for three hours daily. For the first 1½ hours one eye was covered and an opaque collar blocked the open eye's sight of the limbs. During the second 1½ hour period the opposite eye was covered and the forelimbs were visible through a transparent collar. Thus the kitten saw its limbs with only one of its eyes. After many days of this alternating monocular exposure, the kittens were tested with each eye for visually guided reaching to the interrupted surface in Fig. 5.

When using the eye that had previously viewed the limbs, the kittens showed accurate guided reaching, moving their paws to the right or left to land on a prong. When using the same limb but the other eye, which had not viewed the limbs before, the percentage of hits was at a chance level. Thus exposure that sufficed to give one eye precise control over a limb's reaching movements did not help the other eye to achieve such control.

Walking and Reaching: Which One First?

The studies described above have revealed that the development of each component of visually guided behavior depends on a particular form of visual feedback from self-produced movement. Does this mean that a changed sequence of exposure will lead to a changed sequence of development? Not necessarily, because it may be that there are *prerequisites* for the utilization of information in some of the motor-visual feedback loops.

In particular, it seemed to us that to extract useful information from viewing its moving limb, an animal must be able to localize the limb in visual space. Therefore an animal that has not developed a body-centered representation of visual space might be unable to acquire visually guided reaching. This difficulty did not arise in our earlier experiments because in those cases the kittens acquired visually guided reaching by viewing their forelimbs while walking about in a patterned environment. Thus reaching developed concurrently with visually guided locomotion, a capacity which implies a body-centered representation of visual space.

FIG. 5. Pronged surface used for testing visually guided forelimb extension.   (From Hein & Held, 1967.)

Rhea Diamond and I asked what would happen if a kitten received visual feedback *only* from its moving limb, without seeing anything else. Would the results be different for animals that had or had not been allowed previously to locomote in a patterned environment (without at that time seeing their limbs)? Our hypothesis was that there would be a difference: We thought that only kittens that had previously locomoted would develop guided reaching when allowed to see only a moving limb. Accordingly, we gave the kittens behavioral tests after each of three successive exposure periods: visual feedback from one forelimb only, exposure to a visible environment without sight of any limb, and visual feedback from the other forelimb.

Phase 1: Feedback from one forelimb. Experiments on human adjustment to prismatic displacement of vision suggested a convenient way to provide visual feedback from limb movements without sight of anything else in the environment. The research with humans showed that viewing a luminous spot attached to the hand, in an otherwise dark room, served the same function as viewing the hand itself, permitting full compensation for the prismatic displacement (Hein, 1972).

We applied a small spot of luminescent material to one forepaw of each of a group of dark-reared kittens. The animals were then permitted to move about freely in a light-tight enclosure for three hours daily, with the rest of their time spent in total darkness. After ten days of this exposure limited to feedback from one limb, we tested the animals on our usual battery of tests: the visual cliff, obstacle course, and interrupted surface. Although the kittens did display simple visually triggered extension responses, they showed no sign of having acquired either visually guided reaching or guided locomotion.

Phase 2: View of environment. The same animals were next exposed to a normally illuminated room in one of two ways. Some of them were kept in holders that prevented locomotion. The rest were allowed to walk around freely, but wore opaque collars that prevented view of their torso and limbs. This exposure to a visible environment was provided for several hours a day for ten days. Then the animals were again tested on the visual cliff, obstacle course and interrupted surface.

This time, the kittens that had locomoted in normal illumination showed visually guided locomotion. They discriminated the deep and shallow sides of a visual cliff and avoided contact with obstacles. In line with earlier findings, the animals that had been restrained in holders still performed poorly on both tests.

None of the kittens showed visually guided reaching, not even the locomoting ones. They had experienced (sequentially) the same kinds of movement-produced feedback that the kittens in our earlier experiment had experienced concurrently, yet they failed to develop the same capacities. Evidently, the order of exposures is critical.

Phase 3: Feedback from other forelimb. The final phase of our experiment established that it is the sequence of exposures, not their simultaneity, that is crucial. Both groups of kittens (those that had and those that had not acquired guided locomotion in phase 2) were given ten days of exposure with a luminous spot on one forelimb, in an otherwise dark enclosure. As a further test of independence of components, we put the luminous spot on the limb opposite the one it had been on in the first phase of the experiment.

When retested with the interrupted surface, the kittens that had previously walked about in a visible environment now displayed guided reaching, but only with the forelimb that had a luminous spot during the third exposure period.

When using the other forelimb, which had a luminous spot only during the first phase, their performance was at chance level. The kittens that had seen their surroundings only while in holders showed *no* guided reaching with *either* forelimb (though they did show triggered extension).

We drew two conclusions from these results. First, visual feedback from limb movements permits development of visually guided reaching only if an animal has a representation of visual space, such as that obviously available to it when it exhibits visually guided locomotion (Hein & Diamond, 1972). Second, even when *both* forelimbs are being used effectively in visually guided locomotion, restricted exposure can limit the capacity for guided reaching to only *one* limb. In this experiment, the limb from which visual feedback was available only before development of guided locomotion could not be used to reach small targets, even when the other limb could.

Rearing in Dim Light: Performance in Dim and Bright Light

A report by Graybiel and Held (1970) suggested another possible basis for segregation in the acquisition of visually coordinated behavior. They found that if human adults adapted to prisms under normal illumination (photopic range) they showed a reduced degree of adaptation when tested in dim illumination (scotopic level). Apparently there was some dissociation between scotopic and photopic sensorimotor mechanisms.

We wondered whether kittens would display an analogous dissociation. If visually guided behaviors were acquired in dim light, would they be evident when tested at normal illumination levels? Rhea Diamond and I raised kittens for 10 to 17 days in an enclosure that was so dimly illuminated that light reflected from the paws was well below the photopic threshold (Hein & Diamond, 1971b).

When tested in dim light, the kittens negotiated the obstacle course readily and guided their paws accurately to the prongs of the interrupted surface. However, when tested in bright light (after 10 minutes of light adaptation), the kittens' performance was seriously deficient. They repeatedly walked into obstacles, and often acted startled at the contact. With the interrupted surface, their performance was at a chance level; they missed the prongs as often as not.

At the end of the experiment we allowed the kittens to run about and view their limbs in a brightly illuminated enclosure. A few hours of such exposure was enough for the development of both visually guided locomotion and reaching in bright light. Together with other control procedures, this convinced us that the rearing in dim light had not damaged the cone system. We concluded that visually guided behavior develops independently in dim and bright light, calling for movement-produced visual feedback at each level of illumination.

CONCLUSIONS

Our studies have offered an increasingly detailed account of the acquisition of motor-visual coordination in young animals. In many respects, this acquisition parallels human adults' adjustment of coordination to prismatic displacement of vision. Information provided by visual feedback from self-produced movement is of prime importance in both processes.

The experiments with kittens have revealed the surprising extent to which components of visually controlled movement may be acquired independently, each demanding its own specific form of motor-visual feedback. Separable components demonstrated so far by appropriately restricted exposure include: triggered vs. guided components of the visual placing response; visually guided locomotion vs. visually guided reaching; visual guidance by one eye vs. the other; visually guided reaching with one forelimb vs. the other; visually guided behaviors in dim vs. bright illumination. In addition, we found that acquisition of certain components forms a necessary basis for the acquisition of others (for example, the development of visually guided locomotion is a prerequisite for acquisition of visually guided reaching).

ACKNOWLEDGMENTS

This research was supported by grants from the Spencer Foundation, the National Aeronautics and Space Administration, and the National Institutes of Health.

REFERENCES

Bauer, J. A., & Held, R. Comparison of visually-guided reaching in normal and deprived infant monkeys. *Journal of Experimental Psychology: Animal Behavior Processes*, 1975, *1*, 298-308.

Bossom, J. Complete recovery of accurate egocentric localization during prolonged wearing of prisms. Paper presented at Eastern Psychological Association, 1959.

Cohen, M., & Held, R. Degrading visual-motor coordination by exposure to disordered re-afferent stimulation. Paper presented at Eastern Psychological Association, New York, April 1960.

Graybiel, A. M., & Held, R. Prismatic Adaptation under scotopic and photopic conditions. *Journal of Experimental Psychology*, 1970, *1*, 16-22.

Hein, A. Acquiring components of visually guided behavior. In A. Pick (Ed.), *Minnesota symposia on child development, 6*. Minneapolis: University of Minnesota Press, 1972.

Hein, A., & Diamond, R. M. Contrasting development of visually triggered and guided movements in kittens with respect to interocular and interlimb equivalence. *Journal of Comparative and Physiological Psychology*, 1971a, *76*, 219-224.

Hein, A., & Diamond, R. M. Independence of the cat's scotopic and photopic systems in acquiring control of visually guided behavior. *Journal of Comparative and Physiological Psychology*, 1971b, *76*, 31-38.

Hein, A., & Diamond, R. M. Locomotory space as a prerequisite for acquiring visually guided reaching in kittens. *Journal of Comparative and Physiological Psychology*, 1972, *81*, 394-398.

Hein, A., Gower, E., & Diamond, R. Exposure requirements for developing the triggered component of the visual-placing response. *Journal of Comparative and Physiological Psychology*, 1970, *73*, 188-192.

Hein, A., & Held, R. Minimal conditions essential for complete relearning of hand-eye coordination with prismatic distortion of vision. Paper presented at Eastern Psychological Association, Philadelphia, April 1958.

Hein, A., & Held, R. A neural model for labile sensorimotor coordinations. In E. E. Bernard & M. R. Kare (Eds.) *Biological prototypes and synthetic systems. Vol. 1.* New York: Plenum, 1962.

Hein, A., & Held, R. Dissociation of the visual placing response into elicited and guided components. *Science*, 1967, *158*, 390-391.

Hein, A., Held, R., & Gower, E. Development and segmentation of visually controlled movement by selective exposure during rearing. *Journal of Comparative and Physiological Psychology*, 1970, *73*, 181-187.

Held, R., & Bauer, J., Jr. Visually guided reaching in infant monkeys after restricted rearing. *Science*, 1967, *155*, 718-720.

Held, R., & Bossom, J. Neonatal deprivation and adult rearrangement: Complementary techniques for analyzing plastic sensory-motor coordinations. *Journal of Comparative and Physiological Psychology*, 1961, *54*, 33-37.

Held, R., & Hein, A. Movement-produced stimulation in the development of visually-guided behavior. *Journal of Comparative and Physiological Psychology*, 1963, *56*, 872-876.

Held, R., & Hein, A. V. Adaptation of disarranged eye-hand coordination contingent upon reafferent stimulation. *Perceptual and Motor Skills*, 1958, *8*, 87-90.

Held, R., & Mikaelian, H. Motor-sensory feedback versus need in adaptation to rearrangement. *Perceptual and Motor Skills*, 1964, *18*, 685-688.

Riesen, A. H. Stimulation as a requirement for growth and function in behavioral development. In D. W. Fiske and S. R. Maddi (Eds.), *Functions of varied experience.* Homewood, Illinois: Dorsey Press, 1961.

The Rediscovery of Adaptability in the Visual System: Effects of Extrinsic and Intrinsic Chromatic Dispersion

Richard Held

Massachusetts Institute of Technology

Not too long ago when visual scientists spoke about adaptability they were almost always referring to light, dark, and color adaptation. The visual appearance of an illuminated area changes during the course of time, even though its actual intensity and wavelength remain constant. A bright light looks dimmer; a colored area looks less saturated. Over the past century, careful and quantitative psychophysical measurements and theories relating to light and color adaptation have been abundant.

Although temporal changes in the perception of more complex dimensions of stimulation—line orientation, size, motion, edge-color, to mention a few—were known, they were not taken very seriously within the domain of the science of vision. Only a few rather unorthodox investigators were inclined to view them with interest: James J. Gibson (1937) and Wolfgang Köhler (1944), for example. The reason for this neglect is rather obvious in retrospect. There simply were no generally convincing conceptions within which the adaptation of complex properties made sense (no pun intended). However, within the last decade or two, appropriate conceptions have appeared with a vengeance. As a result of the new ideas about features encoded by the visual system, old adaptation phenomena that were formerly treated as mere curiosities have now gained scientific respectability. As a consequence, many of the previously known forms of adaptation and aftereffect have been rediscovered and written accounts published, often without recognition of earlier work.

OPTICAL EFFECTS OF PRISMS

To gain some perspective on the present situation, I would like to start with one of the oldest and most productive techniques for inducing a variety of complex adaptations: the wearing of wedge-prism eyeglasses. Many of the modern studies of visual adaptation can be traced back to the results found in prism experiments over the last century. In turn, some of the recent experiments cast new light on poorly understood aspects of prism adaptation.

As shown in Fig. 1, a wedge prism produces a number of related optical effects, with predictable consequences for visual perception. In all cases, the initial effects of the prisms on perception correspond closely to the prism's optical effects on the retinal image.

Overall Displacement

The largest and most evident effect is the overall displacement of the images of objects as a result of the refraction of light rays passing through the prism. The perceptual result is that the objects appear displaced (toward the apex of the prism) relative to where they are seen with the naked eye. The behavioral consequences are errors in the orienting of parts of the body—eyes, head, torso, limbs—towards seen objects.

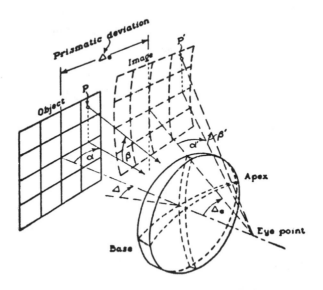

FIG. 1. Displacement and distortions of the image produced by a wedge prism. (From Ogle, 1951.)

Deformation

A uniform displacement does not itself alter the apparent shapes of objects any more than does the image displacement produced by a mirror. However, a prism does alter perceived shapes because the displacement is not uniform; it varies as one looks through different parts of the prism. The differences in displacement result from variation in the amount of refraction when light rays traverse the prism at different angles. The outcome, as seen in Fig. 1, is that straight lines parallel to the base-apex axis of the prism appear to slant and converge, and parallel lines in a frontal plane appear to vary in separation from one side of the visual field to the other. Lines at right angles to the base-apex axis appear curved.

Color Fringes

Finally, because different wavelengths of light are refracted by different amounts, the images of a light-dark boundary displaced to different degrees depending on wavelength, instead of coinciding. The result is that narrow fringes of color appear at the edges of light-dark boundaries. The hue of these color-fringes depends on whether the dark or the light area is nearer the prism base, as shown in Fig. 2.

ADAPTATION TO DISPLACEMENT AND DEFORMATION

From the point of view of adaptation, the interesting result of wearing such a prism in front of the eye is that both the behavioral effects and the appearances of objects seen through the prism gradually change over time. Each of the behavioral errors and visual distortions slowly diminishes, almost as if the visual system were somehow constructing its own internal prism of opposite orientation to cancel the effects of the external one. However, this metaphor is inaccurate in at least one very important way. If the prism-induced errors were corrected by the equivalent of an internal prism, then the amount of correction at a given time would always be the same for every distorted property. But this is not what actually happens. Let us consider, one at a time, the several types of optical distortion produced by prisms and the corresponding adaptive consequences of wearing prism eyeglasses.

Overall Displacement

As mentioned previously, prisms displace all parts of the retinal image by a considerable amount. Considered separately from the local variation in displacement, this overall displacement causes no perceived deformation of ob-

72   Richard Held

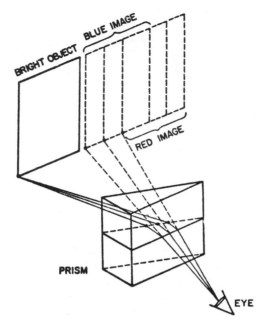

FIG. 2. Production of edge colors by dispersion of white light. Different wavelengths of light from a bright object on a dark background are refracted by different amounts, producing an overlapping set of images. Long-, medium-, and short-wavelength images are shown here.

jects but only a visual-motor discrepancy and intersensory discrepancies. For example, reaching for seen objects will be in error and the seen and felt locations of objects may seem to differ. The reduction of such discrepancies through adaptation has been extensively explored since it was reported more than one hundred years ago (Helmholtz, 1866). Prolonged wearing of prism eyeglasses will result in high degrees of compensation approaching 100%.

In light of the fact that prismatic displacement changes the retinal stimulation that results from movements of the body or its parts, it is not surprising that such movement-induced changes in visual stimulation ("reafference") are primarily responsible for adaptation (Held, 1965; Howard & Templeton, 1966). The investigation of these adaptive behaviors has provided the basis for various theories of sensorimotor coordination, as is discussed by Hardt, Held, and Steinbach (1971) and by Harris (1980), and of the early development of such sensorimotor functions, as discussed by Hein (1980).

Deformation

The deformed appearances of objects seen through the prism have also been the subject of much research over the years. The apparent curvature of straight lines and its reduction with prolonged viewing was first recorded by Wundt (1898) and later studied by Gibson and many others (Gibson, 1933).

One salient result of studies of this form of adaptation is that, unlike adaptation to displacement, it never amounts to more than a fraction of the geometrical distortion produced by the prism. Another difference from adaptation to displacement is the fact that movement of the observer is not at all essential for adaptation to deformation (although there is a special form of curvature adaptation that requires movement-produced visual change in the absence of curved edges [Held & Rekosh, 1963]). A final difference is that, as Gibson (1933) first observed, for curvature adaptation (other than the special form mentioned above) the prism simply acts as a device for producing curved lines—the subject can adapt just as well by viewing curved lines drawn on a surface, without a prism.

These results were probably the first explicit recognition that the visual system can somehow be fatigued, habituated, desensitized, satiated, or otherwise altered by complex properties of stimulation. Related observations that the prism-induced slants of lines, as well as their perceived spacing, show adaptive changes can be regarded as the forerunners of tilt and spatial-frequency-dependent adaptation and aftereffect. The research of Wolfgang Köhler and his associates established aftereffects that entail size changes (Köhler & Wallach, 1944) and depth changes (Köhler & Emery, 1947), clearcut precursors of recent studies of what are now considered feature analyzers of the visual system. In this tradition, I showed how these results could be generalized to the effects of exposure to varied patterns (Held, 1962). I surmised that, "...a pattern sufficiently transformed from normal conditions is an adequate condition for generating aftereffects." But the crucial question remained as to which transformations are necessary and sufficient, since an indefinitely large number of transformations can be performed. The identification of spatial frequency as an important and quite general dimension of effective transformation has given one important answer to this question.

Two Modes of Vision

As mentioned above, compensation for the overall displacement produced by a prism requires, or is greatly enhanced by, movement of the observer. On the other hand, adaptation to the prism-produced deformations occurs without such movement. This difference, among many others, led us to reaffirm an old distinction between two modes of spatial vision: figure-specific and locus-specific analysis (Held, 1968). This distinction appears to be quite pervasive and is marked by many characteristics.

Spatially distributed stimulation on the retina is primarily used for two purposes: (1) for the guidance of movement as in target directed eye movement, in reaching, and in directing locomotion of the body, and (2) in recognition of the forms of objects. But these two functions make antithetical demands upon retinal information.

Goal-directed movement requires information about the location of the target object relative to the eye, limb, or body. Closely related to the guidance of overt movement is the implicit orientation of the body to objects localized in space. In order to indicate a direction from the body either by overt localizing movements of the body or by the use of psychophysical techniques, the visual system must extract a locus from the flux of information received. For recognition of objects, on the other hand, their locations are irrelevant; the goal of form analysis is the extraction of shape independent of its locus in space.

Our finding that adaptation to deformation (figural transformation) entails a process different from that in adaptation to overall displacement is quite consistent with other differences between the two modes of analysis. The opposing demands on the visual system for extracting these two types of information suggest the operations of different neural processes (Held, 1970), and although we are far from an understanding of the mechanisms underlying these differences (Schneider, 1969), they constitute a challenge for future research.

COLOR-EDGE ADAPTATION

Color-Fringe Adaptation

Adaptation to the half-spectra that appear at light-dark boundaries was reported as early as 1883 by an ophthalmologist who prescribed the use of strong lenses which produced appreciable chromatic dispersion (Macfarland, 1883). The "chromatism" along contours, which was prominent when the glasses were first worn, was no longer noticeable to the patient after a few weeks. More recently, Gibson (1937) mentioned the effect after wearing prism glasses and Ivo Kohler (1951) conducted an extensive study of the phenomenon, with strong prisms worn for weeks or months.

Adaptation is specific to the direction of the luminance gradient and hence to the orientation of the edge. No aftereffect is seen on edges parallel to the base-apex axis of the prism worn during exposure. Adaptation to these edge colors is reported to become complete after long periods of exposure, although the situation is complicated by the fact that the degree of adaptation and aftereffect is influenced by the luminance and luminance contrast of the edges being tested (see below).

Until quite recently, little attention was paid to this complex form of adaptation although it was the first to be reported of the genre of contingent aftereffects: the aftereffect in one dimension of stimulation being contingent upon a second dimension.

Orientation-Specific Color Adaptation

Much more research has been devoted to a different but closely related contingent aftereffect discovered by Celeste McCollough in 1965. McCollough had been intrigued by Kohler's reports of color-fringe adaptation and visited Kohler's laboratory in Innsbruck to get information for more detailed quantitative studies. Later, influenced by the discovery in cats of neural units selectively responsive to edges in particular orientations (Hubel & Wiesel, 1958), she had human observers view a vertical grating illuminated by one color alternated every few seconds with a horizontal grating illuminated by a nearly complementary color. After several minutes of such exposure, observers who viewed a black-white grating saw aftereffect colors that differed according to the orientation (horizontal or vertical) of the test grating, being complementary to the hue of each orientation of the exposure gratings. In this way, McCollough demonstrated that the color aftereffect can be made contingent upon edge orientation. (These effects are discussed extensively by Harris, 1980, and Stromeyer, 1978).

McCollough regarded this orientation-specific color aftereffect as fundamentally similar to color-fringe adaptation. One would result from chromatic adaptation of neural mechanisms sensitive to the orientation of a contour; the other, of mechanisms sensitive to the direction of light-dark contrast as well. Both sorts of contour-sensitive cells have been identified neurophysiologically in the visual cortex of animals.

We can go further and speculate, with support from the data reported below, that both forms of color-edge adaptation may simply be special cases of the process by means of which the visual system eliminates the fringe colors produced by the chromatic aberration of the optics of the eye (also discussed below). This interpretation would make teleological sense. The chromatic aberration of the eye is a property which varies widely among eyes of the same as well as different individuals, as a consequence of several uncorrelated optical factors. Therefore it would be difficult to devise a genetically determined correction that would compensate appropriately for the optical defect in all cases. It would be simpler to have an adaptive mechanism which could respond to and nullify whatever color-fringes were produced by the optics of a particular eye.

One general finding of research on color-edge effects is consistent with this teleological thesis. Neither color-fringe adaptation nor the aftereffect discovered by McCollough nor for that matter any of the variety of edge-color aftereffects that have recently been studied (Hajos & Ritter, 1965; Stromeyer, 1978)   show appreciable interocular transfer. That is, when generated by adaptation of one eye, little or no aftereffect can be demonstrated by testing the other eye. This finding is surely consistent with the thesis that such adaptation evolved to color-correct for the ocular aberration of the optics of the eye, since right and left eyes almost invariably differ in their aberrations.

Color-Specific Tilt Adaptation

Color adaptation has been shown to be specific to not only the adapted eye and the locus on the retina which has been exposed, the direction of intensity gradients, and the orientation of edges, but also to other properties of stimulation including spatial frequency and direction of motion (Stromeyer, 1978).

The reverse aftereffect has also been demonstrated. Assuming a close linkage between color and edge processing in the visual system, Held and Shattuck (1971) hypothesized that not only should the color aftereffect be contingent upon edge orientation as McCollough had demonstrated, but it should also be possible to show the reverse, that perceived edge orientation can be made contingent upon color. We used the tilt aftereffect: the observation that after viewing a slightly tilted bar or grating, a vertical edge appears tilted in the opposite direction. For many minutes, observers viewed a red grating tilted off vertical in one direction alternated every few seconds with a green grating tilted equally in the opposite direction. If there were no color-orientation-selective mechanisms, the equal exposure to opposite tilts should create no net tilt aftereffect. However, if edge orientation-color selectivity exists, then opposite directions of the aftereffect would be expected for red and for green test gratings. That is in fact what was found in our experiment (Fig. 3).

We also demonstrated that the orientational tuning of these edge-color selective analyzers approximated that previously found neurophysiologically for luminance-defined edges (Fig. 4). As in the case of McCollough aftereffect, little, if any, interocular transfer was found for the color-selective aftereffect. In fact, opposite aftereffects can be simultaneously generated in the two eyes.

The independence of aftereffects in the two eyes led to a further question. Would opposite tilt aftereffects in the two eyes be equivalent to an "internal stereogram," with binocular disparities that would produce the appearance of tilt in depth (Fig. 5)? We found, as shown by the data in Fig. 6, that such a depth effect can, in fact, be demonstrated (Shattuck & Held, 1975). This depth effect implies that the monocular color-selective channels which process the color-edge information converge onto binocular channels which are not color-selective and which process stereoscopic depth (retinal disparities). This finding is fully consistent with present evidence that it is not possible to induce a color-selective aftereffect in depth (Stromeyer, 1978).

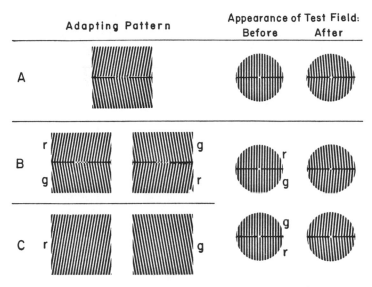

FIG. 3. A: Achromatic tilt aftereffect. After one minute of scanning the adapting pattern by successively fixating the horizontal row of dots, the test pattern appears as shown when fixated at its center. B and C: Color-selective tilt aftereffects. After 10 minutes of scanning the two adapting patterns, alternated at 5-second intervals, the test pattern appears as shown, when fixated at its center (the apparent tilts are exaggerated here). (From Held & Shattuck, 1971.)

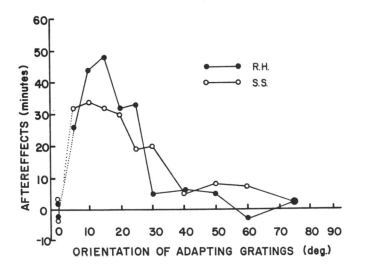

FIG. 4. Magnitude of the color-selective tilt aftereffect as a function of tilt of the adapting patterns. (From Held & Shattuck, 1971.)

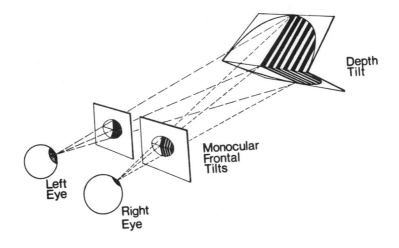

FIG. 5. Stereoscopic depth induced by monocular frontal tilt aftereffects like those diagrammed in Fig. 3. (From Shattuck & Held, 1975.)

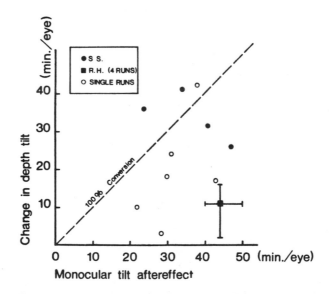

FIG. 6. Shift in perceived stereoscopic depth as a function of shift in perceived frontal tilt after adaptation to opposite frontal tilts in the two eyes. (From Shattuck & Held, 1975.)

ADAPTATION TO COLOR-FRINGES:
SOME EARLY OBSERVATIONS

I became interested in color-edge aftereffects over twenty years ago, motivated largely by curiosity about how these bizarre (as they then seemed) aftereffects relate to the normal functioning of the visual system. I reported many of the following results orally (Held, 1955) and described them in a widely circulated manuscript, but they have not previously been published. It seems to be an appropriate time to publish them now because of the renewed interest in such phenomena and the new conceptualizations now available. There may also be some value in retracing the steps I took in attempting to gain an understanding of a fascinating visual phenomenon about which little was known. Therefore I will describe my initial attempts to determine the stimulus variables that influence color-fringe adaptation and to deal with certain puzzling aspects of the data that emerged. I will conclude with a speculative account that deals with all of my data, including the seeming discrepancies, and allows us to relate the phenomenon to more fundamental functions of the visual system.

Measurement Procedure

As an aftereffect of adapting to the color-fringes that wedge prisms produce along light-dark contours, contours viewed by the naked eye, without prisms, appear to have color-fringes, roughly complementary in hue to those that the prisms had produced. The adaptation itself is manifested as a reduction in the perceptual prominence of the prism-produced fringes. Thus, for both the adaptation and the aftereffect, it is as if the visual system were generating complementary color-fringes that cancel out the optically produced color-fringes.

The basic measurement procedure was to have the observer look at black and white stripes through a variable-strength prism (Fig. 7), and adjust the prism until the optical color-fringes that it produced cancelled out (insofar as possible) the illusory fringes. The variable prism, commonly known as a Risley rotary prism, consisted of two 20-diopter plane-surfaced prisms mounted face to face in bearings that permitted them to rotate at equal speeds in opposite directions when the observer turned a knob. As diagrammed in Fig. 8, this allowed the effective prism strength to change continuously from 40 diopters base-left through 0 diopters to 40 diopters base-right. The symmetrical counterrotation of the two prisms insured that any nonhorizontal component of one prism's effect was exactly balanced by the other prism.

In my early measurements and experiments, the effective base-apex axis of the variable prism was kept constant, usually horizontal (180°). In later studies, the axis was placed in various orientations. The subject, whose head was held fixed by a biting board, monocularly viewed a striped field 20° in diameter through the prism. The field was a 1 cycle/degree black and white square-wave grating, illuminated from the rear by white light from incandescent sources diffused by opal glass. The grating target, as well as other displays used, was viewed from a distance of 60 centimeters, and was always oriented with the stripes perpendicular to the base-apex axis of the prism.

Preliminary Findings

Short-term adaptation. In the course of taking measurements under these restricted conditions, I soon found that when a long series of measurements was taken, the subject's null settings drifted systematically. Similar shifts in prism settings, small but significant, were also found after exposure periods (vision through a prism of some fixed power) of as little as 10 to 20 minutes. It occurred to me that these shifts might represent an early stage of edge-color adaptation, making it possible to study the adaptation in an economical manner by repeated short-term exposures under different conditions.

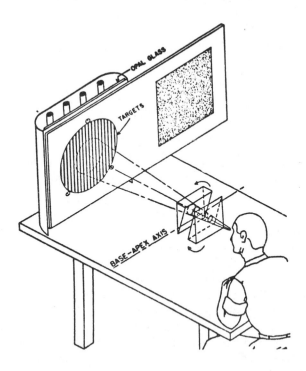

FIG. 7. Variable prism used to null edge colors, with striped grating and speckled exposure field. (From Held, 1962.)

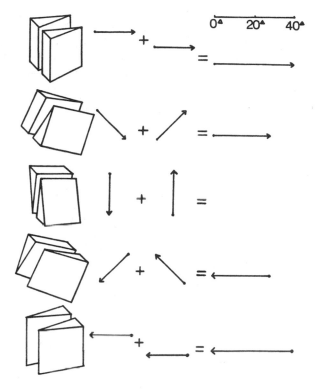

FIG. 8. Apparent displacements and their sums induced by elements of a variable prism.

Using an experimental technique of preexposure measurements followed by exposure and then postexposure measurements, certain qualitative results were obtained merely by consideration of the presence or absence of a significant postexposure shift of the prism settings.

Curvature and color-fringe adaptation. The first question concerned the exposure conditions required for producing the chromatic adaptation as opposed to adaptation to curvature of lines. Are the same conditions of exposure essential to the production of both effects?

When I had subjects scan gratings through a 10-diopter prism for 20 minutes, I found that the two forms of adaptation proceeded at different rates. Curvature adaptation occurred much faster than edge-color adaptation. Although I did not know it at the time (I did not learn about Kohler's research until after completing the experiments reported here), Ivo Kohler (1951) had also found different rates for the two kinds of adaptation, using a cancellation method similar to the one I used.

By varying the exposure stimulus, I found it possible to produce adaptation to the edge spectra without any accompanying adaptation to curvature, and vice versa. If the scanned target consisted of a randomly speckled surface (on the right in Fig. 7), adaptation to the edge spectra (shown by shifts of the prism setting for color) occurred without corresponding shifts for curvature. Shifts for curvature occurred only when the target consisted of linear contours (on the left in Fig. 7) which were given a curved appearance by the prism. On the other hand, if a narrow band color filter was placed over the prism, viewing the stripes gave curvature shifts but no shifts for the edge colors. These results are important because they are evidence against attributing the shifts to physical changes in the optics of the eye: Any optical changes would necessarily entail concomitant and equal shifts for both curvature and chromatic prism settings.

Role of the prism. Further study of the chromatic adaptation showed that the prism plays no role other than as a vehicle for producing edge colors. Similar chromatic adaptation occurred when subjects used their naked eyes to view fringe spectra projected on a screen, or a set of parallel black bars with alternate edges of yellow and blue filter material.

These results eliminate any interpretation in terms of special optical effects involved in scanning through a prism, other than the existence of boundary colors. I nevertheless continued to use the variable prism in my research because of the precision of measurements it afforded. Some idea of this precision can be gained from the fact that the standard deviations of 10 to 20 measurements with the best subject were as small as 0.1 prism diopter and rarely became greater than 0.3 or 0.4 diopter with any subject.

Parenthetically, I should note here that the use of boundary colors, independent of prism dispersion, verged on procedures of the type that McCollough later used to demonstrate the aftereffect that is associated with her name (discussed above). I don't think I am immodest in suggesting that I failed to perform her experiment with orthogonal blue and yellow adapting gratings for only one reason: I simply was not at that time sufficiently impressed by the orientational selectivity of the visual system. It had not yet been conclusively demonstrated as it was to be within the next few years by Hubel and Wiesel (1959).

Adaptation as a Function of Prism Power

Adaptation and test procedure. To study adaptation as a function of prism power, a standardized scanning procedure was adopted. The subject spent 20 minutes looking at the speckled target through the prism at a given setting. He was told to move his glance to a new fixation point of his own choice in continually varied directions, once per second in time to the click of a metronome.

Before and after the scanning period, he viewed the straight-line grating through the variable prism and adjusted the prism power so as to eliminate any color-fringes along the grating contours, making 10 such null settings each time. The difference between the means of the 10 prescan and 10 postscan null settings represented the amount of adaptation produced in 20 minutes.

Each of four subjects went through a series of 12 sessions whose order was permuted among them to reduce possible sequential effects. In each session, the subject scanned the speckled target through a different prism power, ranging from 25 diopters base-right to 25 diopters base-left in eleven steps, with two sessions at 0 diopters. Target luminance was maintained at 7 millilamberts and each subject used his right eye only.

Compensatory adaptation. As shown by the filled symbols and solid curve in Fig. 9, the magnitude of the adaptive shift in null settings increased with increase of the adapting prism power up to 7 diopters base-left or base-right. Further increases of the adapting prism power gave little or no increase of the shift.

In most cases, the shifts in null settings were in a direction which compensated for the adapting prism. To nullify the color-fringes before adapting, a subject looking through a base-right prism would decrease the strength of the prism a great deal, to somewhere near 0 diopters prism power; after 20 minutes of scanning contours through the base-right prism, the subject would tolerate a small amount of base-right prism power when judging that the color-fringes were invisible. That is, in terms of the pre-post difference which

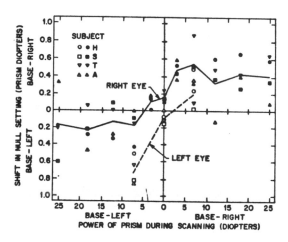

FIG. 9. Adaptation to color-fringes as a function of prism power. Observers set a variable prism to cancel out the illusory color-fringes that resulted from scanning a speckled pattern through a fixed prism. The difference between such null settings before and after scanning is plotted; lines are drawn through the means for four observers.

was the measure of adaptation, scanning through a base-right prism led to an increase in base-right prism power.

Puzzling asymmetry. There were, however, some puzzling aspects of the data, which led to further research. The plotted data show a rather clear-cut asymmetry: After scanning with the right eye through base-right prisms, the shift (shown by the solid curve) rises much higher (reaching a maximum of about 0.5 diopter) than it sinks after scanning through base-left prisms (a shift of slightly less than 0.2 diopter). The upward displacement of the curve is large enough to show a small base-right shift even after scanning at 0 diopters prism power—equivalent to a flat plate of glass which would cause no chromatic dispersion. Another indication of the asymmetry is that the shift in settings did not invariably match the direction of the adapting prism, and therefore was sometimes "antiadaptive"; adapting to a 0.25 diopter base-left prism, for example, led to a small mean shift in the base-right direction.

Left eyes. Suspecting that this asymmetry resulted from using my subjects' right eyes, I repeated the experiment using the same subjects' left eyes, at powers of −7, 0, and +7 prism diopters. The results (open symbols and broken line in Fig. 9) showed magnitudes of adaptation similar to those for the right eyes, but with an opposite asymmetry: a larger shift for base left than for base right.

In addition to these asymmetries, I noticed that when subjects made their first null settings, before adapting, they did not adjust the variable prism to 0 diopters, which would eliminate the actual chromatic dispersion. Instead, their initial null settings (not shown) often deviated from the true 0 diopter prism setting by 0.5 diopter or more. These results led me to examine the chromatic aberration which is produced by the optics of the eye itself.

The "Ocular Prism"

The optics of the human eye suffer considerably from chromatic aberration of several types (Vos, 1960). One source of this intrinsic chromatic dispersion is the fact that the optical axis of the lens system of the eye does not meet the retina at the fovea (Fig. 10). Thus there is a deviation (angle α) of the optical axis of the eye from the fixation axis. This misalignment causes chromatic dispersion which is not unlike that produced by looking through a prism. I will therefore refer to the intrinsic prism-like chromatic dispersion, which is produced by the optics of the eye, as the *ocular prism.*

Explanation of the asymmetries? The presence of chromatic dispersion intrinsic to the eye, the ocular prism, would seem to offer an explanation for the asymmetries of the curves in Fig. 9. The chromatic dispersion due to the ocular prism would either add to or subtract from that caused by the external prism, depending on the orientation of the external prism. Thus the stimulus for adaptation would be augmented for an external prism in one orientation and diminished for the opposite orientation. If the ocular prism is oriented oppositely in the two eyes, the resulting adaptation could display asymmetries like those seen in Fig. 9.

However, a major feature of the data made this simple explanation of the asymmetries highly unlikely. It is well know that in most eyes the optical axis intersects the retina in a nasal direction from (and below) the fixation axis (Fig. 10), producing chromatic dispersion similar to that produced by a base-nasal (and -down) prism (Vos, 1960). In other words, as a general rule we can think of the ocular prism as being base-nasal and -down. (As Vos discusses, there are other sources of aberration and the angle α alone is not always decisive.) If my subjects' eyes were typical, their right eyes would have base-left ocular prisms and their left eyes base-right. Then if adaptation were determined by the algebraic sum of the external prism and the ocular prism, the asymmetries should be exactly the *opposite* of those shown in Fig. 9. Adaptation should be greater for the right eye when the external adapting prism is base-left, matching its ocular prism, and should be greater for the left eye when the external prism is base-right.

Null settings without adaptation. Because it seemed so plausible that adaptation should depend on the algebraic sum of external and ocular prism power, I decided to check on the statistically unlikely possibility that all of my subjects' eyes were atypical, with ocular prisms which were base-temporal instead of the

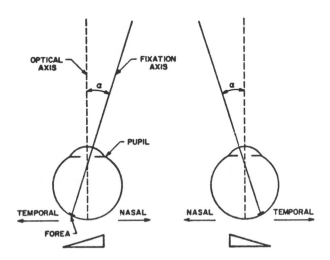

FIG. 10. Misalignment (exaggerated) of the optical axis of the eye from the fixation axis. The misalignment causes chromatic dispersion similar to that produced by looking through base-nasal prisms.

usual base-nasal. To determine the orientation of the ocular prism I had the subjects make null settings of the variable prism *without* any prior exposure through a prism. The variable prism was rotated into various orientations, and the test grating was always oriented so that its bars were perpendicular to the base-apex axis of the prism. Luminances of 70, 0.7, and 0.07 millilamberts were used in addition to the 7 millilamberts employed in the previous experiment. Each of four subjects (three of them from the former experiment) made null settings at each luminance with each eye.

Some of the resulting data for three left eyes, typical of all eight eyes tested, are plotted in Fig. 11. The curves are all rough approximations to half-cycles of a sinusoid, as would be expected if they are tracing out a compensation for ocular prismatic dispersion. Given that the ocular prism has a fixed strength and orientation, it spreads out the different wavelengths originating from each point on a contour by a constant amount, always along its effective base-apex axis. Thus as the grating contours are rotated, the width of the color-fringe measured perpendicularly to that contour varies sinusoidally and requires a correspondingly varying external prism power to counteract the fringe.

Although the sinusoidal curves suggested that I was indeed measuring the effects of a fixed ocular prism, the direction of the results seemed to confirm that in all eight eyes the ocular prism was base-temporal instead of the normal base-nasal. As indicated by the peaks of the curves in Fig. 11, to eliminate visible color-fringes, subjects added base-*nasal* (and -down) external prism power (that is, base-right for the left eye). On the assumption that the external prism was being adjusted to compensate for or nullify the effect of the ocular prism, the implication would be that the ocular prism for all of these eyes is base-temporal and -up.

Chromatic stereoscopy. I now had two sets of data which seemed to imply that all of my subjects had atypical eyes, with base-temporal instead of base-nasal ocular prisms. However, two other kinds of data on two of the subjects yielded evidence which, though not conclusive, suggested that they *did* in fact possess the usual base-nasal ocular prisms!

First I tested for chromatic stereoscopy. If a subject's ocular prisms are both base-nasal (base-right for the left eye and base-left for the right eye), the images of a blue object and a red object are displaced in opposite directions in the two eyes, producing binocular disparity. The result is that if the blue and red objects are actually in the same frontal plane, subjects with base-nasal ocular prisms should see the red one as nearer (see Vos, 1960). For both of my subjects, the red object did appear nearer, thereby indicating a preponderance of base-nasal power.

Ophthalmetric measurements. The second line of evidence consisted of ophthalmetric determinations of the angle α between the optical axis of the eye

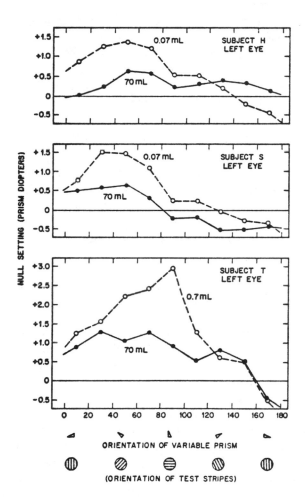

FIG. 11. Subjects' settings of variable prism to cancel out color-fringes seen along test stripes prior to any scanning through a prism. The x-axis and corresponding sketches of prisms represent the orientations for positive settings; negative settings are oriented in the opposite direction (+180°).

and the fixation axis. For both subjects, the optical axis was found to intersect the retina nasally from the fixation axis, which would tend to produce base-nasal ocular prism power.

Now I had a new puzzle: The base-nasal null settings shown in Fig. 11 seemed to imply that my subjects had base-temporal ocular prisms, whereas their color stereoscopy and ophthalmetric measurements implied the opposite. Instead of solving the puzzle of the asymmetric adaptation curves in Fig. 9 by verifying that my subjects all had atypical ocular prisms, the new measurements appeared to disagree with the earlier ones.

The "Neural Prism"

The effect of grating luminance. A clue about how to resolve these mysteries came from an aspect of my procedure that was introduced for no reason other than that it is a variation commonly used in psychophysical experiments: variation of luminance levels. As can be seen in Fig. 11, lower luminance levels (dashed curves) led to higher null settings. Reducing the luminance by a factor of 100 or 1000 raised the maxima of the curves by a factor or 2 or 3. These increases could not have been a direct optical effect of the change in luminance, since the extent of chromatic dispersion is the same for any luminance level.

I began to suspect that the data in Fig. 11 were reflecting not the effects of the ocular prism itself, but rather a habitual *adaptation* of the visual system to the ocular prism. The manifestations of such an adaptive state might well vary with luminance. Again I did not know it at the time, but Kohler (1951) had found a similar variation with luminance level in his observations on color-fringe adaptation.

If my subjects' ocular prisms were actually base-nasal, as for most people, then a compensatory adaptive state would be equivalent to an internal base-temporal prism. For convenience, let me refer to that adaptive state of the visual system as the *neural prism.* Now if for some reason (I will propose one later) the visual system were *overcompensating* for the chromatic dispersion produced by the ocular prism, the neural prism would be stronger than the ocular prism. The net effect would be equivalent to a weak base-temporal prism.

Resolving the puzzles. If the visual systems of my subjects were overcompensating for their base-nasal ocular prisms by, in effect, adding a still larger amount of base-temporal internal prism power, then when asked to adjust an external prism to eliminate all color-fringes, they would make base-nasal settings, as in Fig. 11. Given this reasoning, there is no discrepancy between the implications of the Fig. 11 null settings and of the chromatic stereoscopy and ophthalmetric measurements. The latter two measurements relate only to the physical optics of the eye (the ocular prism) whereas the former depends on both optics and the adaptive state of the visual system (the algebraic sum of the ocular and neural prisms).

The asymmetries in Fig. 9 are also as expected from this analysis. If the algebraic sum of ocular and neural prisms for the left eye is base-left, then the adaptive effects of a base-left external prism would be enhanced, whereas the effects of a base-right external prism would be diminished. This is what is seen in the broken line in Fig. 9. The situation for the right eye would be analogous, but with the asymmetry going in the opposite direction, as seen in the solid curve.

The Effective Internal Prism: Ocular Plus Neural

As a check on the consistency of the above interpretation I ran an additional experiment on subject H's left eye, with a procedure that incorporated aspects of the previous studies. The subject adapted by scanning the speckled target through an external prism, as for Fig. 9, and made null settings with the variable prism and grating stripes in various orientations, as for Fig. 11. Instead of the two orientations of the adapting prism represented in Fig. 9, I used four, deliberately putting the base-apex axis of the external prism either in the same orientation as the inferred ocular prismatic aberration or at right angles to it.

The above interpretation of the data for subject H's left eye suggested that it had ocular prism power equivalent to base-right and -down, with the base-apex axis at 70°, and that his habitual state of adaptation at 70 millilamberts was equivalent to a stronger prism with the same base-apex orientation but pointing in the opposite direction (base-left and -up, 250°). For purposes of adaptation, then, the effective internal prism power should be base-left and -up. Therefore in this experiment subject H adapted by scanning through a 7 diopter prism oriented at 70° (base-right and -down) or 250° (base-left and -up)—adding to or subtracting from his inferred internal prism—or at 160° (base-left and -down) or or 340° (base-right and -up)—perpendicular to the internal prism. In addition, a control condition of scanning at 0 diopters was included. In each of the five conditions, scanning lasted for 20 minutes, at 70 millilamberts.

Scanning at 0 diopters. The results are displayed in Fig. 12. As in Fig. 11, all of the curves are approximately sinusoidal.

The top curve corresponds to the data point in Fig. 9 for scanning with the left eye with the external prism set at 0 diopters, showing a small shift toward base-left (and -up) null settings. Most interestingly the curve is practically a mirror image of the curve of null settings which subject H made at 70 milli-lamberts prior to any scanning through a prism (Fig. 11). In other words, the adaptive shift at each orientation under this condition is proportional to the strength of the preadaptation prism setting in that orientation, but opposite in

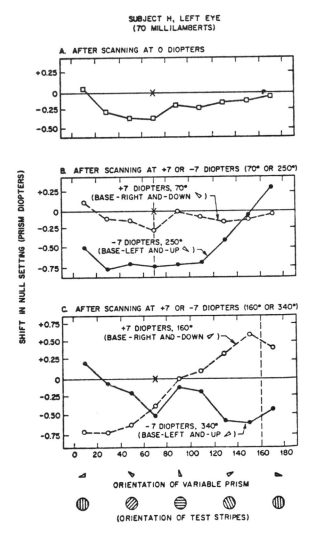

FIG. 12. Effects of scanning the speckled pattern through prisms in various orientations. Same x-axis as in Fig. 11.

90

direction. This is what would be expected if the settings in Fig. 11 represent an excess of base-left neural prism over the base-right ocular prism, producing color-fringes on the speckled target to which the subject then adapts. Thus exposure under this condition actually reduces the compensation for the ocular prism.

Adding or subtracting prism power. The middle graph of Fig. 12 shows the results of scanning through a prism that added to or subtracted from the inferred internal prism power. Confirming the data for the left eye in Fig. 9, the shifts obtained after scanning through a base-right external prism are small, while those obtained after scanning through a base-left prism are quite large.

Estimating the strength of the internal prism. If there were no internal prism power to complicate things, adaptation to external prisms of opposite base orientation (160° and 340°, for example) would result in curves symmetrical about the x-axis of plots of the type shown in Fig. 12. Each curve would approximate a half-cycle of a sinusoid and the two would be out of phase by 180°, with the maximum of one aligned with the minimum of the other and with both curves crossing the x-axis at the same point. Obviously, this is not true of the curves in the bottom graph of Fig. 12. Instead, judging by where the curves cross the x-axis, they appear to be out of phase by only about 110°. The dashed curve would have to be shifted leftward by about 35° and the solid curve rightward by 35° in order for the two to cross the x-axis at the same point and to be approximately mirror images.

A phase relationship like this is just what would be expected if adaptation depends not only on the external prism, but also on the effective internal prism (ocular plus neural), and if that internal prism has its base-apex axis at right angles to that of the external prism. In fact, the phase angle should reveal the effective power of the ocular prism. Since the power and orientation of the external prism are known and the orientation of the ocular prism has been inferred from other data, its effective power is easily derived. A phase shift of 35° for each curve implies the vector sum of the external ±7 diopters at 160° plus 5 diopters at 250° for the effective internal prism.

Interpretation

The above calculation that the effective internal prism power (ocular plus neural) of subject H's left eye is equivalent to a 5 diopter base-up prism in orientation 250° gives a reasonable account of the main features of his data in Figs. 9 and 11 (although the quantitative fit may leave much to be desired).

The analysis I have offered rests on the plausible assumption that adaptation depends on the direction and strength of the color-fringes that a subject sees when looking at contours. The color-fringes in turn reflect the net effect of three influences: chromatic dispersion produced by the optics of the eye (the ocular prism), the state of adaptation of the visual system (the neural prism), and any external prism that is present.

Overcompensation. In order to reconcile all of my data, I had to make two additional assumptions: that the habitual state of adaptation overcompensates for the ocular prism, and that the extent of overcompensation varies with light intensity. I cannot say why the degree of adaptation should vary with light intensity, but there is ample evidence from my own and other investigators' studies that it does. Moreover, this variation is seen both for experimentally produced short-term adaptation (Kohler, 1951) and for the habitual long-term adaptive state measured without external prisms (Fig. 11). It would be nice to believe, therefore, that this adaptive state of the visual system is the outcome of long-term adaptation to its own ocular prism, and that both short- and long-term (habitual) adaptation are one and the same process, a process which normally functions to counteract the color-fringes created by the optics of the eye.

If the function of the adaptive mechanism is to eliminate the unwanted effects of chromatic aberration, why is there in all of my data a mismatch between the strength of this adaptive response and of the ocular prism, with the result that color-fringes *are* seen with the naked eye, opposite in direction to those that the eye's optics produce? I would speculate that the overcompensation which I measured was occasioned by the relatively dim laboratory conditions. I would suppose that the subject brings to the laboratory a habitual adaptive state appropriate for eliminating color-fringes in daylight illumination, brighter by a factor of 10 to 1000 or more than even the highest intensity (70 millilamberts) that I used. In daylight, then, the color-fringes produced by the ocular prism would be nearly neutralized by the opposite ones supplied by the neural prism, whereas in dimmer illumination those supplied by the neural prism would be too strong—yielding the kind of data that puzzled and tantalized me during the course of my research.

CONCLUSION

I have tried to demonstrate, by these many examples, how the new ideas about feature extraction in the visual system have led to new interpretations of the phenomena of adaptation. In turn, both the new and old research on adaptation has led to the postulation of numerous kinds of feature analyzers.

Each instance of adaptation has been said to implicate the existence of analyzers selectively sensitive to the stimulus dimension or combination of dimensions which has been adapted. In other words, visual scientists have been ready, perhaps too ready, to explain their results by freely assuming different species of feature detectors in analogy to the single units discovered by neurophysiologists. (A discussion of this point of view, along with alternative conceptions, is offered by Harris, 1980.) The credo implicit in this work is that if observers can adapt to some particular concatenation of stimuli, then that adaptation is presumptive evidence for the existence of a neural entity selectively responsive to that set of stimulus properties. Consequently, this research is presumed to be a way of dissecting the nervous system into its responsive components.

Whatever may be the ultimate justification of analogies between single units studied neurophysiologically and feature analyzers inferred from psychophysical research, there can be no question about the impetus that they have lent to the rediscovery and further investigation of adaptability in the visual system.

ACKNOWLEDGMENTS

Preparation of this chapter was supported in part by research grants from the National Eye Institute, NIH-5ROI-EY-01191 and NIH-1P30-EY-02621.

REFERENCES

Gibson, J. J. Adaptation, aftereffect, and contrast in the perception of curved lines. *Journal of Experimental Psychology,* 1933, *16,* 1-31.

Hajos, A., & Ritter, M. Experiments to the problem of interocular transfer. *Acta Psychologica,* 1965, *24,* 81-90.

Hardt, M. E., Held, R., & Steinbach, M. J. Adaptation to displaced vision: A change in the central control of sensorimotor coordination. *Journal of Experimental Psychology,* 1971, *89,* 229-239.

Harris, C. S. Insight or out of sight?: Two examples of perceptual plasticity in the human adult. In C. S. Harris (Ed.), *Visual coding and adaptability.* Hillsdale, New Jersey: Lawrence Erlbaum Associates, 1980.

Hein, A. The development of visually guided behavior. In C. S. Harris (Ed.), *Visual coding and adaptability.* Hillsdale, New Jersey: Lawrence Erlbaum Associates, 1980.

Held, R. Adaptation to chromatic dispersion. Paper presented at Eastern Psychological Association, Philadelphia, April 1955.

Held, R. Adaptation to rearrangement and visual-spatial aftereffects. *Psychologische Beitrage,* 1962, *6,* 439-450.

Held, R., & Rekosh, J. Motor-sensory feedback and the geometry of visual space. *Science,* 1963, *141,* 722-723.

Held, R. Plasticity in sensory-motor systems. *Scientific American,* 1965, *213,* 84-94.

Held, R. Dissociation of visual functions by deprivation and rearrangement. *Psychologische Forschung,* 1968, *31,* 338-348.

Held, R. Two modes of processing spatially distributed visual stimulation. In

F. O. Schmitt (Ed.), *The neurosciences: Second study program.* New York: Rockefeller University, 1970.

Held, R., & Shattuck, S. R. Color and edge sensitive channels in the human visual system: Tuning for orientation. *Science,* 1971, *174,* 314-316.

Helmholtz, H. von *Handbuch der physiologischen Optik,* Vol. III. Leipzig: Leopold Voss, 1866.

Howard, I P., & Templeton, W. B. Human spatial orientation, Chapter 15. New York: Wiley, 1966.

Hubel, D. H., & Wiesel, T. N. Receptive fields of single neurones in the cat's striate cortex. *Journal of Physiology,* 1959, *148,* 574-591.

Kohler, I. Über Aufbau und Wandlungen der Wahrnehmungswelt, insbesondere über bedingte Empfindungen. *Osterreich Akademie der Wissenschaft, philosophische-historische Klasse,* 1951, *227,* 1-118.

Köhler, W., & Emery, D. Figural aftereffects in the third dimension of visual space. *American Journal of Psychology,* 1947, *60,* 159-202.

Köhler, W., & Wallach, H. Figural aftereffects. *Proceedings of the American Philosophical Society,* 1944 *88,* 269-357.

Macfarland, S. F. A personal experience with prismatic glasses. *Transactions of the American Ophthalmological Society,* 1883, *3,* 479-480.

McCollough, C. Color adaptation of edge-detectors in the human visual system. *Science,* 1965, *149,* 1115-1116.

Ogle, K. N. Distortion of the image by prisms. *Journal of the Optical Society of America,* 1951, *41,* 1023-1028.

Schneider, G. E. Two visual systems: Brain mechanisms for localization and discrimination are dissociated by tectal and cortical lesions. *Science,* 1969, *163,* 895-902.

Shattuck, S., & Held, R. Color and edge sensitive channels converge on stereo-depth analyzers. *Vision Research,* 1975, *15,* 309-311.

Stromeyer, C. F., III. Form-color aftereffects in human vision. In R. Held, H. Leibowitz, & H.-L. Teuber (Eds.), *Handbook of sensory physiology,* Vol. 8. New York: Springer-Verlag, 1978.

Vos, J. J. Some new aspects of color stereoscopy. *Journal of the Optical Society of America,* 1960, *50,* 785-790.

Wundt, W. Zur Theorie der raumlichen Gesichtswahrnehmungen. *Philosophische Studien,* 1898, *14,* 1-118.

Insight or Out of Sight? : Two Examples of Perceptual Plasticity in the Human Adult

Charles S. Harris

Bell Laboratories, Murray Hill, N.J.

How flexible is the human visual system? When confronted with optical inputs that are systematically distorted, does the visual system become recalibrated (perhaps by making use of undistorted information from other sensory modalities, such as touch), to counteract the distortion and restore perception to normal? When exposed to stimulation that is unchanging and redundant (and therefore less informative than variations) does the visual system become recalibrated to nullify or discount the redundancies?

The evidence for plasticity in the human adult's visual system seems to be abundant and impressive. For example, consider the experiments that George M. Stratton carried out in the 1890's and that Ivo Kohler (1951, 1953, 1964) has been working on in Innsbruck for many years. These investigators used goggles containing lenses, mirrors, or prisms that invert or reverse the retinal image. After wearing such optical devices for a while, people learned to get around successfully; they no longer reached incorrectly, made wrong turns, or blundered into things. In fact, some of Kohler's subjects eventually were able to resume skiing and motorcycle riding while wearing the goggles.

More important, Stratton and Kohler claimed that the adaptation to optical distortion went beyond mere behavioral improvement. They believed that the goggles-wearers' visual perception also improved, so that they were able to perceive things correctly through the distorting goggles.

Stratton reported that after he had been wearing inverting goggles for several days, the world sometimes looked "right side up" or "in normal position." Kohler's reports agreed with Stratton's on adaptation to inversion, and added some bizarre accounts of adaptation to mirror-reversal of the visual field. At an intermediate stage of adaptation to reversal, Kohler says, "inscriptions on buildings, or advertisements, were still seen in mirror writing, but the objects containing them were seen in the correct locations. Vehicles [seen correctly] driving on the 'right'...carried license numbers in mirror writing" (1964, p. 155). In other words, the subject's visual perception at that point seemed to be partly reversed and partly back to normal! After wearing the reversing goggles for several more weeks, Kohler maintained, the subject eventually achieved "almost completely correct impressions, even where letters and numbers were involved" (1964, p. 160).

Such reports certainly give the impression that exposure to radical optical distortions leads to radical changes in visual perception, so that a given retinal image gives rise to a different visual perception.

A somewhat different category of visual plasticity involves changes in the perception of shape or color (see Held, 1980), rather than in overall space perception. Usually such modifications of perception—afterimages, for example, or figural aftereffects—are too fleeting to warrant the label "plasticity." But what if, several hours after looking at green stripes for a few minutes, a person sees white stripes as pink (McCollough, 1965)? Certainly that person's visual system is responding to stimulation differently from before.

I will begin by examining a number of variations on the first sort of adaptation, involving extensive changes in overall spatial perception. The conclusion I will reach is that this striking form of plasticity is not, strictly speaking, *visual* plasticity at all, but instead resides in another perceptual system: the position sense. I will then focus on one example of the second kind of plasticity, a persistent alteration of color perception called the McCollough Effect. I will discuss various plausible interpretations, ending with the intriguing possibility that this instance of plasticity may represent a novel process intermediate between sensory adaptation and learning.

PERCEPTUAL PLASTICITY

Why are psychologists and physiologists so interested in plasticity or modifiability of the visual system? After all, aren't scientists supposed to concern themselves with reliable, repeatable phenomena? Shouldn't they prefer studying a stable system, so that their characterization of it today will still apply tomorrow?

There are a number of reasons why changes in visual system functioning are of special interest:

Perceptual Development

A traditional motivation has been curiosity about how perception develops in the human infant. This is the perennial Nature vs. Nurture, Innate or Learned, Nativism-Empiricism debate. For centuries, there's been a philosophical pendulum swinging repeatedly between the two extremes. Yet it's hard to settle the issue once and for all by doing research on infants; it's hard to carry out the research and hard to draw firm conclusions from it (Rosinski, 1977).

So some psychologists have tried investigating how perception can be modified or rebuilt in the adult, and have then drawn inferences about infant development. Again there's a pendulum that swings from regarding such inferences as reasonable to considering them ridiculous. Parallels between the processes of adult adaptation and infant development, such as those that Held and Hein have been exploring, make the inferences seem reasonable and parsimonious (see Rosinski, 1977; Hein, 1980). On the other hand, the concept of the critical period, taken over from the ethologists, makes them seem unwarranted: The infant (at least during the critical period) is an organism very different from the adult, and generally much more malleable.

Perceptual Physiology

Whether or not one feels justified in drawing inferences from adult to infant, findings on perceptual flexibility in human adults have other broad implications for our understanding of perceptual mechanisms. Most current work on sensory neurophysiology is, of necessity, confined to animals. Generalizing from those findings to humans requires an inductive leap even greater than in generalizing from human adults to infants. Therefore, to bolster our confidence in generalizing from animal to human neurophysiology, we would hope to find parallels between animal and human perceptual performance.

Yet if one accepts the data at face value, there appears to be a disconcerting discrepancy between visual plasticity in animals and in humans. Most physiological research on animals suggests that visual plasticity is strictly limited to an early critical period (Mitchell, 1980). But psychological experiments on human adults, such as those by Stratton and Kohler mentioned above, appear to offer evidence of far-ranging plasticity in the adult's visual perception. So either an early critical period is peculiar to lower animals (and perhaps to certain optical distortions such as astigmatism in humans) or, as I will argue, the findings that appear to demonstrate visual plasticity in human adults are open to a very different interpretation: namely, that our visual systems are as inflexible as other mature animals'.

Perceptual Mechanisms

Findings on plasticity can tell us about the normal operation of perceptual mechanisms. Quite apart from any connection with infants or animals, the presence or absence of visual plasticity in the adult can reveal a lot about the origins and determinants of *our* perceptions, as adults. Finding that a mechanism is changeable will greatly influence our concepts of how the mechanism normally operates, both delimiting and expanding those concepts.

Moreover, if a system is plastic, then we have an opportunity for experimental manipulation. With a plastic mechanism, we can see how the same input is treated before and after the mechanism is altered. We can experimentally *test* hypotheses about the fundamental operations of the mechanism, instead of being restricted to the essentially *observational* approach of feeding stimuli into a fixed mechanism and seeing what comes out.

Perceptual Plasticity Per Se

Of course, some investigators are interested in plasticity in its own right: What does perceptual change consist of, how do you bring it about, how can you facilitate or counteract it? Information about perceptual plasticity is an additional set of facts to add to other knowledge about perception. And applications to treatment and prevention of visual defects may well emerge. For example, Mitchell (1980) discusses a detrimental byproduct, which may become permanent if not treated soon enough, of visual plasticity in children.

Perceptual Illusions

Finally, there is the inherent fascination of seeing perception go astray. We're so used to taking for granted the usual close agreement between perception and reality, it's unsettling and thought-provoking when we find a glaring disagreement.

ADAPTATION TO OPTICAL DISPLACEMENT

To give us insights into perceptual development, physiology, plasticity, and illusion, it would be nice to have a clearcut example of a perceptual change—a substantial change in perception itself rather than in cognition or response, easy to demonstrate, long-lasting, and reasonably general (not tied to the specific stimuli that cause the change).

Adaptation to optical distortions (Welch, 1978, provides an excellent review) fills the bill. My own research on this topic was inspired by that of Richard Held, Alan Hein, and their coworkers (see Hein, 1980; Held, 1980), though the first such experiment was done, of course, by Helmholtz, more than a hundred years ago.

Rapid Adaptation

It's easy to put on a classroom demonstration that resembles Helmholtz's and my experiments. The first thing Helmholtz did, no doubt, was take baseline measurements to find out how accurately his experimental subject (Helmholtz, no doubt) could point at a visual target. He looked at an object and then pointed at it rapidly, as in the top part of Fig. 1. It's important for the rest of the demonstration that the pointing be fast enough to preclude correction of the trajectory when the subject sees the moving hand in relation to the target. To accomplish the same thing, I have used an opaque barrier that blocks the subject's view of the hand, as in the bottom part of Fig. 1. (For a classroom demonstration, a piece of corrugated cardboard will do, with one end bent up and the other supported on the subject's shoulders.)

The next step is to put on goggles containing wedge prisms. In Fig. 2, the goggles contain 30 diopter base-left prisms, which bend the light rays through about 17°, making a target at arm's length appear to be about 5 inches to the subject's right of where it actually is. That's why the rather naive subject in Fig. 2 is pointing 5 inches to his right of the target: He's pointing where he sees the target, and he sees it where the prism optics make him see it.

So far, everything that has happened is a simple consequence of optics. The next step is the crucial one for finding out something about perception. It's clear that the prism goggles are falsifying this subject's perceptions, by making him see things to his right of where they really are. The question is: Can he learn to see accurately again if we give him the chance?

We give him the chance by taking away the opaque barrier and letting him see what he's doing. Now when he points at the target repeatedly, watching his hand through the prisms, his aim quickly improves (Fig. 5). This rapid improvement in accuracy is what is called *adaptation*. When we put the cardboard back and have him point again, as in Fig. 3, he is much closer to the target than in the Fig. 2 baseline measurements.

And finally, the last step, we take off the prisms. The subject's visual input is now back to normal, the same as in the baseline measurements. But now when he tries to point at where he sees the target, he misses. He's a couple of inches off to his left (Fig. 4). His error is called an *aftereffect*. Since the before-after difference is much the same whether measured with prisms off (Fig. 1 vs. Fig. 4) or on (Fig. 2 vs. Fig. 3), I will call either difference the *adaptive shift* (or, for short, *adaptation*).

Let me assure you that this subject's rapid improvement in pointing, when he was permitted to see his hand through the prisms, is not trivial. It is not simply a deliberate conscious correction of his aim—figuring out that he has to point farther left than where he sees the target. We can tell it isn't a conscious correction because when he takes the goggles off, and knows there's nothing to correct for, the leftward shift still occurs—and it is now an *error* in pointing (Fig. 4).

Thus, it appears that the subject is pointing at targets differently because he is now *seeing* them differently. It looks as though we've modified his visual system, producing a new correspondence between location on the retina and visually perceived location.

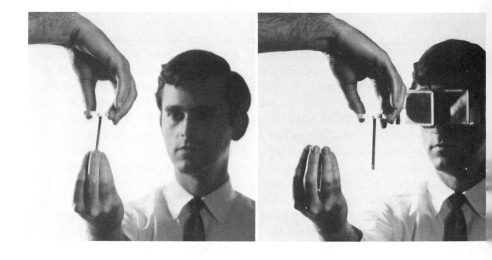

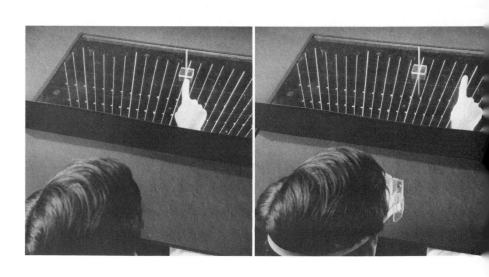

FIGS. 1-4. Above: Reenactment of a century-old experiment on adaptation to sideways displacement of vision (after Helmholtz, 1866). Below: A corresponding recent procedure (after Harris, 1963a). 1: Baseline measurements without prisms show accurate pointing. Visual feedback from the hand is kept from influencing the pointing by (above) having the subject reach rapidly without correction of errors, or (below) using an opaque shield and raised barrier to block the subject's view of

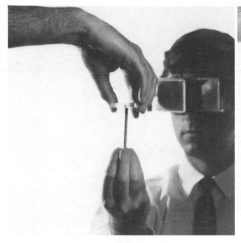

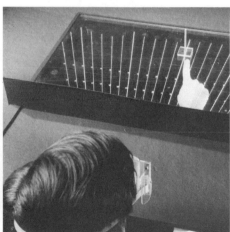

the hand but not of the target rod. 2: When the subject first puts on prism goggles, pointing is displaced. The subject adapts when permitted to see the hand through prisms while repeatedly reaching for the target (Fig. 5). 3: After adapting, the subject points more accurately at targets seen through prisms. 4: When the prism goggles are removed after adaptation, the subject's pointing is in error (the "aftereffect"). The difference between where the subject points in 1 and in 4 is the "adaptive shift." (From Harris, 1968a.)

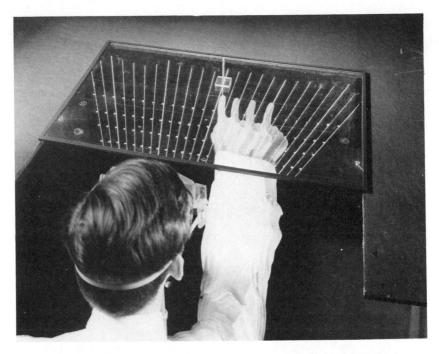

FIG. 5. Adapting to optical displacement. When the opaque shield and barrier are removed from the apparatus, the subject can see the hand through prisms. Accuracy improves rapidly. (From Harris, 1968a.)

Insight or Out of Sight?

This demonstration certainly seems to show that there is remarkable flexibility in the visual system, as if there were a massive rewiring of the connections between retina and visual cortex, or somewhere else in the visual system's mappings (see Dodwell, 1970).

So here we seem to have a perfect example of perceptual plasticity in the human adult, an example that fits all of the desiderata listed above. There's just one problem: It turns out that this plasticity isn't *visual* plasticity at all.

For the simplest kind of adaptation, the kind that results from procedures like those depicted in Figs. 1-4, it's easy to prove that the adaptation is not a change in vision. Suppose that the subject's visual perception of the target got shifted to the left by adaptation, counteracting the prisms' rightward displacement. If the target is now seen, without prisms, to the left of its actual location, pointing should be shifted to the left regardless of which hand does the pointing. That's not what happened in my experiments. On the contrary, adaptation affected only the arm that the subjects saw while wearing prism goggles (Harris, 1963a).

Moreover, pointing with that arm was affected even when the test target was not visual: Figure 6 shows how far off eight subjects were, on the average, after they adapted and tried to point at a visual target without any prisms, and how far off they were when they closed their eyes and tried to point at a clicking sound-source, or simply "straight ahead," with no target at all. All of these findings have been verified in other laboratories, and all confirm that the plasticity is not visual.

Thus, investigators who hope to gain insights into visual plasticity by studying rapid adaptation to prism goggles are likely to be disappointed, because the site of this adaptation is outside the visual system.

Altered Position Sense of the Arm

As Fig. 6 shows, this rapid adaptation has nothing to do with vision and a lot to do with the adapted arm. Does this mean that adaptation is motor-response learning? If the subject has simply learned to move one arm in a new direc-

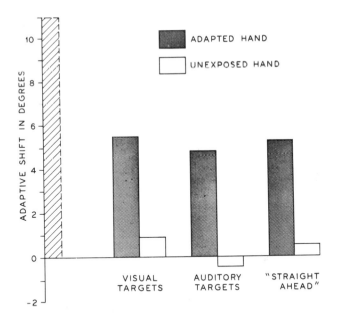

FIG. 6. Results of adapting as in Figs. 1-4 to an 11° displacement. The adaptive shift is the difference between pointing before and after viewing one hand through prisms; all measurements were taken without prisms and without sight of the hand. Eight subjects pointed at visual targets or (while blindfolded) at sounds or "straight ahead." A positive shift means pointing farther left after exposure to rightward visual displacement, or farther right after leftward displacment. (Data from Harris, 1963a.)

tion in order to get it to a given goal, that would indeed account for the results I've just described.

But it wouldn't explain certain other changes involving the adapted arm, changes that have been measured when the arm wasn't even moving. When subjects closed their eyes and estimated the distance between their hands, there was a shift in their judgments after one hand adapted to displacing prisms (Fig. 7). Subjects missed systematically when the motionless adapted hand served as *target* for pointing by the *unexposed* hand (Efstathiou & Held, personal communication, 1964; Harris, 1965; Welch, 1969), even though that hand could point correctly at all other targets (as Fig. 6 shows). Subjects also missed when they tried to point their eyes at the adapted hand in the dark (Hardt, Held, & Steinbach, 1971) and when they tried to judge whether a luminous dot was directly above it (Hamilton & Hillyard, personal communication, 1964). Thus, although the adaptation is specific to the adapted arm, it is not merely a change in the arm's motor programs.

What else might change about the arm? Its position sense. While looking through rightward-displacing prisms, subjects see the hand to the right of its actual location. What I'm saying is that after adapting, they *feel* that the hand is to the right of its actual location, whether they can see it or not. Their position sense has been modified or recalibrated to match the distorted visual perception; a given physical position of the arm now gives rise to a different nonvisual perception of that arm's position, relative to the rest of the body (Harris, 1963a,b; Hamilton, 1964a,b; Hay & Pick, 1966).

If adapted subjects mistakenly feel that the hand is to the right of its actual location, of course they will point farther left than normal regardless of what they're trying to point at—a visual target, a sound, or "straight ahead." Since only one arm is affected, they will also misjudge the separation between their two hands, and will point incorrectly at either one with the other.

In sum, we can conclude that in this sort of experiment the main adaptive change is not just a deliberate correction, since it persists when the subjects know that a correction is inappropriate and believe they are pointing accurately. It is not a visual change, since targets in any modality produce the same test results. It is not a general perceptual change, a new interpretation of all incoming stimuli, because pointing with the unexposed arm remains unaffected. It is not simply a change in arm movements, or a new stimulus-response mapping, or a visuomotor recorrelation, since it shows up when adapted subjects judge the distance between their hands while blindfolded, in the absence of both visual stimulation and motor responses by the adapted arm. Rather, this form of adaptation is a change in the adapted arm's position sense: The arm is consistently felt to be a couple of inches to one side of its actual location relative to the rest of the body.

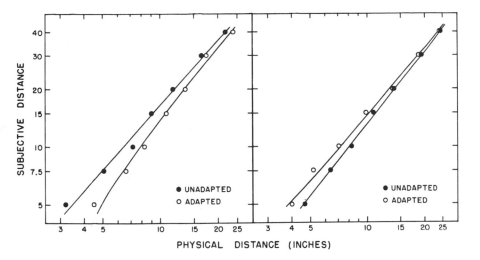

SUBJECTIVE DISTANCE

PHYSICAL DISTANCE (INCHES)

FIG. 7. Blindfolded subjects' judgments of the distance between their hands before and after viewing the right hand through leftward-displacing prisms (left, N = 8) or rightward-displacing prisms (right, N = 7). Subjects were first told to call a certain distance (7 inches) "10" and then to produce separations proportional to other numbers specified by the experimenter. During these measurements, subjects were permitted to move only the hand that had *not* been seen through prisms. The vertical distance between the before and after data is the adaptive shift: A given physical distance felt smaller after adaptating the right hand to leftward displacement (left), and larger after rightward displacement (right). The straight lines through the filled circles are power functions of the form $y = k x^m$, with $m \simeq 1.15$; the slightly curved lines through the unfilled circles result from adding or subtracting a constant (the adaptive shift) from x in the above equation. (From Harris, 1963b.)

Altered Position Sense of the Head or Eyes

Although flexibility of the position sense should be as noteworthy as visual flexibility, some psychologists dismiss the arm-adaptation experiments as uninteresting. All that such experiments show, they might say, is that this procedure is not a good way to produce "real" (i.e. visual) adaptation. After all, the subjects adapted in a very restricted, artificial, laboratory setting—during adaptation, their heads were held fixed by a biting board while they pointed over and over with one hand at one target, seeing nothing but that hand and target. With such restrictions, why expect anything but restricted adaptation, "anomalies such as lack of transfer from one hand to the other" (Gibson, 1969) that tell us nothing about adaptation in more natural conditions?

What does happen in less confined circumstances? As soon as you allow subjects to move their heads and bodies while wearing prisms, you find a form of adaptation that cannot possibly be due to altered position sense of the arm. After removing the prisms, they miss visual targets with *both* arms, regardless of whether they have seen only one hand (Hamilton, 1964a) or neither (Bossom & Held, 1957) through prisms. After walking around for an hour or so with prisms on, when the prisms are removed they walk to one side of their goals (Hamilton, 1964b; Mikaelian, 1970). They appear to have undergone a genuine change in visual perception, quite different from a limited change in position sense of the arm. In fact, with prisms off, these subjects will insist that an object now *looks* straight ahead of them when it is actually slightly off to one side (Kohler, 1951/1964; Held & Bossom, 1961; Hay & Pick, 1966) — seemingly clear evidence of a visual change.

Here too, though, adaptation may involve altered position sense—not of the arm this time, but of the head or eyes (Helmholtz, 1866/1962; Harris, 1963b, 1965; Hamilton, 1964a, b; Mittelstaedt, 1964; McLaughlin & Rifkin, 1965; Hay & Pick, 1966). When people walk around, the images of objects expand on their retinas, creating a visual flow pattern. Normally, this flow pattern is centered on the retina when the eyes and head are pointing along the direction of movement. Prisms displace the flow pattern, requiring subjects to turn their eyes or head in order to get the same retinal flow pattern as they normally do with eyes and head straight ahead. In other words, with eyes or head turned, they are getting visual information that normally indicates that head and eyes are pointing straight ahead.

Could it be that adapted subjects feel that head and eyes are pointing straight ahead, relative to the rest of the body, when in fact either head or eyes are turned a little to the side? If so, of course they will miss when they reach for or walk toward something, and of course their verbal judgments of visual direction will be mistaken. If they see an object directly ahead of their eyes and nose, but incorrectly feel that head or eyes are turned, then they must perceive that object as shifted relative to any other part of the body, such as arms or legs. As with arm-adaptation (Figs. 1-4), the same adaptive change that causes errors without prisms will *improve* accuracy with prisms on: When adapted subjects look off to the side in order to fixate the prism-displaced image of a straight-ahead object, they will feel, appropriately, that they are looking straight ahead.

A change in registration of head or eye position would therefore mimic, on many tests, a genuine change in purely visual perception. To distinguish between the two kinds of change, we need a nonvisual test, in which subjects judge the felt position of the head and eyes instead of a visual target. Kohler (1951/1964) mentions some informal observations along this line: One subject, after walking around for some time while wearing rightward-displacing prisms, "thought he was looking straight ahead when actually his head was turned 6° to 9° to the right of the body median" (p. 38). When the subject was forced to point his head straight ahead, he felt that it was turned to the left. Other evidence of altered perception of head position has been noted by Lotto, Kern, and Morant (1967), Lackner (1973), and Cohen (1972).

Several investigators have reported evidence of modified registration of eye position after adaptation. Subjects who were asked to point their eyes straight ahead, either in the dark or while facing a homogeneous white field, pointed them consistently to one side after adapting (Kalil & Freedman, 1966; Craske, 1967). A similar error was found when the same instructions were given with a visual target present (McLaughlin & Webster, 1967).

It is clear, then, that in some experiments adapted subjects do misperceive which way their head or eyes are pointing, thereby producing just the sort of behavior that supposedly shows a change in purely visual perception. As Kohler noted, "The errors in visual direction disappeared to the same degree that this 'torsion' of the head developed during the first days of the experiment" (1964, p. 38).

ADAPTATION TO INVERTED AND REVERSED VISION

Rapid Adaptation to Reversal

Changes in the position sense of arm, head, or eyes may account for adaptation to sideways displacement, but what about adaptation to optical inversion or reversal? Could changes in position sense possibly compensate for such drastic transformations? It's not too implausible to believe that when subjects see one hand optically displaced from its true position they begin to feel it there, but if they see it moving right-to-left when it's really moving left-to-right, could they actually come to feel that it's moving right-to-left? According to an experiment carried out in collaboration with Judith R. Harris, the answer is *yes* (C. S. Harris & J. R. Harris, 1965; Rock & Harris, 1967).

In this experiment, subjects sat and doodled for 15 minutes a day on four different days, while watching the moving hand through a right-angle prism that was attached to a rigid support. The prism acted like a mirror, reversing the scene right for left. After each 15-minute adaptation period, we covered up the prism, blocking the subjects' vision, and then asked them to write several numbers and letters as we called them out. They had never seen or written any letters or numbers while looking through the prism.

Figure 8 shows examples of what three adapted subjects did when they tried to write normally without visual feedback. What they actually wrote was often backwards. But more important, they usually *thought* that they were writing those letters frontwards. Moreover, when they wrote *frontwards* letters, such as C.R.'s *e* or G.S.'s *s*, they often *felt* that they were writing them backwards!

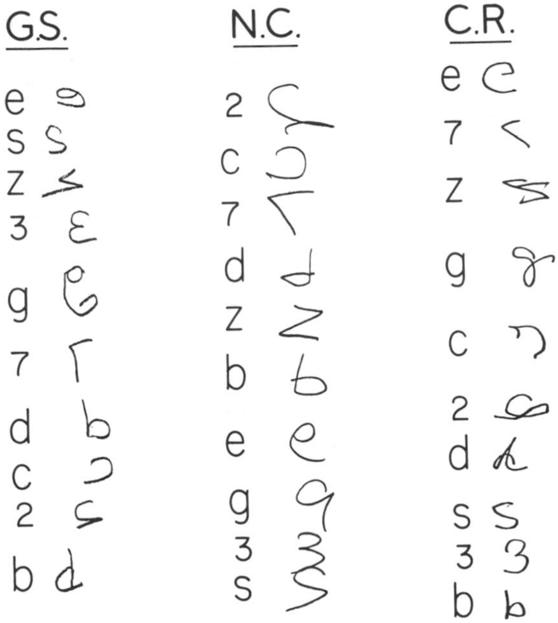

G.S.

N.C.

C.R.

FIG. 8. The letters and numbers on the right side of each column were written by three blindfolded subjects after viewing their hands through mirror-reversing goggles. On the left are the characters they were asked to write. (From C. S. Harris & J. R. Harris, 1965.)

In fact, subject G.S. said that on this trial she thought she had written everything correctly except for the frontwards *s*. Every one of the eight subjects misperceived at least one letter or number, either feeling that it was frontwards when it was really backwards ("unnoticed reversal") or feeling that it was backwards when it was really frontwards ("false alarm").

With our relatively brief exposures, totaling only an hour (Kohler's subjects spent many days adapting to reversal), the adaptation was unstable and disappeared rapidly. This is evident in Fig. 9, which tallies the two kinds of perceptual errors as a function of the number of letters written after the prism was covered, a rough measure of time since exposure. On the first letter after the prism was covered, the subjects made kinesthetic errors nearly one-third of the time; a minute or so later, on the tenth letter, they were seldom wrong. (Incidentally, errors were just as common on "easy" letters as on "confusing" ones such as *z* or *s*.)

What happened here is just like what happened in the experiments with sideways displacement: When vision and position sense supplied conflicting information about the hand's whereabouts, the position sense accommodated itself to the distorted vision. Here the subjects began to feel that the hand was moving as they saw it move, in the opposite direction from its actual movement. This reversal of kinesthetic perception tended to persist after vision through the reversing prism was blocked, as shown by subjects' misperceptions of letters they wrote. Since they couldn't see what they were writing, they had to rely on their kinesthetic perceptions; and those perceptions were often reversed after exposure to the reversing prism.

Long-Term Adaptation to Reversal

Can we generalize from this experiment, with its brief and restricted exposure, to long-term adaptation to reversal? Didn't Kohler say that, after many days, his subjects *saw* objects in their correct locations despite the optical reversal, and didn't he say that eventually even letters and numbers *looked* normal? If, as Kohler reported, partly-adapted subjects saw some things correctly and some things "mirrorwise," doesn't this prove that their visual perception was undergoing a gradual, piecemeal change? No, it doesn't.

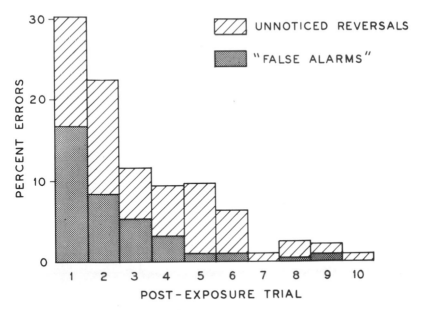

FIG. 9. Decline in errors following adaptation to mirror reversal. The x-axis represents the characters, from the first through the tenth, written after the subjects (N = 8) were blindfolded. "False alarms" are characters written correctly but reported to feel backwards; "unnoticed reversals" are characters written backwards but not reported as backwards. (From C. S. Harris & J. R. Harris, 1965.)

Consider the hypothetical subject shown in Fig. 10A. He is facing a blackboard with an L written on the left side and an R on the right. When we put reversing goggles on him, he sees the letters reversed, as in Fig. 10B, but of course his hands and body feel the same as always. (The four drawings all represent visual perception of the letters and proprioceptive perception of the head, body, and limbs.) If you ask him what he sees, he'll say a backwards L on his right and a backwards R on his left.

Partial adaptation. Now suppose he holds up his right hand and looks at it. Because of the reversing goggles, he sees it on the left. In the experiments on sideways displacement, people who saw their hands in a new location began to feel that their hands were in that location. The same thing might happen when this subject sees his hand on the opposite side of the visual field from usual.

Eventually he should feel that his hands are located as in Fig. 10C. If we now ask which side of the blackboard he sees the R on, he may very well say, as Kohler's subjects did, "on my right-hand side"—because he sees it on the same side (left) as he now feels his right hand to be on. This has nothing to do with everyday confusions over right and left, nor does it imply that the subject's right hand feels like a left hand. On the contrary, his right hand still feels like a right hand—if he's right-handed, it's the strong, skillful one, the one to write with—but it feels as though it's near the other side of his body (where he's been seeing it through the reversing goggles). Since the error in felt location matches the prism-produced error in visual perception, he gives correct answers to many questions: He says he sees the R on his right-hand side, for instance, and that's where it really is. (There's nothing special about the right hand or the word "right"; we'd get an equivalent correct answer by tapping his adapted left hand and asking whether he sees the L on the same or the opposite side.)

Because the subject now gives accurate judgments of the locations of visual objects, we might be misled into thinking that his visual perception is back to normal—except that, as Kohler reported, he still insists that the R *looks backwards.* And he still gives "wrong" judgments about where the R is located relative to his *shoulders* (as Kohler noted) or *head* (as J. G. Taylor, 1962, found in a similar experiment), because he still perceives those parts of his body correctly. Suppose we ask the subject to turn to his right. To make sure he's doing the proper thing, he may wiggle his writing hand (his "right hand") and turn toward where he feels that hand. The result would be, as Kohler reported about his partly-adapted subjects, that "A subject trying to turn 'right' with his eyes closed actually turns left" (1964, p. 153).

Complete adaptation. Eventually the subject's feet should adapt, and the rest of his body also; he should then feel that they are arranged as in Fig. 10D. At this stage, his behavior should be, by and large, back to normal. With

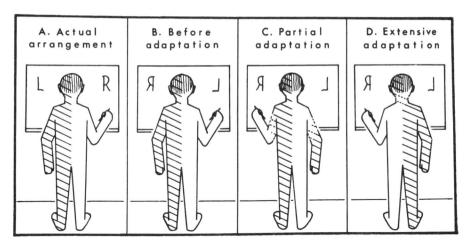

FIG. 10. Adaptation to reversal interpreted as changes in position sense.
A. The actual physical arrangement. B. The subject's initial impressions after putting on reversing goggles. Perception of the letters is by vision; of the head and body, by position sense. C. The subject's impressions at an intermediate stage, with only the arms adapted. D. The subject's impressions after extensive adaptation, with changes in felt position of arms, legs, and body relative to the head. (From Harris, 1965.)

proprioceptive and kinesthetic perceptions of his arms and legs reversed, so that they now agree with the reversed visual field, he can behave successfully by simply doing what feels appropriate to what he sees.

But if all the changes are kinesthetic, not visual, why did Kohler say that finally even letters and numbers viewed through the reversing goggles looked "normal" or "natural," no longer like mirror-writing? Note that Kohler reported that the letters never looked the *same* as before the subject put on the goggles. Rather than demonstrating a reversal of vision, then, this return to "normal" appearance is just what happens without any reversing goggles when people practice reading mirror-writing for a long time. They end up able to read mirror-writing almost as easily as normal writing (Kolers, 1968), and the backwards words and letters look familiar and "normal," no longer "strange" and "backwards." In fact, Kohler's own evidence suggests that this supposed last step in "learning to see right way round" is merely a process of familiarization: The first words that looked normal to Kohler's subjects were the ones they saw most frequently through the reversing goggles.

Thus adaptation to mirror-reversal seems to be fundamentally the same as adaptation to sideways displacement. In both cases, we can conclude that there is no change in subjects' purely visual perception, but that their position sense and movement sense are modified, so that they incorrectly feel their arms and legs to be where the reversing goggles make them appear to be.

Adapting to Inversion

Stratton's classic experiments seem to offer the most compelling evidence of genuine, far-ranging, visual plasticity. His lens system rotated his retinal image 180°, making the world look both inverted and reversed. Although Stratton didn't persevere long enough to achieve complete and stable adaptation, he did find that from time to time, toward the end of both of his experiments, the world seen through the lenses appeared to be "in normal position," "rather upright than inverted," or simply "right side up" (1896, p. 616; 1897, pp. 354, 358, 469). It sounds almost as though his brain had taken his "reinverted" retinal image and rotated it back to its normal orientation.

However, Stratton's detailed experimental diary makes it clear that, as with displacement and reversal, the major component of his adaptation was changes in position sense. When Stratton first looked through the inverting goggles, he saw the floor and his feet up above his forehead. In the experiments on displacement and reversal, subjects who saw their hands optically displaced to a new location soon came to feel that their hands were actually in that location. Stratton says the same thing happened to his feet: "...the limbs began actually to feel in the place where the new visual perception reported them to be.... I could at length *feel* my feet strike against the seen floor..." (1896, p. 615).

Gradually, he began to feel that his legs, his arms, and more and more of his body, were all "that way" from his chin. Which way was "that way"? He could feel his feet pressing against the floor; he could feel the tensions in his legs, fighting against gravity; he could feel gravity pulling from "that way." So he had to feel that "that way" was downwards. And since "that way" was where he saw the floor through the lenses, the floor appeared to be downwards, just as it should. Thus the visual scene looked "right side up" again — because of a changed perception of the direction of his legs, not a change in visual registration.

Stratton recorded some unusual details about these changes in position sense. He says "I could...at times feel that my arms lay between my head and this new position of my feet; shoulders and head, however...kept the old localization they had had in normal vision, in spite of the logical difficulty that the shape of the body and the localization of hands and feet just mentioned made such a localization of the shoulders absurd" (1896, p. 615). Such a localization should not only have seemed absurd, it should have made Stratton feel that his head was on upside-down! And so it did: Stratton noted that the objects he saw "frequently seemed to be in normal position, and whatever there was of abnormality seemed to lie in myself, as if head and shoulders were inverted and I were viewing objects from that position, as boys sometimes do from between their legs" (1896, p. 616). Stratton's simile conveys precisely the sense in which things seen through inverting lenses could look upright: If you look at an upright book from between your legs, you'll see the bottom of the page as "below" the top, yet the words will look like upside-down print. So even with as drastic a transformation as optical inversion, the position sense manages to accommodate itself to vision.

IMPLICATIONS OF PLASTICITY IN THE POSITION SENSE

Inflexibility in Vision

We started out with a picture of virtually unlimited plasticity in the visual system. People were wearing glasses that turned the visual scene upside-down or into its mirror image, and yet they were having no trouble at all walking around, reaching for things, riding motorcycles, or skiing. They seemed to be telling us that their vision was back to normal, that in spite of the optical distortion the world now looked just the same as it had looked before with undistorted inputs. Given so much apparent flexibility, it was easy to conclude that the neural links between eye and brain could be reconnected in radically new ways, or that the brain could in effect construct its own internal "inverse spectacles" to undo the optical distortion, or even that there is no stable connection at all between retinal stimulation and visual perception. Any one of those views, in turn, made it easy to believe that newborn infants start out with a welter of meaningless visual sensations, to which they later learn to attach the spatial properties that they ascertain through movement, touch, and position sense. And it seemed that human beings retain into adulthood the visual plasticity that lower animals quickly outgrow.

We now have quite a different picture. First, in many experiments with optical distortion it turned out that there was *no* compensatory change at all in *visual* perception. When people see one hand optically displaced or reversed, it is often only the position sense for that hand that changes to match the distorted vision. On this point there is now widespread agreement (Welch, 1978). Second, in a number of cases where the adaptation surely is not reducible to changes in the arm's position sense, there is probably a change in position sense of the head or eyes relative to the rest of the body. In such cases, so many visual judgments and visually guided behaviors are affected that one *could* talk about a modification of visual perception, as long as one bears in mind that here too what is actually modified is the interpretation of nonvisual information about positions of body parts. (Although I can't claim that the convention of referring to this variety of adaptation as "visual adaptation" is mistaken, I do think that it is misleading; see the Addendum.)

A growing weight of evidence encourages me to venture a more sweeping claim: It seems that whenever there's a really major change in space perception, it's due to changes in the position sense, rather than being purely visual. Although there apparently *are* some genuine examples of plasticity in visual space perception (see the Addendum), it seems that the clearer it is that the change is purely visual, the smaller the magnitude of change—and the less useful it is as a basis for empiricist theories of visual space perception.

Development of Perception

This change in our picture of how people adjust to optical distortions should foster changes in some widespread beliefs about how infants develop visual perception in the first place.

If adults could readily modify their optically distorted visual perceptions to conform to the information provided by touch, kinesthesis, and motion, it would be reasonable to suppose that the same sort of information initially shapes vision in newborn infants, as the philosopher Berkeley (1709) proposed long ago. If, on the other hand, there are no major changes in purely visual space perception in adults, this line of reasoning would imply that visual perception is more stable, more likely to be well-structured at birth, than is often thought.

Infants and adults *may,* however, be very different creatures. What does direct investigation of infants tell us about their perception? The burgeoning literature is vast enough to provide some support for almost any conclusion one wishes to draw. Any attempt to evaluate this literature and determine a consensus runs into a serious obstacle: There is doubtless a bias to report *changes* in perception with age, rather than stability. Investigators interested in perceptual development are likely to search for developmental changes, and will be understandably reluctant to accept (or publish) data that fit the "null hypothesis" of no change with age. Nevertheless, a variety of evidence suggests that much of the basic spatial structure of visual perception is present in the infant (Rosinski, 1977, offers a good review). Other lines of research that were once thought to indicate that visual perception is learned rather than innate, such as the deficits found in animals raised in the dark or in people whose sight has been surgically restored (see Hebb, 1949), have since been given rather different interpretations (Wertheimer, 1951; Hochberg, 1962; Hubel & Wiesel, 1963), consistent with a large innate component.

The Plastic Position Sense

Whatever the origins of visual space perception are, it is now clear that in adults the position sense is continually calibrated by vision. In contrast, there is no evidence for calibration of vision by position sense. Certainly it makes sense for organisms to use the very precise information that vision offers, to recalibrate their vaguer position sense as the body grows.

In some ways, this is a disappointing conclusion. Here we had an exemplary instance of plasticity in perception, and it turned out that the perception that's

plastic is the position sense, not vision. Now of course plasticity in the position sense is news too—maybe even more so than plasticity in vision, since so
many people have assumed that the position sense is a stable and trustworthy
guide to reality. An infallible position sense has often been invoked in
theories about how we build up or rebuild any puzzling aspects of visual space
perception. And of course flexibility in the position sense has just as exciting
implications for plasticity in the central nervous system as visual flexibility
would have. Although we have lost the picture of unlimited visual adaptability
that we started out with, we have gained an awareness of remarkable flexibility
in a sensory modality that formerly appeared stable, reliable, and rather uninteresting.

THE McCOLLOUGH EFFECT

With the most striking evidence for visual plasticity shown to result from nonvisual alterations, let us turn to a phenomenon that unquestionably occurs
within the visual system: the McCollough Effect. Although more limited in
scope and strength, this phenomenon is equally thought-provoking because of
its surprising longevity and its implications for the nature of elementary
stimulus-analyzing mechanisms.

Most individual cells in the visual cortex are known to respond only to certain very specific patterns of light. For example, a particular cell may respond
only to lines that are straight, vertical, and red. Early neurophysiological studies of such "feature detectors" in animals promised to reveal in detail the
steps between stimulus and perception.

A discovery by Celeste McCollough (1965) seemed to provide a link
between animal neurophysiology and human perception, by demonstrating
psychophysically the orientation- and color-specificity that characterize many
cortical cells. (Reviews of the extensive literature on the McCollough Effect
have been provided by Anstis, 1975; Skowbo, Timney, Gentry, & Morant,
1975; MacKay, 1978; and Stromeyer, 1978.)

In order to experience the McCollough Effect, you spend five or ten minutes
staring alternately at vertical red stripes and horizontal green stripes, switching
from one to the other every ten seconds or so. (You can look through red and
green cellophane at the gratings in Fig. 11.) Then you look at a black-and-
white test pattern, such as those in Fig. 12. You'll probably notice that the
horizontally striped letters in Fig. 12 look pinkish, and the vertically striped
background may look greenish. When you rotate the book or tip your head
90°, the colors change places.

Here we have real *visual* plasticity. Before your exposure to the colored
stripes, the achromatic patterns look colorless; after, they look colored. In
fact, after viewing the colored stripes, you experience a perceptual
phenomenon that doesn't ever occur under normal conditions: color percep-

tions that change as you tilt your head, dependent on the orientation of stripes on your retina.

Edge Detectors

Color adaptation of edge detectors. McCollough attributed her orientation-specific color aftereffect to "color adaptation of edge-detectors in the human visual system" (McCollough, 1965). (The term "edge-detector," as commonly used, implies not just sensitivity to contours, but to contours within a narrow range of orientations.) If we humans, like cats and monkeys, have separate mechanisms for detecting vertical and horizontal contours, she reasoned, then red vertical stripes would red-adapt only the vertical-edge detectors and green horizontals would green-adapt only the horizontal-edge detectors. After adaptation, the vertical-edge detectors would give a less-red (i.e. greener) response to verticals, and the horizontal-edge detectors a less-green (i.e. pinker) response to horizontals.

Thus McCollough took her observations as evidence that humans do possess orientation-specific visual mechanisms. In addition, her observations led her to infer three properties of these edge-detectors, besides their sensitivity to contour orientation. First, they are subject to color adaptation. Second, they must respond to contours over some range of retinal locations, since the aftereffect colors (unlike color afterimages) don't move when the observer's gaze shifts from place to place on the test pattern; they stay put on the appropriately oriented contours. Such invariance with displacement of the retinal stimulus is

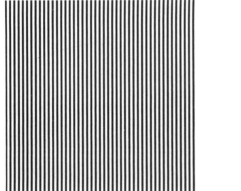

FIG. 11.   Vertical and horizontal gratings for producing the McCollough Effect. The two gratings should be viewed alternately through colored filters, red for vertical and green for horizontal, for several minutes.

FIG. 12. Test stimuli for viewing the McCollough Effect. After exposure to red verticals and green horizontals, the horizontally striped regions will appear pink and the vertically striped regions greenish. Rotating the picture or one's head 90° will cause the colors to exchange
places. (Left: courtesy of Public Relations Department, Bell Telephone
Laboratories. Right: from Harris & Gibson, 1968a, suggested by the
painting "Square of Three" by Reginald Neal.)

characteristic of the cortical cells that Hubel and Wiesel (1959) called "complex cells." ("Simple" cells, on the other hand, require a stimulus that has
both the appropriate orientation and retinal location.) Finally, since she was
able to induce opposite aftereffects in the two eyes by having one eye view
orientation-color pairings that were the opposite of those seen by the other eye,
she concluded that the relevant detectors must be monocular, located at a level
in the visual system where inputs from the two eyes have not yet been combined.

Adaptation of colored-edge detectors. An additional specificity was ascribed to
these edge detectors by my willful misinterpretation (made public by Gibson &
Harris, 1968, and Harris, 1968b) of McCollough's model. Instead of postulating, as McCollough did, just two kinds of detector to mediate the aftereffects, I
decided for didactic reasons to talk about *four*: red-vertical detectors, green-
vertical detectors, red-horizontal detectors, and green-horizontal detectors.
The McCollough Effect would result from adaptation of two of these four
kinds of doubly-selective mechanism.

For some reason, many people now think that this is what McCollough was
proposing. The misinterpretation has virtually driven the original out of circu-
lation (an illustration, perhaps, of Gresham's Law). Other people claim that

the two different proposals—color adaptation of edge detectors and adaptation of colored-edge detectors—are indistinguishable. Actually, though, they should be easy to distinguish physiologically: McCollough's hypothesis says there should be horizontal- and vertical-edge detectors that normally respond to a broad range of wavelengths but that show appropriate distortions of their wavelength-response curve after prolonged exposure to colored horizontals or verticals. The colored-edge-detector hypothesis says you should find units that normally respond well only to a particular combination of color and orientation—which indeed is what was soon reported (Hubel & Wiesel, 1968).

Spatial Frequency

Research soon revealed another property that detectors underlying the McCollough Effect must have: spatial-frequency specificity.

The first discovery about the effect (beyond what was reported in McCollough's original paper) was that the aftereffect colors are determined not only by the orientation of contours, but also by their spacing. In fact, the Mc-Collough Effect was probably the first example of spatial-frequency-specific adaptation, antedating the experiments with colorless stripes (see Julesz, 1980). In demonstrations at the University of Pennsylvania in 1965 and 1966, I had students adapt to colored grids while standing at various distances from the projection screen. Then a black-and-white striped test pattern was projected and the students were asked to walk toward and away from the screen to find the distance at which the aftereffect colors looked strongest. The distance each person picked was generally about the same as while adapting to the colored grids, which means that the best aftereffect was seen when the test contours had about the same spacing on the retina as the adapting stripes. At much smaller or greater viewing distances, the aftereffect colors weakened or disappeared.

Perceived vs. retinal spacing. A later study provided more precise confirmation of this dependence on retinal spacing. I had subjects adapt to a green vertical grating with stripes 0.1° wide, alternating with a red grating, also vertical, with stripes half as wide. They were then tested with vertical black-and-white gratings of various stripe widths, suspended from an overhead track.

By using a pulley to move the grating forward or back, the subjects could vary the spacing of contours in their retinal images of the grating. They found that at some distances (depending on the stripe spacing) the grating looked pink, whereas at some greater distances the same grating looked greenish. At an intermediate distance, it looked white. The subjects were asked to position each test grating at this "neutral point," where it turned pink if brought any closer and green if moved farther away. The neutral-point technique proved quite sensitive: Each test grating looked white over only a small range of distances.

The result was that regardless of the actual and perceived spacing of stripes in a test grating, subjects almost always positioned it so that the *retinal* spacing was the same, as indicated by the straight lines passing through the origin in Fig. 14. (If the aftereffect depended on *perceived* bar width, and size constancy were perfect, the data points would have fallen along a horizontal line.)

Stripe width vs. spatial frequency. Using this sensitive "neutral-point" judgment, we can ask a question even more pertinent to a spatial-frequency analysis: Does the McCollough Effect depend on the *width* of the black or white stripes, or on their *spatial frequency*? The studies I have cited don't provide an answer to that question because all three spatial parameters—black stripe width, white stripe width, and spatial frequency—were varied together (if at all).

Suppose we adapt subjects as before, using widely spaced green stripes and closely spaced red ones, and then ask them to adjust the retinal magnification of a test stimulus by moving it nearer or farther, until it looks neither pink nor green. This time, instead of a 1:1 ratio between the widths of the black and the white test stripes, we use some other ratio, such as 1:3. If what matters is spatial frequency, a 1:3 grid should appear neutral when it has the same spatial

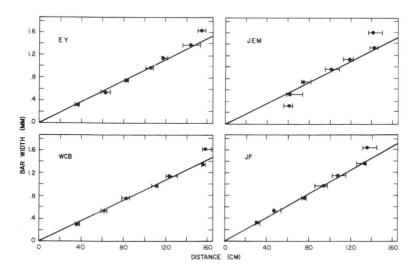

FIG. 14. Viewing distances chosen by four observers to make test gratings with various bar widths appear colorless after adaptation to wide green and narrow red stripes. The lines represent constant retinal width. (From Harris, 1970.)

frequency as a 1:1 grid—in other words, it should have the same cycle-width. So should a 3:1 grid, with black stripes three times as wide as the white (horizontal dotted line in Fig. 15). But if the aftereffect instead depends on the width of the black bars, then to get a neutral point with a 1:3 black/white grid we would need a much wider cycle-width, in order to get black bars as wide as those in the colored adapting gratings (Fig. 15, upper left). For a 3:1 black/white grid we'd need a narrower total cycle-width (Fig. 15, lower right). Likewise, if all that mattered was white-bar width, a 1:3 black/white test stimulus would have to be much narrower in order to look neutral (lower left) and a 3:1 test stimulus would have to be wider (upper right).

The experiment's outcome is shown in Fig. 16. It is clear that black/white ratio had no systematic effect whatever: The subjects' neutral-point settings gave the same cycle-width for all three black/white ratios. Thus, we can conclude that the major influence on this aftereffect is spatial frequency, rather than width of white or black stripes. (For lower spatial frequencies, though, Uhlarik and Osgood, 1974, found black stripe width to be the controlling variable.)

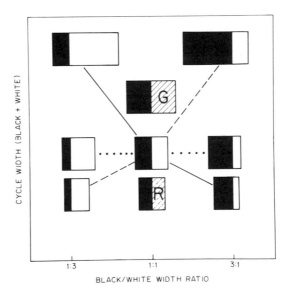

FIG. 15. Possible results of adapting to wide green and black stripes and narrow red and black stripes. If the aftereffect is determined entirely by the width of the white test stripes, the same white stripe would yield a colorless perception regardless of the width of the black stripes (diagonal dashed line). Dependence on black stripe width would produce the unbroken diagonal line. Dependence on spatial frequency would produce a horizontal line, like the dotted one, indicating a constant period or cycle width. (From Harris, 1971a.)

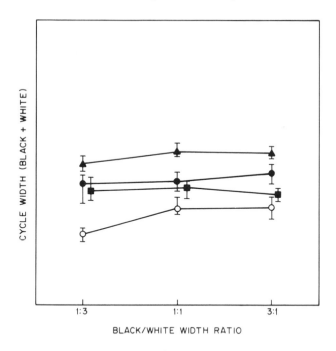

FIG. 16. Cycle widths chosen by four subjects to make grids with various black/white ratios appear colorless, after adaptation to wide green and black stripes and narrow red and black ones. (From Harris, 1971a.)

Localized Color Adaptation

At this point, it seemed that McCollough's discovery had provided us with direct and detailed insights into the workings of the human visual system. Apparently we have visual mechanisms that are very selective in what they respond to, requiring contours with a certain orientation, color, and spatial frequency. The similarities to properties found by recording from cortical cells strengthened the rationale for generalizing from animal to human vision. And the location-invariance displayed by both the McCollough Effect and complex cells pointed the way to an understanding of important attributes of complex pattern perception.

However, all of the findings cited above, which seemed to offer direct testimony to the operation of multiply selective, narrowly tuned, highly structured, complex edge detectors in human perception, could be accounted for by a well-known, much simpler, mechanism—one lacking in selectivity and spatial organization.

The simpleminded hypothesis that Alan Gibson and I proposed (Gibson & Harris, 1968; Harris & Gibson, 1968a, 1968b) ascribed the McCollough Effect to localized color adaptation resulting from biased fixation. It is often referred to as the "afterimage," "retinal," or "killjoy" hypothesis. (All three labels are a bit misguided.)

Evidence against afterimages. McCollough had a number of reasons for believing that her aftereffect is *not* due to ordinary negative afterimages, the kind that you get by staring at any brightly colored pattern and then looking at a blank surface. First, to get an ordinary afterimage you have to stare fixedly at some point in the colored adapting pattern or else use a very intense, briefly presented pattern; for the McCollough Effect you don't. Second, the color of an ordinary afterimage would be neutralized by alternate exposure to complementary colors such as red and green; the McCollough Effect is enhanced by such exposure. Third, to see an afterimage best, you look at a homogeneous surface; to see the McCollough aftereffect, you must look at stripes, and the stripes must have the proper orientation. Fourth, when you move your eyes around, an ordinary afterimage moves with them, because it is tied to a particular location on the retina; McCollough colors stay attached to the appropriately oriented stripes regardless of eye movements. The letters in Fig. 12 remain pink and the background stays green no matter what part of the figure you look at. And finally, afterimages normally fade away in a matter of seconds or at most minutes; the McCollough Effect can persist for hours.

Biased fixation and localized adaptation. These five distinctions certainly seem more than adequate to establish that the McCollough Effect is something very different from ordinary afterimages. However, it occurred to me that the issue is not so cut-and-dried: These distinctions hold up only if you scan the stimuli completely *randomly.* Suppose instead that you tend to look at the colored stripes more than the black background. Then, whenever you fixate on a green horizontal stripe, you're adapting horizontal strips of the retina to green. Since the stripes are evenly spaced, it doesn't matter which green stripe you fixate; even if you switch around from one to another, you're green-adapting the same retinal strips (Fig. 17A and B). Likewise, whenever you fixate on any red vertical stripe, you're red-adapting vertical strips of the retina. That means that the alternate exposures to complementary color grids, instead of cancelling out, contribute systematically to building up a plaid pattern of color adaptation (Fig. 17C). The less consistent you are in fixating, the weaker and blurrier the plaid is, but it's still there.

What happens now if you look at a black-and-white striped test pattern? Figure 17D shows part of a test pattern, enlarged to the same scale as Fig. 17A and B. If you again tend to fixate on the brighter stripes rather than on the dark background, the image of a white stripe will pass through the center of the retina, as indicated by the fixation mark in Fig. 17D. That means that the horizontal white stripes fall on strips of retina that are mostly adapted to green,

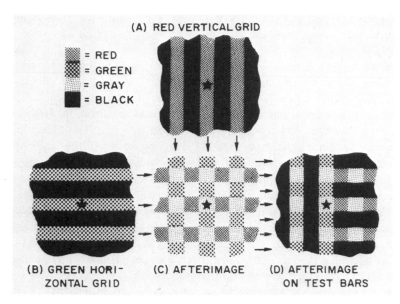

(A) RED VERTICAL GRID

= RED
= GREEN
= GRAY
= BLACK

(B) GREEN HORI-   (C) AFTERIMAGE   (D) AFTERIMAGE
    ZONTAL GRID   ON TEST BARS

FIG. 17. How localized color adaptation could produce illusory colors
like the McCollough Effect. Fixating a red stripe (A) red-adapts vertical
strips of retina and fixating a green stripe (B) green-adapts horizontal
strips. The result is a plaid pattern of adaptation (C). (The star marks
the center of the fovea.) When a white stripe in the test pattern is fixated (D), the portions of the plaid adaptation pattern that are visible are
predominantly green on vertical stripes and pink on horizontals. (From
Gibson & Harris, 1968.)

and they therefore look pink. Vertical white stripes stimulate regions mostly
adapted to red, and so look greenish. Again because of the regular spacing of
the test stripes, you can move your gaze from one stripe to another without
changing the correspondence with the plaid adaptation map, so the horizontally
striped areas remain pink. On the other hand, if you rotate either the test pattern or your head, you dilute or abolish the preponderance of one color on
each stripe.

With very intense adapting stimuli, subjects may actually see the plaid pattern for a while. With the usual procedure, though, they don't; test stripes
look homogeneously colored, and a blank surface looks colorless. I would assume that this is merely an instance of the averaging or assimilation that occurs when *real* brightness or color gradients are very blurred—see, for example, Krech and Crutchfield (1958, p. 86), Krauskopf (1967). Nevertheless, if
the plaid pattern is usually not visible, it is misleading to refer to it (as Gibson
and Harris and others have) as an "afterimage." It's also worth noting that
although I've been talking about adaptation in the retina, such a pattern of local adaptation might build up at any place in the visual system that preserves a

topographic mapping of the retina—the lateral geniculate body, for instance, or the visual cortex—not just in the retina itself.

Evidence against localized adaptation. With only a little ingenuity, the plaid adaptation model can be applied to most other findings on the McCollough Effect. Sometimes an additional assumption or two is required, but the total number probably doesn't exceed that required by other current models.

There is, however, one conclusive bit of evidence against this Gibson-Harris model: the Gibson-Harris experiment (1968). We modified the usual McCollough procedure by using brief (80 millisecond) flashes of the red and green adapting stripes. Each grating appeared randomly in one of two locations; in one position the colored bars fell where the black bars fell in the other position. With this random-location procedure, no relevant inhomogeneities in retinal adaptation can develop, regardless of what eye-movements a subject makes.

If the McCollough aftereffect depends on a pattern of local color adaptation, we should have found that this procedure doesn't produce any McCollough Effect. But it does, in all subjects (graph on the left in Fig. 18). And the aftereffect grows steadily stronger with increasing total exposure time (graph on the right in Fig. 18). It even occurs with much shorter flashes that definitively rule out stimulus-linked eye-movements (Stromeyer & Dawson, 1974).

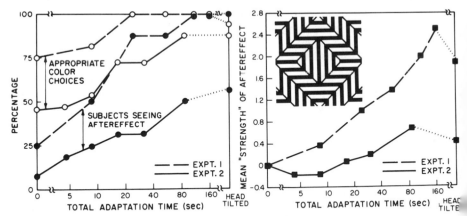

FIG. 18. Growth of the McCollough Effect produced by randomly located adapting flashes. •: Percentage of subjects who reported seeing an appropriate color. ○: Percentage of forced-choice color reports that were appropriate, regardless of whether the subject reported seeing any color (chance level = 50%). ■: "Strength index" calculated by adding 1 each time a subject called the aftereffect color "stronger than on the preceding test" and subtracting 1 each time it was called "weaker" (possible range: −6 to +6). Eight subjects who had previously seen a demonstration of the McCollough Effect took part in Experiment 1; 16 naive subjects participated in Experiment 2. (From Harris & Gibson, 1968a.)

I must admit to a lingering fondness for the elegance and precision of the local-adaptation model. So let me make explicit the lesson that this model, right or wrong, has to offer: Simple as it is, a pattern of differential point-by-point adaptation could account for precisely the same findings that at first looked like direct proof of the role of more complex mechanisms in the Mc-Collough Effect. In fact, careful consideration of local adaptation actually yielded successful predictions of the outcomes of quite a few subsequent experiments, experiments that were often intended to provide support for some other, more elaborate, model. Thus, even when there seems to be a close match between some psychophysical data and some physiological mechanism, psychological investigation ought to be pursued thoughtfully and imaginatively, to determine whether some other physiological mechanism—perhaps simpler, perhaps not yet discovered—shows an even better fit (see Teller, 1980).

Some people are impatient with psychological theorizing and analytic experimentation. Why bother with speculative models, they say, when we already know the physiological *facts*? Because physiological "facts" are facts only about physiology; when you invoke them to explain psychological phenomena, they become a theory or model. And when physiological facts are turned into psychological theories, they need the same critical scrutiny and empirical testing that we give to other unproven theories (Harris & Barkow, 1969).

Intensity Differences and "Dipoles"

Having ruled out localized color adaptation as an adequate explanation for the McCollough Effect, must we conclude that the effect originates in highly selective edge detectors after all? Alan Gibson and I were reluctant to go that far, since even though localized adaptation was too simple to explain all the findings, it *nearly* did the job. So instead of going all the way to mechanisms as complex as orientation-specific spatial-frequency-tuned colored-edge detectors, we decided to ask what was the simplest kind of mechanism that could handle the available data.

What we wanted was a mechanism that could respond differentially to grossly different orientations and spacings, but that wouldn't care much about the precise location of a contour, a mechanism that might reside low enough in the visual system to be monocular and precede any size-constancy operation. How far along the continuum from point-by-point adaptation to highly structured edge detectors would we have to go? Just one step: to a mechanism that deals with pairs of retinal regions instead of single points.

The simplest adequate mechanism would be a cell that receives inputs from two nonconcentric locations of the retina, responding in proportion to the intensity difference between the two regions. Since the defining feature of such cells is that they are connected to two retinal locations, we called these hypothetical difference-detectors "dipoles." The dipole receptive areas are assumed to be small and scattered densely all over the retina in random orienta-

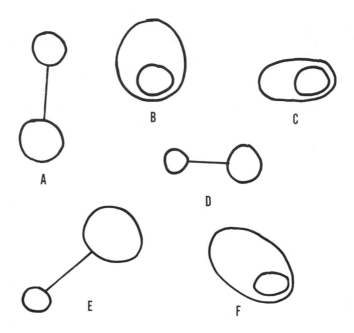

FIG. 19. "Dipoles": hypothetical neural units that respond to differences in intensity of stimulation of two nonconcentric regions of the retina. The pairing of regions is indicated by overlap or by a connecting line. Each such unit would respond to a wide range of orientations and curvatures of an intensity edge. (Based on Gibson & Harris, 1968; Harris & Gibson, 1968b.)

tions. Figure 19 shows some examples of possible arrangements of dipoles' receptive fields.

Given a set of vertical stripes, a dipole arranged like A or B in Fig. 19 would be unlikely to respond—because both receptive areas would be exposed to the same stripe, and there would be no difference in intensity between the dipole's two receptive areas. On the other hand, a horizontal grid *would* produce an intensity difference for some proportion of dipoles arranged like A and B. Similarly, dipoles with receptive areas like C and D are more likely to respond to vertical stripes. If we assume that dipoles vary randomly not only in their spatial arrangements but also in their spectral sensitivities—some more sensitive to red, others to green—then a vertical red grid would adapt one population of dipoles, and a horizontal green grid would adapt a different (though overlapping) population. Of course, some dipoles (E and F, for example) would not respond to either stimulus or would respond to both; these cells would not contribute to the aftereffect.

Our definition of dipoles allows them to have either separate or overlapping receptive fields. Cells that fit this definition have been found at various levels of the visual system. For example, many of the so-called "concentric field cells," in the lateral geniculate nucleus and elsewhere, actually have somewhat nonconcentric receptive fields (see, for example, the receptive-field maps presented by Kuffler, 1953, such as the one shown on the right in Fig. 20; the perfectly concentric diagrams that are usually printed are idealizations). Alternatively, they could be cells with separated fields, like those that Bishop and Spinelli, for example, have reported finding in the visual cortex.

Since a dipole can respond to edges, *is* a dipole an edge detector? No. Dipoles are too unspecialized to fit either the psychological or the physiological definition of an orientation-specific "edge-detector." The ability of dipoles to respond to edges is, so to speak, an accident: Edges work only because they delineate two areas of different intensity. An orientation-specific edge detector is, by definition, a cell that responds most strongly to a straight stimulus in a particular orientation. For a dipole, however, there is no optimal stimulus: Stimuli with a wide variety of shapes and orientations will work equally well. That's why a single dipole cannot possibly produce a perception of a straight line. (Of course, a *set* of dipoles could do so, but for that matter so could a set of rods or cones.)

It is not clear at this point whether there is any advantage in thinking about dipoles rather than edge detectors. Perhaps the only testable difference between the two is the amount of orientation selectivity predicted for the McCollough Effect. Unfortunately, the question of orientation selectivity is at present unresolved. Physiological data offer little guidance: De Valois, Albrecht, and Thorell (1978) note that microelectrode recordings from single cells in the visual cortex reveal "enormous variability...in the fineness of the orientation tuning....Our most narrowly-tuned cell had a bandwidth...of 6°; the median is about 40°; and there are numerous broadly tuned cells with

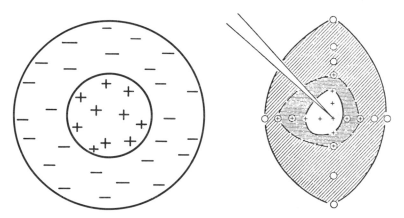

FIG. 20. Left: A typical idealized diagram of a concentric receptive field. Right: Sensitivity map of an actual receptive field. (From Kuffler, 1953.)

bandwidths up to 100° and more." Psychophysical data are also equivocal. Stromeyer (1969) reported that the McCollough Effect can be obtained only if the test stimulus is quite close in orientation to the adapting stimulus. Fidell (1969), on the other hand, found that a green adapting grating weakens the aftereffect of a red adapting grating even when their orientations are as much as 45° apart. Other data indicating broad generalization across orientation has been reported by Ellis (1977), who noted that psychophysical measures of the McCollough Effect's orientational selectivity underestimate the breadth of tuning of the underlying mechanisms. His data suggest that these mechanisms respond appreciably to orientations even 90° apart. Ellis concluded that his findings "rekindle suspicion that physiological mechanisms with the properties of Harris and Gibson's (1968) 'dipoles' may prove adequate to subserve the aftereffect."

THE McCOLLOUGH EFFECT AS ASSOCIATIVE LEARNING

The models I've dealt with so far vary considerably in what they assume or imply about the neural organization, locus, and function of the units responsible for the McCollough Effect. Yet when contrasted with the next model, the previous ones can all be seen to fall into the same general class. They all assume some sort of weakened response by some kind of prewired neural units. That is, they all assume that the McCollough Effect results from something like fatigue, adaptation, changed operating level, inhibitory after-discharge, or the like, occurring within single neural units in a population with rather specific and limited responses to particular subsets of stimulus patterns.

Associative Models of Perception

Associative models instead rely on *strengthening* of connections *between* mechanisms. According to this kind of model, the McCollough Effect depends not just on preexisting characteristics of the units, but on linkages that may not even have existed before exposure to colored stripes.

The associative model (or class of models) is a venerable one among philosophical and psychological theories of perception. It has often been invoked when some aspect of perceptual experience seems surprising in the light of the retinal stimulus or the known visual mechanisms. This kind of model has been particularly appealing whenever there appears to be a change in visual system functioning, so that a given stimulus produces a perception that is different from before.

The basic notion is that the perceptual experience in question is elicited by the seemingly inadequate or irrelevant stimulus because that stimulus was around when that perception was elicited by some *other* stimulus that *does* seem adequate. For example, as applied to adaptation to prismatic distortion (or to the origin of visual space perception in general) an associative account might say that signals from the retina acquire their spatial significance by co-occurring with nonvisual spatial perceptions that are directly evoked by tactile and kinesthethic stimulation (cf. Berkeley, 1709; Kohler, 1951/1964; Taylor, 1962).

Associative Models of the McCollough Effect

As applied to the McCollough Effect, an associative model would say that after repeated pairing of color and orientation, orientation alone can elicit the perceptual response of seeing color. Such a model was first made explicit by Mary Viola (1966), an undergraduate working with John Hay at Smith College. Since then, a number of investigators have proposed various conditioning, learning, or associative models. (See reviews by Skowbo, Timney, Gentry, & Morant, 1975; MacKay, 1978; Stromeyer, 1978. Recently Montalvo, 1976, has developed a novel associative model for the McCollough Effect, with some properties quite different from its predecessors'.)

Why Associative Models?

What makes associative models for the McCollough Effect so appealing? Three things:

Stimulus pairing. First, the procedure for producing the McCollough Effect *looks* like an ideal one for associative conditioning. A color and an orientation are repeatedly presented together, and then an orientation alone is able to elicit a color perception. Schematically, the procedure looks just like classical conditioning: A stimulus that starts out as ineffective in eliciting a certain response is repeatedly presented along with one that does elicit it (the unconditioned stimulus); thereafter the previously ineffective stimulus (now a conditioned stimulus) elicits the response when presented alone.

Yellow Volkswagen detectors. A second reason for resorting to an associative model is the continuing proliferation of *contingent aftereffects,* in which perception of one aspect of a test pattern is contingent on the presence or value of another aspect, which is normally thought to be irrelevant to that perception. A popular pastime among vision and perception researchers in recent years has been drawing up a table that has the rows and columns labeled with visual dimensions such as hue, luminance, motion, orientation and spatial frequency. Each compartment in the table represents a possible contingent aftereffect analogous to the McCollough Effect. For example, perception of a motion aftereffect can be made contingent on the color of the test stimulus, perception of orientation can be made contingent on spatial frequency, and so on (see Mayhew & Anstis, 1972; Wyatt, 1974; Skowbo, Timney, Gentry, & Morant, 1975; Stromeyer, 1978). As soon as an empty space is noticed in such a table, there's a rush to fill it in by setting up a new contingent aftereffect and dashing off a publication announcing its existence and ascribing it to a new double-duty cortical unit—or a triple- or quadruple-duty unit.

Years ago, I fabricated the "yellow Volkswagen detector" to draw attention to the unpalatable inventory that this approach seemed to be heading toward: one hypothetical detector for each distinctive perception (Harris, 1968b, 1971b). For certain types of experiments, Graham (1980) has proposed an elegant solution to the proliferation of inferred special-purpose detectors. She argues that the data that led to the postulation of numerous diverse detectors can in fact be accounted for by the same spatial-frequency channels that handle so many other findings. Unfortunately, that kind of simplification is not possible for contingent aftereffects like the McCollough Effect. No one type of detector or channel can possibly deal with the myriad contingent aftereffects. The only obvious way to cut down markedly on the number of special mechanisms is to find some way to ascribe all of the different aftereffects to a common associative mechanism, capable of connecting any of a wide range of attributes of stimuli and perceptions.

Longevity. Doubtless the strongest spur to invoking conditioning models is the amazing longevity of the McCollough Effect (and other contingent aftereffects). McCollough noted that 10 minutes' exposure to the colored gratings can give aftereffects that last hours. Riggs, White, and Eimas (1974) have found that with 2½ hours' exposure, the aftereffect colors are easily measurable more than a *week* later. They pointed out that this seems to be well outside the range of durations of adaptation of units in the retina or visual cortex. Such a long-lasting effect seems more like memories or synaptic modifications than like a transient weakening of responsiveness of some sensory unit.

Difficulties for Associative Models

A number of findings raise difficulties for associative models.

Longevity. Some recent findings call into question the assumption that the longevity of the McCollough Effect implicates an associative rather than a sensory mechanism.

Frome and her collaborators have shown that inspecting a colorless grating leads to a change in perceived squareness of a rectangle (Frome, Danielson, & Levinson, 1974; Frome, Levinson, Danielson, & Clavadetscher, 1979). This is apparently a simple, noncontingent aftereffect. However, the persistence of this simple aftereffect is comparable to that of the McCollough Effect (Frome, Harris, & Levinson, 1975). After 5 minutes of adaptation the effect lasts at least 2 hours; after 15 minutes of adaptation the effect is in full strength 24 hours later (Fig. 21). Other evidence of very long-lasting noncontingent aftereffects has been reported by several investigators (e.g. Gibson, 1933; Blakemore & Campbell, 1969; Masland, 1969; Blakemore, Nachmias, & Sutton, 1970; Kalfin & Locke, 1972; Hansel & Mahmud, 1978).

Thus, given the proper conditions, various simple aftereffects can be as long-lasting as the McCollough Effect. There are two possible conclusions. One is that all of these seemingly noncontingent aftereffects are actually contingent upon some undetermined attribute of the adapting stimulus or the experimental situation. The other is that *non*associative aftereffects can also be very persistent, and therefore longevity cannot be taken as evidence for an associative model of the McCollough Effect.

Wrong colors. The most obvious embarrassment for an associative model of the McCollough Effect is the colors themselves. In other kinds of conditioning, what gets associated is whatever was paired during the conditioning process. In the McCollough Effect, what gets associated is the *opposite* of what was paired—the complementary color. Exposure to green horizontals makes neutral horizontals look pink, not greenish.

But this is not a fatal problem. In fact, Ivo Kohler (1951/1964) and James G. Taylor (1962) had an answer to it even before the McCollough Effect was

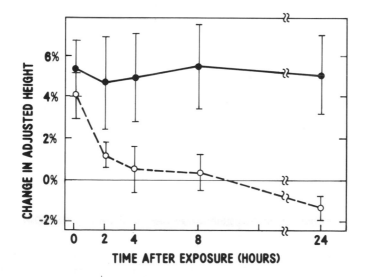

FIG. 21. A long-lasting aftereffect. Viewing a colorless vertical sinusoidal grating leads to a change in perceived squareness, as measured by subjects' adjustments of the height of a rectangle to make it appear square. After 15 minutes' exposure to the grating, the misjudgments persisted for at least 24 hours (filled circles). After a 5-minute exposure, the aftereffect dissipated much more rapidly (open circles). (From Frome, Harris, & Levinson, 1975.)

discovered. In line with their theorizing, we can say that what gets conditioned to the adapting stimulus is not the initial perception, but rather the initial *response* to the stimulus: A green stimulus elicits an unconditioned *neutralizing response*, namely "adding red" (this is what we normally call "color adaptation" or "negative afterimage"). It is this neutralizing response that gets conditioned to contour orientation and is then elicited by the test stimulus.

Too much generalization. More serious difficulties for an associative model arise when we think about typical examples of learning and then try to make predictions about the McCollough Effect by analogy, especially about how it will generalize to test stimuli that differ from the adapting stimuli. Just where we'd expect good generalization, we find that the McCollough Effect is narrowly restricted; just where we'd expect it to be restricted, it generalizes.

As an example of surprisingly broad generalization, consider the BTL test pattern or the concentric-diamonds Op Art design in Fig. 12. They have very little overall similarity to the striped adapting grids, yet the McCollough aftereffect shows up even better on those complex patterns than on a full-field grating that is geometrically identical to the adapting stimulus. Similarly, McCollough mentioned that when she looked at a pattern of concentric circles—with little resemblance to her straight adapting stripes—she saw wedge-shaped sectors of aftereffect colors (wherever the curved contours were roughly vertical or horizontal).

Probably the most extreme example of generalization between dissimilar patterns is seen after prolonged viewing of colored *random-dot* patterns: small black dots scattered on a green background alternating with large dots on red. Even though exposure was only to *dots*, colored aftereffects were seen on *striped* gratings (Harris, 1972). Thus, the McCollough Effect generalizes quite well to test patterns that no one would be likely to treat as "equivalent stimuli."

Too little generalization. Now consider the McCollough Effect's unexpected specificity. Any other kind of learning that is achieved with only one eye open shows up when tested with only the other eye open. But McCollough noted (a bit uneasily, given the large proportion of cortical cells that receive inputs from both eyes) that her effect is confined to the eye that viewed the colored stripes. In fact, presenting opposite orientation-color pairings to the two eyes made the apparent colors of a test pattern change when one or the other eye was closed. Numerous attempts by highly-motivated experimenters have failed to find convincing evidence of transfer of the McCollough Effect from one eye to the other. (There have been some recent reports of partial—or reversed—transfer under special conditions, but nothing like what's found in typical learning experiments.)

Not only is the McCollough Effect tied to the eye of origin, it is tied to the particular patch of retina that was adapted. By having subjects adapt by fixating in the center of patterns like those on the left in Fig. 22, we were able to produce oppositely colored McCollough Effects simultaneously on adjoining retinal regions, using test patterns like those on the right. Stromeyer (1972) went further and showed that, after adapting with a fixation point and small adapting grids, aftereffect colors could be seen only if the test pattern fell on the adapted retinal region. Using our concentric-diamonds test pattern (Fig. 12), Barkow and I were able to show that the McCollough Effect follows Emmert's Law: That is, just like an afterimage, after a small patch of retina is adapted, the aftereffect colors appear to cover less and less of a large test pattern as one gets closer and closer to it (Harris, 1970).

Dependence on retinal geometry. In fact, just about *everything* about the McCollough Effect is strictly tied to the geometry of the retinal image. If you adapt to green verticals, McCollough noted, then test stripes appear pink only if they are *retinally* vertical—for example, when physically horizontal stripes are viewed with your head tipped 90°. There's no trace of an influence of *perceived* orientation (Ellis, 1976). Similarly, as explained above, after you adapt to colored grids with different stripe widths, the colors that you see on test pat-

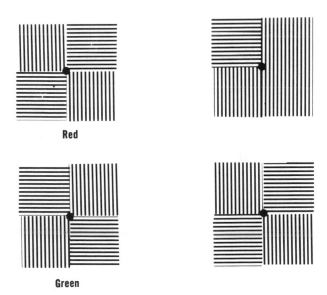

Red

Green

FIG. 22. Retinal localization of the McCollough Effect. Subjects fixated in the center of the field while the two colored patterns on the left were alternated. When they then fixated in the center of various test patterns, as illustrated on the right, the color that they saw on vertical stripes depended on which quadrant the verticals fell in. (From Harris, 1969.)

terns at different viewing distances depend entirely on contour spacing in the retinal image, regardless of how wide or narrow the stripes look; there's no trace of size constancy in the aftereffect (Fig. 14).

This dependence on retinal geometry is a serious problem for a learning model, since learning normally depends on objects *as perceived* rather than on details of the proximal stimulus pattern. That's why learning theorists can usually take all the workings of the sensory systems for granted and talk about *objects* as stimuli, without considering how the invariant properties of those objects get detected from diverse patterns of light on the retina.

Dependence on stimulus attributes. Other details of the retinal stimuli also play an important role. As mentioned above, if you vary the ratio of black-stripe width to white-stripe width, the aftereffect is governed by the spatial frequency rather than by either black or white stripe width (Fig. 16). And if you lighten up the black stripes in the colored adapting grids, approaching a luminance match between gray and colored bars, you knock out the McCollough Effect altogether (Fig. 23), even though it's still easy to see the bars and their orientation. You wouldn't think that an associative learning mechanism would be so finicky about such stimulus details as contrast and spatial frequency.

Finally, and perhaps most informative, it seems as though there are certain varieties of contingent color aftereffect that are very easy to get (such as the McCollough Effect itself), others that are difficult (such as curvature-color or random-dot-color effects), and others that reportedly are impossible. Barkow, Fidell, Mayhew and Anstis, Riggs, and Stromeyer are among those who have tried pairing colors with a wide variety of patterns and have been unable to get any color aftereffects for most of them.

New Ideas About Learning

Where does that leave us? Haven't I just made an overwhelming case against an associative learning model? Doesn't it sound as though the McCollough Effect has all the stimulus specificities you'd expect from special-purpose visual detectors, rather than the broad range of arbitrary connections you'd expect to be possible through conditioning? I used to think so, but now I think we shouldn't give up so quickly.

It's been said that psychologists often struggle to find behavioral correlates for neurophysiology that's ten years out of date (whereas neurophysiologists, a more cautious breed, ignore behavioral data until it's at least 40 years out of date). Could it be that vision people are uneasy about associative models of the McCollough Effect only because our notions about learning are out of date? It seems that most of the principles and findings in learning that I memorized in graduate school have since been either challenged or reinterpreted. In particular, there's been a strong movement, led by such people as Gar-

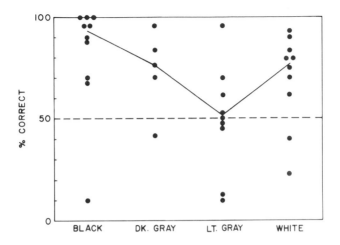

FIG. 23. Dependence of the McCollough Effect on brightness contrast. Subjects adapted to red and green gratings in which the colorless stripes were black, dark gray, light gray, or white. They were then shown black-and-white test patterns and asked to assign the label pink or green to each striped area. Each point plotted represents a different subject's proportion of color names that agree with the McCollough Effect (i.e. the complement of the color that had previously been viewed on stripes of the same orientation). (From Harris & Barkow, 1969.)

cia, Rozin, Seligman, and Shettleworth, to stress the *nonarbitrariness* of stimulus-response connections.

Associations between certain stimuli and certain responses seem to be remarkably easy to form in certain species—a prime example is rats' rapid learning to avoid poisoned bait, an avoidance always based on taste, not visual appearance. Other connections are difficult or impossible to produce—such as teaching a pigeon to peck a key to turn off a stimulus that signals electric shock, or teaching a cat to respond to hue (cats do have color receptors, but for years they acted color-blind). A book called *Biological Boundaries of Learning* (Seligman & Hager, 1972) and another entitled *Constraints on Learning: Limitations and Predispositions* (Hinde & Stevenson-Hinde, 1973) contain several dozen chapters on these newer views of learning.

It seems as though the nervous system comes with built-in predispositions to form certain connections and to avoid forming others. What we may have in the McCollough Effect is learning that is circumscribed by definite visual system predispositions. Contingent aftereffects may represent a very basic form of memory, the product of a low-level mechanism. If so, contingent aftereffects may offer a new avenue for unraveling the psychology and physiology of learning. The preconditions and stimuli can be precisely controlled;

there is low variability in the build-up and decay of the effects; and it may be comparatively easy to locate, stimulate and record from the brain cells that are involved.

Whether or not we accept a learning model for the McCollough Effect, we do now have a valid example of visual plasticity in the adult, with many of the features that make plasticity interesting. And in this case, the plasticity exhibits a new, unexpected, and therefore potentially illuminating, combination of properties.

ADDENDUM: GUIDELINES FOR FURTHER READING ABOUT ADAPTATION TO VISUAL DISTORTIONS

If one delves into the vast literature on adaptation to visual distortions (Welch, 1978, lists more than 500 relevant references), it is easy to get the impression that controversy and unresolved disputes abound. The guidelines that follow should help the reader appreciate that there is actually far less disagreement than meets the eye.

Terminology

Many prevalent confusions and apparent contradictions stem from differences in how terms are used by different authors (and sometimes by the same author at different times). Often it takes careful and insightful reading to ascertain what meaning is being assigned to a term.

"Perception." Does "perception" or "perceptual" specifically imply *visual* perception, or does it refer to *any* sensory modality? Some authors, for instance, ask whether an adaptive change is proprioceptive *or* perceptual—by which they mean visual. I would say that an alteration in position sense *is* a perceptual change.)

"Sensorimotor." Does "sensorimotor" mean *visual*-motor only? It often does in papers about visual distortion. Or does it also cover all aspects (sensory or motor or their linkages) of *any* sensory-motor system, including auditory-motor and perhaps proprioceptive-motor? Alternatively, is "sensorimotor" used as a noncommittal but all-inclusive term that *contrasts* with

"visual" and alludes to the coordination of bodily movements (without attributing priority to either position sense or motor commands)? As a final alternative, is "sensorimotor" virtually a synonym for "position sense" as I use it, with "sensori-" and "motor" referring to afferent and efferent components? For example, the most recent development of Held's sensorimotor theory ascribes adaptation to "the system that controls and assesses coincidence of the directions indicated by the exposed arm with those of objects, including other members of the body" (Hardt, Held, & Steinbach, 1971). How such a "sensorimotor" change would differ from alterations in position sense is problematic (see Hochberg, 1971; Howard, 1971; Kaufman, 1974), and the empirical findings that might justify making a distinction are open to other interpretations (see Hardt, Held, & Steinbach, 1971; Hochberg, 1971; Harris, 1974; Welch, 1978).

A similar range of usages can be found for "reafference." Although reafference can designate any kind of sensory feedback that results from self-produced movements, in the literature on visual distortions, it almost always denotes *visual* feedback, not kinesthetic.

"Motor" or "efferent." Does "motor" or "efferent" imply overt movements, or only intentions, plans, or readiness that may or may not result in physical movement? Are "motor commands" or "efference" assumed to dictate the direction and extent of movements, or to specify their end positions (as recent physiological data [Polit & Bizzi, 1978] may imply)? If end positions, the information derived from monitoring the motor command may be functionally equivalent to a "felt position" given by the position sense (Harris, 1965). "Motor control system" is another term that sometimes encompasses passive position sensing, when no movement is being made or planned, and sometimes is restricted to the determination of overt movements.

"Proprioceptive." When I called changes in felt position "proprioceptive" ("...for want of a better adjective...," Harris, 1965), I unwittingly set the stage for a continuing string of misunderstandings. I defined "proprioceptive change" as a change in the relation between physical position of a body part (relative to other parts) and perceived or registered position, regardless of whether afferent input or efferent outflow provides the necessary information.

For many people, though, "proprioceptive" and "kinesthetic" (and even "position sense") connote only sensory inflow from receptors. Accordingly, the evidence most often cited as contradicting the proprioceptive-change or position-sense hypothesis is the ability of monkeys with deafferented arms to adapt to displacing goggles, without proprioceptive feedback from the limb (e.g. Taub, 1968). But Taub himself concluded that his findings *support* the position-sense hypothesis: "We have previously presented evidence that kinesthesis consists of two independent and redundant components—one peripheral (proprioception) and one central (central feedback?)... In monkeys with deafferented forelimbs, the peripheral component is absent; there is thus less resistance to recalibration, and accordingly the process proceeds to completion more rapidly than in normal animals. One might say that the less there is of position sense, the easier it is to alter" (Taub, 1968, p. 97). (It now appears that the major site of adaptation in Taub's monkeys was actually the neck rather than the arm, as they were allowed head movements but not sight of the arm. Since the deafferentation affected the neck as well as the arms, Taub's conclusion still holds.)

Some people find the notion of altered position sense acceptable for the arms or head but not for the eyes, because (according to many textbooks) "the eyes have no position sense." However, the evidence does not support this assertion unless we give "position sense" a very narrow meaning. It is true that some experiments suggest that awareness of the position of the eyes is based on monitoring of efferent outflow to the eye muscles rather than afferent inflow from them; subjects can be deceived about the eye's position if it is moved passively. But in order to be so deceived, the subjects must have some impression of where their eyes are pointing. Indeed, Merton (1961) found that judgments of eye position made in the dark are just as accurate as judgments of arm position in the dark. We still don't know whether the physiological basis for felt position is the same for eyes as for limbs, or different. The same three sources of information—afferent input, efferent outflow, and efferent triggering or enhancement of afference—have been proposed from time to time for limbs (Rose & Mountcastle, 1960; Festinger, Burnham, Ono, & Bamber, 1967; Hamilton, 1964b) and for eyes (Skavenski, 1972; Helmholtz, 1866/1962; Shebilske, 1977). But we don't have to wait for a resolution of the physiological question before labeling the psychological process of adaptation. Given that the nervous system does register the positions of the arms and eyes, it is possible that the registration can be altered, and "change in position sense" is an apt label for that kind of alteration.

To some readers, "proprioceptive change" and "altered position sense" imply not only afference, but a peripheral or distal site rather than a central one—a change "in the limb" rather than "in the brain." Although one could imagine that arm, head, or eye adaptation to optical displacement affects the output of receptors in the joints or muscles, such peripheral changes could hardly account for the changes in position sense that appear to underlie adaptation to optical inversion and reversal. My assumption has been that all of the changes occur within the brain—within whatever mechanisms deal with positions of body parts rather than specifically with vision or movements.

Some changes in position sense *may* be traceable to peripheral mechanisms. If the eyes or head are kept turned to one side for a while, they are felt to be less turned than at first. Such "fatigue" or "muscle potentiation" effects (Hein, 1965; Ebenholtz, 1976) may well have a peripheral locus. Since wearing displacing goggles may induce asymmetric postures of the head or eyes, this sort of effect may well account for some or even all of the observations in some adaptation experiments. However, this kind of alteration in position sense dissipates quickly when the affected body part returns to a neutral position, or is moved about.

One final usage of "proprioceptive" should be mentioned. Gibson (1966) has pointed out that information about positions and movements of the body can come through the eyes as well as from the muscles and joints. Therefore he proposed extending the term "proprioceptive" to any perception of the self. If one accepts that broadened definition, though, one is obliged to introduce modifiers (such as "articular proprioception" and "visual proprioception") in order to discuss intelligibly the research dealt with here.

Changes in Position Sense, in Visual Perception. or in the Relationship Between Modalities?

"Visual." A dichotomy that is often encountered in the literature is "proprioceptive vs. visual" adaptation. This dichotomy obscures the possibility that altered position sense can pertain to the head and eyes, not just the limbs. (Quite a few writers use "proprioceptive change" to mean only a change in the arm.) Misperceiving the orientation of the head or eyes of necessity affects visual perception and visually-guided behavior: If the head or eyes are mistakenly felt to be turned when they are really pointing straight ahead, then an object straight ahead of the nose must be *seen* as off to one side of the body midline. So calling this change "visual" is defensible, but is nonetheless misleading. When early investigators (and some recent ones) talked about "visual" learning, they had in mind some sort of rerouting or reinterpretation of visual signals from the retina to the visual cortex. (Rewiring of this sort does occur in frogs whose eyes have been rotated after their optic nerves are severed: The optic nerve fibers make new connections in the brain, so that each retinal receptor is once again connected to the same region as in a normal frog [Sperry, 1944].) More recent believers in truly "visual" adaptation would be likely to relate it to the kinds of rewiring that may occur in the receptive fields of young animals exposed to abnormal visual inputs (see Mitchell, 1980), or to visual aftereffects such as the McCollough Effect.

If adaptation to displacement, inversion, and reversal were really visual, we might expect people to be able to adapt to a great variety of twistings, shearings, and other nonuniform distortions of the retinal image. On finding that adaptation to such distortions is minimal at best, we might then cast about for some characterization of the class of visual distortions that can be nullified by adaptation (Dodwell, 1970). But if we believe that adaptation affects the registration of head or eye position, not retinal information per se, then we don't expect much versatility in what distortions can be adapted to. In general, sizable reduction in perceptual distortion is expected only if altered evaluation of head or eye position will do the trick, without changes within the retinal geometry.

Some people have argued that head and eye adaptation should be called "visual" because they *do* affect visual perception, whereas arm adaptation *doesn't*. Even that claim is misleading. A person who is misperceiving head orientation of course misperceives the location of a visual target relative to the torso; but visual location is *not* misperceived relative to the nose. This situation is not qualitatively different from what happens when a person is misperceiving the location of a hand: The location of all visual targets is misperceived then, too — *relative to that hand* — though not, of course, relative to nose, head or torso. The same analysis applies to adaptation of the eyes, although in this case the only judgment that can be made on the "unadapted side" is of visual locations relative to the direction of the gaze. Thus calling head or eye adaptation "visual," and contrasting it with "proprioceptive adaptation" (of the arm), obscures the fact that in all cases the nonvisual perception of the relative positions of body parts has altered; the particular locus of the change determines how various visual judgments and behaviors are affected.

Talking about "visual" adaptation also overlooks the fact that altered position sense of the head or eyes can be measured while subjects face a homogeneous surface (without any landmarks to visually localize) or even in the dark, without any visual input at all. Subjects may be asked, in the dark, to point their eyes straight ahead, at their forefinger, or at their big toe (Kalil & Freedman, 1966; Craske, 1967; Templeton, Howard, & Wilkinson, 1974). Just as it seems strange to speak of "motor learning" when an effect can be measured in the absence of any motor response, so it seems inappropriate to apply the label "visual adaptation" to a change that is manifested in the absence of vision.

"Intermodal relationships." Some of my colleagues have chided me for saying that the adaptive changes take place *within* the position sense. Why not be more cautious, they've asked, and say that adaptation is simply a changed *relationship* between vision and proprioception, or between vision and motor responses, instead of a change within one modality? My answer is that by talking only about altered relationships I would be ignoring all the evidence we now have that the major changes take place *within* the nonvisual sense that registers positions and movements. Subjects' misperceptions of the locations of their arms, legs, head, and eyes can be demonstrated even with their eyes closed; thus it would be strange to ascribe these misperceptions to an altered relationship between vision and proprioception. The changes can be measured with appropriate nonvisual targets (auditory, proprioceptive, or remembered) as well as with visual ones. Indeed, there are changes in the structure of

proprioceptive space—in the perceived relation between one body part and others—with no sign of any comparable changes in the structure of visual space.

Preconditions vs. end-products. It is important to point out that this discussion concerns only the *outcome* of adaptation (the nature of the end-product), not what *causes* it (what its necessary and sufficient preconditions are). There is still no consensus on the influence of many variables on each of the various forms of alteration in position sense; active vs. passive movement vs. intermodal disagreement; sight of body parts vs. visual flow patterns; conscious beliefs vs. error information vs. information about veridicality; visual input vs. imagery vs. hypnotic anesthesia; attention vs. sensory dominance (see summaries by Welch, 1978; and see Rock, 1966; Wallach, 1968; Canon, 1971; Wallace & Garrett, 1973; Finke, 1979). Nevertheless, we have come a long way in understanding *what* changes, even if we don't always know how to predict whether and when those changes will occur.

Other Effects Produced by Wearing Prisms

Prism goggles produce various optical and behavioral effects (see Held, 1980) and correspondingly a number of different, but often simultaneous, reactions by subjects. Adaptation at the various sites I have been discussing—arm, head, or eyes—produces diverse sets of behavioral changes, but all can be understood as changes in position sense. However, there are other observations in experiments with prism goggles that do not fit this description. For example, straight lines are slightly curved or tilted by prisms; exposure to such stimuli may produce figural aftereffects (Gibson, 1933; Köhler & Wallach, 1944; Morant & J. R. Harris, 1965), which appear to be genuine (though limited) visual modifications.

Another possible component in the adaptation procedure is motor learning, as the subject becomes practiced in making the movements demanded by the experimental task (Freedman, Hall, & Rekosh, 1965; Harris, 1965, p. 437; Taub, 1968; Kornheiser, 1976). Although such motor learning may add to the measured changes in performance, it is not likely to contribute very much without a corresponding change in position sense, because then subjects would feel that their movements were in error (Harris, 1963a; Kornheiser, 1976).

The straight-ahead shift. One particularly deceptive change that appears to be prevalent in prism-adaptation experiments is a nonperceptual, cognitive change that I have called the "straight-ahead shift" (Harris, 1974). The straight-ahead shift is a change in which spatial direction is treated as "straight-ahead" by an observer. No prisms are needed in order to produce a straight-ahead shift. Consider a "thought experiment" in which you are facing down a long corridor, but turned 5° or 10° to the left of the corridor's main axis. Asked to point straight ahead, you might take your body's median plane as defining straight ahead, and therefore point to the left of the center of the corridor; or you might adopt an environmental standard, pointing straight down the corridor's main axis.

The actual data from such an experiment revealed a compromise between these extremes for most subjects (Harris & Gilchrist, 1976). Instead of a long corridor, we restricted the subjects' visual environment to the interior of a corrugated cardboard box (Fig. 24). We then compared their performance on three tasks while the box was aligned with the median plane vs. while it was rotated 10° to the right or left. When subjects used a lever system to position a visual target within the box to appear straight ahead, they positioned it an average of 3° in the direction of the box's rotation. Similarly, when asked to reach below the box and point straight ahead, they deviated by about 3° in the direction of the box's rotation. The third task, however, was not significantly influenced by rotation of the box: When the subjects reached under the box to

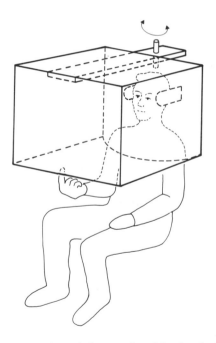

FIG. 24. Apparatus used to induce a "straight-ahead shift" without prisms. The corrugated cardboard box could be positioned either with its back wall perpendicular to the subject's median plane (as shown here) or rotated 10° to the right or left. In contrast to the experiments with prism goggles, the subjects did not see any part of their bodies at any time during the experiment. (From Harris & Gilchrist, 1976.)

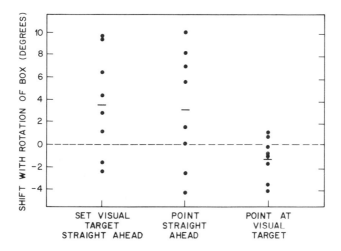

FIG. 25. Effects of the "straight-ahead shift" on three tasks. The plotted points represent 8 subjects' differences between performance while looking at a wall perpendicular to the line of sight (Fig. 11) and rotated 10°; dashes indicate means. A positive shift means pointing (or positioning the target) farther right with exposure to rightward visual displacement, or farther left with leftward displacement (the opposite of Fig. 6). Subjects' impressions of which direction was straight ahead shifted in the direction of rotation, thereby affecting their pointing straight ahead and their positioning of a visual target to look straight ahead, but not how they pointed at the visual target. (From Harris & Gilchrist, 1976.)

point at the visual target within it, they were about as accurate with the box rotated as with it straight (Fig. 25). Thus, in this and other related experiments, the only kind of visual task that was affected was the one that involves judgments of straight ahead. A reasonable inference is that the subjects' visual and proprioceptive perception were unchanged—all that was changed was their subjective median plane.

The same experiment can be performed by having subjects face the wall of a room or experimental apparatus squarely, and then putting wedge prisms over their eyes. No movements of the head of body are permitted, so there are none of the usual prerequisites for prism adaptation, such as active movement, visual feedback from movements, or sight of a body part. But the optical effect of 10° prisms is pretty much the same as rotating the box 10°, and the asymmetrical visual scene has the same effect on judgments of the median plane. The result (C. S. Harris, J. R. Harris, & Karsch, 1966; Bauer & Vandeventer, 1967; Wilkinson, 1971) is a shift in pointing straight ahead that goes in the same direction as the prismatic displacement (in the *opposite* direction from the "adaptive" shifts shown in Fig. 6), and a shift in setting a visual target to appear straight ahead that also goes in the same direction as the prismatic displacement (like the "adaptive" shifts found for this task when there is head or eye adaptation).

The straight-ahead shift may be a pervasive and deceptive intruder into many adaptation experiments (see Harris, 1974, for numerous examples). As I have noted, "By altering performance on a number of often-used tests of perception, a straight-ahead shift can masquerade as a change in vision, audition, or position sense. It can affect judgments of the visual straight ahead, creating the illusion that there is a change in visual perception when there is none, or inflating estimates of the magnitude of change when there is one. It can influence subjects' behavior when they are asked to point straight ahead, giving the impression that there is a 'maladaptive' change in position sense when there is none, or that there's no change when there really is. A straight-ahead shift may be the culprit when one encounters failures to replicate, inequality of adaptation and aftereffects, negative intermanual transfer, absence of expected correlations and presence of peculiar ones, unduly rapid or evanescent adaptation, disagreement among related measures (converging operations), departures from additivity of components and their variances, nonmonotonic growth or decay curves, uninterpretable individual differences, and other suchlike perplexities" (Harris, 1974, p. 473-474).

ACKNOWLEDGMENTS

I thank Irvin Rock, Robert B. Welch, Naomi Weisstein, and especially Judith R. Harris and Francine S. Frome, for their thoughtful suggestions.

REFERENCES

Anstis, S. M.   What does visual perception tell us about visual coding?   In M. S. Gazzaniga & C. Blakemore (Eds.), *Handbook of psychobiology.* New York: Academic Press, 1975.

Bauer, J. A., Jr., & Vandeventer, M.   Changes in pointing straight ahead following displaced vision result from a process independent of that which produces adaptive shifts in eye-hand coordination.   Paper presented at Eastern Psychological Association, Boston, April 1967.

Blakemore, C., & Campbell, F. W.   On the existence of neurones in the human visual system selectively sensitive to the orientation and size of retinal images. *Journal of Physiology,* 1969, *203,* 237-260.

Blakemore, C., Nachmias, J., & Sutton, P.   The perceived spatial frequency shift: Evidence for frequency-selective neurones in the human brain. *Journal of Physiology,* 1970, *210,* 727-750.

Bossom, J., & Held, R.   Shifts in egocentric localization following prolonged displacement of the retinal image. *American Psychologist,* 1957, *12,* 454. (Abstract)

Canon, L. K. Directed attention and maladaptive "adaptation" to displacement of the visual field. *Journal of Experimental Psychology*, 1971, *88*, 403-408.

Cohen, M. M. Changes in auditory localization following prismatic exposure under continuous and terminal visual feedback. *Perceptual and Motor Skills*, 1974, *38*, 1202.

Craske, B. Adaptation to prisms: Change in internally registered eye-position. *British Journal of Psychology*, 1967, *58*, 329-335.

De Valois, R. L., Albrecht, D. G., & Thorell, L. G. Cortical cells—bar and edge-detectors, or spatial-frequency filters? In S. J. Cool & E. L. Smith (Eds.), *Frontiers in visual science*. New York: Springer-Verlag, 1978.

Dodwell, P. C. *Visual pattern recognition*. New York: Holt, Rinehart and Winston, 1970.

Ebenholtz, S. M. Additivity of aftereffects of maintained head and eye rotations: An alternative to recalibration. *Perception & Psychophysics*, 1976, *19*, 113-116.

Ellis, S. R. Orientation constancy of the McCollough effect. *Perception & Psychophysics*, 1976, *19*, 183-192.

Ellis, S. R. Orientation selectivity of the McCollough Effect: Analysis by equivalent contrast transformation. *Perception & Psychophysics*, 1977, *22*, 539-544.

Festinger, L., Burnham, C. A., Ono, H., & Bamber, D. Efference and the conscious experience of perception. *Journal of Experimental Psychology Monograph*, 1967, *74*, *(4, Whole No. 637)*.

Fidell, L. S. Orientation specificity in chromatic adaptation of human "edge-detectors." *Perception & Psychophysics*, 1970, *8*, 235-237.

Finke, R. A. The functional equivalence of mental images and errors of movement. *Cognitive Psychology*, 1979, *11*, 235-264.

Freedman, S. J., Hall, S. B., & Rekosh, J. H. Effects on hand-eye coordination of two different arm motions during adaptation to displaced vision. *Perceptual and Motor Skills*, 1965, *20*, 1054-1056.

Frome, F., Danielson, J. T., & Levinson, J. Z. Shifts in perception of size after adaptation to gratings. Paper presented at Association for Research in Vision and Ophthalmology, Sarasota, April 1974.

Frome, F., Harris, C. S., & Levinson, J. Z. Extremely long-lasting shifts in perception of size after adaptation to gratings. *Bulletin of the Psychonomic Society*, 1975, *6*, 433. (Abstract)

Frome, F., Levinson, J. Z., Danielson, J. T., & Clavadetscher, J. E. Shifts in perception of size after adaptation to gratings. *Science*, 1979, *206*, 1327-1329.

Gibson, A., & Harris, C. S. The McCollough effect: Color adaptation of edge-detectors or negative afterimages? Paper presented at Eastern Psychological Association, Washington, April 1968.

Gibson, E. J. *Principles of perceptual learning and development*, New York: Appleton-Century-Crofts, 1969.

Gibson, J. J. Adaptation, after-effect, and contrast in the perception of curved lines. *Journal of Experimental Psychology*, 1933, *16*, 1-31.

Gibson, J. J. *The senses considered as perceptual systems*. Boston: Houghton Mifflin, 1966.

Graham, N. Spatial-frequency channels in human vision: Detecting edges without edge detectors. In C. S. Harris (Ed.), *Visual coding and adaptability*. Hillsdale, New Jersey: Lawrence Erlbaum Associates, 1980.

Hamilton, C. R. Intermanual transfer of adaptation to prisms. *American Journal of Psychology*, 1964a, *77*, 457-462.

Hamilton, C. R. *Studies on adaptation to deflection of the visual field in split-brain monkeys and man*. Doctoral dissertation, California Institute of Technology, 1964b.

Hansel, C. E. M., & Mahmud, S. H. Comparable retention times for negative color afterimage and McCollough effect. *Vision Research*, 1978, *18*, 1601-1605.

146   Charles S. Harris

Hardt, M. E., Held, R., & Steinbach, M. J. Adaptation to displaced vision: A change in the central control of sensorimotor coordination. *Journal of Experimental Psychology,* 1971, *89,* 229-239.

Harris, C. S. Adaptation to displaced vision: Visual, motor, or proprioceptive change? *Science,* 1963a, *140,* 812-813.

Harris, C. S. *Adaptation to displaced vision: A proprioceptive change.* Doctoral dissertation, Harvard University, 1963b.

Harris, C. S. Perceptual adaptation to inverted, reversed, and displaced vision. *Psychological Review,* 1965, *72,* 419-444.

Harris, C. S. Coping with visual distortions. *Bell Laboratories Record,* 1968a, *46,* 297-304.

Harris, C. S. The McCollough color aftereffect: Edge-detectors, afterimages, or what? Talk given at Cornell University, September 1968b.

Harris, C. S. Retinal localization of orientation-specific color aftereffects. *Journal of the Optical Society of America,* 1969, *59,* 504. (Abstract)

Harris, C. S. Effect of viewing distance on a color aftereffect specific to spatial frequency. *Psychonomic Science,* 1970, *21,* 350. (Abstract)

Harris, C. S. Orientation-specific color aftereffects dependent on retinal spatial frequency, rather than on stripe width. *Journal of the Optical Society of America,* 1971a, *61,* 689. (Abstract)

Harris, C. S. Orientation-specific color adaptation: A consideration of four possible models. Paper presented at Canadian Psychological Association, St. John's, Newfoundland, June 1971b.

Harris, C. S. Color adaptation dependent on contours but not on orientation. Paper presented at Association for Research in Vision and Ophthalmology, Sarasota, April 1972.

Harris, C. S. Beware of the straight-ahead shift—a nonperceptual change in experiments on adaptation to displaced vision. *Perception,* 1974, *3,* 461-476.

Harris, C. S., & Barkow, B. Color/white grids produce weaker orientation-specific color aftereffects than do color/black grids. *Psychonomic Science,* 1969, *17,* 123. (Abstract)

Harris, C. S., & Gibson, A. R. Is orientation-specific color adaptation in human vision due to edge detectors, afterimages, or "dipoles"? *Science,* 1968a, *162,* 1506-1507.

Harris, C. S., & Gibson, A. R. A minimal model for McCollough's orientation-specific color aftereffect. Paper presented at Psychonomic Society, St. Louis, November 1968b.

Harris, C. S., & Gilchrist, A. Prism adaptation without prisms: A nonvisual change with implications about plasticity in the human visual system. Paper presented at Association for Research in Vision and Ophthalmology, Sarasota, April 1976.

Harris, C. S., & Harris, J. R. Rapid adaptation to right-left reversal of the visual field. Paper presented at Psychonomic Society, Chicago, October 1965.

Harris, C. S., Harris, J. R., & Karsch, C. W. Shifts in pointing "straight ahead" after adaptation to sideways-displacing prisms. Paper presented at Eastern Psychological Association, New York, April 1966.

Harris, C. S., & Krauskopf, J. Absence of color specificity in adaptation to colored gratings. *Bulletin of the Psychonomic Society,* 1973, *2,* 325. (Abstract)

Hay, J. C., & Pick, H. L., Jr. Visual and proprioceptive adaptation to optical displacement of the visual stimulus. *Journal of Experimental Psychology,* 1966, *71,* 150-158.

Hebb, D. O. *The organization of behavior.* New York: Wiley, 1949.

Hein, A. Postural after-effects and visual-motor adaptation to prisms. Paper presented at Eastern Psychological Association, New York, April 1960.

Hein, A. The development of visually guided behavior. In C. S. Harris (Ed.), *Visual coding and adaptability.* Hillsdale, New Jersey: Lawrence Erlbaum Associates, 1980.

Held, R. The rediscovery of adaptability in the visual system: Effects of intrinsic and extrinsic chromatic dispersion. In C. S. Harris (Ed.), *Visual coding and adaptability.* Hillsdale, New Jersey: Lawrence Erlbaum Associates, 1980.

Held, R., & Bossom, J. Neonatal deprivation and adult rearrangement: Complementary techniques for analyzing plastic sensory-motor coordinations. *Journal of Comparative and Physiological Psychology,* 1961, *54,* 33-37.

Helmholtz, H. von. *Handbuch der physiologischen Optik,* Vol. III. Leipzig: Leopold Voss, 1866.

Helmholtz, H. von. *Treatise on physiological optics. Vol. 3.* New York: Dover, 1962.

Hinde, R. A., & Stevenson-Hinde, J. (Eds.) *Constraints on learning: Limitations and predispositions.* New York: Academic Press, 1973.

Hochberg, J. Nativism and empiricism in perception. In L. Postman (Ed.), *Psychology in the making.* New York: Knopf, 1962.

Hochberg, J. Space and movement. In J. W. Kling & L. A. Riggs (Eds.), Woodworth & Schlosberg's *Experimental psychology. (3rd ed.)* New York: Holt, Rinehart and Winston, 1971.

Howard, I. P. Perceptual learning and adaptation. *British Medical Bulletin,* 1971, *27,* 248-252.

Hubel, D. H., & Wiesel, T. N. Receptive fields of single neurones in the cat's striate cortex. *Journal of Physiology,* 1959, *148,* 574-591.

Hubel, D. H., & Wiesel, T. N. Receptive fields of cells in striate cortex of very young, visually inexperienced kittens. *Journal of Neurophysiology,* 1963, *26,* 994-1002.

Hubel, D. H., & Wiesel, T. N. Receptive fields and functional architecture of monkey striate cortex. *Journal of Physiology,* 1968, *195,* 215-243.

Julesz, B. Spatial-frequency channels in one-, two-, and three-dimensional vision: Variations on an auditory theme by Bekesy. In C. S. Harris (Ed.), *Visual coding and adaptability.* Hillsdale, New Jersey: Lawrence Erlbaum Associates, 1980.

Kalfin, K., & Locke, S. Evaluation of long-term visual motion after-image following monocular stimulation. *Vision Research,* 1972, *12,* 359.

Kalil, R. E., & Freedman, S. J. Intermanual transfer of compensation for displaced vision. *Perceptual and Motor Skills,* 1966, *22,* 123-126.

Kaufman, L. *Sight and mind.* New York: Oxford University Press, 1974.

Kohler, I. Über Aufbau und Wandlungen der Wahrnehmungswelt, insbesondere über bedingte Empfindungen. *Österreich Akademie der Wissenschaft, philosophische-historische Klasse,* 1951, *227,* 1-118.

Kohler, I. Umgewöhnung im Wahrnehmungsbereich. *Die Pyramide,* 1953, *3,* 92-96, 109-113, 132-133.

Kohler, I. The formation and transformation of the perceptual world. Translated by H. Fiss. *Psychological Issues,* 1964, *3(4),* 1-173.

Köhler, W., & Wallach, H. Figural after-effects: An investigation of visual processes. *Proceedings of the American Philosophical Society,* 1944, *88,* 269-357.

Kolers, P. A. The recognition of geometrically transformed text. *Perception & Psychophysics,* 1968, *3,* 57-63.

Kornheiser, A. S. Adaptation to laterally displaced vision: A review. *Psychological Bulletin,* 1976, *83,* 783-816.

Krauskopf, J. Heterochromatic stabilized images: A classroom demonstration. *American Journal of Psychology,* 1967, *80,* 634-637.

Krech, D., & Crutchfield, R. S. *Elements of psychology.* New York: Knopf, 1958.

Kuffler, S. W. Discharge patterns and functional organization of mammalian retina. *Journal of Neurophysiology,* 1953, *16,* 37-68.

Lackner, J. R. The role of posture in adaptation to visual rearrangement. *Neuropsychologia,* 1973, *11,* 33-44.

Lotto, D., Kern, A., & Morant, R. B. Prism induced tilt after-effects and changed felt head position. Paper presented at Eastern Psychological Association, Boston, April 1967.

MacKay, V. *Associative responses to colour and pattern in the human visual system.* Doctoral dissertation, University of Keele, 1978.

Masland, R. H. Visual motion perception: Experimental modification. *Science,* 1969, *165,* 819-821.

Mayhew, J. E. W., & Anstis, S. M. Movement aftereffects contingent on color, intensity, and pattern. *Perception & Psychophysics,* 1972, *12,* 77-85.

McCollough, C. Color adaptation of edge-detectors in the human visual system. *Science,* 1965, *149,* 1115-1116.

McLaughlin, S. C., & Rifkin, K. I. Change in straight ahead during adaptation to prism. *Psychonomic Science,* 1965, *2,* 107-108.

McLaughlin, S. C., & Webster, R. G. Changes in straight-ahead eye position during adaptation to wedge prisms. *Perception & Psychophysics,* 1967, *2,* 37-44.

Merton, P. A. The accuracy of directing the eyes and the hand in the dark. *Journal of Physiology,* 1961, *156,* 555-577.

Mikaelian, H. H. Adaptation to rearranged eye-foot coordination. *Perception & Psychophysics,* 1970, *8,* 222-224.

Mitchell, D. E. The influence of early visual experience on visual perception. In C. S. Harris (Ed.), *Visual coding and adaptability.* Hillsdale, New Jersey: Lawrence Erlbaum Associates, 1980.

Mittelstaedt, H. The role of movement in the origin and maintenance of visual perception: Discussion. *Proceedings of the Seventeenth International Congress of Psychology.* Amsterdam: North-Holland, 1964. (Abstract)

Montalvo, F. S. A neural network model of the McCollough effect. *Biological Cybernetics,* 1976, *25,* 49-56.

Morant, R. B., & Harris, J. R. Two different after-effects of exposure to visual tilts. *American Journal of Psychology,* 1965, *78,* 218-226.

Polit, A., & Bizzi, E. Processes controlling arm movements in monkeys. *Science,* 1978, *201,* 1235-1237.

Riggs, L. A., White, K. D., & Eimas, P. D. Establishment and decay of orientation-contingent aftereffects of color. *Perception & Psychophysics,* 1974, *16,* 535-542.

Rock, I. *The nature of perceptual adaptation.* New York: Basic Books, 1966.

Rock, I., & Harris, C. S. Vision and touch. *Scientific American,* 1967, *216,* 96-104.

Rose, J. E., & Mountcastle, V. B. Touch and kinesthesis. In J. Field (Ed.), *Handbook of physiology. Section 1. Neurophysiology.* Vol. 1. Washington, D.C.: American Physiological Society, 1960.

Rosinski, R. R. *The development of visual perception.* Santa Monica: Goodyear, 1977.

Seligman, M. E. P., & Hager, J. L. *Biological boundaries of learning.* New York: Appleton-Century-Crofts, 1972.

Shebilske, W. L. Visuomotor coordination in visual direction and position constancies. In W. Epstein (Ed.), *Stability and constancy in visual perception: Mechanisms and processes.* New York: Wiley, 1977.

Skavenski, A. A. Inflow as a source of extraretinal eye position information. *Vision Research,* 1972, *12,* 221-229.

Skowbo, D., Timney, B. N., Gentry, T. A., & Morant, R. B. McCollough effects: Experimental findings and theoretical accounts. *Psychological Bulletin,* 1975, *82,* 497-510.

Sperry, R. W. Optic nerve regeneration with return of vision in anurans. *Journal of Neurophysiology,* 1944, *7,* 57-70.

Stratton, G. M. Some preliminary experiments on vision without inversion of the retinal image. *Psychological Review*, 1896, *3*, 611-617.

Stratton, G. M. Vision without inversion of the retinal image. *Psychological Review*, 1897, *4*, 341-360, 463-481.

Stromeyer, C. F. Further studies of the McCollough effect. *Perception & Psychophysics*, 1969, *6*, 105-110.

Stromeyer, C. F., III. Contour-contingent color aftereffects: Retinal area specificity. *American Journal of Psychology*, 1972, *85*, 227-235.

Stromeyer, C. F. Form-color aftereffects in human vision. In R. Held, H. Leibowitz, & H.-L. Teuber (Eds.), *Handbook of sensory physiology*, Vol. VIII. New York: Springer-Verlag, 1978.

Stromeyer, C. F., III, & Dawson, B. W. McCollough colour after effect. *Nature*, 1974, *249*, 777-778.

Taub, E. Prism compensation as a learning phenomenon: A phylogenetic perspective. In S. J. Freedman (Ed.), *The neuropsychology of spatially oriented behavior*, Homewood, Illinois: Dorsey Press, 1968.

Taylor, J. G. *The behavioral basis of perception*. New Haven: Yale University Press, 1962.

Teller, D. Y. Locus questions in visual science. In C. S. Harris (Ed.), *Visual coding and adaptability*. Hillsdale, New Jersey: Lawrence Erlbaum Associates, 1980.

Templeton, W. B., Howard, I. P., & Wilkinson, D. A. Additivity of components of prismatic adaptation. *Perception & Psychophysics*, 1974, *15*, 249-257.

Uhlarik, J. J., & Osgood, A. G. The role of some spatial parameters of gratings on the McCollough effect. *Perception & Psychophysics*, 1974, *15*, 524-528.

Viola, M. Color adaptation contingent upon the geometry of the inducing stimulus. Senior honors thesis, Smith College, 1966.

Wallace, B., & Garrett, J. B. Reduced felt arm sensation effects on visual adaptation. *Perception & Psychophysics*, 1973, *14*, 597-600.

Wallach, H. Informational discrepancy as a basis of perceptual adaptation. In S. J. Freedman (Ed.), *The neuropsychology of spatially oriented behavior*. Homewood, Illinois: Dorsey Press, 1968.

Welch, R. B. Adaptation to prism-displaced vision: The importance of target pointing. *Perception & Psychophysics*, 1969, *5*, 305-309.

Welch, R. B. *Perceptual modification: Adapting to altered sensory environments*. New York: Academic Press, 1978.

Wertheimer, M. Hebb and Senden on the role of learning in perception. *American Journal of Psychology*, 1951, *64*, 133-137.

Wilkinson, D. A. Visual-motor control loop: A linear system? *Journal of Experimental Psychology*, 1971, *89*, 250-257.

Wyatt, H. J. Singly and doubly contingent after-effects involving color, orientation and spatial frequency. *Vision Research*, 1974, *14*, 1185-1193.

Locus Questions
in Visual Science

Davida Y. Teller

University of Washington

If you're a scientist, you can study some aspect of nature for a long time, ask yourself the same question day after day, and keep working on experiments to pin down the answer. And then one morning in the shower, you ask yourself, "What does that question really mean?" You scrub your back some more, and you begin to wonder what it is you're trying to find out from the experiments you're doing. And then you may wish you had skipped your shower, because you realize that now you can't go back to the lab and just collect more data. You're going to have to spend some time thinking, and thinking is very hard work indeed.

That's what happened to Joseph Sturr and me one summer a couple of years ago. We were working on some studies of Westheimer's spatial sensitization effect. The data looked exciting, and everyone we told about it always said, "That's a great experiment! It'll really tell us a lot about vision."

What we wanted it to tell us was whether the sensitization effect is central or peripheral. But then one day, we found ourselves asking, "Is sensitization central or peripheral? What does *that* mean?" Now, that's the kind of question you don't usually ask yourself. It can interfere with your research productivity.

The Causal Chain vs. the Causal Locus

The problem is this: We know light gets into the eye of an organism and gets absorbed in the receptors. The receptors process and transmit the information, which makes the horizontal cells and bipolars do the same. That, in turn, makes the amacrines and retinal ganglion cells do their job. And so the information gets transmitted along the axons in the optic nerve and loops around and around in the brain. Eventually a response comes out of the organism, through the mouth or through the hand.

In other words, we know there's a *causal chain* between the light hitting the eye and the response. We know that all information that gets through to the output must be present, in some disguise or other, at every link of the chain. We know that if almost any link or loop in that chain didn't work, the response wouldn't happen (at least not in the same way). Each link is just as much a part of the causal chain as any other.

Nevertheless, people in visual research like to ask things like: "What is the site of light and dark adaptation?", or "Are contrast effects central or peripheral?", or "Is the frequency-response function optical or neural?", or "Where do Mach bands, or contrast-modulation thresholds, or visual illusions, or the Bezold-Brucke hue shift, or masking, or whatnot, occur?" And when we ask *locus* questions like those, we seem to be making a peculiar slip of the mind. It is as though we wanted to believe that some parts of the physiological system or its activity are more to blame for that particular visual effect than other parts are; or that the causes of the effect reside in some parts of the physiological chain more than in other parts. But how can you say that one link is responsible for the properties of the chain?

An easy out, of course, is to say that locus questions are just meaningless and ill-conceived questions, and kick them out of the science. But questions that are just kicked out have a way of slipping back into the discourse anyway, often in disguised form. And it may be better, rather than deciding a question is meaningless, to try very hard to track down and isolate the conceptual puzzle that caused the itch that made us ask the question in the first place.

What I want to do here is present some of the ideas I've come up with in my attempts to deal with the apparent peculiarity of "Where?" questions. I'd like to offer some thoughts about what we mean when we ask where a given visual phenomenon takes place, or when we ask what physiological mechanism explains or underlies some visual phenomenon.

In the first section of this paper, I will step back to get an overall picture of visual science. In the light of that picture, I will propose a seat-of-the-pants meaning that I think many of us have in the backs of our minds when we ask locus questions: the "Looking More Like the Response" criterion. I will remind you of the indispensible but tricky role of linking hypotheses. In the second section, I will introduce Westheimer's spatial sensitization effect as a specific context for examining the kinds of questions we ask and what we may be driving at. I will discuss the constraints that the sensitization effect places upon models of the visual system, and two logically-separable operations it implies. In the third section, I will describe the Center-Surround model, an informal model commonly used to account for sensitization by ascribing the effect to a certain kind of cell in the visual system. I will try to unearth some of the important assumptions that are needed to make this simple single-cell model work, including a set that I group together as the "Nothing Mucks It Up" proviso. Finally, I will ask how we would go about looking for a physiological locus for each of the operations implied by the sensitization effect. In the process, I will come up against some limitations of the "Looking More Like the Response" criterion.

CAUSE AND LOCUS QUESTIONS IN VISUAL SCIENCE

We visual scientists are trying to study a system that extends through three realms of discourse: stimuli, responses, and the intervening physiological system. It seems to me that that's where the problem of understanding locus questions really starts. The representation of these three realms of discourse at the top of Fig. 1 may give you some idea of the network we are trying to untangle.

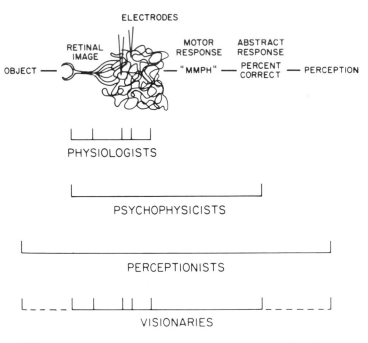

FIG. 1. Overview of visual science. The upper part of the figure shows the three realms of discourse—the visual input, the neural network, and the subject's responses—that make up the terrain of visual science. Different schools of visual scientists tend to concern themselves with different parts of the terrain, as shown in the lower part of the figure.

Three Realms of Discourse

At the input end of the science, we're lucky, because at the beginning, God apparently said, "Let there be light," and there is light. That is, there's something whose properties some people, at least, claim to understand quite precisely. It makes me feel good to know that there's something so solid at the input end (especially if I avoid thinking about whether it's waves or quanta, and about how a single quantum can interfere with itself).

At the output end of our science is the second realm of discourse, the behavior of an organism. Under normal circumstances, behavior is a hard thing to study because it's so complicated. In visual research we reduce the problem somewhat, by making the subject sit still and bite a bite bar. And often we only let him give out one of two responses at a time, such as "Yes" or "No"; or rather, since he's biting the bite bar, "MMph" or "MM-MMph".

Even then the behavior end of the science isn't very simple, because actually we don't care at all about the specific responses the subject makes. We don't care what language he uses, or what muscles he twitches. If we're defining a threshold carefully, for example, we want to know what percent correct responses he gives for each of a series of intensities of a test flash. But we don't care how he does it; we don't care whether he's correct by speaking, pressing a button, wiggling his ears, or whatever. We're interested in an abstract property, percent correct, that we believe many responses would have in common if we control the stimulus situation carefully enough.

In between the stimulus and the response is the third realm of discourse: an enormous mess of neurons, bossing each other around by means of neural spikes, slow potentials, and so forth.

Visionaries and Other Kinds of Scientists

Different kinds of scientists look at this complicated situation in different ways. The *visual physiologists* usually listen in on the physiology, and try to understand how the activities of cells are related to the stimulus and to each other. That is, they deal with the front end of the system, and this may be why they often seem to be closer to God than the rest of us are. *Visual psychophysicists* typically look at the stimulus and the response, and try to find regularities relating the input and the output of the system. People in *visual perception* are usually interested in relations between more global aspects of the stimulus and more global aspects of the response; in my diagram, their interests are more far-out than the psychophysicists', at both ends.

The bottom line represents the group of scientists who sometimes call themselves *visionaries*, of which I count myself one. Visionaries are distinguished by a peculiar fascination (some would say obsession) with the whole system.

We want to find out anything we can about how the physiology brings about the behavior, how the system manages to transform some particular stimulus condition into some particular response or response pattern. We seem to be happy only when' we are dealing with all three realms of discourse at once. This broad interest moves us to a new plane of complexity, sometimes even including near escapes from the mind-body problem; so perhaps it's no wonder that we end up feeling the need to call ourselves visionaries.

The "Looking More Like the Response" Criterion

What, then, do visionaries mean when they ask, "Is brightness contrast central or peripheral?" or when they say, "The Stiles-Crawford effect is located in the receptors"? When faced with a conceptual question like this, a standard technique is to examine several cases in which we use the concept with some confidence, and try to ferret out the rules that guide our usage. So let me start with a working proposal, a general meaning I think many of us may have in mind, and then illustrate this interpretation with several examples.

When we ask, "What is the locus of the such-and-such effect?" I think we may mean something like, "At what level of the visual system do the signals caused by the stimulus first start *looking more like* the *response* than they do like the *stimulus*?"; or, "At what level of the physiological system do the signals become *more similar* to the response than they are to the stimulus?"; or maybe even, "At what level of the visual system do the signals look the *most* like the response?" (Remember that "response" here means the abstract property that we would draw on a graph, such as percent correct, rather than the motor specifics of the subject's "MMph"'s.)

Let me give some examples, and try to explain more about what I mean. Here I find that Brindley's distinction between Class A and Class B experiments is very useful. As an example in Class A, take the case of color mixture. By picking the proper mixture, we can concoct two patches of light that are physically quite different, but behaviorally indistinguishable. An appropriate mixture of "red" light plus "green" light looks exactly like a "yellow" light, and no matter how hard you try, you can never learn to respond differently to the two. We say that this is *because* the two light patches lead to statistically identical states of the nervous system, probably right at the receptor level.

In Class A (or information-loss) experiments, like color matching, two physical stimuli are different; the responses to the two are the same. Information about the difference between the stimuli is lost. In this case, we all seem to agree to localize the effect at the place where the physiological signals stop being like the stimuli—that is, different from each other—and start being like the two responses—the same.

156   Davida Y. Teller

Linking Hypotheses

The case is much harder when we are asking about the locus of a really subjective, or Class B, effect. For instance, consider Mach bands. You see illusory bright or dark bands when you look at certain patterns—intensity ramps—that don't contain any corresponding high- or low-intensity bands. A common explanation is this: Suppose we could put a Mach-band-producing pattern on the retina, and look at the firing rates of many neurons (say, retinal ganglion cells) at some rather peripheral level of the visual system. We might well find that neurons in the topological position where we see the bright band are firing faster than their neighbors, and neurons in the topological position where we see the dark band are firing slower than their neighbors, so that a sketch of firing rates across a row of cells would *look like* a sketch of the brightness perceived across the Mach band-producing pattern of light. Many people would probably be willing to say that Mach bands are caused at the first neural layer where the firing rates across the layer have relative maxima and minima in the right locations. Others might instead single out the layer in which the maxima and minima are the most pronounced.

But as Brindley pointed out, to say you've found the locus of Mach bands in either of these two places, you must be making an analogy, formulating a *linking hypothesis*, between two different realms of discourse. You must be making a guess about how subjective brightness (measured by the subject's responses) is represented in the physiological system. In the case of Mach bands, the most common linking hypothesis (often implicit) is that the relative firing rates of neurons across a neural layer cause the perception of relative brightnesses across a visual field. The higher the firing rate, the linking hypothesis says, the higher the perceived brightness.

Yet it's clear that reasonable people could disagree about the plausibility or adequacy of a particular linking hypothesis. And as Brindley pointed out, if we search for the locus of Mach bands and fail to find what we expected where we expected it, we don't know whether we're failing because the Mach bands aren't located where we're looking, or because we're using the wrong analogy or linking hypothesis, and looking at the wrong aspect of the physiological signals.

As a general rule, visionaries use crucial linking hypotheses all the time, usually in casual, implicit (and often unacknowledged) ways. On the other hand, the explicit formulation of linking hypotheses is a risky business, and I suspect that one reason that linking hypotheses are so often implicit is that when we make them explicit they usually sound oversimplified, premature, and downright silly. Also, over the course of a decade or two, as knowledge and models change, particular linking hypotheses can go in and out of fashion. Even within a decade, a linking hypothesis that appeals to one person can seem silly to another; one person's pet linking hypothesis can be another person's laughingstock.

As an historical example: Many early visionaries used to believe that, since we are able to see the two-dimensional visual world, there should be a two-dimensional point-for-point representation of the visual world on the visual cortex; and others believed that since we see contours and objects there should be extracellular current flows of certain kinds in the brain. As a modern example: Do you really believe that the firing of cortical "line detectors" causes the perception of lines; or that the relative firing rates of neurons across a neural layer cause the perception of relative brightness across the visual field; or both?

To summarize: So far I've suggested that when we ask, "What is the locus of a particular psychophysical effect?" we probably mean something like, "When does the signal caused by the stimulus first stop looking like the stimulus and start looking like the response?" Although this may capture the essence of what we mean, it by no means makes the question completely straightforward. In particular, we're still stuck with defining "looking like." "Looking like" differs for different attributes of our perceptions. We always have to define "looking like" by means of a linking hypothesis. Linking hypotheses are a sticky wicket, especially in the case of Class B phenomena, but I don't know any way for visionaries to avoid them and still ask locus questions. We'll see more examples of various linking hypotheses later, in relation to the sensitization effect.

THE SPATIAL SENSITIZATION EFFECT

Let's turn now to the spatial sensitization effect, also known as the Westheimer effect. I'm devoting a lot of space to it because I've devoted a lot of thought and research to it, and it *was* the topic that triggered my puzzlement over locus questions and spoiled my shower. But I'm not really concerned here with the details of the sensitization effect itself. I'm just going to be using it as a vehicle for exploring what locus questions mean.

The Basic Experiment

To do a sensitization experiment, you present a very small, brief test flash at the center of a background disk of light (Fig. 2). Then you vary the diameter of the disk, and find out what intensity of the test spot is needed to make the test spot just barely visible on disks of different sizes.

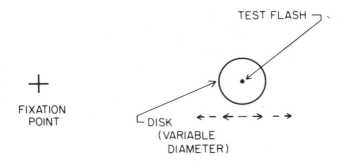

FIG. 2. The stimulus configuration used in generating the sensitization (Westheimer) effect. The subject's task is to detect a small test flash presented at the center of a background disk, for various diameters of the background disk.

Figure 3 shows the kind of results you get once you've learned how to do the experiment right. The threshold intensity for the test spot rises with increasing background-disk diameter, reaches a maximum at some intermediate background-disk diameter (say, 45 minutes of arc), and then falls again. The threshold may drop as much as a factor of 10 as the disk diameter increases to, say, 2°. This drop is what we call "sensitization." As the disk diameter increases, up to 45 minutes, the observer becomes less and less sensi-

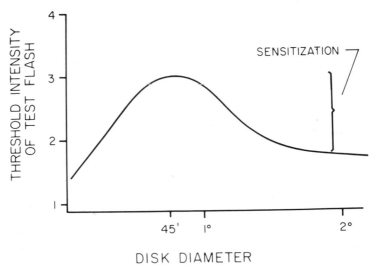

DISK DIAMETER

FIG. 3. Schematic results in a sensitization experiment. The threshold intensity for the test flash rises with increasing disk diameters, reaches a maximum, and then falls again. The fall in the threshold (increase in sensitivity) over the range of larger disk diameters is called the sensitization effect.

tive to the test spot; but beyond that diameter, increasing the disk size makes the observer more and more sensitive—the extra light "sensitizes" the observer.

There are a number of ways to describe the sensitization effect, all of them nearly equivalent, yet each offering a slightly different slant. First, we can capture the essence of the effect by simply saying that the threshold for a small test flash is higher on a disk of light that's 45 minutes wide than on one that's 2° wide. Putting it in a somewhat broader context, we can say that a small test flash is always harder to see when there's a disk of light present as background than when there's none, but an intermediate size disk makes the test flash *much* harder to see, whereas a larger disk makes it only moderately harder to see.

Another useful way to conceptualize the effect, tying the concept of threshold down to the concept of detection, is this: We can choose a fairly dim intensity for the test flash, somewhere between the threshold intensities needed on the 45 minute and 2° disks, and then find that the flash is detected almost every time on a 2° disk and almost never on a 45 minute disk. (This procedure also makes a persuasive demonstration.)

Why are we focusing our attention on just the downhill part of the curve, from 45 minutes to 2°, and giving it a special name? One reason is suggested by drawing a comparison with a more traditional kind of threshold experiment. If we start with a disk of light and then increase its intensity while keeping its size the same, we find that over a large range of intensities, the threshold for a small test flash increases monotonically with the intensity of the disk. Increasing disk intensity makes the observer steadily less and less sensitive to the test flash. In a sensitization experiment, we put extraneous light into the eye in a different way, increasing the disk's size instead of its intensity. At first, we observe the same thing as when we increase intensity: the more light, the higher the threshold. But beyond 45 minutes in diameter, we start to get the opposite: More light lowers the threshold. It is this departure from the familiar precedent that attracts our attention.

System Properties

Why do we do psychophysical experiments like this? One answer is that we simply want to know how particular changes in the stimulus change the responses of the observer—we want to define the *system properties* of the organism. But a deeper answer is that we wish to use these system properties to place constraints on possible models of how the underlying physiology must work. That is, the results of a psychophysical experiment give us some facts about information flow within the organism. These facts act to rule out an infinity of potential models of the organism's physiology, and allow another infinity to remain as potentially applicable. (Of course, we're usually not smart enough to be able to specify what the two infinities are. The best we usually do is to specify one model or maybe two, and hope the infinity that we rule out doesn't include the model we hold closest to our hearts.)

So now the question is: What system properties must be embodied in any model with pretensions toward predicting (or rather, postdicting) sensitization? We've just said that a flash that's visible on a large background disk may be invisible on an intermediate-size disk. So we can say that, under these conditions, the visual system performs a *disk-size-dependent test-flash-detection* operation.

If we dissect this hyphenated monster somewhat, we can say that the existence of the sensitization effect implies two conceptually separable system properties, as schematized in Fig. 4. First, there is some neural representation of the size or spatial pattern of the background disk. If the threshold varies with the size of the background disk, something about the overall state of the nervous system must vary with the size of the disk; information about the size or spatial pattern of the background disk must be preserved within at least the early part of the system. Second, there is a neural detection or threshold operation, whose inputs and properties either allow or fail to allow detection of the test flash on any given trial. In addition, the detection operation must have an input from, or be modulated by, the disk-information-preserving operation. We could make a block diagram of these two operations and their order and interaction, something like Fig. 4. In fact, flirting with the nominal fallacy, we could make simpler labels for the boxes, calling the disk-information box a "size coder" or "pattern analyzer," and calling the test-flash-detection box a "detector," as shown in Fig. 5.

We have to watch out for labels and block diagrams, though. They can lure us into assuming that simple-sounding operations must be performed in a simple way or at a single locus. We might do better to throw away our blocks and draw a sloppier diagram, like Fig. 6, to remind ourselves that systems can do

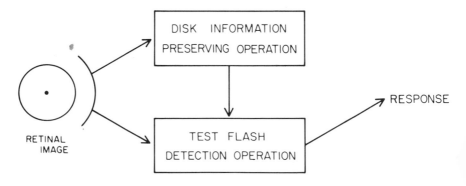

FIG. 4. The two operations implied by the sensitization effect.

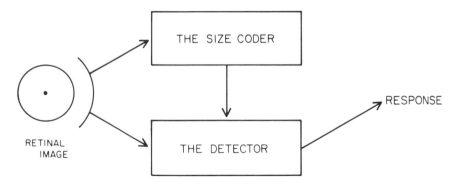

FIG. 5. Simplified version of Fig. 4, drawn by a psychophysicist with mental blocks.

simply-definable operations in complex and roundabout ways. (To further drive home this point, I had planned to display an infinite number of figures, all more or less like Fig. 6. But luckily for the draftsperson, common sense prevailed.)

The Faith of a Visionary

Does the basic sensitization effect place any more constraints on physiological models than the ones mentioned so far? Unfortunately, no. Although good psychophysical data reveal system properties, such data seldom tell us how or where the nervous system performs particular operations. We don't know whether to expect any individual operation to be performed in a simple way or at a single locus, or early or late in the system. We don't know whether to expect either operation to be carried out by single cells, or by the pattern of activity across layers of cells, or in some other way. We don't even know whether to expect logically separable operations to be readily separable physiologically: A single cell or layer may be carrying out both operations, intertwining them so thoroughly that it may become silly to ask which part of the physiology is doing which operation or which comes before which. Indeed, even if we can agree on a meaning for the question "What is the locus of the operations implied by a given psychophysical or perceptual effect?", the answer could in the end still be, "There isn't any locus; the operations are performed diffusely, with no one locus any more salient than any other."

And here the incipient visionary comes to a choice point. The visionary wants to know how the subparts of the underlying physiological and anatomical system combine to produce the system properties defined by behavioral experiments. Yet the visionary must also face the fact that, maybe, neatly definable and separable operations, deduced from psychophysical effects, won't correspond to neatly definable and separable physiological events or anatomical

162   Davida Y. Teller

FIG. 6. Ugly and realistic version of Fig. 4, drawn to accommodate known neurophysiological complexities.

loci. If the correspondences you seek need not even exist, then why search? The only possible response to this uncertainty is an affirmation of faith. If you're going to be a visionary, you have to have faith that the neural causes of visually guided behaviors are somehow simple enough to be conceptualized, and recognized if they are found.

THE CENTER-SURROUND MODEL

After pushing logical analysis about as far as it can go in revealing system constraints, and convincing ourselves that simple correspondences between behavior and substrate are worth seeking, what do we do? Some of us try to find more system constraints by doing more psychophysics. That's what the psychophysical literature on sensitization is about. Some of us try to dream up at least one or two conjectures (sometimes called "models") about how the physiological system, as currently conceived, could produce the psychophysical effect. And some of us, guided by such conjectures or models, start poking about with electrodes in the visual system, to try to find out how or whether individual cells in the system carry out these operations. The models that guide us may not be very explicit, but they're there; and without them we wouldn't know how to start looking.

To a visionary there's a very obvious model or analogy that comes to mind as soon as we look at a sensitization curve. I'll call it the *Center-Surround model.* It comes to mind because when modern visual physiologists explore the properties of cells in the visual system, they find that there are many cells that are affected in opposite ways by light, depending on where the light hits the retina.

An idealized mapping of the responses of such a cell is shown in the diagram

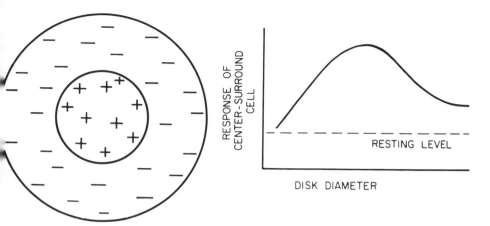

FIG. 7. Left: Plot of the receptive field of a center-surround cell. Right: Response of a center-surround cell to disks of light of various diameters, centered on the cell's receptive field, drawn to the same size scale as the receptive field at the left. The cell is maximally activated by middle-sized disks of light, which just fill the center of the receptive field.

on the left in Fig. 7. This diagram means that there is a cell whose activation level increases when light falls on a certain part of the retina, the *center* of the receptive field (marked by +'s), and decreases when light falls nearby, in the *surround* (marked by −'s). (More generally, light falling within the center of a concentric receptive field causes the state of the cell to deviate one way or the other from its resting level, while additional light falling in the surround will oppose the influence of light in the center, and return the cell toward its resting level. For the following discussion, it doesn't really matter whether the cell produces neural spikes or slow potentials, nor which way the light-induced deviations go.)

We can now imagine how this cell might respond to disks of light of various diameters, centered on the receptive field. As the disk grows in size, the cell deviates more and more from its resting level. The deviation reaches a maximum with a disk that just fills the center of the receptive field. Then, as the disk of light invades the inhibitory surround of the receptive field, the cell returns toward its resting level.

If we plot the level of activation for each disk diameter, we get something like the U-shaped *area-response curve* shown in the diagram on the right in Fig. 7. You don't have to be a visionary to notice that if you squint a little and maybe rescale and relabel some axes, Fig. 7 *looks like* the psychophysical sensitization curve in Fig. 3. Both curves are U-shaped, both horizontal axes represent the diameter of a disk of light, and in both cases the vertical axis represents something having to do with the response of a cell or a person to light.

So concentric, spatially-opponent receptive fields provide a general class of physiological models with immediate intuitive appeal for explaining psychophysical sensitization. If such models stand up under further scrutiny, we may well have a context in which to ask our locus questions. Maybe we will be able to say that sensitization could be caused by, or located in, some class of cells with center-surround receptive fields, at some particular level of the visual system.

Two Assumptions

But now let's censor our intuition. In order to explain the sensitization effect with such a model, one must be making at least two simple but crucial hidden assumptions, which respectively link the cell's activation level to the cell's threshold, and the cell's threshold to the person's threshold.

The first assumption links the two U-shaped curves by linking their vertical axes, relating the cell's threshold for a small test flash to the cell's response to the background disk. The assumption must be that the cell's threshold for a small test flash is higher, the greater the cell's deviation from its resting state. Or, to put it another way, the greater the deviation of the cell from its resting state, the more light is needed in the test flash to get the test-flash information through the cell. This assumption has a testable ring to it, and it's always a plus for a model if the assumptions behind it are themselves potentially testable.

The second assumption links the cell's threshold for the test flash to the whole organism's response to the test flash. This assumption says that the responsiveness of this cell is reflected more or less directly in the psychophysically measured threshold. This is, when you think about it, a rather remarkable assumption. In my less poetic moments, I like to call it the *"Nothing Mucks It Up"* proviso. It means that under the highly controlled conditions of the psychophysical experiment, nothing else in the system interferes with the control this cell exercises over the choice of a psychophysical response—the entire remainder of the subject's visual system and brain have no effect at all other than to convert a single cell's activity into "MMph" or "MM-MMph".

For example, this assumption implies that no other cell or channel has a lower threshold for the test flash, over the whole range of disk diameters used in the experiment. So before we go further, we'd better look at some other cells and think some more about whether we can live with this assumption. So far we've been thinking about only a single center-surround cell at a time. And it's been one specific single cell, at that: the cell on whose receptive field the test flash and disk are centered. But in fact, the light in our experiments is hitting the receptive fields of a lot of other cells at the same time. This realization might well make us suspicious that our intuition chose this particular cell for a reason we haven't yet figured out; or maybe even that, if we didn't choose the centered cell and studiously ignore the rest, the model wouldn't work.

Neural Images

So let's try thinking a bit about "neural images"; that is, about the pattern of activity in a set of similar cells when disks of light are present. To give us something specific to look at, let's say that there is a row of cells with overlapping receptive fields, with excitatory centers 45 minutes in diameter and with concentric inhibitory surrounds that extend out to 2°. Let's draw a diagram of the responses of this row of cells in the presence of, first, a 2° disk of light.

In Fig. 8 you see a row of schematic retinal ganglion cells with overlapping receptive fields. A 2° disk of light is falling on a particular place on the retina. Cell A's receptive field is too far to the left to get any input from the disk of light, so Cell A remains at its resting level, as indicated by the circle plotted below A. The disk of light covers part of Cell B's receptive field, about half of

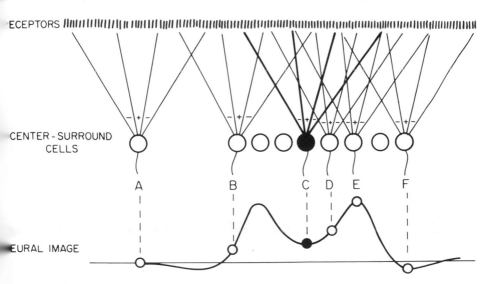

FIG. 8. Responses of a row of six center-surround cells (A, B, C, D, E, and F) to a 2° disk of light centered on the receptive field of cell C. The response of each cell depends on the position of the disk of light with respect to the cell's receptive field. The plot of the responses of the row of cells, shown at the bottom, can be called a *neural image* of the disk.

the center and half of the surround. Since light has opposite effects in center and surround, Cell B also remains near its resting level. For Cell C the disk of light is centered on its receptive field, covering all of the center and surround. Again center and surround tend to cancel, so cell C also stays near its resting level. For cell D, the disk of light is slightly eccentric. It covers all of the center but misses a little of the surround, so cell D is a little more excited than is cell C. For Cell E the disk of light covers all of the center and only part of the inhibitory surround, so cell E is way above its resting level. And for Cell F light falls in part of the surround and no light hits the center, so Cell F is below its resting level. Everything is symmetrical about the center of the disk, so we can fill in symmetrical points on the two sides of Cell C.

What we've come up with in Fig. 8 is a neural image of the 2° disk: a plot of the activity level for each cell in the row of hypothetical ganglion cells, all with receptive fields of the same size, when a 2° disk of light is present. The obvious and crucial point is that the various cells in the row are in different states, because the response of each individual cell depends on the position of the disk as well as its size. (From considerations like these it is clear that, although the response of a ganglion cell varies with the size of a disk of light, any individual ganglion cell is a very poor coder of disk size information per se. A disk of light of a given size can produce very different responses in a single ganglion cell, depending on the disk's position, intensity, wavelength, fine-grained texture, and so on. Any single cell confounds all of these parameters. Size information is preserved, through the early layers of the retina, by the pattern of activity across the neural image, and not by individual isolated cells. If we wanted to search for individual cells that could be candidates for the locus of size perception, we would want to look elsewhere.)

In the same way as in Fig. 8, we can plot the neural images caused by disks of different sizes. This is shown in Fig. 9. The neural image has a different

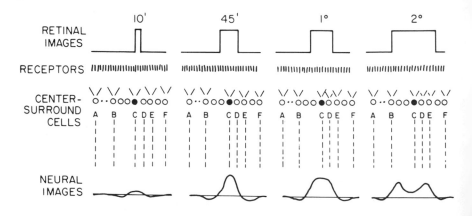

FIG. 9. Neural images for disks of various diameters.

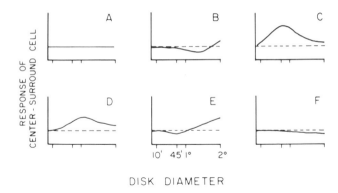

DISK DIAMETER

FIG. 10. Response of six center-surround cells (A, B, C, D, E, and F) to disks of light of various diameters. As in Fig. 7, cell C gives an elegantly U-shaped curve, with its peak at a 45-minute disk diameter. But the other cells do not. If center-surround cells like these are to provide a model for the sensitization effect, the system must ignore all the cells except cell C.

shape for each different size of the disk of light; and for each disk size, the neural image contains cells in lots of different states, depending on the relative positions of the disk and the cell's receptive field.

Now, suppose we take cells A, B, C, D, E, and F, and plot the variation in response of each one of these cells with variation in the size of the disk. This is shown in Fig. 10. For cell C, the cell on which the disks are centered, we get a familiar U-shaped curve, with a maximum response at 45 minutes disk diameter. But for the eccentrically placed cells, we get a variety of curves, none of which look much like the psychophysical sensitization curve.

In other words, the consideration of neural images has revealed that indeed, our intuition became infatuated with the centered cell, C, for a good reason. If the system pays attention to the centered cell, then the Center-Surround model works; if not, it doesn't. The other, noncentered cells don't provide any ready analogy to the sensitization effect.

Is Cell C the Most Sensitive Channel?

When we choose one cell and ignore the rest in model building we assume that the nervous system chooses that cell and ignores the rest in real information processing. To say that the centered cell does the detecting of the test flash is to say that the centered cell is the most sensitive channel in its layer of the system, under the conditions of the experiment, over the whole range of disk diameters used in sensitization experiments. This is to assert that no other parallel cell or channel has a lower threshold for the test flash, or contributes to the detection of the test flash.   And this assertion in fact implies that there are a lot of otherwise plausible events that are assumed not to happen. To drive this point home, I will develop three examples of things that the other, noncentered cells are implicitly being assumed not to do.

First, we must be asserting that at this level of the system, at threshold, only one cell (or a small group of cells) passes on the information from the test flash. Suppose we believed that, instead of passing just through the one (centered) cell, information about the test flash passes through many or all of the cells within whose receptive fields the test flash falls. We might then think that detection is based, one way or another, on pooling the responses of all of those cells. If we had to pay attention to what other cells besides the centered cell are doing, the Center-Surround model would lose much of its appealing simplicity. As Fig. 9 illustrated, cells at different positions across the row give very different responses to the same disk. Since there's no simple relation between the response of an individual cell and the size of the disk, there would be no obvious relation between the responses of all these cells and the threshold in the sensitization effect. The response of the cells wouldn't *look like* the response of the organism, and we'd want either to look at cells at a different physiological level, or to abandon the Center-Surround model altogether.

Second, when making the original Center-Surround model, and thinking only of the centered cell, C, we got stuck with assuming that the cell's threshold varies with the cell's deviation from its resting state. This assumption now comes back to haunt us in the context of the neural image. In the hypothetical ganglion cell layer in Fig. 9, all of the cells deviate from their resting levels less than Cell C does, and there are even a couple of cells *at* the resting level, Cell B and the one between E and F. Why don't we expect these cells to have the lowest threshold for the test flash? We must be assuming that somehow, even though these cells are nearer their resting level than is Cell C, they are less sensitive to the test flash. We could attribute this to the eccentric placement of either the disk or the test flash, or both. In other words, we must have built into our model some quantitative features, to the effect that either an asymmetrically placed disk desensitizes a cell a lot, or the sensitivity of a cell to the test flash decreases rapidly with displacement of the test flash from the exact center of the receptive field, or both. These are statements about the quantitative properties of receptive fields, and the point is that the Center-Surround model implicitly involves such assumed properties, to allow us to ignore cells like A, B, D, E, and F.

And third, this discussion has assumed that for a given position in a given neural layer of the visual system, all the receptive field centers are the same size, 45 minutes wide in our example. If they're not all the same size, it's possible that while we're busy looking at cells with receptive fields with 45 minute centers, the test flash may be slipping through by way of cells having receptive fields of some other size. We might have guessed, a priori, that 5 minute test spots would be detected by cells with 5 minute receptive-field centers. But what we're assuming, to make the Center-Surround model work, is that under the conditions of the experiment, there's no detector that's more sensitive to a 5 minute test spot than the detectors with 45 minute receptive-field centers. There may well be cells with very small receptive-field centers, but if so they just aren't as sensitive to small spots as our 45 minute friends. Indeed, some people have suggested that the sensitization effect reveals to us the spatial tuning of the particular detection channel that is most sensitive to extremely small spots of light.

And Nothing Mucks It Up

Now, all of the things I've just been saying are in essence a list of things that we assume *don't* happen. If a simple single-cell model like the Center-Surround model is to work, the information from the test flash can't sneak through the system in any way other than through the cell whose properties we choose to specify. And this cell must be the weakest link and impose its selective information-loss characteristics on the neural signals in a permanent way. To put forward the Center-Surround model is to claim that a particular cell is the *weakest link in the most sensitive channel* of the visual system, under the conditions of the experiment. So after describing a cell whose output looks like the subject's responses, we find ourselves adding, "...and nothing mucks it up." If we're going to claim that this cell is the locus of the sensitization effect, we have to say that the sensitivity of the whole system—the determination of the threshold—depends upon the information-transmission properties of this cell only; we can't let the information slip through in any other way.

This kind of problem is common when you ask questions about causality. If you think about it hard enough, you find yourself compiling a list (often a very instructive list) of complications that don't happen. Usually, though, it turns out that the list is large or infinite, and can't be specified completely. In the end, you just have to say, "This is what causes the effect, and nothing else interferes; nothing mucks it up." Why does the sun rise in the east? Because the earth turns west-to-east, and nothing mucks it up.

In summary, this detour through neural images makes me understand the Center-Surround model and its underlying assumptions more poignantly than I did before. It has generated some specific and interesting items for the list of things that one has to assume don't happen. If one is interested in the Center-Surround model, it would be worthwhile to test and make sure that some of these things in fact don't happen, at the physiological level.

SEARCHING FOR THE LOCUS OF SENSITIZATION

When I discussed the system constraints implied by the sensitization effect, I made the case that two logically separable operations might be involved: a disk-information-saving operation, and a test-flash-detection operation (for brevity, the disk and detection operations). I noted that, if you want to search for these operations in the physiological system, you have to cut down your task by adopting a set of working assumptions, or a model of some kind, implicit or explicit. I discussed a common class of models, called center-surround models, that start from the similarity between psychophysical sensitization curves, on the one hand, and cells with center-surround receptive fields on the other. Now, within the context of center-surround models, let's go back and consider what it would mean to search for the physiological locus of the *disk* and *detection* operations that might be involved in Westheimer's sensitization effect.

The Detection Operation

The detection operation should be the easier case. We're dealing with retention or loss of test-flash information, by the cell and by the organism; and the meaning of "looking like" seems fairly clear. For the sensitization effect, "What is the locus of detection?" means "Where is the earliest or most salient level of the physiological system, at which information about a small test flash is lost in the presence of a 45 minute field but retained in the presence of a 2° field?" If we've agreed to pay attention only to cells with center-surround receptive fields, on which the stimulus pattern is centered, it sounds as though all that's left to do is start poking electrodes into various likely places, and find out.

However, at the practical level, when you're sitting there with an electrode on a cell, things still aren't simple. How do you decide whether information about the test flash is passing through a cell? Various criteria, or linking hypotheses, are used by various researchers. And we might not all agree about which ones are legitimate. You have to remember that whatever you, the experimenter, do to get information out of a cell's responses—count, subtract, average, take ratios, draw envelopes, calculate standard errors, compute d', or whatnot—you have to claim that the rest of the animal's physiological system can do something similar. In a way, what you do to the cell's output to find a correspondence with the psychophysical response *is* a *model* of one thing the rest of the system does. And we might not all agree about what it's reasonable to assume the rest of the system can do.

This point can be exemplified by an interesting study by Ken Nakayama. First Nakayama mapped out the receptive fields of individual cells in the cat's lateral geniculate nucleus. Then he recorded the responses produced by centering different sized disks of light on the receptive field. One of these area-response curves is shown in the upper part of Fig. 11; as you'd expect, it's U-shaped. Next, he turned on disks of various sizes. While each disk was steadily presented, he flashed a small test spot, of a fixed intensity, at the center of the disk, and recorded the average number of extra neural impulses

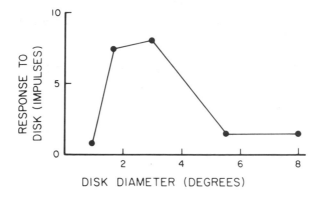

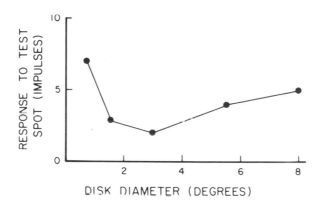

FIG. 11. Responses of a real cell in a cat's lateral geniculate nucleus. The upper curve shows the response of the cell to disks of various diameters centered on the cell's receptive field. The lower curve shows the response to a small test spot of a fixed intensity, when it was flashed at the centers of the background disks of various diameters. (Replotted from Nakayama, 1971.)

caused by flashing the test spot. This is shown in the lower part of Fig. 11 for the same cell that's represented in the upper part. You can see that the greater the response of the cell to a given size disk, the fewer extra impulses were produced by adding a small test flash to that size background.

Nakayama found several cells like the one represented in Fig. 11, where it was easy to see an obvious correspondence between the cell's deviation from resting level and its transmission of test-flash information (extra impulses triggered by the test flash). He found two other cells in which a correspondence could be uncovered only by applying subtle statistical analysis and a sophisticated criterion for information transmission. And there were several cells in

172 Davida Y. Teller

which, within the realm of linking hypotheses he considered, he did not find an appropriate variation in information transmission with changes in size of the background disk.

If you're willing to accept any of several fairly reasonable linking hypotheses, you would conclude from Nakayama's observations that *some* cells in the cat's lateral geniculate do have the properties that the Center-Surround model calls for. You can't be sure what proportion of cells work the right way. That depends on whether the later parts of the nervous system are applying more powerful analytic techniques than Nakayama did, or less powerful ones. That is, you'd have to know the capacity of the later parts of the system for detecting and transmitting test-flash information.

At any rate, I find it comforting to know that, even if we apply a very simple criterion for information transmission (number of extra impulses), there are some cells somewhere, in cats at least, with the right properties to provide the detection operation in the form called for by the Center-Surround model. And until I hear a better proposal, I think it would be reasonable to say that the locus of the detection operation in sensitization is the earliest level at which such cells are found in the human visual system or, alternatively, the level at which the behavior of such cells is most distinctive.

The Disk Operation

Now let's turn to the disk, or spatial pattern, operation. In this case, the problem of the cell's activity *looking like* the response is in some ways paradoxical. On the one hand, the invention of the Center-Surround model was triggered by the fact that the U-shaped area-response curve of a center-surround cell looks like the U-shaped sensitization curve, so it should be easy to define *looking like* for the disk operation.

On the other hand, I am troubled by the fact that the area-response curve of the cell describes the cell's response to the background disk, while the sensitization curve describes the organism's response to the test flash. That is, in a sensitization experiment, we ask the subject to tell us about the presence or absence of the test flash; we ask him absolutely nothing about the background disk. So naturally the subject's response contains no direct reference to the size of the disk. That means that there's probably no direct or universally appealing linking hypothesis that will let us all readily agree that the cell's respons (to the disk) has come to look like the subject's response (to the test flash).

In making the Center-Surround model, we have already encountered this problem in another form, when we noted that we had to link the vertical axes of two curves by an assumption. We bridged the gap between the cell's response to the disk and the subject's response to the test flash by assuming that the cell's response to the test flash covaried with its response to the disk — the greater the deviation of the cell from its resting state, the higher its threshold, we assumed; and Nakayama's experiment has shown us that in some cases this is actually so. So perhaps, in the case of the pattern operation, our criterion of *looking like* is just that the response of the cell to disks of increasing diameter should be U-shaped, like the sensitization curve. And in that case, to search for the locus of the disk operation, all we need do is search for the earliest or most salient level in the system at which neurons demonstrate center-surround receptive fields, and U-shaped area-response curves, with the right spatial dimensions.

As in the case of detection, we will have to decide what our criterion of response in the cell is, and what we mean in detail by the most salient level, especially since some cells respond by means of slow potentials and others by means of spikes. And as in the case of detection, the more robustly the cells demonstrate U-shaped area-response curves across variations in the exact definition of the response of the cell, the more satisfied we will be that we are approaching a meaningful answer.

The Locus of Sensitization

Now that we've discussed the meaning of the locus question for each of the two operations implied by the sensitization effect, we return to the question of the locus of the effect itself. If we should happen to locate both operations in the same cell, we're home free; with no further discussion, we would all locate the effect there too. But pronouncedly U-shaped area-response curves may well appear earlier in the system than do U-shaped test-spot-detection curves. If so, where will we locate the sensitization effect?

In the context of the Center-Surround model, we expect to find a cell in which both things happen, and we would locate the sensitization effect in that cell, even though we might locate the disk operation at an earlier level.

But what if we set the simplest center-surround model aside for the minute. Suppose that, in our poking about with electrodes, we found some center-surround cells with U-shaped area-response curves, but found that their sensitivity to a small additional test spot didn't follow their deviations from their resting thresholds. And suppose we found other cells, perhaps later in the system, which had U-shaped test-spot-detection curves, but whose area-response curves bore no resemblance to a U? In other words, suppose we found cells that looked like they performed our two operations, but no single cell that combined the two operations. (The latter might even be shown to have an input from or be modulated by the former.) In this case, where would we want to locate the sensitization effect?

More generally, any particular psychophysical effect may imply the existence of more than one operation, and these operations may be located at different levels of the system. In that case, wher (if anywhere) do we want to locate the effect itself? The answer here may be that, in each case, *one* of the operations implied will be more similar to, or provide a more direct analogy to, the psychophysical response than any of the other operations. I would speculate that we would call the locus of that characteristic operation the locus of the whole effect.

As an example, consider the question of the locus of dark adaptation. Various models include the concept of "dark light"—the operation that supplies the information that a bright light was on in the past—and suggest that in dark adaptation this memory operation is located in the receptors; but that the detection operation is located later in the system. Within the context of these models, I suspect a majority of visual scientists would agree that dark adaptation should be located at the locus of its detection operation, since the subject's task is defined to be detection of the test flash. Similarly, sensitization should be located at the locus of its detection operation, for the same reason.

But there are some alternatives here, too. It may be that we think of the detection operation as a general one, which is involved in many kinds of psychophysical experiments; or as a flexible one, whose locus may vary with the parameters of the test flash. And maybe we would want to locate psychophysical phenomena such as adaptation and sensitization at the locus of their most unique operation: at the locus of the memory operation in adaptation, and at the locus of the disk operation in sensitization.

Another alternative here is that, since suboperations aren't always clearly separated conceptually, the question of which locus is *the* locus hasn't come up very often. If that's so, there probably isn't any consensus on the meaning of this question.

The "Looking More Like" Criterion: Limitations

In the attempt to isolate a meaning for locus questions, I put forward a proposal: that many visual scientists achieve intellectual satisfaction by locating a psychophysical effect at the level, within the physiological chain of events, at which the neurally coded signals stop looking like the stimulus and start looking like the psychophysical response. But the locus question is a difficult one, and we have been running up against the complexities of its conceptualization at every turn. We immediately noted that "looking like" involves a linking hypothesis or analogy between a bit of behavior and the properties of a cell. We noted that we have to operate within the confines of an implicit or explicit model, and within all the explicit or implicit assumptions involved in the model, and we have to be willing to turn our backs on all the things the model assumes not to happen. We have to distinguish between the concept of the locus of each of the operations implied by the psychophysical effect, and the concept of the locus of the effect. And we have to admit that any particular operation, and any particular effect, may in fact be diffusely accomplished, and in the end may not be localizable to a single level or cell type.

Aside from all of these internal kinds of problems, I am sure there are limitations on the breadth of applicability of the "Looking More Like the Response" interpretation of the locus question. These will surely be discovered if people try to apply the criterion in various real contexts. For example, the work I did in straightening out my thoughts about size coding, and the disk operation, led me to think of another limitation: The criterion may not be useful in cases where the stimulus and the response themselves look a good deal alike. For instance, suppose we presented a subject with a set of disks of various sizes, all at the same distance, and asked him to judge their sizes. He would probably do fairly well, and his average size estimate might well increase linearly with object and retinal size. If so, we could ask how size information passes through each level of his system, but we couldn't ask where the transformation between *looking like the stimulus* and *looking like the response* occurred, because the stimulus and the response already look alike, and there would be no transformation to locate.

This impasse would not necessarily arise for all experiments concerning size. If the subject's judgments increased nonlinearly with retinal image size, we could ask where the neural information undergoes a similar nonlinear transformation. As an even clearer example, suppose we were perceptionists studying size constancy. When we placed our test pattern at different distances from the subject, we'd find that there was a clear difference between the retinal-image size and judgments of size. So it would make sense to ask where in the physiological system the size information becomes less closely related to retinal-image size and more closely related to perceived size, or to the subject's response.

Thus, for the "Looking More Like the Response" criterion to work, the stimulus and the response can't be too similar. I suspect that the stimulus and the response can't be too different from each other either. That's why this criterion wouldn't be useful in many other fields of physiological psychology. But I think that many of us visionaries work on problems in which the stimulus and the response are just different enough so that we can think about transforming the stimulus into the response, and be interested in locating the transformation within the physiology.

CONCLUSION

This paper has been an attempt to look at a progressing science, and to see what we mean by one kind of question we often pose. In fact, it is probably true that sometimes the meaning of the question is ambiguous, or at least very difficult to spell out; and also that different people have different implicit meanings in mind, even when they phrase their questions the same way. This state of affairs is not as bad as it sounds. You can't insist that working scientists limit their thought processes with any particular set of rules all the time, or work on definitions at the same time they're working on data. You have to let them keep on being creative, doing experiments that are exciting and insightful in one way or another, even if the premises that generated the insight and excitement are not always perfectly clear.

Nevertheless, I hope that some of the ideas I've discussed will prove useful when you're working at the definitional and conceptual level. It's important to recognize linking hypotheses, and see whether they're silly or sensible. (There are lots of silly ones around.) It's also illuminating to think about the "Nothing Mucks It Up" proviso whenever you're dealing with simple models of the visual system. It can be very instructive to start listing things that have to not happen in order for a simple, elegant theory to do the work one wants it to do. And it may be important to carry out tests to make sure that those things aren't happening.

While in the process of thinking through these questions, I've developed a funny nervous tic. I used to blithely ask, "What is the locus of such-and-such effect?" like any normal visionary. Now I still ask it, but I peek over my shoulder to make sure no one was listening. If anyone was, I can't help muttering "...whatever *that* means." I'd hate to think that this nervous habit is contagious, because it does make people look at you kind of funny. At the same time, I hope that now you'll share a bit of my feeling of uncertainty and guilt whenever you ask, "Is such-and-such central or peripheral?" or "What is the locus of such-and-such?" Just so long as it doesn't make you quit taking showers.

ACKNOWLEDGMENTS

This chapter is based on a paper that was first presented as an invited address at the Lake Ontario Visionary Establishment (LOVE) conference, Niagara Falls, Ontario, Canada, March 2-4, 1972. Many persons contributed knowingly or unknowingly to the emergence of this paper. Among them were Michael Scriven, who taught me the fundamentals of modern philosophy; Giles Brindley, who developed the concept of a linking hypothesis; Tom Cornsweet and my fellow students at Berkeley, who shared many lunchtime debates about the meanings of psychophysical data; Dick Rose, who helped formulate the concept of "looking like the response"; Naomi Weisstein, who insisted that I think through the problem of neural images; and my long-term intellectual playmate Gordon Bermant, who reminds me that pursuit of the philosophy of mind is like jogging: The exercise is good for you even if you always end up where you started.

REFERENCES

Brindley, G. *Physiology of the retina and visual pathways.* Baltimore: Williams and Wilkins, 1960.
Nakayama, K. Local adaptation in cat LGN cells: Evidence for a surround antagonism. *Vision Research,* 1971, 6, 501-510.
Sturr, J., & Teller, D. Sensitization by annular surrounds: Dichoptic properties. *Vision Research,* 1973, 13, 909-918.
Westheimer, G. Spatial interaction in the human retina during scotopic vision. *Journal of Physiology,* 1965, 181, 881-894.

Neural Images:
The Physiological Basis
of Spatial Vision

J. G. Robson

Physiological Laboratory, Cambridge University

One approach to the study of human spatial vision is through psychophysical experiments designed to explore the way in which we see spatial patterns. Another approach can be made through a study of the physiological mechanisms that underlie visual perception and it is this latter approach we shall adopt here. In particular, we shall look at some of the things that have been found out about the physiology of the visual system by studying the behavior of individual nerve cells at different stations along the main visual pathway from the retina through to the visual cortex.

Of course, there are problems in deciding what physiological knowledge is pertinent. For one thing, we really have very little idea how perception is related to the activity of nerve cells (see Teller, 1980), so we cannot know what aspects of neural activity are relevant to an understanding of the psychophysical findings. For another thing, we do not really know that the nature of visual perception is determined exclusively by the behavior of nerve cells in the retino-cortical pathway. There is another major division of the visual system, connecting the retina to the midbrain. This pathway may also play a role in certain sorts of perception. However, the integrity of the visual cortex is certainly essential for normal vision in humans, since damage to the visual cortex can cause virtually complete blindness in man (see Brindley, 1970). It should also be borne in mind that much of our knowledge of the behavior of individual nerve cells is based upon studies in sub-human species (e.g. the cat) whose visual systems are certainly organized rather differently from that of man.

Nevertheless, even though the interpretation in terms of human perception of what we find out about the behavior of nerve cells in animals must always be hedged around with caveats, it still seems worthwhile to ask how nerve cells in the visual system respond to the kinds of stimuli that are employed in human psychophysical experiments and to attempt to answer the question by direct examination. In particular, it is of interest to see how visual neurones respond to sinusoidal grating patterns of the kind that have become so popular with psychophysicists in the past few years. We can also usefully consider how neural responses to sinusoidal gratings are related to responses to the kinds of stimuli that have been more commonly employed by neurophysiologists, for instance, spots, bars, and edges.

THE STIMULUS PICTURE AND THE RETINAL IMAGE

Before describing how the neurones of the visual system respond to visual stimulation, we shall probably find it helpful to look at the very first steps in the visual process. The first steps are, of course, the formation of an optical image on the retina and the conversion of the light into signals that can be transmitted and processed by the nervous system.

There are two reasons for considering the formation of the retinal image when we are really interested in the later stages of signal processing in the visual system. First, it is the retinal image that is, so to speak, the real input to the neural mechanism; it is therefore important to know how the retinal image is related to the actual visual scene. Second, it has frequently proved tempting to think of the activity of the arrays of neurones at each level in the visual system as constituting a "neural image," analogous to the retinal image. Therefore, when we come to consider the neural transformations that result in the successive neural images, it will be helpful to know something of the available, well-defined methods for describing an optical image and the behavior of optical image-forming devices.

The Stimulus Picture

Although the retinal image is in real life usually formed as a projection of the three-dimensional external world, it is always possible to produce an equivalent retinal light distribution by providing an appropriate two-dimensional external picture. Since this is so, we can, without loss of generality but with considerable gain in simplicity, use pictures rather than objects as visual stimuli. Such pictures are often for experimental purposes produced either by projecting light at a reflecting screen or by projecting electrons at a fluorescent screen. This latter technique, the use of cathode ray tube displays, has made practicable many of the recent psychophysical and neurophysiological investigations of spatial vision that have used the contrast of the stimulus pattern as an important experimental variable.

Our stimulus, then, is a two-dimensional picture. This picture we can imagine to be composed of an array of infinitesimally small areas, each emitting light towards the eye. If, as a simplification, we assume that each element of the picture emits light of the same wavelength composition, then we can specify the picture completely by specifying the luminance of each of its elementary areas.

Point-Spread Function

If the optical system of the eye were ideal, then the retinal image of our stimulus would be an exact copy of it (save for some uniform magnification) and the illuminance of each elementary area of the retina would be directly proportional to the luminance of the corresponding element of the stimulus picture. However, the optical system of the eye is not ideal, so the light emerging from each element of the stimulus picture does not affect only the corresponding element of the retinal image. Instead, the light entering the eye from each point of the stimulus is spread out on the retina (Fig. 1A). This spreading is partly the inevitable result of diffraction at the pupil and partly the

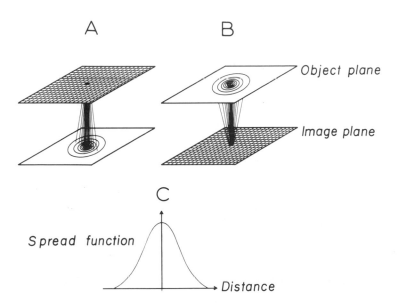

FIG. 1. A. Light from each elementary area of the object spreads out to form a blur circle in the image plane. B. Light reaching an elementary area of the image comes from a circular area of the object. C. The intensity of the light in the image of a point source is greatest at the center and falls off with distance from the center. The same spread function describes the relative significance of contributions from different points of the object to the light falling on a point in the image plane.

outcome of focus errors, aberrations, and imperfections in the optical components of the eye.

Although the retinal image is a blurred version of the original picture, the blurring can be precisely described in terms of how the light from each point in the stimulus is distributed in the retinal image; that is, in terms of the *point-spread function* of the optical system (Fig. 1C). This spread function fully characterizes the image-forming process.

There is an alternative, but equivalent, way to think about the relation between the blurred retinal image and the original stimulus picture. We can consider the light falling on each elementary area of the retina as coming not just from the corresponding element of the stimulus picture, but also in part from neighboring elements (Fig. 1B). The contributions from remoter elements in the stimulus are relatively less important. In this case the extent of the blurring can be thought of in terms of a *point-weighting function*, which describes how much each element of the stimulus contributes to the illuminance of an element in the retinal image. In other words, the point-weighting function summarizes the variation in the contribution made by a point stimulus as its distance from the location in the stimulus plane that corresponds geometrically to a given retinal element is varied. If distances between points in both the retinal image and the stimulus are expressed as angular subtenses at the appropriate nodal points of the eye, then the point-spread and point-weighting functions are the same function.

The point-spread function can in principle be measured directly by forming the image of a point source and scanning the image with a photocell having a very small aperture. Similarly, the point-weighting function can be measured by keeping the photocell aperture in a fixed position in the image plane while moving the light source about in the stimulus plane.

Since the illuminance at each point in the retinal image is the sum of the contributions from all the elements of the stimulus picture, then, if we know the point-weighting function of the eye, we can calculate the retinal illuminance distribution for any luminance distribution in the stimulus plane. This is done by adding together, for each image element, the calculated contributions made by all the picture elements—that is, by convolving the luminance distribution in the stimulus picture with the point-weighting function. It is worth emphasizing that our ability to calculate the retinal light-distribution in this simple way comes about because, in the case of incoherent optical image formation, a given amount of light coming from a given point makes the same contribution to total illuminance regardless of how much other light is also present. In other words, the simple calculation is feasible because the superposition principle holds exactly; like any other optical system, the eye is operating linearly in forming the retinal image.

It should be noted that this discussion has so far assumed that the optical system of the eye is both *isotropic* and *isoplanatic*; that is, that the blurred image of a point is circular and the blurring has the same form irrespective of its position in the visual field. Although it is unlikely that either of these assumptions is quite correct even in an eye with its best spectacle correction, limitations in the resolving power of the visual nervous system keep the deviations from ideal behavior from being perceptually significant.

Line-Spread Function

Although the point-spread function of an optical system is the most obvious measure of its performance, it is frequently easier to measure and use the line-spread function instead. This function describes how the illuminance in the blurred image of a long, thin, luminous line falls off as a function of distance from the middle of the image.

In an *isotropic* optical system the line-spread function is the same for lines in any orientation. An optical system that produces astigmatic images demonstrates *anisotropy*; its line-spread function is different for different orientations of the line. If the imaging system is isotropic, then the point-spread function is rotationally symmetric and is a function of only one variable, distance from the center of the image. In this case the line-spread function is also a function of a single variable, distance from the center, and is independent of the orientation of the line.

The point- and line-spread functions are simply related mathematically and either may equally well be used to describe the behavior of the system.

Modulation Transfer Function

We have so far been treating the stimulus picture as an array of elementary areas of different luminance. This may seem natural and convenient, permitting the imaging of each stimulus element to be considered separately, without regard to the luminances of any other elements. On the other hand, it is not necessary to think of the stimulus picture divided up into independent points in this way. There may in fact be advantages in regarding the stimulus not as a large number of dispersed points of light, but rather as a large number of superimposed *patterns* of light. In particular, we may consider our stimulus picture to be the sum of a large number of sinusoidal grating patterns (Fig. 2), each grating having a specified spatial frequency, orientation, contrast and spatial phase. One advantage of this way of decomposing the stimulus picture is that each of the elementary (grating) components of the stimulus independently produces an image that is itself a sinusoidal grating. Thus the total retinal image is the sum of a number of grating components each corresponding exactly to a component in the stimulus picture except insofar as the contrast of the image components will always be less than that of the stimulus components.

FIG. 2. A sinusoidal grating pattern. When evenly illuminated the luminance across the pattern perpendicular to the bars has the form $L = L_0(1 + m \cos 2\pi fx)$, where L_0 is the mean luminance, m is the contrast, x is the distance across the grating and f is the spatial frequency. When the pattern is used as a visual stimulus, x is usually expressed in terms of the angle subtended at the eye. The grating, here shown with the bars vertical, could have any other orientation.

The reduction in the contrast of each grating component in the image (with respect to the corresponding component in the stimulus picture) varies with spatial frequency, generally becoming more pronounced at higher spatial frequencies. Indeed, above some particular spatial frequency (the cutoff frequency, which depends upon the pupil diameter and the wavelength of the light) the image contrast becomes zero; the light is spread uniformly over the whole image.

The behavior of an imaging system can be described completely by specifying the ratio of image contrast to stimulus contrast at all spatial frequencies; this ratio as a function of spatial frequency is the system's *modulation transfer func-*

tion. If the system is not isotropic the modulation transfer function will depend upon the orientation of the gratings.

One way of measuring the modulation transfer function is to do it directly by forming successively the images of sinusoidal gratings of different spatial frequencies, measuring for each one the contrast of the grating stimulus and its image, and calculating the ratio. Since optical systems behave linearly, it does not matter what the contrast of the stimulus grating is. The image/stimulus contrast ratio is the same for any level of contrast, though the measurements may be easier to make if the contrast is high.

Because the image/stimulus contrast ratio is independent of the level of contrast, there are two equivalent methods that can be adopted when measuring the modulation transfer function. As the spatial frequency of the stimulus is varied, its contrast can be kept fixed and the varying contrast of the image measured. Alternatively, the image contrast can be set at a convenient level and then, for each spatial frequency, the contrast in the stimulus that is required to produce the designated image contrast can be found. (The resulting data plot, comparable to the "contrast-sensitivity function" measured psychophysically or neurophysiologically, is the inverse of the modulation transfer function, a plot of stimulus/image contrast.) The second method will prove useful later, when we come to consider the spatial frequency response of visual neurones.

In practice, it is not necessary to measure the modulation transfer function in any of these direct ways, because it can always be deduced from the line- or point-spread function by an appropriate Fourier transformation. For an optical (and therefore linear) imaging system, the point-spread, line-spread and modulation transfer functions all provide identically the same information. Which function is used to describe the behavior of the system is only a matter of which is most convenient in a particular case.

Modulation Transfer Function of the Optical System of the Eye

Various methods of measuring how well they eye performs as an optical image-forming device have been employed in both man and animals. In man, the method least open to problems of interpretation is probably that adopted by Arnulf and Dupuy (1960) and Campbell and Green (1965). In this method a pattern of light and dark bars is formed directly on the retina by the interference of light from two small images of a coherent light source, focussed at the subject's pupil. By changing the distance between the two images, the spatial frequency of the retinal pattern can be changed. The contrast of an interference pattern formed by a (nonscattering) optical system in this way is largely unaffected by optical aberrations and focus errors and may be assumed to be 1.0. By superimposing a uniform field on the interference pattern a retinal image of reduced but known contrast can be generated. It is thus possible to compare the visibility of sinusoidal interference gratings of different spatial frequencies and calculated retinal contrast with the visibility of external gratings viewed normally. It is found that in order to produce the same visibility, the contrast of the external test grating always needs to be higher than the calculated retinal contrast of an interference image of the same spatial frequency on the retina, presumably because defects of the eye's optics reduce the contrast in the retinal image of the normally viewed test stimulus. The ratio of the contrasts required to give equal visibility of normal and interference patterns at different spatial frequencies is the modulation transfer function of the eye's optical system.

The modulation transfer function of the human eye depends upon the size of the pupil, aberrations being the dominant contributor to degradation of the image when the pupil is large and diffraction when it is small. At some intermediate size (about 2-3 millimeters diameter in man), the optical system produces the least blurred image. Arnulf and Dupuy's (1960) estimate of the modulation transfer function for a 2.5 millimeter pupil and best focus is shown by the filled circles in Fig. 3. At high spatial frequencies the contrast of the retinal image falls rapidly towards zero while at low frequencies the contrast of

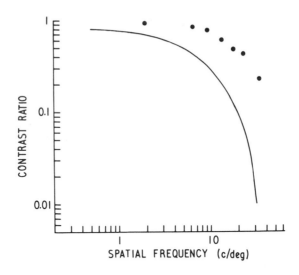

FIG. 3. The ratio of the contrast of the retinal image to the contrast of an external test grating is shown as a function of the spatial frequency. The continuous curve is for a cat eye with a 1 millimeter diameter pupil (Robson & Enroth-Cugell, 1978); filled circles are measurements made by Arnulf and Dupuy (1960) in man with a pupil of 2.5 millimeters diameter. In both cases the image was in best focus and the pupil size was approximately optimal. The human data may be spuriously high because they do not take account of scattered light (see text).

the retinal image approaches that of the external stimulus. It seems likely, however, that the modulation transfer function of the human eye does not really approach so close to 1.0 at low frequencies as these results suggest, since the method used by Arnulf and Dupuy does not properly take into account the effects of light-scattering in the eye. Light scattered onto the retina by the ocular media reduces the contrast of the retinal image; both interference and normal images are equally affected. Therefore Arnulf and Dupuy's method conceals the effect of scattered light because it measures the ratio of the contrasts of equally visible normal and interference images.

The retinal image quality in animal eyes can be measured by methods in which the retinal image is examined directly (e.g. DeMott, 1959; Robson & Enroth-Cugell, 1978). For the cat the optimal pupil diameter is about 1 millimeter and the modulation transfer function for this pupil size is shown by the curved line in Fig. 3. That the optics of the cat's eye are not quite as good as those of the human eye is clearly shown by the rapid fall in the modulation transfer function occurring at somewhat lower spatial frequencies for the cat's eye than for the human eye. It also appears that the performance of the cat's eye at low spatial frequencies is not as good as that of the human eye. However, it is again possible that this discrepancy is no more than a reflection of the failure of the method used to obtain the human measurements to show the effects of light scattering. The direct method used to obtain the modulation transfer function of the cat's eye should more accurately demonstrate the effects of preretinal scattering at least.

PHOTORECEPTORS AND THE RETINAL IMAGE

The retinal image is of significance for vision only insofar as the retinal photoreceptors respond to the light falling upon them and we should therefore inquire how well the photoreceptors respond to the incident light. We might expect that the magnitude of a photoreceptor's response would be directly determined by the luminous flux falling on the end of the receptor. But retinal photoreceptors (cones, at least) respond less well to light coming from directions away from their axis, that is to light coming through the outer part of the pupil. Thus, the illuminance of the retina is not really quite the appropriate measure of the input to the photoreceptors, since it does not take account of the directional difference in the effectiveness of incoming light (the Stiles-Crawford effect). It follows from this that, to the extent that the blurring of the retinal image is due to aberrations, the directly measured spread function of the eye will not exactly correspond to the physiologically effective spread function.

The Photoreceptor Image—Spatial Sampling

Since the photoreceptors in the retina are spread out in a more or less uniform array, each responding to the light falling on it, we can reasonably think of the pattern of activity in the whole array of photoreceptors as a photoreceptor image homologous with the retinal image. The photoreceptor image differs from the retinal image in two respects.

The first difference arises because the photoreceptors are not infinitesimally small. Each one collects the light falling on an extended (albeit rather small) area of retina. The resulting pooling over finite collecting areas slightly reduces the contrast of the photoreceptor image compared with the retinal image that we have been examining. However, because the collecting areas are very small, this reduction is significant only at spatial frequencies high enough to be approaching the limit of visual resolution. If we want to take account of the collecting area when determining the activity of the photoreceptors, we can lump its effect in with the optical factors that affect the light distribution in the retinal image, treating it simply as another factor causing a slight increase in width of the effective spread function.

The second difference between the photoreceptor image and the retinal image is of a more fundamental nature; whereas the illuminance of the retinal image is, like the external stimulus luminance, a continuous function of position, the activity of the photoreceptor array is essentially a discrete function. Although we have already discussed the stimulus picture and the retinal image in terms of an array of elementary illuminated areas, these were infinitesimal areas—essentially just theoretical constructs. Now we are faced with the fact that there is a limited number of photoreceptors (and, of course, of other neurones in the visual system) each transmitting a single output signal, the array of such signals being most simply thought of as a set of point samples of a hypothetical continuous function. The continuous function effectively sampled at different points by the photoreceptors is, of course, the retinal image slightly modified by the effect of integrating over a collecting area equal to the entrance aperture of a photoreceptor.

One might suppose that this discrete sampling would mean that the photoreceptor image would lack some of the information that was available in the retinal image. However, the sampling process actually does not, *per se*, cause any loss of information, so long as all spatial-frequency components in the retinal image have periods (i.e. cycle widths) at least twice as great as the distance between adjacent photoreceptors (see Bracewell, 1965). Indeed, if we knew the extent to which each photoreceptor is activated, we could reconstruct the retinal light distribution exactly, or at least within the limits set by the noisiness of the signals from the photoreceptors.

The Human Photoreceptor Mosaic

In the center of the human fovea, the spacing between adjacent photoreceptors (center-to-center) is about 0.002 millimeter, subtending a visual angle of a little less than 0.5 minute of arc (Polyak, 1957, p. 269). Thus, the photoreceptor mosaic in this region is capable of transmitting all the information in a retinal image with spatial frequencies up to at least 60 cycles/degree. The retinal image contains no components at any significantly higher spatial frequency than this (the absolute diffraction-determined cutoff limit for a 2 millimeter pupil and a light of wavelength 560 nanometers is 63 cycles/degree). Therefore, it is unlikely that the coarseness of the foveal mosaic interferes with full use of all the information in the retinal image.

Indeed it may well be advantageous that the optical system of the eye does not transmit spatial-frequency components beyond about 60 cycles/degree. If it did, these components could produce spurious signals, because of the phenomenon of *aliasing* (see Bracewell, 1965). Aliasing occurs whenever a continuous function is sampled too infrequently (less that twice per cycle of the highest frequency component). Its effect is to introduce spurious frequency components into the sampled signal. In fact, such spurious components may sometimes be faintly visible close to the fixation point when very high-frequency interference fringes are formed upon the retina (Campbell & Green, 1965).

Away from the center of the fovea the retinal mosaic becomes coarser and the maximum spatial frequency that it can properly transmit becomes lower. It might be expected that the disturbing effects of aliasing would concomitantly become greater. However, this does not seem to be a real problem. In the regions outside the foveal center, the signals from several neighboring cones are pooled, so that the effective spread function becomes broader. The result is that there is less effective contrast at those high spatial frequencies that might give rise to aliasing. In addition, the spread function of the optical system itself probably becomes broader farther away from the central fovea, thereby further diminishing the aliasing problem.

The Cat's Retinal Mosaic

In the cat the maximum spatial frequency that can be significantly transmitted to the retina even under optimal conditions appears to be only about 30 cycles/degree (Robson & Enroth-Cugell, 1978). But in the cat's *area centralis*, the retinal receptors are spaced less than 0.5 minute of arc apart (Steinberg, Reid & Lacy, 1973). They could in theory transmit signals up to 60 cycles/degree, so that sampling of the image would entail no loss of information.

However, it is the rods that are spaced so closely in the cat retina, while it is the cones that will almost certainly be the operative photoreceptors under natural conditions in which pupil size is optimal. The cone separation, even in the *area centralis*, is around 1.5 minutes of arc (equivalent to .005 millimeter on the retina; Steinberg, Reid, & Lacy, 1973). Thus, only spatial frequencies up to about 20 cycles/degree can be properly transmitted by the cones to the cat's nervous system. There must be some loss of information because of the inadequate sampling of the retinal image.

We might also expect the cat to have aliasing problems when looking at scenes containing high spatial-frequency components. However, the cat's ability to discriminate fine gratings is very limited. The spatial-frequency resolution limit is usually reported to be well under 10 cycles/degree (Bisti & Maffei, 1974; Blake, Cool, & Crawford, 1974). This is much less than the limit set by either the optical system or the photoreceptor sampling. Hence there must be substantial spatial integration occurring within the nervous system, which will certainly reduce, if not completely eliminate, aliasing effects for the cat.

RETINAL GANGLION CELLS AND NEURAL SIGNALS

We now turn our attention from the photoreceptors to the nerve cells in the visual system, starting with the ganglion cells in the retina.

The ganglion cells are not the cells that are immediately affected by signals from the photoreceptors. Rather, they are the final output cells of the retina, connected to the photoreceptors by a complex arrangement of intermediate cells (Fig. 4). Although a great deal of elegant work has been done in the past few years unravelling the connections and examining the interactions between these intermediate cells, we shall not consider here either the structure of the retina or the signals transmitted by the horizontal, bipolar or amacrine cells. Instead we shall see how the overall function of the retina is expressed in terms of the relation between the stimulus picture and the signals that leave the retina.

First, however, let us look at the nature of the signals transmitted by the ganglion cells of the retina to the brain. As is universally the case when information has to be conveyed over long distances in the nervous system, the signals in the optic nerve are trains of discrete nerve impulses. Retinal ganglion cells normally generate a continuous though rather irregular train of impulses even when they are not subjected to specific visual stimulation. The average frequency of the discharge is usually in the range of 10 to 100 impulses per second. When a ganglion cell responds to visual stimulation, the frequency of the discharge is usually altered, though sometimes only transiently. The strength of the stimulus is reflected in the magnitude of the change in frequency of the discharge. Although it is possible to describe the response of a gan-

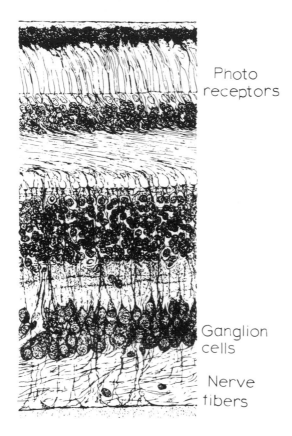

Photo receptors

Ganglion cells

Nerve fibers

FIG. 4. A section of a primate retina from a region close to the fovea. The photoreceptors are connected to the ganglion cells by large numbers of intermediate horizontal, bipolar and amacrine cells having extensive lateral extensions. The nerve fibers from the ganglion cells travel across the inner surface of the retina before leaving the eye to run in the optic nerve. The total thickness of the retina is about 0.3 millimeter. (From Polyak, 1941.)

glion cell in terms of changes in the frequency of its discharge, it may be more appropriate, in view of the fact that the ongoing discharge of the cell approximates a random process, to consider that the effect of a stimulus is to change the instantaneous probability that the cell will fire.

The irregularity in timing of the nerve impulses and the probabilistic nature of the response to a stimulus create a problem for the investigator. Unless rather intense stimuli are used, we may be unable to distinguish a stimulus-produced change in firing rate from the inevitable spontaneous fluctuations (Barlow & Levick, 1969a). Therefore we often have to resort to averaging the responses to many repetitions of the stimulus. In this way it is possible to increase the effective signal-to-noise ratio of our measurements to the required extent.

But if a cell's responses to a stimulus are so unreliable that we have to average responses to dozens or even hundreds of stimulus presentations in order to see that the cell *is* responding to the stimulus, then what do our measurements have to do with vision (see Teller, 1980)? Certainly the perceiving animal is not usually averaging over successive presentation of the stimulus. Rather, if human experience is anything to go on, the stimulus is either seen or not seen on each presentation. In a sense, then, it might seem that our physiological measurements may be dealing with stimuli so weak that they are below the visual threshold.

However, the averaged responses may in fact be more pertinent to visual perception than that. We should bear in mind that usually signals from many cells in the visual system converge onto each of the cells at a higher level. It may well be that individual cells at higher levels can respond reliably to visual stimuli which could not be detected by examining the activity of any one of the lower-level cells. Although I do not know that this has ever been directly demonstrated neurophysiologically, I strongly suspect that it must be so. In effect, what the neurophysiologist does with a single cell, by summing the responses to many successive presentations of a stimulus, the visual system may accomplish by summing the responses of many cells to a single presentation.

In addition, it is possible that a weak visual stimulus which would significantly change the discharge of a single cell on only a small proportion of trials might well be detected much more frequently by an animal having a large number of cells, even if all the cells respond on average equally poorly to the stimulus. If there is some spontaneous variation in the cells' sensitivity, one cell may signal the occurrence of a stimulus on some trials when the others are temporarily too unresponsive. The overall detection rate may therefore be increased because of "probability summation" (see Graham, 1980). Thus, we do have reasons for being interested in how nerve cells respond to single stimuli that are too weak to produce changes in the cell's firing that are readily measurable, or even clearly detectable, on a single trial.

Receptive Fields of Retinal Ganglion Cells

We can now look in more detail at the way retinal ganglion cells respond to visual stimulus patterns, so that we can discuss the characteristics of the "ganglion cell image."

The neural impulses produced by an individual ganglion cell can be recorded at their site of origin by pushing a microelectrode through the vitreous body of an animal's eye and advancing it until it just touches the body of the ganglion cell. Alternatively, it is possible to record the nerve impulses as they pass along the fibers of the optic nerve or tract.

The former method was employed by Kuffler (1953). He was the first to investigate how mammalian (cat) retinal ganglion cells respond to patterned visual stimulation and he has provided the classical description of their behavior. As we saw earlier, each ganglion cell is connected indirectly to a number of photoreceptors, so it is not surprising that Kuffler found that he could influence the activity of a retinal ganglion cell from a relatively extensive area of the retina. This retinal area, or the corresponding area on a screen whose image is formed on the retina, is the cell's *receptive field*.

Kuffler observed that in many instances turning on a small spot of light in the middle of a cell's receptive field caused an increase in the cell's discharge rate. On the other hand, he also observed some cells whose discharge rate increased briefly whenever he turned *off* a light-spot that had been shining on the middle of the receptive field for some time. These two basic types of ganglion cell are found in roughly equal numbers in the retina and are generally referred to as *on-center* and *off-center* cells respectively.

An off-center cell's response to turning *on* a light in the center of its receptive field is impossible to observe unless the cell has a well maintained resting discharge (that is, unless the cell generates action potentials at a fairly high frequency in the absence of specific visual stimulation). Then the response to light onset is seen as a reduction in the maintained rate (Fig. 5C).

The middle of a ganglion cell's receptive field can be readily identified: It is the point at which turning a small spot of light on or off has the greatest effect. If the stimulating spot is moved away from this point, the cell's responsiveness is found to become progressively less. Usually it is possible to keep the response constant by increasing the intensity of the spot as it is moved into less sensitive regions of the receptive field (e.g. Cleland & Enroth-Cugell, 1965).

When the stimulating spot moves sufficiently far from the middle of the receptive field, it begins to produce the opposite kind of response. Thus, if a stimulus spot is turned on in the outer region of an on-center receptive field, it will reduce the discharge rate of the cell. Shining a light on the outer part of an off-center receptive field will increase the cell's firing rate (Fig. 5A).

As might be expected, if the strength of two stimuli that fall separately on the center and surrounding areas are suitably balanced, it is possible to leave the cell's firing rate virtually unaffected. In fact changing the luminance uniformly over the whole receptive field has only a minimal effect on many ganglion cells, because the center and antagonistic surround regions are more or less equally and oppositely affected by such a stimulus (Fig. 5B).

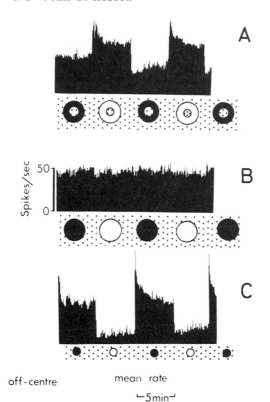

FIG. 5. Discharge of an off-center ganglion cell in the cat retina with different stationary patterns of light and dark in its receptive field. A. Successive 5 minute intervals while alternating black and white annuli in the receptive-field surround. B. Alternating large black and white discs each covering the whole receptive field. C. Alternating small black and white discs each confined to the receptive field center. All stimuli were presented against a gray background. (From Bishop & Rodieck, 1965.)

Response of Ganglion Cells to Grating Stimuli

Now we can see how such a cell would respond if we were to use a sinusoidal grating as a stimulus rather than a spot of light (see Enroth-Cugell & Robson, 1966).

Consider, for example, an off-center cell onto whose receptive field we project a grating pattern with a half-period roughly as wide as the excitatory receptive field center. If the grating is positioned as in Fig. 6A, with a bright bar lying across the center of the receptive field, then we can expect the cell to be strongly excited when the grating is turned off (i.e. when a homogeneous field with the same mean luminance is substituted for the grating). Conversely, if the grating is shifted in phase so that a dark bar falls across the center of the receptive field as in Fig. 6C, then the activity of the cell should be correspondingly depressed when the grating is turned off.

Now suppose that the stimulus pattern is shifted by an intermediate amount, so that it falls as in Fig. 6B or 6D. If the system behaves linearly, we would expect no response to turning the grating on or off. Any increase in activity

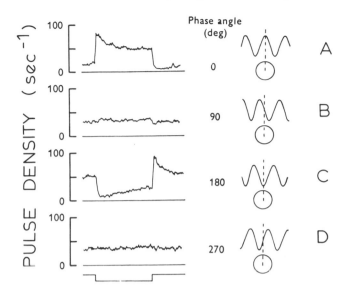

FIG. 6. The response of an off-center cat retinal ganglion cell to a static grating pattern. The diagrams on the right indicate how the luminance pattern fell in relation to the central (in this case inhibitory) region of the cell's receptive field. The peripheral surround region (in this case excitatory) of the receptive field is not shown. On the left is shown the firing rate of the cell when the contrast of the pattern goes from 0.32 to 0 for 1.1 seconds and then returns to 0.32. When the pattern lies with odd symmetry relative to the receptive field center (phase angles of 90° and 270°) the cell does not respond to the pattern.

due to one half of the stimulus pattern should be cancelled out by an equivalent decrease due to the other half. This is exactly what happens for most ganglion cells, as the response records in Fig. 6B and 6D demonstrate.

This is an important observation. It implies that, at least to a first approximation, the response of a ganglion cell is related to the weighted sum of contributions, proportional to luminance, from the photoreceptors within its receptive field. Although not all ganglion cells behave in this way, a majority do. It is these cells which show more or less linear spatial summation (first called *X-cells* by Christina Enroth-Cugell and myself in 1966 and later referred to as "sustained" cells by Cleland, Dubin & Levick, 1971) that form the major component of the retino-cortical system. The behavior of the other type of ganglion cells (Y-cells) that transmit signals via the lateral geniculate nucleus to the visual cortex is more complicated and less easily characterized. However, two features of Y-cells should perhaps be noted. First, the receptive fields of Y-cells are considerably larger than those of X-cells in the same part of the retina. Second, although Y-cells demonstrate very obvious signs of nonlinear behavior with stimuli of high spatial frequency, they behave much more nearly linearly when responding to stimuli of low spatial frequency.

Do Ganglion Cells Signal Contrast?

The earlier discussion about optical image-forming devices was sometimes couched in terms of the relation between the *luminance* at each point in the stimulus and the illuminance at each point in the image. At other times reference was made instead to the relation between the *contrast* of the stimulus and the contrast of the image (and implicitly the mean luminance or illuminance). These two measures could be used more or less interchangeably because optical systems behave linearly.

But what of ganglion cells, whose behavior we have already seen is not completely linear? In talking about a ganglion cell, is it better to examine the way in which its output is related to the luminance distribution of the stimulus or is it better to think of the cell's output as a function of the contrast (and mean luminance) of the stimulus? For a nonlinear system, the two approaches are not equivalent.

There are two reasons why it seems more appropriate to choose contrast as the measure of stimulus strength for ganglion cells. First, "contrast" automatically bears the implication that is is spatial *differences* in stimulus luminance that are important in determining the response of a ganglion cell. We have already seen that differential stimulation of center and surround regions of a ganglion cell's receptive field (Fig. 5) can have a large effect on the cell's firing rate, whereas equal stimulation of the two antagonistic regions does not. This shows up in contrast-sensitivity plots as a much smaller sensitivity at zero spatial frequency than at intermediate frequencies. Clearly it is the existence of some *contrast* between one region of a receptive field and another that is signalled by the cell. When there is no contrast and the stimulus is uniform, the luminance can be varied over a wide range without having much effect on a ganglion cell's firing rate. The insensitivity of ganglion cells to relatively small changes in luminance of a homogeneous field probably depends mainly on the spatial differencing effect of center-surround antagonism. However, a large change in luminance does generally produce some, albeit short-lived, change in firing rate, implying that there are also time-dependent adaptation processes at work to minimize the effects of sustained changes of luminance.

An adaptation process is probably also partly responsible for that aspect of ganglion cell behavior which provides the second reason for preferring to describe the stimulus pattern in terms of its contrast. This behavior is best appreciated by considering the result of a simple experiment; at least it is a simple experiment if you are already recording the response of a ganglion cell to a drifting grating pattern of roughly optimal spatial frequency and fairly high luminance (see Fig. 7). The experiment consists of listening to the discharge

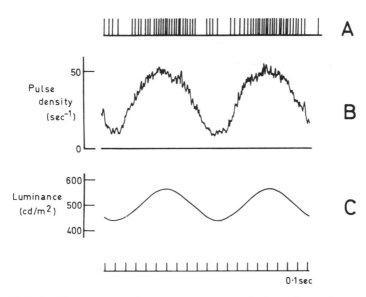

FIG. 7. The response of an on-center cat retinal ganglion cell to a sinusoidal grating pattern (contrast 0.12) drifting across its receptive field. The lower sinusoid (C) is a measure of the luminance at the very center of the receptive field, while the top record (A) shows a sample of the train of nerve impulses generated by the cell. At B is shown the fluctuation in frequency of the cell's discharge, the record being obtained by finding the probability of getting a nerve impulse in different short intervals of time relative to the stimulus (probability estimated over 200 seconds of stimulation). Note the harmonic distortion in the response. The spatial frequency and drift velocity were approximately optimal. (From Cooper & Robson, 1968.)

of the cell (whose frequency will be rising and falling as the light and dark bars of the grating pass across the center of the cell's receptive field) while a colleague slips a neutral density filter (of, say, 1 or 1.5 log units) in front of the animal's eye. This will reduce the retinal illuminance by 10 or 30 times without changing the contrast of the pattern. It will be observed that there is no obvious change in the way the discharge frequency fluctuates in synchrony with the passing bars of the grating, though there may be a slight hiccup as the filter is put in or taken out. Indeed the cell's firing may be so little affected it may not even be possible to tell when the filter is inserted. In other words, the response of ganglion cells seems to be much more dependent upon the contrast of the stimulus pattern than upon its mean luminance.

Another way to show that the behavior of ganglion cells can be largely independent of retinal illumination is to measure contrast sensitivity at different luminance levels (Enroth-Cugell & Robson, 1966). It can be seen from Fig. 11 that (at least in the normal, photopic range) changing the illumination by a factor of 30 has little effect upon the cell's sensitivity, except at high spatial frequencies (high for this cell, that is).

We can interpret this finding by saying that, at spatial frequencies up to at least its optimum, a retinal ganglion cell may best be thought of as being sensitive to the *contrast* (luminance variation as a fraction of the mean luminance) rather than to the absolute luminance variation of the stimulus pattern. At higher spatial frequencies (above the optimum) the sensitivity rises with increasing luminance. Barlow and Levick (1969b) found that the incremental sensitivity of a ganglion cell (measured with a flashing spot centered on its receptive field) was approximately proportional to the square root of the luminance and a similar relationship would not be inconsistent with the grating sensitivity results.

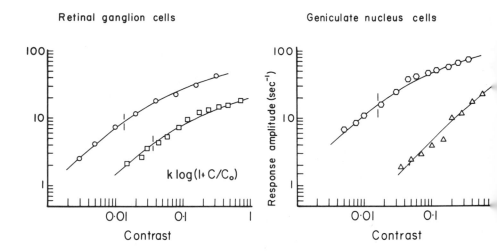

FIG. 8. The magnitude of the response of retinal ganglion cells and cells in the lateral geniculate nucleus (cat) to grating patterns of optimal spatial frequency drifting across the receptive field at approximately optimal velocity. The response is measured as the amplitude of that variation in discharge frequency which is synchronized with the passage of gratings bars across the receptive field. All curves have the same form: response amplitude $= k \log(1 + C / C_0)$ where k and C_0 are constants. C_0, which can be considered as the upper limit of the contrast at which the cell's behavior is approximately linear, is indicated by the small vertical lines against each curve. (The three curves on the right are redrawn from Maffei & Fiorentini, 1973; the left-hand curve from Enroth-Cugell & Robson, unpublished results.)

It is interesting to note that, although the human contrast threshold for detecting grating patterns of intermediate and high spatial frequencies is inversely related to the square root of the retinal illumination level at low levels, the contrast threshold for all spatial frequencies becomes independent of the illumination at photopic levels (Van Nes & Bouman 1967). It is not clear if this effect would also be seen in ganglion cells at sufficiently high retinal illuminance levels.

But how linear is the behavior of even these cells if we think of them as signalling the *contrast* of the stimulus pattern? (The contrast, m, of a grating is defined by the equation $L = L_0(1 + m \cos 2\pi fx)$, describing the luminance across a grating pattern, where L_0 is the mean luminance, f is the spatial frequency of the pattern and x is the distance across the pattern.) In order to answer this, and indeed questions about how the cells respond to changes in the spatial frequency of the stimulus, it is technically more convenient to use as a stimulus a drifting grating pattern, rather than a stationary pattern whose contrast is varied with time.

Figure 7 shows the response of a cat retinal ganglion cell to a sinusoidal grating pattern drifting across its receptive field. Clearly the discharge is modulated in synchrony with the passage of the bars of the grating across the center of the cell's receptive field and we can use the amplitude of the modulation of the discharge frequency to measure how well the cell responds to the pattern.

Let us now see how the size of the response varies with the contrast of the grating pattern. Figure 8 shows some typical results. Since the results are shown on log-log plots, the fact that the relationship between contrast and response is curvilinear implies that the response is related to contrast neither by a linear nor any simple power-law relation. In fact the simplest description of these results is that at low contrast levels the response amplitude is proportional to the contrast while at higher levels the response amplitude becomes more nearly proportional to the logarithm of the contrast. The contrast level at which the change from linear to a logarithmic relation occurs seems to vary considerably from cell to cell in no very obviously systematic way.

Now we can look at the way in which ganglion cells respond to grating stimuli of different spatial frequencies. We noted earlier that we should expect a ganglion cell to respond particularly well to patterns whose spatial half-period is roughly equal to the diameter of the central part of its receptive field. Moreover we have already seen that at zero spatial frequency (a change in the luminance of a uniform field) the response can be very small while at high spatial frequencies it is inevitable that the response becomes attenuated. This is amply confirmed by experimental observation (Fig. 9). But how do we quantify this behavior?

We could simply measure the amplitude of the ganglion cell's response to various gratings of the same contrast but different spatial frequencies. Howev-

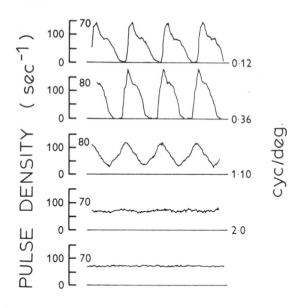

FIG. 9. The response of a cat retinal ganglion cell to sinusoidal grating patterns (contrast 0.4) of different spatial frequencies (indicated at right) drifting at such a velocity that, in each case, four bars of the pattern pass across the center of the receptive field every second. (cf. Fig. 7B). (From Enroth-Cugell & Robson, 1966.)

er, since we have already seen that ganglion cells do not exhibit a proportional relationship between response amplitude and stimulus contrast we would not expect to obtain a unique relationship between response amplitude and spatial frequency of the stimulus. However, if we determine, for a number of different spatial frequencies, how great a contrast is required to produce a certain constant response, then, since the system appears to behave linearly except for a nonlinearity at the output, we shall obtain a measure of the modulation transfer function (spatial frequency response function) of the underlying spatial summation process.

Figure 10 shows the result of just such a measurement. As expected there is a well defined optimal spatial frequency. The sensitivity becomes substantially less at low spatial frequencies, while the sensitivity is rapidly and profoundly reduced as the spatial frequency is raised above the optimum. We can obtain a good description of the contrast sensitivity function (in effect the modulation transfer function of the retinal spatial summating mechanism) by assuming that it is the difference of two Gaussian functions, one of these being several times broader than the other. This suggests a simple model in which the center and antagonistic surrounds of a ganglion cell's receptive field reflect the

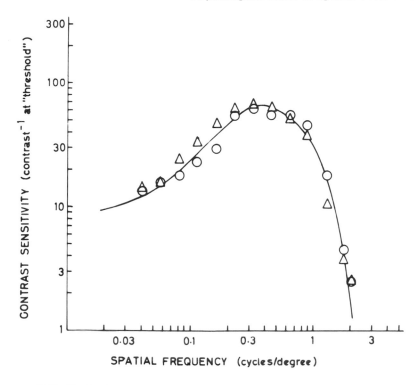

FIG. 10. Typical contrast sensitivity function of a cat ganglion cell. The cell is stimulated by a grating drifting at 4 Hertz across its receptive field. For each spatial frequency of the grating the contrast level at which the cell's discharge frequency is detectably modulated at 4 Hertz is determined by an experimenter who listens to the discharge relayed over a loudspeaker. Cells with different size receptive field centers give similar curves displaced along the logarithmic spatial frequency axis. The curve drawn through the experimental points (two determinations) is the difference of two Gaussian functions. (From Enroth-Cugell & Robson, 1966.)

local predominance of one of two spatial summating mechanisms which are concentric but have opposite effects on the ganglion cell. There are possible objections to this being a true description of the actual retinal mechanism but it is probably worth retaining as a useful heuristic device.

The exact form of the spatial-frequency response functions of retinal ganglion cells depends upon the mean level of retinal illuminance at which it is measured (Fig. 11). At low illuminance levels the sensitivity generally becomes less and the low-frequency attenuation becomes less marked, or even more or less disappears.

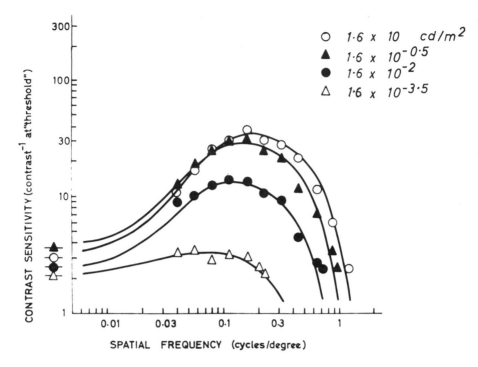

FIG. 11. The contrast sensitivity function of a cat retinal ganglion cell measured at different levels of illumination. The pupil size was fixed at 3.5 millimeters diameter. (From Enroth-Cugell & Robson, 1966.)

The Ganglion-Cell Image

We now know enough about the behavior of individual ganglion cells to visualize the pattern of activity, the ganglion-cell image, that would be produced in an array of such cells by a visual stimulus.

But we have not yet looked at how the receptive fields of the ganglion cells are actually distributed over the retina or how their characteristics vary with retinal location. In fact the ganglion cells are much more densely packed together in the central part of the retina than in the periphery (e.g. Stone, 1965), so we would expect the sampling of the ganglion-cell image to be different in different regions. Many investigators (e.g. Wiesel, 1960; Cleland & Levick, 1974) have found that the centers of ganglion-cell receptive fields are substantially smaller (on average) in the central retina than they are in the periphery. Thus we must expect the ganglion-cell image to demonstrate a marked anisoplanatism in terms of both the density of sampling and the extent of the "blurring" introduced by summation over the area of the ganglion cell's receptive-field center.

Fischer (1973) has pointed out that the average distance between ganglion-cell receptive fields increases with retinal eccentricity in the same way as their average diameter increases. It is not surprising that such a relationship should exist between receptive-field size and cell separation, because the diameter of its receptive-field center determines how high a spatial frequency a ganglion-cell will respond to while the separation between the cells determines how high a spatial frequency the array of cells can properly transmit. Now it is not desirable for the diameters of the receptive-field centers to be so small that ganglion cells respond to spatial frequencies that cannot be properly represented by the activity of the array of cells, because the image is too infrequently sampled. On the other hand, there would be little point in sampling more frequently, in a given retinal region, than is needed to transmit the highest frequency to which the individual cells there can respond. Thus, since the spatial-frequency response limit is roughly equal to the reciprocal of the diameter of the receptive-field center, we might expect to find that the receptive fields are spaced at a distance approximately equal to the radius of their field centers. This spacing would insure that individual cells would not respond to higher frequencies than could be adequately transmitted by the cell array. Unfortunately we still do not have precise enough information about the size of ganglion-cell receptive fields and the spacing between them to be certain whether or not the retinal ganglion cells are really arranged in quite this way. The information we do have suggests that there may be rather more cells (of both X and Y types separately) than are minimally necessary to sample the image adequately (see Robson, 1957).

If all the X-cells in any one retinal region have receptive-field centers of the same size, then the range of spatial frequencies transmitted by X-cells from that region will be rather restricted, since X-cells act as bandpass filters whose optimal spatial frequency is inversely related to their field size. However, this may not be a serious limitation on the spatial information transmitted from the region, since the Y-cells (which, like X-cells, also send signals to the visual cortex via the geniculate body) have receptive-field centers that are substantially larger than those of the X-cells in any given retinal region and respond to lower spatial frequencies. The Y-cells may therefore supplement the X-cell signals by transmitting information about the lower spatial frequencies.

Another aspect of the arrangement of retinal ganglion cells about which we lack information is the form of the lattice in which the ganglion-cell receptive fields are arranged. Although the photoreceptors in the central fovea are known to be more or less hexagonally packed (Polyak, 1957) there is no particular reason for believing the ganglion cells are arranged in this same way, as they are not obviously subjected to the same kind of physical constraints. In view of the known anisotropy of human vision (lower resolution and contrast sensitivity in oblique orientations than in either the vertical or horizontal one) it is tempting to speculate that the neural images in the visual system may be more closely sampled in the vertical and horizontal than in the oblique directions, that is to suppose that the receptive fields of nerve cells in the visual system are arranged on a rectangular lattice.

THE LATERAL GENICULATE BODY

The main waystation along the pathway from retina to cortex is the lateral geniculate nucleus. Although the behavior of the cells of this nucleus has been quite extensively studied, we shall not pause to consider geniculate cells in detail, because their behavior is qualitatively so similar to that of retinal ganglion cells. Geniculate cells have similar circular receptive fields divided into antagonistic center and surround regions and they appear to exist with the same X and Y variants as retinal ganglion cells. The output of the lateral geniculate nucleus constitutes a "geniculate image" or "images" and forms the input to the visual cortex. Each geniculate image can be expected to be much like one of the ganglion cell images.

Contour Enhancement in the Neural Image

Because the spatial-frequency response function of retinal ganglion cells and of the cells in the lateral geniculate nucleus (Maffei & Fiorentini, 1973) is of bandpass type, the neural images at the retinal and geniculate levels show marked contour enhancement. This can be seen very clearly in Fig. 12, which shows how a retinal ganglion cell responds to a light/dark border as the border is moved across the retina relative to the middle of the receptive field (Enroth-Cugell & Robson, 1966). The figure can also be interpreted as the response of an array of similar cells to an edge in a fixed position. Kaji, Yamane, Yoshimura, and Sugie (1974) have demonstrated experimentally that the contours of simple two-dimensional shapes are similarly emphasized by lateral geniculate cells (Fig. 13).

These contour enhancing effects in the retinal and geniculate neural images are often taken as "explanations" of the appearance of Mach Bands and related phenomena, but what may strike the reader as particularly remarkable is really how little similarity there is between the distribution of activity in an array of retinal or geniculate nerve cells and the distribution of brightness in the visual percept of simple figures.

THE VISUAL CORTEX

It has been clear since the pioneering work of Hubel and Wiesel (1959, 1962, 1968) that the behavior of cells in the visual cortex is very different from that of retinal ganglion cells and cells of the lateral geniculate nucleus. Cortical

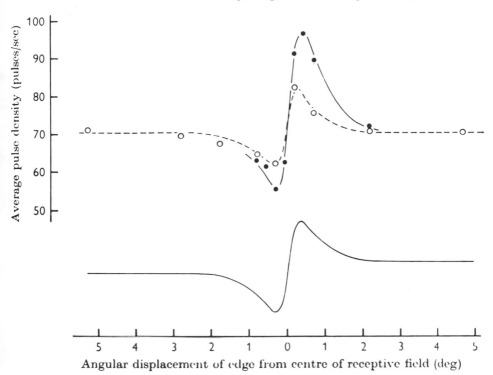

FIG. 12. The activity (firing rate) of an on-center retinal ganglion cell as a function of the position of the boundary between the lighter and darker halves of a bipartite stimulus pattern. When the boundary is well to either side of the receptive field, or exactly bisects the receptive field (displacement = 0), the cell fires at the same rate as it would if the stimulus were a uniform field. Maximum change in firing rate is obtained when the stimulus edge is just to one side of the middle of the receptive field. Filled circles are for a stimulus contrast of 0.4, the open circles for a stimulus contrast of 0.2. The lower curve shows the edge sensitivity of the cell calculated from measured values of the cell's spatial-frequency-response function assuming linearity. (From Enroth-Cugell & Robson, 1966.)

receptive fields typically do not have a circular organization, but rather are arranged linearly. For some cortical cells (but only some, the ones called "simple cells" by Hubel & Wiesel, 1959), it is possible to map out receptive fields with a flashing spot of light. Such maps reveal that the excitatory and inhibitory regions form parallel strips.

    Because the boundaries between the excitatory and inhibitory regions of their receptive fields are more or less straight, it is not surprising that these cells respond best to stimuli that are also linearly arranged, stimuli whose orientation corresponds to that of the receptive field. Nor is it surprising that

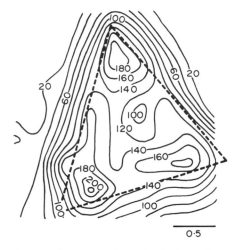

FIG. 13. Iso-response contour map for an on-center cell (whose receptive field center was 0.74° in diameter) in response to a bright triangle with sides 2.1° long. The stimulus triangle is indicated by the dashed lines. Note that the response of the cell was greatest when the middle of the receptive field fell just inside one of the apices of the stimulus. (From Kaji, Yamane, Yoshimura, & Sugie 1974.)

these cells respond particularly well to appropriately oriented grating patterns when the spacing in the pattern matches the separation between the excitatory or inhibitory strip-like regions of the receptive field.

Simple cells in the primary visual cortex of the cat appear to receive inputs mainly from X-cells in the lateral geniculate nucleus (Stone & Dreher, 1973) and hence from the X-cells of the retina. Like the X-cells of the retina and lateral geniculate nucleus, the response of a simple cell to an optimally oriented stationary grating stimulus is a sinusoidal function of its phase with respect to the receptive field. The maximum positive response is obtained when the brighter parts of the stimulus pattern fall predominantly on excitatory regions of the receptive field. This makes it convenient to measure the spatial frequency-response function of cortical cells, like that of retinal X-cells, by using drifting grating patterns as stimuli. But to characterize the cortical cell's behavior fully, the orientation of the grating pattern, as well as its spatial frequency, must be varied.

Complete measurements on cortical cells have not yet been published but some results are available. For instance, Fig. 14 shows how changing the orientation of a drifting grating of optimal spatial frequency affects the magnitude of a typical cortical cell's responses while Fig. 15 shows how the response to an optimally oriented grating can depend upon its spatial frequency. (Very similar results have been obtained by De Valois, Albrecht, & Thorell, 1978, recording from nerve cells in the cortex of monkeys.) It should be stressed, however, that not all cells are exactly as selective as this one. Many cells respond well over a different range of orientations and to a broader range of spatial frequencies.

There is another important class of cortical cells, rather different in behavior from the simple cells. Hubel and Wiesel (1959) called them "complex cells."

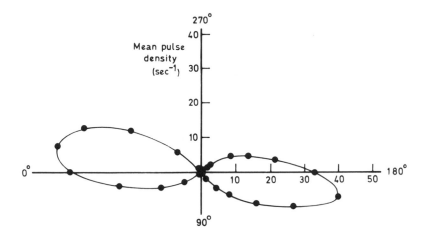

FIG. 14. The magnitude of the response of a cat cortical cell as a function of the orientation of a drifting grating pattern. Contrast of the pattern was fixed and the spatial frequency and drift velocity were about optimal. This cell showed no sign of direction specificity, responding equally well when the direction of movement of the pattern was reversed. (From Cooper & Robson, 1968.)

FIG. 15. The response of a cat cortical cell as a function of the spatial frequency of a drifting grating (filled circles). The contrast was fixed and the orientation and drift frequency were about optimal. This cell was the most highly frequency-selective one seen (Cooper & Robson, unpublished results). Also shown is a measure (open circles) of the frequency selectivity of a human mechanism functionally isolated by the technique of specific adaptation (see Graham, 1980). The two data sets have been arbitrarily shifted relative to each other so as to coincide. (From Campbell, 1974.)

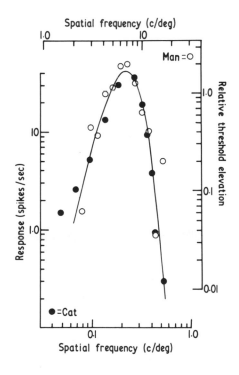

Complex cells do not respond at all well to a spot of light, and their receptive fields can be easily explored only with elongated stimuli. Compared with simple cells, they do not seem to show such a high degree of selectivity for either orientation (Watkins & Berkley, 1974) or spatial frequency (Maffei & Fiorentini, 1973). Moreover, they probably are largely indifferent to the phase of stationary grating stimuli that are turned on and off and they respond at a steady level rather than with a modulated discharge to moving gratings despite their changing location on the receptive field. Some complex cells may respond peculiarly well to moving gratings, as opposed to stationary flickering ones (Cooper & Robson, 1968).

It appears that at least some complex cells may receive direct input signals from Y-cells in the geniculate nucleus, rather than from X-cells (Stone & Dreher, 1973). While this could certainly explain some of the differences between simple and complex cell behavior, it seems inevitable that some of the complex cells are, as Hubel and Wiesel originally suggested, hierarchically higher in the cortical organization and receive their input from those cortical cells that in turn receive input from the lateral geniculate nucleus.

The Cortical Image

Now let us see to what extent it is possible to describe the activity of the cells in the visual cortex as an "image" of the visual stimulus. As at the lower levels in the visual system, what we are dealing with is an array of discrete neural signals. Each signal is some spatial function of the stimulus picture, evaluated over a region whose location corresponds to the location of the signal in the cortical array.

However the cortical image is certainly more complex than the images at lower levels. At the cortex, each region of the visual field is represented many times over by the activity of cells which presumably each compute a different function of the stimulus picture occupying this region. Certainly they must do so insofar as each region is represented by the activity of cells with widely varying receptive-field sizes (Hubel & Wiesel, 1974). Thus the cortical image clearly cannot be thought of as a single, two-dimensional image. Even if we consider only simple or only complex cells, we must think either of a quite large number of very different cortical images or of a single cortical image that is multidimensional.

One extra dimension in which this cortical image must extend represents orientation. As we have seen, each cortical cell responds to patterns having only a limited range of orientations, the full range of orientations being covered by different cells having different optimal orientations. A further dimension in which one can imagine the image to extend represents spatial frequency. As with orientation, cortical cells respond selectively to a limited range of spatial frequencies, cells with a variety of optimal frequencies being found in each cortical region (corresponding to each region of the visual field).

One other characteristic of cortical cell behavior that shows a considerable range of variation is the bandwidth of the spatial-frequency-response function. It is known that while some simple cells have only one or two excitatory and inhibitory regions within their receptive fields, other cells may have more. Bishop, Coombs, and Henry (1971) report finding cells with receptive fields having three (and occasionally more) distinct excitatory regions presumably alternating with inhibitory ones. It may be supposed that the greater the number of antagonistic regions in a receptive field, the better the match must be between the stimulus and the receptive field in order to yield a strong response (see Graham, 1980; Weisstein & Harris, 1980). Thus cells with a larger number of parallel receptive-field regions can be expected to have greater spatial-frequency selectivity. Tolhurst, Thompson, and Movshon (1978a, 1978b) have recently been able to show that the bandwidth of the spatial-frequency-response function of cortical cells is related in the appropriate way to the independently determined organization of their receptive fields. They have also been able to show that the response of simple cells (allowing for the fact that the resting discharge may be zero and discharge frequencies cannot be negative) is more or less proportional to stimulus contrast up to quite high levels of stimulus contrast.

Since the cortical image is multidimensional (even if we ignore the representation of binocular disparity and color), it is difficult to visualize it in its entirety. However, we can easily look at a cross section through the image. In particular, let us look at a section across which there is no variation in optimal spatial frequency, bandwidth or orientation. The array of cells transmitting this image has sometimes been thought of (often implicitly) as a "spatial-frequency channel" (see Graham, 1980; Julesz, 1980; Weisstein & Harris, 1980), it being assumed that this array has special significance for perception. However, at the moment it is not at all clear whether the subset of cells comprising such an array has any particular claim to consideration as a physiological entity, as it would have if we knew that the signals from these cells were somehow associated at a higher level.

The distribution of neural activity in a spatial-frequency channel can be computed if we know the spatial transformation effected by cells in the array. We can get some idea of the image by assuming that the cells operate linearly and have orientation and spatial-frequency selectivity comparable to those measured neurophysiologically in cortical cells. Figure 16 shows a plausible point-weighting function for a cortical cell, based on the orientation and spatial-frequency-response functions shown in Figs. 14 and 15 (and assuming that the two functions are independent). The distribution of activity in the image of any visual scene can now be calculated by convolving the object distribution

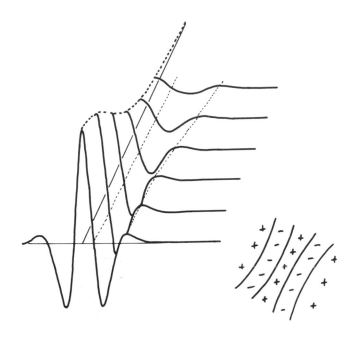

FIG. 16. The two-dimensional weighting function of a hypothetical cortical cell having the orientation selectivity of Fig. 14 and the spatial-frequency selectivity of Fig. 15. The cell was assumed to operate linearly and the orientation and spatial-frequency selectivities were assumed to be independent. Only one quarter of the function is sketched on the left. On the right is a diagrammatic plan of the receptive field of such a cell showing nearly parallel inhibitory (−) and excitatory (+) regions. For this synthesis the weighting function was assumed to have even symmetry. This is an arbitrary assumption and it is worth noting that the receptive fields of real cortical cells may show either even or odd symmetry (see Hubel & Wiesel, 1962). However, when the frequency selectivity is high, the spatial weighting functions with odd and even symmetry look rather similar, apart from a lateral displacement equivalent to a phase angle of 90°.

with the weighting function. An example of such an image (computed by Eugene Switkes) is shown in Fig. 19.

It must be stressed that Fig. 19 is not a representation of *the* cortical image which might exist in your cortex when you look at Fig. 17 (or, if you visit Cambridge, at Fergus Campbell's college rooms themselves). It is simply an indication of how one particular (possibly arbitrary) *subset* of your cortical neurones may respond. (Since the neurones are discrete, it would perhaps have been more correct to show a discretely sampled version of the transform.)

As may be guessed, the choice of which transform of the picture to display was not entirely accidental. Figure 19 represents the image in one of the most

FIG. 17. St. John's College, Cambridge: a view in Second Court (photograph courtesy of P. Starling).

active "spatial-frequency channels," possibly the channel whose activity may be the most important in recognizing the picture for what it is. Readers can judge for themselves how much useful information a single channel may carry (try backing away from the figure).

Spatial Image or Fourier Transform?

The cross sections of the multidimensional cortical image that we have been thinking about depend on considering together particular sets of the cells in the visual cortex. Each cross section corresponds to a two-dimensional array of

FIG. 18. The same view as in Fig. 17, after isotropic filtering. The filter function has the form shown in Fig. 15 with a center frequency corresponding to the periodicity of the mullions of the window. The weighting function is assumed to be radially symmetric.

cells, with all the cells in each array sharing the same characteristics (bandwidth, frequency, orientation selectivity, etc.) and differing only in the retinal locations of their receptive fields. Thinking in this way encourages us to generate pictures such as Fig. 19, which represents the activity in one such array, but is it really appropriate to think of cortical activity in terms of a large number of grossly anisotropic images? Although we cannot answer this question with certainty, we can be certain that it is not *necessary* to think in this way. We can instead conceive of the cortical cells grouped into sets having in

FIG. 19. The filter used here has the same frequency selectivity as the cell of Fig. 15 and the same orientation selectivity as the cell of Fig. 14; the optimal orientation is assumed to be vertical. This picture is therefore Fig. 17 convolved with the function shown in Fig. 16. Figure 19 can be thought of as the output of a two-dimensional array of cells all having the same orientation and spatial-frequency selectivity. (The transforms were prepared by Eugene Switkes.)

common the outline of their receptive-fields but varying in their other characteristics. (Again, there are no neurophysiological data implying that such a grouping has any structural basis.) If a set of cells all have coincident receptive · fields but different numbers of pairs of excitatory and inhibitory regions, then the cells will differ from each other in being maximally sensitive to grating pat-

212   John G. Robson

terns having different spatial frequencies, and the bandwidths of their spatial-frequency-response functions will be inversely related to the optimal frequency. Of course, a complete set of cells having coincident receptive fields will contain cells maximally sensitive to many different orientations.

If within such a set of cells a sufficiently large number of different optimal orientations and spatial frequencies are represented, and if the orientation and spatial-frequency selectivities are sufficiently great, then the activity of the whole set of cells can reasonably be thought of as a discrete Fourier transform of a patch of the retinal image (the patch corresponding to the receptive-field area that all the cells share). The activity level of each cell represents the amplitude of that component of the stimulus picture having a particular orientation and spatial frequency.

The information available at the moment suggests that it is only among the simple cells that it is possible to find cells having the requisite selectivity for orientation and spatial frequency. It therefore seems most appropriate to consider the simple cells as the most likely contributors to a discrete Fourier transform representation. In addition, simple cells (unlike complex cells) respond differently to stimuli falling in different positions in their receptive fields. Thus, it is possible for pairs of simple cells having slightly differently organized receptive fields to represent by their activities the coefficient of one component in a complex Fourier transform.

Other suggestions that the activity of the cells of the visual cortex might be considered as a Fourier transform have emphasized the role of the complex cells and the importance of their insensitivity to phase (Glezer, Ivanoff, & Tscherbach, 1973; Pollen & Taylor, 1974). However, it seems to me more appropriate to think of the simple cells as the possible mediators of a complete and useful discrete Fourier transform of the luminance variations in the visual stimulus. If this is a reasonable interpretation, it remains to explain the role of complex cells. As a speculation only, it may be worth suggesting that the complex cells could be concerned not with the analysis of visual patterns defined in terms of gross luminance variations but with the analysis of patterns defined by variations in local texture.

If we want to think of the simple cells of the visual cortex as performing a discrete Fourier analysis of the visual image, we are faced with data that suggest that the analysis can only be a rather crude one. Just how crude can probably be most simply expressed by saying that, if the visual image is analyzed patch by patch into its Fourier components, the highest order harmonic components that could be selectively registered in any patch would seem to be the third-order ones. This limitation is set by the greatest degree of orientation and spatial-frequency selectivity achieved by simple cells, a limitation dependent upon the maximum number of excitatory and inhibitory subdivisions present in the cells' receptive fields.

How useful such a crude Fourier analysis would be, even granting that the visual system could perform simultaneously the same analysis of many image patches of different sizes and in different locations, I do not know. However, I have a hunch that the answer to this question may take us another step on the way to understanding how we see.

REFERENCES

Arnulf, A., & Dupuy, O. La transmission des contrastes par le système optique de l'oeil et les seuils des contrastes rétiniens. *Comptes Rendus de l'Academie des Sciences, Paris,* 1960, *250,* 2757-2759.

Barlow, H. B., & Levick, W. R. Three factors limiting the reliable detection of light by retinal ganglion cells of the cat. *Journal of Physiology,* 1969a, *200,* 1-24.

Barlow, H. B., & Levick, W. R. Coding of light intensity by the cat retina. In W. Reichardt (Ed.), *Data processing by organisms and by machines.* New York: Academic Press, 1969b.

Bishop, P. O., Coombs, J. S., & Henry, G. H. Receptive fields of simple cells in the cat's striate cortex. *Journal of Physiology,* 1973, *231,* 31-60.

Bishop, P. O., & Rodieck, R. W. Discharge patterns of cat retinal ganglion cells. In P. W. Nye (Ed.), *Symposium on information processing in sight sensory systems.* Pasadena: California Institute of Technology, 1965.

Bisti, S., & Maffei, L. Behavioural contrast sensitivity of the cat in various visual meridians. *Journal of Physiology,* 1974, *241,* 201-210.

Blake, R., Cool, S. J., & Crawford, M. L. J. Visual resolution in the cat. *Vision Research,* 1974, *14,* 1211-1218.

Bracewell, R. *The Fourier transform and its application.* New York: McGraw-Hill, 1965.

Brindley, G. S. *Physiology of the retina and visual pathway.* London: Edward Arnold, 1970.

Campbell, F. W. The transmission of spatial information through the visual system. In F. O. Schmitt & F. G. Worden (Eds.), *The neurosciences, third study program.* Cambridge, Massachusetts: MIT Press, 1974.

Campbell, F. W., & Green, D. G. Optical and retinal factors affecting visual resolution. *Journal of Physiology,* 1965, *181,* 576-593.

Cleland, B. G., Dubin, M. W., & Levick, W. R. Sustained and transient neurones in the cat's retina and lateral geniculate nucleus. *Journal of Physiology,* 1971, *217,* 473-496.

Cleland, B. G., & Enroth-Cugell, C. Quantitative aspects of sensitivity and summation in the cat retina. *Journal of Physiology,* 1968, *198,* 17-38.

Cleland, B. G., & Levick, W. R. Brisk and sluggish concentrically organised cells of the cat's retina. *Journal of Physiology,* 1974, *240,* 421-456.

Cooper, G. F., & Robson, J. G. Successive transformations of spatial information in the visual system. In *IEE/NPL conference on pattern recognition,* IEE conference publication 42, 1968.

DeMott, D. W. Direct measures of the retinal image. *Journal of the Optical Society of America,* 1959, *49,* 571-579.

De Valois, R. L., Albrecht, D. G., & Thorell, L. G. Cortical cells: Bar and edge detectors or spatial frequency filters? In S. J. Cool & E. L. Smith (Eds.), *Frontiers in visual science.* New York: Springer, 1978.

Fischer, B. Overlap of receptive field centers and representation of the visual field in the cat's optic tract. *Vision Research,* 1973, *13,* 2113-2120.

Glezer, V. D., Ivanoff, V. A., & Tscherbach, T. A. Investigation of complex and hypercomplex receptive fields of visual cortex of the cat as spatial frequency filters. *Vision*

214   John G. Robson

Research, 1973, *13,* 1875-1904.

Graham, N. Spatial-frequency channels in human vision: Detecting edges without edge detectors. In C. S. Harris (Ed.), *Visual coding and adaptability.* Hillsdale, New Jersey: Lawrence Erlbaum Associates, 1980.

Hubel, D. H., & Wiesel, T. N. Receptive fields of single neurones in the cat's striate cortex. *Journal of Physiology,* 1959, *148,* 574-591.

Hubel, D. H., & Wiesel, T. N. Receptive fields, binocular interaction and functional architecture in the cat's visual cortex. *Journal of Physiology,* 1962, *160,* 106-154.

Hubel, D. H., & Wiesel, T. N. Receptive fields and functional architecture of monkey striate cortex. *Journal of Physiology,* 1968, *195,* 215-243.

Julesz, B. Spatial-frequency channels in one-, two-, and three-dimensional vision: Variations on an auditory theme by Bekesy. In C. S. Harris (Ed.), *Visual coding and adaptability.* Hillsdale, New Jersey: Lawrence Erlbaum Associates, 1980.

Kaji, S., Yamane, S., Yoshimura, M., & Sugie, N. Contour-enhancement of two-dimensional figures observed in the lateral geniculate cells of cats. *Vision Research,* 1974, *14,* 113-117.

Kuffler, S. W. Discharge patterns and functional organization of mammalian retina. *Journal of Neurophysiology,* 1953, *16,* 37-68.

Maffei, L., & Fiorentini, A. The visual cortex as a spatial frequency analyser. *Vision Research,* 1973, *13,* 1255-1268.

Movshon, J. A., Thompson, I. D., & Tolhurst, D. J. Spatial summation in the receptive-fields of simple cells in the cat's striate cortex. *Journal of Physiology,* 1978a, *283,* 53-77.

Movshon, J. A., Thompson, I. D., & Tolhurst, D. J. Receptive-field organization of complex cells in the cat's striate cortex. *Journal of Physiology,* 1978b, *283,* 79-99.

Pollen, D. A., & Taylor, J. H. The striate cortex and the spatial analysis of visual space. In F. O. Schmitt & F. G. Worden (Eds.), *The neurosciences, third study program.* Cambridge, Massachusetts: MIT Press, 1974.

Polyak, S. L. *The retina.* Chicago: University of Chicago Press, 1941.

Polyak, S. L. *The vertebrate visual system.* Chicago: University of Chicago Press, 1957.

Robson, J. G., & Enroth-Cugell, C. Light distribution in the cat's retinal image. *Vision Research,* 1978, *18,* 159-173.

Steinberg, R. H., Reid, M., & Lacy, P. L. The distribution of rods and cones in the retina of the cat *(Felis domesticus). Journal of Comparative Neurology,* 1973, *148,* 229-248.

Stone, J. A quantitative analysis of the distribution of ganglion cells in the cat's retina. *Journal of Comparative Neurology,* 1965, *124,* 337-352.

Stone, J. Sampling properties of microelectrodes assessed in the cat's retina. *Journal of Neurophysiology,* 1973, *36,* 1071-1079.

Stone, J., & Dreher, B. Projection of X- and Y-cells of the cat's lateral geniculate nucleus to areas 17 and 18 of visual cortex. *Journal of Neurophysiology,* 1973, *36,* 551-567.

Teller, D. Y. Locus questions in visual science. In C. S. Harris (Ed.), *Visual coding and adaptability.* Hillsdale, New Jersey: Lawrence Erlbaum Associates, 1980.

Van Nes, F. L., & Bouman, M. A. Spatial modulation transfer in the human eye. *Journal of the Optical Society of America,* 1967, *57,* 401-406.

Watkins, D. W., & Berkley, M. A. The orientation selectivity of single neurones in cat striate cortex. *Experimental Brain Research,* 1974, *19,* 433-446.

Weisstein, N., & Harris, C. S. Masking and the unmasking of distributed representations in the visual system. In C. S. Harris (Ed.), *Visual coding and adaptability.* Hillsdale, New Jersey: Lawrence Erlbaum Associates, 1980.

Wiesel, T. N. Receptive fields of ganglion cells in the cat's retina. *Journal of Physiology,* 1960, *153,* 583-594.

Spatial-Frequency Channels in Human Vision: Detecting Edges Without Edge Detectors

Norma Graham

Columbia University

One early approach to the study of vision was to investigate the appearance of small patches of light and to try to explain the appearance of the whole visual field as the juxtaposition of the appearances of many small patches. A theoretical model that can be viewed as a natural descendant of this early approach, made appropriately more rigorous for the case of threshold experiments, is what I will call a single-channel model.

Despite considerable success in accounting for a variety of visual data, it now appears that a single-channel model is an inadequate description of visual perception. Moreover, a currently prevalent view is that trying to describe the appearance of a whole visual field as the juxtaposition of appearances of single points is doomed to failure from the start. Rather, according to this current view, the appearance of things depends on many stages of complicated information processing. The initial stages occur in the retina and further stages extend throughout the highest parts of the central nervous system.

A popular candidate for one of the earliest stages in this chain of visual information processing is a collection of *feature detectors* that simultaneously process different kinds of information in the visual stimulus. Each feature detector is presumed to respond vigorously only when the stimulus situation contains the appropriate "feature"—for example, an "edge detector" would respond only when there is an edge in the appropriate place on the retina.

What I intend to do here is describe the role one kind of psychophysical experiment has played in the rejection of single-channel models of the visual system and in the exploration of feature-detection models. In this kind of experiment, the visibility of compound patterns composed of two or more simpler patterns is compared to the visibility of the simpler patterns alone.

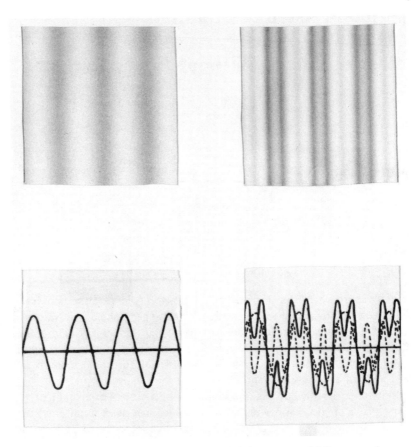

FIG. 1. A simple sine-wave grating containing one spatial frequency is shown on the top left, and a compound grating containing two spatial frequencies is on the top right. Underneath are the intensity profiles of the gratings, showing intensity of the grating at each horizontal location across the pattern. From Graham and Nachmias (1971).

In the first section I will review early experiments on the detection of compound patterns made up only of sinusoidal components (examples of a simple and a compound sine-wave pattern of this type are shown in Fig. 1). These early experiments produced strong evidence against the single-channel model for threshold vision. The findings can instead be interpreted as evidence for the existence of a rather odd type of feature detector—a detector or channel which responds only to patterns containing spatial frequencies within a limited range. Very roughly, being sensitive to a limited range of spatial frequencies means responding best to a particular size of element in the pattern (e.g. width of stripe); a more precise definition of spatial frequency is given below. I'll refer to this kind of channel as a *spatial frequency channel.*

In the second section I will discuss some recent experiments by Shapley and Tolhurst and by Kulikowski and King-Smith. These elegant experiments used patterns made up of sinusoids plus aperiodic stimuli (for example, sinusoids plus lines, sinusoids plus edges) as well as various combinations of aperiodic stimuli. These authors interpreted their results as evidence for the existence of several additional kinds of feature detectors—things like edge detectors and line detectors. The crucial distinction between these new feature detectors and the spatial frequency channels, as will be described later, is that each of these new feature detectors is supposed to respond to a broader range of spatial frequencies than does any spatial frequency channel.

I will argue, however, that these experiments do not actually provide persuasive evidence for the existence of additional feature detectors. On the contrary, my conclusion is that these new findings can probably be explained in terms of the same spatial frequency channels that were inferred from the earlier sinusoid-plus-sinusoid experiments. To reach that conclusion, I will reexamine the newer data in the light of a model that allows for probability summation among spatial frequency channels.

Much of the work referred to here is not mine and I will mention the authors in the appropriate places. Much of the work that is mine has been done in collaboration with Jacob Nachmias of the University of Pennsylvania.

A SINGLE-CHANNEL MODEL

Sine-Wave Gratings

Let's begin by looking at examples of gratings containing one sinusoidal component (the sine-wave pattern in Fig. 1 left) or two sinusoidal components (Fig. 1 right). Below each pattern is a graph that shows how the intensity of the grating varies as you move horizontally across it. For the left pattern, the graph depicts a single sinusoid added to a constant intensity (the mean luminance). For the right pattern, the graphed function is the sum of two sinusoids added to a constant intensity.

For patterns such as these, it is easy to specify and understand what *spatial frequency* is: The spatial frequencies contained in a pattern are the frequencies (cycles per unit distance) of the sinusoids that add up to equal the function relating intensity to distance across the pattern. Thus the left pattern contains only one spatial frequency and the right pattern contains two frequencies, having a ratio of three to one. For the pattern on the left, the spatial frequency is the number of peaks (bright bars) per unit of horizontal distance. We define the *contrast* of a stimulus (a measure of how different the light and dark bars are) as half the distance between the peak and trough intensities divided by the mean intensity.

First, let's describe a typical single-channel model of the visual system and then we can see what such a model predicts for the responses to simple sine-wave gratings, gratings containing only one sinusoidal component. At the same time we can review a few of the basic facts about sinusoidal stimuli.

A Single Channel

Those of you who like physiological analogues can think of a single channel as an array of retinal ganglion cells or lateral geniculate cells or even simple cortical cells. Each cell in the array has the same kind of receptive field (the same shape, the same orientation, the same size, everything the same except the position on the retina). But the receptive fields of different cells in the array, although they overlap, cover different portions of the visual field.

More abstractly, we can consider a single channel to be a two-dimensional array of "weighting functions" (defined below) corresponding point-by-point to the visual stimulus. (My use of the term "channel" is different from some other people's uses. Readers interested in a discussion of this terminology should see page 258.)   For the purposes of models like this, the visual stimulus is considered to be two-dimensional as it is on the retina rather than three-dimensional as it is in the world. In fact, we will be dealing only with stimuli that are effectively *one* dimensional: The striped gratings vary in intensity only along the horizontal axis; they maintain the same intensity along any vertical line. Therefore we need consider only a one-dimensional cut across the two dimensions of the single channel. In general, then, the response of a channel is a two-dimensional array corresponding point-by-point to the visual stimulus. But we'll usually be considering a one-dimensional cut across the response: the *response profile*.

The Weighting Function

The magnitude of the response at any point in the single channel's response profile can be specified by a *weighting function*. The weighting function indicates the extent to which light falling at various points on the retina adds to or subtracts from the response at the given point in the single channel. (The weighting function is so named because it describes how the light falling on different points is weighted in determining the response.) In terms of the physiological analogue, the weighting function would be a quantitative description of a cell's receptive field, and the response at a point in the channel would be the output from the cell connected to that receptive field.

One kind of hypothetical weighting function is represented by the small sketches in the top line of Fig. 2. The line as a whole represents a one-

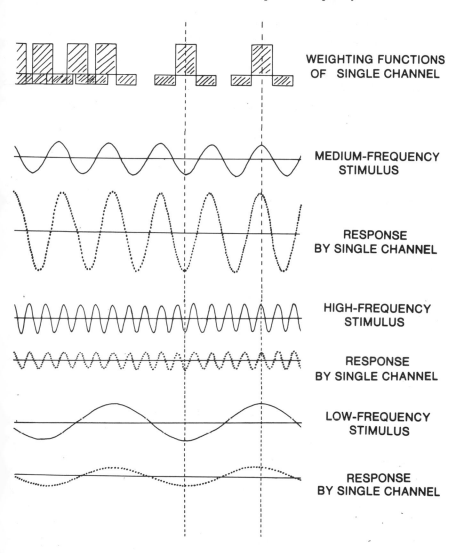

WEIGHTING FUNCTIONS
OF   SINGLE CHANNEL

MEDIUM-FREQUENCY
STIMULUS

RESPONSE
BY SINGLE CHANNEL

HIGH-FREQUENCY
STIMULUS

RESPONSE
BY SINGLE CHANNEL

LOW-FREQUENCY
STIMULUS

RESPONSE
BY SINGLE CHANNEL

FIG. 2.   Diagram of some of the weighting functions that determine the
responses of a single channel (top row). The channel's responses
(third, fifth, and seventh rows) to three gratings of different spatial frequencies (second, fourth, and sixth rows).

dimensional cut across the single channel. Each of the small sketches of the
weighting function indicates that the response at a given point of the channel is
increased by light falling anywhere within some small area of the retina and is
decreased by light falling anywhere within a surrounding area. (The weighting
function shown in the figure has a somewhat artificial "rectangular" distribu-

tion for the center excitatory area and for the surrounding inhibitory area. It is easy to substitute other, more plausible configurations.) The weighting functions should really be pictured as being densely distributed all along the top line, with many of them overlapping at any given point, but they have been thinned out for clarity here. Notice that the weighting functions at all points across the channel are assumed to be the *same*; this is an important assumption of the single-channel model.

Response to Different Spatial Frequencies

Your intuition may suggest that this single-channel model should produce big responses for gratings in which the bar-widths match the dimensions of the weighting function, and smaller responses for gratings of other bar-widths. The rest of Fig. 2 shows that such an intuition is approximately correct. Here we see the intensity profiles of three stimuli and the response at each point across the single channel to each of the three. Notice first that, conveniently, the response to any sine-wave stimulus is itself sinusoidal, as long as you are considering linear systems. (We are assuming that the single channel is linear: All it does is add and subtract.)

The second row of the figure shows the intensity profile of a sinusoidal grating of intermediate spatial frequency. Consider the response (third row in Fig. 2) at the middle of the bright bar at the extreme right end of the figure. There is a lot of excitation because a bright bar is illuminating the center of the weighting function (or receptive field on the retina). There is little inhibition because most of the surround of the weighting function is illuminated by dark bars. Little inhibition and a lot of excitation produces a big net response. When the peak response is large (compared to the mean response) we say the channel is responding well to this stimulus pattern.

Now consider the response at the middle of the dark bar. There is a lot of inhibition because most of the negative surround of the weighting function is illuminated by bright bars. The more strongly illuminated the inhibitory surround is, the less the net response. Furthermore, there is little excitation, because the excitatory center is getting little illumination from the dark bar. Thus there is very little response at this point in the channel. So the total difference between the peak response (the response in the middle of the bright bar) and the trough response (the response in the middle of the dark bar) is very large. A large difference between peak and trough also indicates that the channel is responding well to the grating.

However, when you consider a higher spatial frequency grating (such as that for which the intensity profile is shown in the fourth row of Fig. 2), the bars are so closely spaced that *many* bright and dark bars fall within the center of each weighting function. Likewise, many bright and dark bars fall within the surround. Thus the response at any point in the array is approximately the same as that at any other point, because there are always approximately the same number of bright bars as dark bars in both the center and surround. The peak response is small, and so is the difference between peak and trough. That is, the channel does not respond well to this high frequency grating.

Finally, consider what the response (seventh row) to a low spatial frequency grating (sixth row) is like. At the center of the bright bar, there is a lot of excitation (as for the medium spatial frequency) because the center of the weighting function is illuminated by a bright bar. But there is also a lot of inhibition (unlike the case for the medium spatial frequency) because the negative surround of the weighting function is also illuminated by the bright bar. A lot of excitation and a lot of inhibition leads to a smaller response than a lot of excitation and a little inhibition, so the peak response to the low-frequency grating is smaller than to the medium spatial frequency. We say that the channel is not responding well.

Like the peak response, the difference between the peak and *trough* response is also smaller for a low-frequency grating than for a medium frequency. In the middle of the dark bar there is little excitation (like the medium frequency case) but there is also little inhibition (unlike the medium frequency case). Little excitation coupled with little inhibition leads to a trough that is not as deep as for the medium spatial frequency. Therefore the difference between the peak response and trough response is relatively small for the low spatial frequency.

In short, a single-channel model with a center-surround type of weighting function predicts bigger responses to gratings of intermediate frequency than to gratings of lower or higher frequencies.

Psychophysical Data

In predicting the greatest response to intermediate frequencies, a single-channel model does agree well with psychophysical data. A human observer's responsiveness to a grating is often measured by finding the *contrast threshold*, the smallest light-dark contrast that enables the observer to tell there is a grating present rather than a blank field. (In these experiments, the average intensity is held constant while the contrast is varied.) Another measure of the same sort is *contrast sensitivity*, which is defined as the reciprocal of the contrast threshold; the higher the contrast threshold, the lower the contrast sensitivity.

Consider what should happen if a human observer were well described by a single-channel model and if we made the additional assumption that the contrast threshold is the smallest contrast necessary to produce a sufficiently large response somewhere across the single channel. In other words, we assume the contrast threshold is achieved when the contrast is high enough for the channel's peak response to exceed some criterion. Then we would expect the

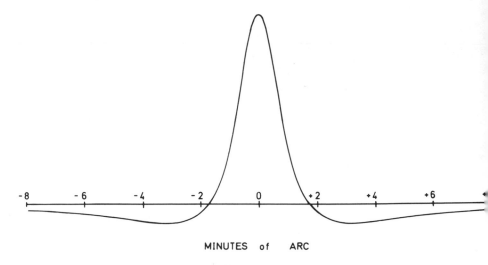

MINUTES of   ARC

FIG. 3. The weighting function for a single channel model which leads to accurate predictions of the data on human contrast sensitivity for gratings. From John Robson.

contrast threshold to be lowest (contrast sensitivity to be highest) for gratings of intermediate frequencies, since it is at intermediate frequencies that the channel produces the biggest response (for any given amount of stimulus contrast). This is just what does happen: It is well known that human contrast sensitivity is greatest at intermediate frequencies. In fact, you can make the single-channel model agree perfectly with human psychophysical data by simply picking out a weighting function with an appropriate shape. Figure 3 shows a weighting function that works well for human contrast threshold data.

Effect of Changing the Weighting Function

For future reference, it will be useful to consider now how changing the weighting function changes the channel's response to different spatial frequencies. The kind of weighting function we've already looked at, one central excitatory area flanked by surrounding inhibitory areas, always leads to a frequency response function something like the broadest one (B) shown in Fig. 4. It is a rather wide function—the maximum sensitivity is to a spatial frequency of 14 cycles/degree, yet sensitivity is substantial even to spatial frequencies as different as 5 or 30 cycles/degree. With this sort of weighting function, there is a sizable response to spatial frequencies that differ from the best frequency by a factor of two or more. (The function that gives the peak response to various frequencies is the same as what's called "the amplitude characteristic of the Fourier transform." It can be computed easily using the methods of Fourier analysis. It is important to note that although using the methods of

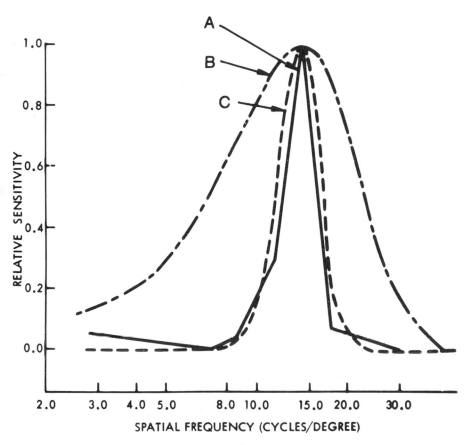

FIG. 4. Theoretical frequency response curves (B and C) for two different channels centered on the same spatial frequency but having different bandwidths. The third curve (A) is a frequency-response curve estimated from data. The vertical axis, marked "relative sensitivity," gives the peak response of the channel to a grating of some fixed criterion contrast (relative to the peak response produced by a 14 cycle/degree grating at the criterion contrast). Or equivalently, since we are considering linear channels, the vertical axis gives the reciprocal of the amount of contrast necessary to produce a peak response that reaches a criterion (relative to the contrast necessary at 14 cycles/degree). From Sachs, Nachmias, and Robson (1971).

Fourier analysis seems to imply analyzing a compound stimulus into its sinusoidal components, it does not in fact imply the use of a multiple-channels model.)

If you change the size of the weighting function (if, for example, you double the widths of both the center and surround but leave the shape unchanged), you will change the channel's best frequency (for example, from 14 cycles/degree to 7 cycles/degree) but you will not change the breadth of the response function. For example, if the original weighting function gave a response to frequencies between 5 and 30 cycles/degree, a ratio of 1 to 6, a weighting function twice as wide will give a response to frequencies between 2.5 and 15 cycles/degree, again a ratio of 1 to 6. This means that when you change only the size of the weighting function, the channel's frequency response function will keep the same shape when plotted against a logarithmic frequency scale as in Fig. 4, but it will be shifted horizontally.

Suppose you wanted to construct a channel that responds only to a very narrow range of spatial frequencies, something more like curves A and C of Fig. 4. These curves depict a sizable sensitivity only to spatial frequencies between 12 and 18 cycles/degree; a 10 or 20 cycles/degree grating gives only a negligible response. What kind of a weighting function would you need in order to produce such a narrow response curve? Figure 5 gives the rather peculiar answer: a multilobed weighting function with *several* evenly spaced excitatory and inhibitory areas.

A channel that is an array of such multilobed weighting functions is sensitive to a much narrower range of spatial frequencies than is the channel of Fig. 2.

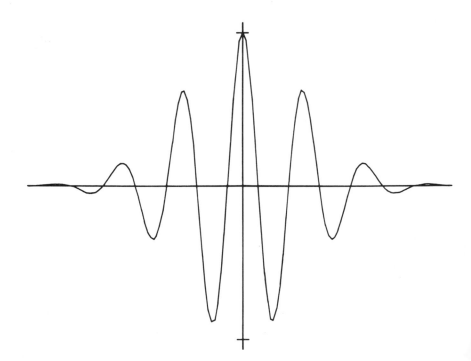

FIG. 5. The weighting function for a channel having a frequency response like that of curve C in Fig. 4. From John Robson.

To see why, first imagine a grating stimulating the channel with multilobed weighting functions, with a bright bar illuminating the central excitatory part of one particular multilobed weighting function. If the grating has the best spatial frequency for this weighting function, bright bars will fall in all the excitatory areas and dark bars will fall in all the inhibitory areas. Therefore there will be a very large response at this point in the channel. The large peak response means that the channel is very sensitive to this stimulus. (Similarly, the channel's response at the point where a *dark* bar falls on the central excitatory part of a multilobed weighting function will be a very small response, so the difference between the peak and trough responses of the channel will be large.)

Now imagine a grating with slightly narrower, more closely spaced bars, again with a bright bar falling on the central excitatory part of the weighting function. You don't need to imagine much of a change in the grating's frequency before dark bars start creeping inward into the outermost excitatory areas, thereby reducing the response. Slightly widening the bars has the same effect, as dark bars creep outward into the outermost excitatory areas. In short, any slight mismatch between the bar-spacing of the grating and the dimensions of the multilobed weighting function will lead to a much reduced response by the channel; thus the channel is sensitive to only a narrow range of spatial frequencies.

Response of a Linear Channel to Other Stimuli

Also for future reference, let's look at another convenient fact about sine waves. Knowing how the channel (or any linear system) responds to sine waves is enough to tell you how the channel responds to any stimulus at all. This apparently magical fact is true because two other facts are true: One—any stimulus at all can be treated as the sum of a number of sinusoidal stimuli; and two—a linear channel's response to a stimulus which is the sum of various component stimuli can be shown to equal the sum of the responses to the various component stimuli. So to calculate the channel's response to any arbitrary stimulus, you just need to know which sine waves the stimulus is the sum of, and then you add up the responses to those sine waves.

Sine Waves Added to Sine Waves

Let's go back to the main discussion. What does a single-channel model of the visual system predict for the response to sine waves? We have shown that a single-channel model can deal very well with thresholds for single sinusoidal gratings if an appropriate weighting function is chosen (Fig. 3). But how well can it do with thresholds for a compound grating composed of two sinusoids added together?

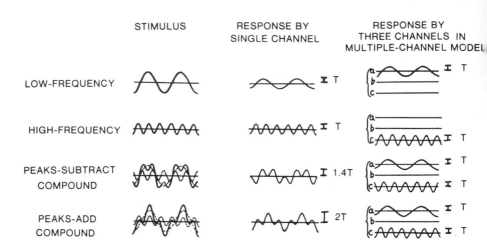

FIG. 6. Four grating patterns (left column) and the responses to them predicted by the single-channel (middle column) and multiple-channels models (right column—three channels are shown). The broken lines indicate the sinusoidal components of the compound gratings. From Graham and Nachmias (1971).

The left column of Fig. 6 presents the intensity profiles of several stimuli and the middle column shows the responses of the single channel to these stimuli. The top stimulus is a simple grating (a sine wave added to a constant luminance), with a contrast selected to put the grating at psychophysical threshold. Remember that we are assuming that "to be at psychophysical threshold" means "to produce a peak response that is as big as a certain criterion." This criterion size is labelled T (for "threshold") in Fig. 6. (In this model of the detection process, the threshold is determined entirely by the peak response. Therefore the spatial ordering of the response magnitudes in the response profile is of no importance. That is, if you took the set of response magnitudes and scrambled them into a new spatial order, you would still predict the same threshold. Another way of saying this is that in the kind of channel models that I am discussing, *all* of the spatial interactions (i.e. all the interactions that depend on distances between points) are a result of the weighting function.)

The second row shows a simple sinusoidal grating of three times the frequency of the first stimulus. Its contrast, too, was chosen to put the grating at threshold; that is, it has been adjusted so that the peak response matches the criterion T.

The third and fourth rows in Fig. 6 show two compound gratings that are combinations of the simple sinusoidal stimuli in the first and second rows. (In both combinations, the two component sine waves have been added together, and added to the same mean luminance as in the simple gratings.) In the compound grating shown in the third row, the two sine waves were positioned so that the darkest point of one coincided with the brightest point of the other (the *peaks-subtract* phase). In the fourth row, the component sine waves were positioned with the *brightest* point of one coinciding with the brightest point of the other (the *peaks-add* phase).

The single channel's response to each of these compound gratings can easily be computed from its responses to the simple gratings. Since the single channel is a linear device and each compound grating is a sum of the simple gratings, the response to the compound grating is just the sum the responses to the simple gratings. (Of course you have to position the simple response functions appropriately, so that they correspond with the positions of the simple sinusoidal components in the compound grating. In this discussion, all patterns are adjusted to have the same mean intensity. This means that, for a linear channel, the mean response across the channel is the same for all patterns and therefore can be ignored in deriving predictions that compare different patterns.) The responses shown in the second column were computed in this way. As you can see, the peak response to each of the compound gratings is now greater than T, the criterion for detection. In fact, it is 1.4 times T for the stimulus in the third row (the peaks-subtract stimulus) and 2.0 times T for the stimulus in the fourth row (the peaks-add stimulus). Therefore, according to this single-channel model, you should be able to reduce the contrast in each component of the peaks-add pattern by a factor of 2.0 and find that the peaks-add pattern would then be at threshold, because the peak response would then just equal T. You should be able to reduce the contrast in each component of the peaks-subtract pattern by a factor of 1.4 and find that the peaks-subtract pattern would be at threshold.

To put it another way, according to the single-channel model, the two compound gratings should be more visible than either simple grating, and further, the peaks-add compound should be more visible than the peaks-subtract. The brightest part of the peaks-add compound is brighter than the brightest part of the peaks-subtract compound, and both are brighter than the brightest parts of the simple gratings.

Evidence Against a Single-Channel Model

What happens when you actually measure the thresholds of humans for such simple and compound gratings? Rather strangely, but definitely, the compound gratings are *not* much more visible than the simple ones—certainly nothing like the predicted factors of 1.4 or 2.0. Moreover, relative position (phase) makes no difference—the peaks-add pattern is no more visible than the peaks-subtract.

This experimental finding is definitive evidence against the version of the single-channel model presented above. Is there some easy way to modify the single-channel model to make it fit this finding? Apparently not. Postulating compressive nonlinearities before or after the single channel doesn't help much. Instead of assuming, as we did above, that the peak response must reach some criterion in order for a pattern to be at psychophysical threshold, you might try some other assumption about the detection process. However, none of the obvious alternatives works, although some alternatives (such as probability summation across space, which will be discussed later in another context) do move the predictions closer to the data—that is, some relatively simple detection processes do lead to single-channel predictions of a difference between simple and compound stimuli that is somewhat less than the factors of 2 and 1.4 predicted by the peak-response criterion (but *not* as much less as found in the experimental data).

Of course, postulating a sufficiently *complicated* detection process as a substitute for the peak detector (which would be like postulating a large number of other stages of processing occurring after the single channel) might predict these data well and also might make an interesting model, but it would be a rather different model from those considered to date.

It should be mentioned that James Thomas and his colleagues at UCLA have done a series of experiments similar to these, involving the detection of disks of different sizes rather than gratings of different spatial frequencies. Their experiments also produced results inconsistent with a single-channel model.

MULTIPLE SPATIAL-FREQUENCY CHANNELS

So now we are left with the problem of explaining the unexpectedly low visibility of two sinusoidal gratings added together. On the basis of preliminary results somewhat similar to these results from adding up sine waves, Fergus Campbell and John Robson advanced a new model in 1968 as an alternative to the single-channel model. They proposed that the important part of the visual system for experiments like these is not a single channel but a collection of *many* channels.

Each of these multiple channels responds only to a relatively narrow range of spatial frequencies. One channel might respond only to low spatial frequencies, another only to high frequencies. The sensitivity of the whole visual system to any pattern is determined by whichever one of the multiple channels is most sensitive to the pattern. In particular, a pattern will be above threshold for the whole visual system whenever it is above threshold for *at least one* of the spatial-frequency channels.

Although one can certainly talk about these channels without specifying any particular physiological mechanism, I find it helpful to think of the multiple channels in more concrete terms. One can consider each channel as an array of receptive fields, or weighting functions, just like the single channel of the single-channel model. Each channel is specialized for a different range of spatial frequencies, so the weighting function (or the receptive field) for each channel has a different size—the channel for low spatial frequencies has a weighting function with much wider excitatory and inhibitory areas than the channel for intermediate spatial frequencies has, and so forth for other channels. This multiple channels model is quite similar to a model proposed by James Thomas, although Thomas's model was not developed to deal with sine-wave grating experiments.

Sine Waves Plus Sine Waves

To see what this multiple-channels model will predict for the threshold of two sine-wave gratings added together, let's look at the right hand column of Fig. 6. The lines labelled A, B, and C represent the responses of three different channels. Channel A is the channel that responds to the low-frequency sine wave in the left column, and it does not respond to the high frequency at all; channel C responds to the high frequency, and not at all to the low frequency; channel B doesn't respond to either one. Since the top stimulus in this figure is assumed to be at threshold and only channel A responds to it, the response in channel A must be at threshold—that is, the peak response by channel A must equal the criterion for threshold, marked T. Similarly for the second pattern: Channel C, in reacting to the second pattern, must give a peak response equal to T.

Now consider the peaks-subtract compound grating shown in the third row. How will channel A respond to it? The compound grating is the sum of the low-frequency and high-frequency sine waves pictured above it (and repeated as dotted lines in the third row). Therefore channel A's response to the compound grating is the sum of its response to the low-frequency component plus its response to the high-frequency component. Since channel A doesn't respond at all to the high-frequency component (its response profile is a flat line), its total response to the sum of the two components looks just like its response to the low-frequency grating alone. We've already said that the low-frequency grating is at threshold for channel A so the compound grating, which gives exactly the same response, must also be just at threshold. Similarly for channel C: Its response to the compound grating looks just like its response to the high-frequency component alone, so the compound grating is just at threshold for channel C. Since the compound grating is just at threshold for each channel individually, it is (according to the multiple-channels model's assumptions) just at threshold for the visual system as a whole. (The analysis differs somewhat if response variability is considered, as is done in the next section.)

So, unlike the single-channel model, and in much better accord with the psychophysical data, the multiple-channels model predicts that the peaks-subtract compound grating should be no more detectable than one of its components. We can go through the same analysis and reach precisely the same conclusion for the compound grating shown in the fourth row, the peaks-add stimulus. It is just at threshold for each channel individually and hence for the visual system as a whole. Therefore this compound grating should be no more detectable than either of its sinusoidal components, and the peaks-add and peaks-subtract gratings should be equally detectable. In other words, relative position or phase of the two components shouldn't matter at all. And that was one of the surprising aspects of the psychophysical data: Peaks-add and peaks-subtract gratings gave the same results.

Even this simple version of the multiple-channels model does quite a good job of predicting a human observer's performance when detecting these kinds of pattern: Compound gratings are (to a first approximation) no more detectable than their most detectable component, and the relative phase between components in a compound grating makes no difference to its detectability. In the next section we will find that when we take response variability into account, the multiple-channels model fits the data even more closely.

Probability Summation Among Multiple Channels

I have been talking as if there were no variability in the visual system, as if a grating with a contrast just below the threshold were invisible every time the subject looked at it and a grating with a slightly higher contrast, just above the threshold, were visible every time. But in fact there is a whole range of contrast levels for which a grating is sometimes visible and sometimes invisible. The "threshold" is arbitrarily defined as that contrast level at which the grating is seen a certain percentage of the time, usually 50%.

As Sachs, Nachmias, and Robson showed, in order to predict the thresholds for compound gratings exactly, one has to take the visual system's variability into account. It turns out that a very simple way of dealing with the variability will do, a way often referred to as "probability summation."

Consider again the response of the multiple channels to the gratings in Fig. 6. Remember that each of the sinusoidal components is individually at threshold; we've picked the appropriate amount of contrast to make that so. Thus on 50% of the trials with the low-frequency component alone, channel A's response is big enough for the observer to see something. Likewise, on 50% of the trials with the high-frequency component alone, channel C's response is big enough for the observer to see something. What happens when the compound grating is presented? According to the multiple-channels model, just the same thing as when its two components are presented separately: On 50% of the trials channel A responds to the compound grating and on 50% of the trials channel C responds. But the trials on which channel A responds are not all trials on which channel C responds (unless the variability in the two channels happens to be perfectly correlated). So on *more* than 50% of the trials *either* channel A or channel C (or both) gives a response big enough to meet the criterion for threshold. Therefore, according to the multiple-channels model, the observer sees something on *more* than 50% of the trials with the compound grating. This means the compound grating is somewhat more detectable than either of its components; how much more depends on the degree of correlation between the channels.

In fact, an assumption of complete independence (no correlation) between channels produces predictions that agree quantitatively with the data. This independence is ordinarily implied by the term probability summation. In general, *probability summation* among channels refers to the increase in the detectability of a pattern that results when two or more uncorrelated channels rather than one respond to the pattern ("summation" because there is an increase in detectability and "probability" because the increase is a direct result of the probabilistic nature of the process). Notice that probability summation can make a compound pattern more detectable than any of its components even if there is no "real" summation among components within any one channel— that is, even if, as far as the response of any one channel is concerned, presenting two (or more) components is no better than presenting one alone.

Thus, within the framework of a multiple-channels model, there are two possible causes of an increased detectability of a compound pattern relative to its components: "probability summation" resulting when channel responses are uncorrelated and more channels respond to the compound pattern than respond to any one of its components alone, and "summation within a channel" resulting when one of the channels responds better to the compound pattern than to any of its components. This distinction between kinds of summation will be very important in the next section.

An Example of Probability Summation

Probability summation can sometimes make a compound grating *substantially* more visible than either of its components. Let me give an example. The data shown in Fig. 7 come from a two-alternative forced-choice experiment that John Robson and I ran, comparing the detectability of compound gratings containing three components (rather than two as in Fig. 2) to the detectability of each of the three components alone. The components' frequencies were in the ratio of 1 to 3 to 9. In the compound gratings, the three components were arranged in either of two phases, and the relative contrasts in the three com-

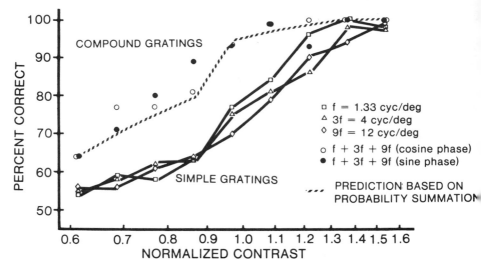

FIG. 7. Percent correct in a two-alternative forced-choice experiment for three simple gratings and two compound gratings containing the three frequencies of the simple gratings but in two different phases. In the compound gratings, the components were arranged so that their peaks coincided (cosine phase) or so that the combination approximated a square-wave grating (sine phase). The broken line is the prediction for the compound gratings based on probability summation among the three simple components.

Each of the curves in the figure has been horizontally translated (which is why the horizontal axis is marked "normalized contrast" instead of "contrast") so that the compound grating represented by any one of the circles is made up of the three components whose detectabilities are given by the three symbols directly below the circle. Notice that the contrasts of the three components in any one of the compound gratings were chosen so that all three would be approximately equally detectable.

The mean luminance of the 7.25° × 4.5° desaturated green (P31) display (29 × 18 centimeters at a distance of 2.28 meters) was 100 millilamberts, and the display was surrounded by a homogeneous white screen of approximately the same mean luminance with outer dimensions of 60 by 60 centimeters. Each trial consisted of two 600 millisecond presentations of a tone, separated by 300 milliseconds; during one tone a grating was presented and during the other the display remained unpatterned. The onset and offset of the grating were gradual, the contrast of the grating during the 600 millisecond period being proportional to $e^{-(t/100)^2}$ where t varied from −300 milliseconds to 300 milliseconds. Trials were initiated by the subject. In any one block of trials, 40 patterns (eight contrast levels in each of the three simple and two compound gratings) were presented once each in a random order. In accordance with a "staircase" rule, contrast levels were sometimes changed between blocks to keep performance at a fairly constant level. Each data point in the figure comes from between 60 and 150 trials. The observer was John Robson, viewing the display binocularly with normal spectacle corrections.

ponents were adjusted so that all three were about equally detectable when presented alone. (In accord with this adjustment of relative contrasts, the horizontal axis in Fig. 7 is labelled "normalized contrast." The normalization was done by dividing the actual contrast by a different factor for each component frequency. Each point on the horizontal axis represents three different frequencies' contrasts in the same ratio in which they appear in the compound gratings. The value of 1.0 was assigned for convenience to that normalized contrast closest to the one producing 75% correct.)

On each trial the observer had to say whether the grating was in the first or second interval. The three lower curves in Fig. 7 show the improvement in seeing each of the three simple gratings as contrast is increased. The circles up above give similar data for a compound grating. Each circle gives the detectability for a compound grating made up of the three simple components whose detectabilities are represented by the three symbols directly below the circle. The dashed line shows the predictions for the compound grating's detectability based on probability summation among the three simple components. As you can see, the fit is quite good, considering the binomial variability inherent in the data.

In a two-alternative forced-choice experiment like this one, a subject will be correct on 50% of the trials if he simply guesses randomly. The 50% guessing rate has to be taken into account when computing the probability-summation predictions. Thus, if a subject is correct on each component 50% of the time (no more than chance), the prediction from probability summation alone is that he will be correct on the complex grating only 50% of the time.

The threshold in forced-choice experiments is typically defined as the contrast needed for 75% correct. For each of the three simple components in Fig. 7, then, the threshold is at a normalized contrast of about 1.0. The threshold for the compound grating is quite a bit lower, at a contrast of about 0.8, lower than the lowest of the thresholds for any of the three components. This substantial difference, a ratio of about 0.8 (0.1 log unit), is fully explained by probability summation among the multiple channels.

It's important to bear in mind that even though the compound gratings in this experiment did have thresholds considerably lower than any of their components' thresholds, the data are still far from consistent with a single-channel model. A single-channel model would predict that when you add up three components in peaks-add phase, you should need only one-third as much contrast to put the resulting compound grating at threshold. In Fig. 7 that would be a contrast of 0.33, off the graph to the left.

Measuring the Bandwidth of a Spatial-Frequency Channel

So far I haven't said anything specific about the *bandwidth* of each of the multiple channels. How wide a range of spatial frequencies does a given channel respond to? All I've said is that the range is considerably narrower than for the single-channel model. In that model, the single channel responds to the entire visible range of spatial frequencies, so it predicts that a compound pattern should be more detectable than any one of its component frequencies, no matter how far apart they are. We know that the channels can't be *that* broadly responsive, because the data show that for widely separated frequencies, a compound pattern is no more detectable than you'd expect from probability summation among independent detectors that each respond to only one component frequency.

There is a way to estimate more precisely the range of responsiveness of an individual channel. Once Sachs, Nachmias, and Robson had shown that (allowing for probability summation among channels) the multiple-channels model accurately predicts the findings for two widely separated frequencies (which were assumed to stimulate completely separate channels), they could use this model to estimate the bandwidth of an individual channel by choosing frequencies that were quite close together.

When two neighboring frequencies were used, they found that the compound pattern was more detectable than probability summation predicts. The "extra" detectability could be attributed to summation within individual channels—to individual channels' having responded to both frequencies. They assumed that only two channels were significantly involved in the detection of any two-component grating—the two, independent channels with center frequencies equal to the two frequencies in the compound grating.

To calculate backwards from the amount of extra detectability for compound patterns to the sensitivity of individual channels, Sachs, Nachmias, and Robson had to use some assumption about the combined effect of neighboring frequencies on an individual channel, that is, about the exact form of the summation within each individual channel. For the patterns used in their experiments, their assumption was equivalent to the following model of a channel (a model that is consistent with everything said about channels so far): Each channel is a linear system exactly like the single channel of Fig. 6's middle column, except that it is sensitive to a narrower range of frequencies; a pattern is at threshold for a channel whenever the peak response across the channel meets a criterion; and the variability in a channel's response (which leads to probability summation among channels) comes from one of two equivalent sources—either the criterion varies from time to time, or the whole response profile of a channel is raised or lowered by a noise signal added to it, which varies from time to time.

In their study, Sachs, Nachmias, and Robson measured the detectability of compound gratings containing two components, one of which always had a frequency of 14 cycles/degree, and so they were able to estimate the frequency response of the channel centered at 14 cycles/degree. You've already seen their estimate of the frequency response of that channel; it is the extremely narrow curve in Fig. 4. Remember that there is nothing mysterious about an extremely narrow frequency-response curve. If you think of a channel as an array of receptive fields or of weighting functions, the frequency-response curve is narrow if the weighting function has not only an excitatory central area and an inhibitory surrounding area, but also auxiliary areas of excitation and inhibition (like Fig. 5).

Studies by Quick and by Sachs, Nachmias, and Robson suggest that, for channels centered at lower spatial frequencies, the estimated bandwidth (on a log frequency axis) may be a good deal broader than for the channel at 14 cycles/degree. If so, then for the lower spatial frequency channels, this estimated bandwidth implies that the weighting functions may be simple center-surround weighting functions.

Discrepant Estimates of Bandwidth

The bandwidth that Sachs, Nachmias, and Robson estimated for the 14 cycles/degree channel is a good deal narrower than the bandwidth usually deduced from a different type of experiment, involving adaptation or masking. The explanation of this difference is not at all clear. It could be that the channels revealed by summation experiments are not the same channels as those revealed by adaptation/masking experiments. Another possibility is that the models currently used to deduce bandwidth from summation and adaptation/masking experiments are inadequate. For instance, perhaps adaptation itself could cause an increase in bandwidth; this possibility was considered and rejected by Lange, Stecher, and Sigel (1973).

Inadequacies in the models that are used (either explicitly or, more often, implicitly) to deduce bandwidth from adaptation/masking experiments are beyond the scope of this discussion. But a possible shortcoming of the model used to deduce bandwidth from summation experiments was alluded to earlier, in the discussion of the single-channel model. There are other plausible assumptions, besides those described above, that we could make about the detection process and about the variability in the channel's responses. Some of these alternative assumptions (one example is discussed in the next section) would lead us to derive a broader bandwidth estimate from summation experiments, an estimate more in line with those from adaptation/masking experiments. However, precise quantitative agreement between such estimates based on the different kinds of experiments remains to be shown, and trying to show it may well reveal more problems. (The assumption that only two channels are involved in the detection of a two-component compound grating may well be another inadequacy of the model used by Sachs, Nachmias, and Robson. But if more than two channels are involved, using the assumption of only two probably makes the estimated bandwidth broader than the actual bandwidth. Thus, changing this assumption could only make the bandwidth estimated from summation experiments even narrower.)

Probability Summation Across the Spatial Extent of a Channel

I will now give an example of a possible detection process other than the simplest form of peak-response detection. The example is particularly appropriate because it involves another instance of probability summation. However, understanding the example is not necessary for understanding the material that follows this section.

In the models described earlier, all of the variability in a channel's responses was assumed to come from one of two equivalent sources—variability in the threshold criterion for each channel or variability in a noise signal that is added to the *whole* response profile of the channel, thereby raising or lowering the profile as a whole. Neither source of variability changes the basic shape of the response profile; points that have equal responses at one time (the peaks, for example) also have equal responses at any other time. In other words, neither of these two sources of variability entails any variation in the relative magnitudes of responses at different points across a channel.

But other sources of variability in a channel's responses are possible and are perhaps even more reasonable. After all, why shouldn't the relative response magnitudes at different points across a channel vary? In the physiological analogue, the responses at different points across a channel are produced by different neurons. If the sensitivity of neurons varies over time, and if the sensitivities of different neurons are not perfectly correlated, there would have to be variation over time in the relative response magnitudes at different points.

Let's try assuming that all the variability in a channel's responses comes from the variability of response magnitudes at individual points across the channel (and not from the two spatially uniform sources of variability mentioned above). At any one moment, the response profile will look more irregular than those in Fig. 6; some "bumps" will be higher than others, for instance. On different trials, the peak response (the highest bump) will occur at different locations—sometimes at a location that doesn't even correspond to a peak in the stimulus.

We can still assume that a pattern is at threshold whenever the peak response reaches a criterion, but now the particular location in the channel that produces the peak response will vary from trial to trial. In this model of the detection process, there will, therefore, be probability summation across the spatial extent of a channel: When there are *more* locations at which a very large response often occurs, there are more chances on any particular trial to get a very large peak response. Therefore, the channel will be more likely to detect the stimulus, and will be more sensitive to the pattern. (In this model of the detection process, as in the simple peak-response model described earlier, the spatial ordering of the response magnitudes is of no importance.)

So, for example, as the number of bars in a grating is increased, a channel's sensitivity to the grating will increase, because more points in the channel will have a chance to detect the grating. (In addition, of course, there will still be probability summation among different channels, because whether or not each channel's peak response exceeds the threshold criterion will still vary from trial to trial.)

As Granger (1973) pointed out, this new model of a detection process, including probability summation across space, predicts that a channel will show *less* summation between components of a compound grating than predicted by the simple peak-detection model. Why this is so can be seen by carefully comparing a channel's responses to simple and to compound gratings. Figure 8 shows the profiles of a channel's responses to a single grating of 12 cycles/degree and to a compound grating of 12 cycles/degree combined with 11 cycles/degree. The contrasts in the gratings were chosen so that the peak response would be the same height in both profiles. If a channel had a simple peak-detection process, therefore, it would be equally sensitive to both patterns.

However, according to the new model, the profiles in Fig. 8 represent only *average* responses. The probability of getting a peak response that meets the criterion on a particular trial does not depend solely on the peak in the average response profile. Rather, it depends on the *number of different locations* across the channel that produce large average responses (and, of course, on how large those responses are). As is clear in Fig. 8, the "beating" between components produces only a few high points in the compound grating's average response profile, whereas there are many high points in the simple grating's profile. Therefore, according to the new model, the channel will be a good deal less likely to detect the compound grating than to detect the simple grating. In short, a model allowing for probability summation across space predicts much less detectability for the compound grating relative to the detectability of the component frequencies (that is, much less summation within a channel) than does the simple peak-detection model.

The upshot is that if we were now to assume that there is probability summation across the spatial extent of a channel, then we would expect compound stimuli to be less detectable than we expected when we were assuming simple peak detection. So when we find experimentally that a compound stimulus is not very much more detectable than its components, we would no longer assume that this means each channel is very insensitive to frequencies other than its optimal one. We would conclude instead that the channel is more sensitive to nonoptimal frequencies than we had previously thought. And saying that a channel is more sensitive to nonoptimal frequencies than we had thought is the same as saying that the channel's bandwidth is broader than we had thought.

Preliminary calculations suggest that, when probability summation across space is considered, the data from Sachs, Nachmias, and Robson's experiment may be consistent with an estimated bandwidth almost as large as that of the broadest curve shown in Fig. 4. This bandwidth is substantially larger than

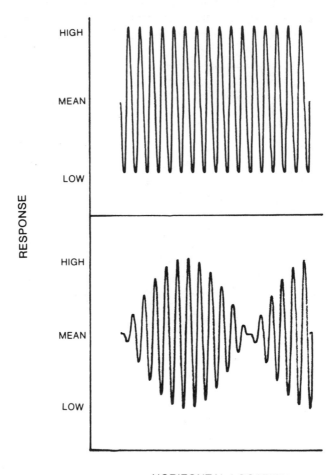

HORIZONTAL LOCATION

FIG. 8. The top graph is a channel's response profile to a simple grating of 12 cycles/degree, and the bottom graph is the response profile to a compound grating containing components of 11 cycles/degree and 12 cycles/degree. The contrasts of the gratings were chosen so that the two response profiles would have the same peak height. In particular, the contrasts in the two components of the compound grating were chosen so that the responses to each component alone would have the same peak height. Hence, the contrast in the 12 cycles/degree simple grating was twice the contrast of the 12 cycles/degree component in the compound grating.

that originally estimated and, if correct, the weighting function for the 14 cycles/degree channel might be of the center-surround type. However, it is an open question whether or not probability summation across space should be included in the model of a spatial frequency channel. And it is worth emphasizing that this broader bandwidth still is not nearly wide enough to make the multiple-channel model into a single-channel model.

Summary

What I have said up to this point can be summarized as follows: To explain the measured thresholds of compound gratings composed of several sinusoidal components, it is not sufficient to assume a single-channel model. It *is* sufficient to assume probability summation among multiple channels each of which responds to only a relatively narrow range of spatial frequencies. Exactly how narrow a range depends on the particular model of a channel's detection process that is assumed. The range is narrower, for example, when simple peak detection is assumed than when probability summation across spatial extent is considered. When I refer to a channel as "narrow" in what follows, I mean only that the range of frequencies to which the channel responds is narrow enough to require at least several such channels to span the range of frequencies to which a human observer is sensitive.

EDGE DETECTORS AND OTHER NEW FEATURE DETECTORS

In the rest of the chapter I would like to discuss some recent interesting experiments by Shapley and Tolhurst and by Kulikowski and King-Smith. These experiments were interpreted by their authors as evidence for other kinds of feature detectors in addition to spatial-frequency channels of the sort discussed above. First I'll review the interpretations given by the authors and then I'll go on to look at an alternative explanation that assumes there are no feature detectors other than the spatial-frequency channels.

Sine Waves Plus Broadband Stimuli

Rather than adding sine waves only to sine waves as in the experiments described above, Shapley and Tolhurst and Kulikowski and King-Smith added sine waves to broadband "test stimuli," such as edges and lines. (A *broadband stimulus* is a stimulus that can be considered to be the sum of a large number of sine-wave components, with a fairly large range of different frequencies. All nonrepetitive or aperiodic stimuli are broadband. An edge stimulus is a bright homogeneous field next to a dark homogeneous field. A line stimulus is a bright stripe superimposed on a dark field. The intensity profiles of an edge and of a line, as well as of the other aperiodic stimuli that were used, are shown in the insets of Fig. 11).

They did their experiments in the following way: They set the contrast in the sine-wave grating at some level below threshold. They then had the subject adjust the contrast in the superimposed test stimulus (in the edge, for example) until the subject could just barely see that there was a pattern present instead of a blank field. (The mean intensity of the pattern was held constant while the contrast was being adjusted.) This procedure was repeated with several subthreshold values (including zero) of sine-wave contrast.

The data they obtained were plotted as in Fig. 9: The test-stimulus contrast needed to make the compound pattern visible was plotted for each level of contrast in the subthreshold sine wave. Their actual data looked much like the fictitious data in Fig. 9. The points fell on a straight line, and the line intersected the horizontal axis at a contrast far above the threshold for the sine-wave grating alone (here called 1.0).

Frequency Responses of the New Detectors

The investigators interpreted these results within the framework of the following model: A large number of different feature detectors exist, each of these detectors is a linear system, and a stimulus is always detected by the detector that has the lowest threshold for that stimulus. Notice that there is no provision for probability summation in their model—that is, it never happens that the relative sensitivities of feature detectors fluctuate so that a stimulus is sometimes detected by one feature detector and sometimes by another.

Using their model, they could easily interpret data like that of Fig. 9. The data were gathered using added sine waves with low contrasts, including zero. All of the data points fall on a straight line as would be true if only a single linear feature detector were acting. Therefore they assumed that a single feature detector did determine all the data points. That detector would be the one with the lowest threshold for the test stimulus alone (i.e. the detector that determines the point on the plot where the sine-wave contrast is zero) and so will be called the "test-stimulus detector."

Then they could infer the test-stimulus detector's sensitivity to sine waves of various frequencies by using data like that in Fig. 9. (Why not directly measure the detector's sensitivity for a sine wave by presenting a sine wave to the observer? You can't, according to this kind of model, because when you present a sine wave by itself, its threshold is determined by whatever detector is most sensitive to the sine wave rather than by the test-stimulus detector.) The way to infer the test-stimulus detector's sensitivity is to see where the straight line through data like that in Fig. 9 cuts the horizontal axis: That intercept should tell what contrast in the sine wave would produce a threshold

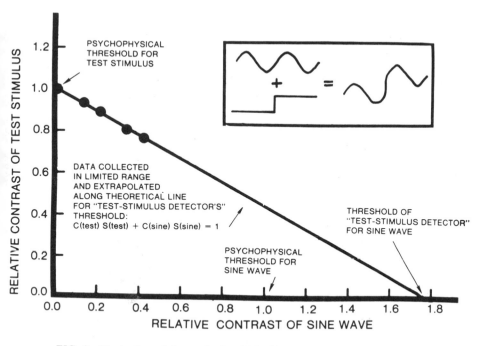

FIG. 9. Illustration of the method used by Shapley and Tolhurst and by Kulikowski and King-Smith to measure the "sensitivity of a test-stimulus detector to sine waves." Inset at upper right shows the intensity profile for one kind of stimulus they used—a combination of an edge and a sine wave. Data points are fictitious points typical of their actual data, showing, for each amount of contrast in the sine wave, how much contrast in the edge is necessary to make the compound pattern just visible to the observer. The straight line drawn through the data points is assumed to represent the responses of a linear "test-stimulus detector" whose behavior is described by the equation given in the figure, where C(test) and C(sine) are the contrasts in the test stimulus and sine, respectively, and S(test) and S(sine) are the sensitivities of the test-stimulus detector for the test stimulus and sine, respectively. (Sensitivity is, as usual, the reciprocal of threshold.)

response by the test-stimulus detector when there is no contrast at all in the test stimulus (0.0 on the vertical axis). So the reciprocal of this intercept is the test-stimulus detector's sensitivity to that sine wave.

For each test stimulus, Kulikowski and King-Smith and Shapley and Tolhurst used sine waves of a number of different spatial frequencies, finding the intercept for each one, as shown for the fictitious data in Fig. 10 (left). Then, by plotting the reciprocals of the values of those intercepts against the spatial frequency, they produced a *frequency-sensitivity curve* like that in Fig. 10 (right). This curve shows, for each frequency of sine wave, the inferred "sen-

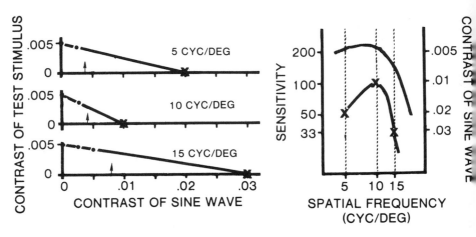

FIG. 10. The three plots on the left are the fictitious results of adding sine waves of three different frequencies (5, 10, and 15 cycles/degree) to a test stimulus. See Fig. 9 for more details about the method. The plot on the right shows the "frequency-sensitivity curve of the test-stimulus detector" that is derived from the plots on the left (and from similar plots for other frequencies). For each spatial frequency, the curve gives the reciprocal of the intercept from a plot like those on the left. (The righthand axis shows the actual value of the intercept.)

sitivity of the test-stimulus detector" for that sine wave. Notice that the steeper the line on one of the plots in Fig. 10 (left), the greater the corresponding sensitivity on the frequency-sensitivity curve in Fig. 10 (right). I will sometimes refer, therefore, to the inferred sensitivity of the test-stimulus detector for a sine wave as "the effectiveness of a sine wave in reducing the threshold for the test stimulus," as a reminder of what was actually measured.

Figure 11 shows the actual frequency-sensitivity curves from Kulikowski and King-Smith's data for six different test stimuli (one of which was a sine-wave grating as in the earlier experiments). The lower curve in each panel shows the data for the sensitivity of the test-stimulus detector. The upper curve is the psychophysical contrast-sensitivity function. Shapley and Tolhurst's curve for an edge, not shown here, is similar to Kulikowski and King-Smith's. As you can see in Fig. 11, there are at least five different curves for the six different test stimuli. (The curves for the two lines shown in the upper right and lower left panels are very similar and might be considered identical.) By these investigators' interpretation, this indicates the existence of five different detectors.

Weighting Functions of the New Detectors

Now, if these detectors are indeed linear systems (as was suggested by the straightness of the data plotted as in Fig. 9), the curves in Fig. 11 are just the

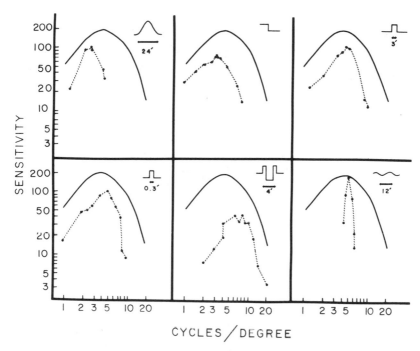

CYCLES / DEGREE

FIG. 11. Data from Kulikowski and King-Smith's experiments adding sine waves to six different test stimuli. The top curve in each panel is shown for reference and is the usual psychophysical contrast sensitivity function; it gives the reciprocal of the threshold contrast for a simple sinusoidal grating as a function of the spatial frequency of the grating. The lower curves connect the data points for the sensitivity of six "test-stimulus detectors" calculated by the method illustrated in Figs. 9 and 10. The test stimuli were a blurry bar (upper left), an edge (upper middle), a 3-minute wide line (upper right), a 0.3-minute line (lower left), a triphasic light-dark pattern (lower middle) and a sine-wave (lower right).

frequency responses of linear systems. So the curves in Fig. 11 can easily be transformed mathematically to reveal the spatial weighting functions that characterize the various detectors. (Just as the spatial weighting function can be transformed to give the frequency response by taking the Fourier transform, you can take the inverse Fourier transform of the frequency response (if you are willing to assume something about the phase characteristics of the system) in order to get the spatial weighting function.)

The results of this transformation are shown in Fig. 12. The weighting function of the edge detector consists of one excitatory region next to an inhibitory region; the grating detector has a multilobed weighting function much like that shown earlier for the original interpretation of the Sachs, Nachmias, and Rob-

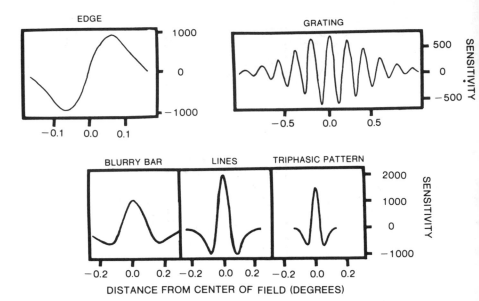

FIG. 12. The weighting functions characteristic of the detectors for which the frequency responses are shown in Fig. 11. There are only five weighting functions shown because the data for the two widths of line (upper right and lower left in Fig. 11) were so similar. These weighting functions were calculated from the data in Fig. 11 by using the assumptions that the detectors were linear and that certain kinds of symmetry would be found in the weighting functions. Notice that the scales on the axes are different for the different stimuli.

son data (Fig. 5); and the other detectors have various versions of a center-surround weighting function.

These weighting functions, strictly speaking, describe the detection of the test stimulus when the test stimulus occupies a particular location in the visual field (since the test stimulus was presented only in one location in these experiments). Presumably, however, similar responses could be evoked over a wide area of the visual field. Then you could describe the detection of an edge, for example, by an array of the appropriate weighting functions (each weighting function being an excitatory region next to an inhibitory region) spread over a large part of the visual field. You might refer to this whole array as the "edge detector" or you might refer to each weighting function as an "edge detector." Either usage will make sense in everything that follows. In any case, in line with the previous definition of a "channel," you might well refer to the whole array of weighting functions as a channel.

The channel deduced from the case where the test stimulus was a grating is akin to a spatial-frequency channel. (It might not be exactly the same as a spatial-frequency channel, because the logic used in deducing it, which ignored probability summation, might not be quite right.) The channels deduced from cases where the test stimuli were nonrepetitive (and therefore broadband) are distinguished from the spatial-frequency channels by their responsiveness to a much broader band of spatial frequencies.

Other Predictions

If the detectors are linear, one can make two kinds of testable predictions from the above data. The expected results for various other combination stimuli, like edges and lines added together, are predictable from the weighting functions (or equivalently from the sine-wave sensitivity profiles). And the actual threshold of the visual system for a test stimulus alone is also predictable. The investigators made these predictions and checked some of them against data; the predictions fit the data quite well.

BROADBAND FEATURE DETECTORS OR PROBABILITY SUMMATION AMONG SPATIAL-FREQUENCY CHANNELS?

Shapley and Tolhurst's and Kulikowski and King-Smith's experiments and interpretations make rather a pretty story, explaining quantitatively a variety of interesting results. And in some ways, edge detectors and line detectors are more appealing to common sense than are the spatial-frequency channels. We've all seen and drawn lines and edges, whereas sinusoidal gratings are a laboratory curiosity.

Too Many Channels?

However, two things bothered us about these studies. First, almost any time a new test stimulus is used a new feature detector—a new channel—is found. How many channels are we going to end up with? Somehow it seems wrong to end up with an infinite number of them. In some sense of the word, of course, there *must* be a different channel for each stimulus that we can *name* differently; if we can recognize two things as different, then somewhere in the nervous system the responses to these two things must be different; the information about the two things must be channeled differently at some point. But that is not the kind of channel I thought we were studying and it is not the kind of channel people talk about studying—we talk as if we were dealing with a limited number of feature detectors which form an early stage in visual information processing.

Probability Summation

The second bothersome thought was: "What would happen if you tried to take probability summation into account?", or in other words, "Where have all the spatial-frequency channels gone?" Shapley and Tolhurst and Kulikowski and King-Smith's logic assumes that there is no probability summation, that whatever detector has the lowest threshold for the pattern will always detect the pattern (i.e. there will be no variability from trial to trial in the relative magnitude of the responses from various detectors and thus it will never happen that on one trial one detector has the biggest response and on another trial another detector does). Using this assumption, they could indeed rule out the possibility that any of the spatial-frequency channels detects the broadband test stimulus. According to their logic, if a spatial-frequency channel *ever* detects the broadband test stimulus (or the combination of test stimulus with a very low contrast sine wave), then it must *always* detect the broadband test stimulus. And the kind of curve plotted in Fig. 11 would look like the narrow frequency response of a spatial-frequency channel, just like the data from a sine-plus-sine experiment. Obviously, the broadband-stimulus curves don't look narrow, so it does seem that the spatial-frequency detectors play no role in detecting broadband stimuli.

The assumption that there is no probability summation was certainly a reasonable one to begin with, especially since it led to such good quantitative predictions. But we know that probability summation does occur in the sine-plus-sine experiments, so a model that ignores probability summation (like Shapley & Tolhurst's or Kulikowski & King-Smith's) cannot explain those experiments completely.

Threshold for an Edge

Once you acknowledge the presence of probability summation, it becomes much more difficult to decide whether various test stimuli are being detected by new kinds of feature detectors or by conglomerates of spatial-frequency channels. For example, you might try to make a straightforward calculation of what probability summation among spatial-frequency channels would predict about the threshold for an edge. To perform such a calculation you'd need to know how many channels there are (which we do not know), what their frequency response is (which we do not know, except at 14 cycles/degree), and what the lower part of their psychometric function looks like. With such a large area of ignorance in which to make auxiliary assumptions it is, as you might expect, possible to construct a model, involving only probability summation among spatial-frequency channels, that does accurately predict the threshold for an edge. The problem, though, is that when so many auxiliary assumptions are used to predict so little data, you cannot claim the successful prediction as a clear validation of the model.

Sine Waves Plus Broadband Stimuli

So it seemed worthwhile to see whether we could devise a testable model with fewer auxiliary assumptions, which could be checked against some other kind of data. In particular, we asked what probability summation among spatial-frequency channels would predict about the experiments using broadband test stimuli combined with sine waves. If these predictions had disagreed with Shapley and Tolhurst and Kulikowski and King-Smith's data (no matter what kind of auxiliary assumptions were made), we would at last have had a conclusive demonstration of the insufficiency of spatial-frequency channels. As it turned out, the predictions agreed with all their data using only a few reasonable auxiliary assumptions. This agreement gives considerable support to the view that the only kind of channels involved in the detection of threshold stimuli are spatial-frequency channels.

Qualitative Predictions from a Probability-Summation Model

Let's consider at a qualitative level (before going on to some quantitative predictions) what you might expect to happen when a sine wave is added to a broadband test stimulus, if you think the only relevant part of the visual system is a set of spatial-frequency channels and if you allow for probability summation.

The broadband test stimulus activates a certain subset of the spatial-frequency channels: the subset that responds to the spatial frequencies of which the test stimulus is composed. What happens when you add a sine wave to the test stimulus? If the sine wave's spatial frequency is *not* contained in the test pattern, the sine wave will not affect the channels that are responding to the test stimulus. So at low contrasts the added sine wave will have no effect at all on the threshold for a combination of itself and the test stimulus. The sine wave will not contribute anything to the detection of the test-plus-sine combination until the sine wave's contrast is high enough to strongly activate its *own* spatial-frequency channel. And then the sine wave will contribute only because its own channel is probability summating with the channels that are responding to the test stimulus, not because it is increasing the response of any of the channels that the test stimulus is activating.

However, you would expect something quite different to happen if you add a sine wave of a frequency that *is* a substantial component of the test stimulus. As soon as you add any of the sine wave at all, no matter how low its contrast, you increase the likelihood of detection. When the sine wave is added, the response of the channel tuned to the sine wave's frequency goes up from a low level (due to the test stimulus alone) to a higher level. So the threshold for detecting the test-plus-sine combination is lower than the threshold for the test stimulus alone.

Of course, if the test pattern were a sine wave with the same frequency as the sine wave you are adding, the threshold would be even lower. In that case you would be adding a sine wave to a sine wave of the same frequency, so only one channel would be involved in detecting either the test stimulus or the test-plus-sine combination. For a broadband test stimulus, though, containing many frequencies, a large number of different spatial-frequency channels is involved in detecting the test stimulus. Adding a sine wave increases the response of only one (or a few) of them, so there is only a small effect on the threshold.

More generally, if only spatial frequency channels are involved, the effectiveness of adding a sine wave to a test stimulus should depend directly on how much of that sine wave's spatial frequency is present in the test stimulus—the greater the relative amount of the spatial frequency present, the greater the effectiveness of adding it. Notice that, qualitatively, this is what does happen in the experiments (Fig. 11). When a blurry bar (which contains only low spatial frequencies) was used, only sine waves with low spatial frequencies were effective; when a triphasic light-dark-light pattern (which contains only high spatial frequencies) was used, only sine waves with high spatial frequencies were effective.

Predictions for Simple Test Stimuli

Can we calculate *quantitative* predictions from a model with probability summation among spatial-frequency channels and no other feature detectors? For the kind of experiment in which a sine wave is added to a test stimulus, it is rather easy to calculate predictions, *if* you choose a certain kind of test stimulus. Figure 13 shows the results of some calculations for four specially selected test stimuli. For these four stimuli, the calculations are easy because we don't have to worry about how many channels there are and what their bandwidths are.

One of the four test stimuli was a sine wave grating. The other three test stimuli consisted of two, three, or five sine waves added together. The sine waves in any one test stimulus were very different in frequency, so each sine wave would affect a different channel. The contrasts in the sine waves were adjusted so that each of the two, three, or five channels involved was presumably responding at the same level. (It was assumed, for convenience, that a sine wave affects only one channel.) To carry out the calculations, it is necessary to assume *some* form for a channel's psychometric function. Purely for convenience, the psychometric function used was a log-linear function that spanned a range of seven log units on the log contrast axis. Neither of these assumptions used for convenience is crucial.

Each line in Fig. 13 represents the predictions for adding a sine wave of a frequency contained in the test stimulus to one of the test stimuli. (The label

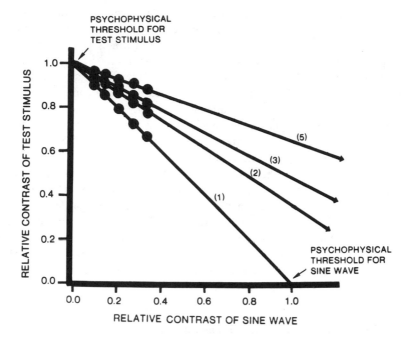

FIG. 13. Quantitative predictions for the thresholds of combinations of sine waves and certain test stimuli, assuming that there are only spatial-frequency channels with probability summation among them. The four hypothetical test stimuli consist of one, two, three, or five sine-wave components (as indicated by the numbers next to the lines). See text for further details.

next to each line identifies the test stimulus, by specifying the number of frequencies it contains.) The symbols show, for various amounts of contrast in the added sine wave, how much test-stimulus contrast is necessary to put the test-plus-sine combination at threshold.

The plots in Fig. 13, depicting predictions from a model of probability summation among spatial-frequency channels, look just like plots of data from a Shapley and Tolhurst or Kulikowski and King-Smith experiment (see Fig. 9). The points fit quite well onto straight lines (although in fact the linearity is only approximate). When the lines are extended, they hit the horizontal axis far beyond the threshold for the single sine wave. The approximate linearity simply shows there are many ways of getting a straight line.

The positions of the intercepts in Fig. 13 make sense according to the qualitative argument given earlier. To repeat briefly: When the intercept is at a higher contrast than the threshold contrast for a sine wave alone, that means that the sine wave is less effective in reducing the threshold for a broadband stimulus than it is in reducing its own threshold (i.e. when the test stimulus is also a sine wave, with the same frequency). The reason, according to a model of probability summation among spatial-frequency channels, is that the test stimulus is detected by several spatial-frequency channels (two, three, or five channels for the test stimuli used here) whereas a sine wave is detected by only one channel. Thus, when you add a sine wave to a broadband test stimulus, you assist only one of *several* channels that each contribute to detection at one time or another (producing probability summation). When you add a sine wave to a single sine wave of the same frequency you affect the one channel that is completely responsible for the detection. So, reasonably enough, the sine wave helps more in the latter case.

Figure 13 displays another property of the predictions from the model of probability summation among spatial-frequency channels: The larger the number of channels involved in detecting a test stimulus, the less it helps to add a sine wave to that stimulus (that is, the farther out the intercept of the data line with the horizontal axis). The reason for this is an extension of the argument above: When more channels contribute to detecting the test stimulus, any one channel contributes less, so the less the effect of adding a sine wave which affects only one channel.

Assumptions for a Quantitative Probability-Summation Model

The remaining sections of this chapter are for those readers who would like a more detailed derivation of quantitative predictions for the test stimuli actually used by Shapley and Tolhurst and by Kulikowski and King-Smith, instead of predictions that are qualitative or restricted to a special kind of test stimuli, as discussed so far. The derivation will show that, using only a small set of reasonable assumptions, we can calculate very good fits to the previously obtained data.

We are going to assume that the data result from probability summation among a set of spatial-frequency channels without any other, specialized, broadband detectors at work. The calculations plotted in Fig. 13 show that probability summation among spatial-frequency channels does predict the *general* type of results found experimentally when a sine wave is added to *certain* broadband stimuli. But we haven't yet demonstrated that such a probability-summation model can predict quantitatively the results for various other test stimuli as you vary the spatial frequency of the sine wave. To do so requires either some assumptions about the number of channels, their bandwidth, and their psychometric functions, or a general assumption that avoids those problems. I've chosen to make such a general assumption here because, although it produces only an approximation of the predictions of a complete model, the general assumption conveys a better idea of why the model makes the predictions it does. And anyway the approximation is not too bad.

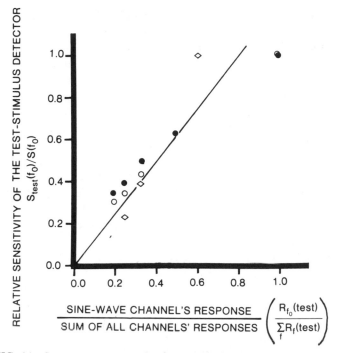

FIG. 14. Some results from sample calculations assuming only spatial-frequency channels with probability summation among them. The horizontal axis gives the proportion of the sum of the responses of all channels that is being contributed by the channel responding to the sine wave. The vertical axis shows the effectiveness of adding the sine wave to the test stimulus relative to the effectiveness of adding the sine wave to itself (or, in other words, the sensitivity of the test-stimulus detector to a sine wave divided by the sensitivity of the visual system to that sine wave). See the lower left section of Fig. 15 for definition of the symbols used on the axes.

To explain the motivation for the particular assumption I used (Assumption 1 in Fig. 15), the predictions from Fig. 13 are plotted in a different way in Fig. 14. The horizontal axis of Fig. 14 gives the contribution by the one channel that the added sine wave activates, as a fraction of the sum of the average magnitudes of all channels' responses to the test stimulus. (The average magnitude of a channel's response is simply the average peak in the channel's response profile, because, in terms of the models presented in the first half of this chapter, the peak response determines whether a channel detects a stimulus.) When the test stimulus has two sinusoidal components adjusted to affect two channels equally, and the added sine wave affects one of those two channels, the quantity on the horizontal axis is 1/2. When the test stimulus has three components adjusted to affect three channels equally, the quantity is

1/3, and so on. (For definitions of the symbols on Fig. 14's axes, see the bottom of Fig. 15.)

Figure 14's vertical axis gives the effectiveness of adding a sine wave to the test stimulus, relative to the effectiveness of adding the sine wave to itself. In other words, the vertical axis gives the "sensitivity of the test-stimulus detector" to a sine wave, divided by the sensitivity of the visual system to the sine wave. The solid points in Fig. 14 were determined from the intercepts of the lines drawn in Fig. 13. (The other points come from other kinds of sample calculations. The open circles come from calculations like those of Fig. 13 but using a log-linear psychometric function spanning 5 decibels rather than 7 decibels on the log contrast axis. The diamonds come from calculations using a test stimulus composed of two sine waves far apart in frequency where the contrasts were *not* adjusted to produce equal responding in the two affected channels but to produce several different ratios of responding; a 7 decibel psychometric function was used.)

Assumption 1 in Fig. 15 is a more general form of the relation suggested by the straight line in Fig. 14. The fact that the points in Fig. 14 fall roughly along a straight line suggests that the relative effectiveness of the added sine wave is approximately proportional to the fraction of the total response of all the channels that is contributed by the channel that the added sine wave activates. I am assuming that the proportionality shown in Fig. 14 for a few sample calculations is true for all cases of probability summation among multiple channels. (See Fig. 15 for a formal statement of this assumption.) Such an assumption has the great advantage of circumventing the problems of how many channels there are, their exact psychometric functions, etc. It is not completely accurate, because the relative effectiveness depends not only on what proportion of the total response a given channel contributes but also on the *distribution* of the responses across the other channels. And even in the case of test stimuli composed of equally balanced components, the relative effectiveness is not strictly a linear function of the fraction of total response contributed by the added sine wave's channel. However, this assumption is quite accurate enough for an investigation of whether probability summation among spatial-frequency channels can predict the kind of results found when sine waves are added to broadband stimuli.

The other assumption used here, Assumption 2 in Fig. 15, is that the average magnitude of the response of any channel to the test stimulus (more precisely, the average peak response) is proportional to the maximal sensitivity of that channel (taken to equal the contrast sensitivity of the visual system for that channel's center frequency) multiplied by the amount of that channel's center frequency which is contained in the test stimulus (the magnitude of the test stimulus spectrum at that frequency). Because this assumption is based entirely on what happens at one spatial frequency (the channel's center frequency), it is necessarily an approximation for any channel that is not extreme-

Assumption 1:

$$\frac{S_{test}(f_0)}{S(f_0)} = A \cdot \frac{R_{f_0}(test)}{\sum_f R_f(test)}$$

(justified by sample calculations)

Assumption 2:

$$R_f(test) = B \cdot F_{test}(f) \cdot S(f)$$

(narrow channels with equal widths
on linear frequency axis)

Conclusion:

$$S_{test}(f_0) = \frac{A \cdot B}{\sum_f R_f(test)} \cdot F_{test}(f_0) \cdot [S(f_0)]^2$$

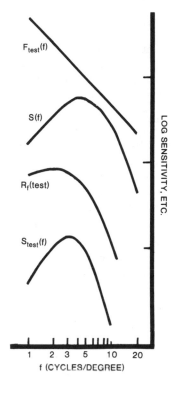

$S_{test}(f_0)$ = sensitivity of "test-stimulus detector" to frequency f_0 as derived by Shapley-Tolhurst-Kulikowski-King-Smith method
= effectiveness of a sine wave of frequency f_0 in reducing threshold of test stimulus

$S(f_0)$ = psychophysical contrast-sensitivity function
= sensitivity of channel centered at frequency f_0 to sine wave of frequency f_0

$R_{f_0}(test)$ = average magnitude of the response of channel centered at frequency f_0 to the test stimulus

$F_{test}(f_0)$ = amount of frequency f_0 contained in test stimulus
= spectrum of test stimulus

A and B are constants, the values of which are not known

FIG. 15. (Left) The assumptions and conclusions of a model of probability summation among multiple spatial-frequency channels for predicting the results of experiments in which sine waves are added to broadband test stimuli.

(Right) Illustration of the calculations involved in the probability summation model. The top curve shows the spectrum of an edge—the function giving the amount of each spatial frequency present in an edge. The second curve is the psychophysical contrast-sensitivity function (from Kulikowski & King-Smith)—the function giving the reciprocal of the contrast threshold for simple sinusoidal gratings. The third curve is the product of the first two and, according to Assumption 2 of the probability-summation model, is proportional to the responses that an edge produces in channels centered at different spatial frequencies. The fourth curve is the product of the second and third and is proportional to the "sensitivity of the edge detector" as predicted by the probability summation model.

ly narrow (any channel with greater than zero bandwidth). But it is a very good approximation for the spatial-frequency channels since, as can easily be shown by direct calculation from the models described in the first part of this chapter, the approximation is good even for quite wide channels.

The relation of the constant of proportionality, B, to the bandwidth of the channel does depend on the particular detection process that is assumed. To predict a given value for the constant of proportionality, B, you need to assume a larger channel bandwidth when using the detection-process model that allows for probability summation across space than when using simple peak detection (in which case bandwidth will actually equal B if you define the spectrum of test stimuli carefully). The additional assumption, embodied in Assumption 2, that the same constant of proportionality B holds for every channel across the whole frequency range is tantamount to the assumption that every channel has the same bandwidth, measured on a linear frequency axis (thus on a log frequency axis the bandwidth is broader for a low-spatial-frequency channel than for a high). Quick's study suggests that this assumption is quite reasonable.

Assumption 2's specification of the average magnitudes of the spatial-frequency channels' responses to an edge is illustrated by the top three lines in the right half of Fig. 15. The topmost line is the spectrum of an edge—how much of each spatial frequency is present in the edge. The second, curved line is the psychophysical contrast-sensitivity function (from Kulikowski & King-Smith's study), which also tells us the peak sensitivities of the channels centered at various spatial frequencies. The third line is the product of multiplying the functions in the first two. By Assumption 2, the value of this product at a given spatial frequency is proportional to the average magnitude of the response to an edge by the channel centered at that spatial frequency.

Quantitative Predictions from a Probability-Summation Model

Putting Assumption 1 together with Assumption 2, we can easily derive a quantitative prediction (see Fig. 15): The "sensitivity of the test-stimulus detector" (what I've been calling "the effectiveness of a sine wave in reducing the threshold for the test stimulus") should be proportional to the spectrum of the test stimulus multiplied by the square of the contrast-sensitivity function. Or in other words, the sensitivity of the test-stimulus detector to a given frequency is predicted to be proportional to the average response magnitude of the channel centered at that frequency multiplied by the psychophysical contrast sensitivity for that frequency.

The predicted "sensitivity of the edge detector" is given by the bottom curve in Fig. 15, which is the product of the second and third curves. Similar predictions can easily be made for the other test stimuli used in Shapley and Tolhurst's and Kulikowski and King-Smith's experiments.

The constant of proportionality for these predictions of test-stimulus detector sensitivity, as can be seen in Fig. 15, is equal to the product of the two unknown constants of proportionality from Assumptions 1 and 2 (the constants do not depend on which test stimulus you are considering) divided by the sum of all the channels' average responses to the test stimulus (this sum does, of course, depend on which test stimulus you are considering). Thus, if you cannot estimate the sum of all the channels' average responses, you are left with a different constant of proportionality for each test stimulus. In that case, you'd have to fit the predicted sensitivities (e.g. bottom curve, Fig. 15) to the actual data (Fig. 11) separately for *each* test stimulus, by finding the constant of proportionality that produces the best fit. (In practice, you plot both the predicted sensitivities and the actual data on log-sensitivity axes and shift the predictions vertically to get the best possible fit to the data.)

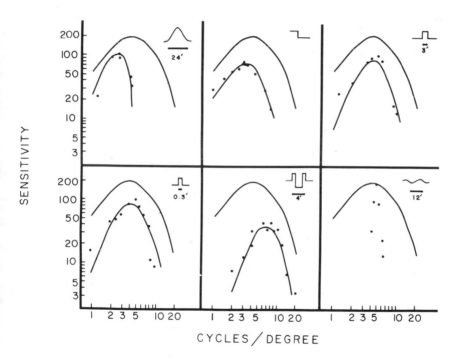

FIG. 16. Comparisons between predictions from the probability-summation model and data from Kulikowski and King-Smith's experiments. The solid points are the "sensitivities of the test-stimulus detector" to sine waves of different frequencies, as calculated from the experimental data. (The same data points were shown in Fig. 11.) The lower curve gives the predictions from the probability-summation-among-spatial-frequency-channels model. (The upper curve is the usual psychophysical contrast-sensitivity function.)

(A) Data and predictions for experiment using a blurry bar. (B) Edge. (C) 3.0-minute wide line. (D) 0.3-minute line. (E) Triphasic light-dark-light pattern. No predictions are made for the sine wave grating since it is not a broadband stimulus.

Figure 16 shows how well the data collected by Kulikowski and King-Smith are fit by predictions based on probability summation among spatial-frequency channels. In each section, the top curve is the visual system's overall contrast-sensitivity function, shown for reference. The points are the experimental data. The bottom curve is the prediction from probability summation among spatial-frequency channels. (There are no predictions for the sine-wave grating since it is not a broadband stimulus.) As you can see, the predictions are a very good fit to the data. They are not perfect, of course, but neither are the data. (By making an additional assumption, you can fit the data almost as well with just one free parameter. See the note on page 260-261.)

Remaining Problems

As mentioned earlier, Shapley and Tolhurst and Kulikowski and King-Smith showed that a few examples of two other kinds of data were quantitatively consistent with their results from the test-stimulus-plus-sine experiment: the results from test-stimulus-plus-another-test-stimulus experiments (such as edge-plus-line) and the thresholds for each test stimulus alone. It can easily be argued, on the basis of some sample calculations, that the consistency found between the data from the test-stimulus-plus-sine experiments and the data from the test-stimulus-plus-test-stimulus experiments would be expected from a model of probability summation among spatial-frequency channels. What cannot be quantitatively predicted on the basis of probability summation among spatial-frequency channels using the approach presented here are the actual threshold contrast values for various test stimuli alone.

If instead of the assumptions used here, an explicit model of probability summation among channels is constructed, then the thresholds for test stimuli can be predicted and, in the process, estimates of channel density and bandwidth are obtained (Graham, 1977). This estimate of channel bandwidth is in good agreement with the estimate from the sine-plus-sine experiments like those of Sachs, Nachmias, and Robson and of Quick. Both kinds of estimates depend in similar ways on the exact model assumed for the channel; that is, on whether or not probability summation across space is included in the model.

A possible shortcoming of the probability summation model is that, in the long run, even one free parameter to fit data is one too many—its value may prove to be inconsistent with some other kind of data.

Finally, even if the collection of spatial-frequency channels *could* detect broadband stimuli, it might not actually do so. An observer might, for example, ignore the spatial-frequency channels when engaging in tasks for which some other part of the visual system seemed more appropriate. Or there might be inhibition among spatial-frequency channels, so that when many of them are responding, none responds very well.

Conclusion

At the moment, despite some remaining questions, I feel there is no way to rule out the hypothesis that only relatively narrowband spatial-frequency channels, with probability summation, are involved in the detection of the various kinds of stimuli used in these experiments. That hypothesis means that data of the kind shown in Fig. 16, for example, from an experiment in which sine waves of various frequencies were added to a broadband test stimulus, might be better viewed as the result of probability summation among several relatively narrowband channels than as the frequency response of a single "test-stimulus detector."

As was explained earlier, however, these "relatively narrowband" spatial-frequency channels may not be as narrowly tuned as was originally deduced from the sine-plus-sine experiments. If probability summation across space does occur, the bandwidth of these channels may turn out to be much broader than we at first thought.

To put this last point another way, suppose that we knew that an early stage of the visual system consists of a set of spatial-frequency channels. Suppose that each channel is an array of identical receptive fields (identical in all characteristics except location in the visual field), but the characteristics of the receptive fields (size, in particular) vary from channel to channel. Suppose further that there is probability summation across space (across different locations) and across channels (across different kinds of receptive field). What, then, would be the bandwidths of these channels (what would be the Fourier transforms of the weighting functions associated with the various channels)? The answer is not yet known. But this much can be said. The bandwidths will probably be greater than those deduced from sine-plus-sine experiments when probability summation across space was ignored (although probability summation across channels was considered). But the bandwidths will probably be narrower than those deduced for test-stimulus detectors from broadband-test-plus-sine experiments when probability summation across channels was ignored (probability summation across space was not very important because all the test stimuli occupied fixed locations in the visual field). And such an intermediate bandwidth is what I mean by "relatively" narrowband.

Perhaps we are wrong to consider the results of detection-summation experiments like those described here as telling us anything about a limited set of parallel feature detectors (spatial-frequency channels) early in the chain of visual information processing. Perhaps we would do better to consider all the data as resulting from much more complex processes. But if we are going to consider these experiments as revealing the existence of parallel feature detectors, it seems possible to explain all the psychophysical data described above quite simply: You do *not* need to conclude that there are broadband detectors, like edge detectors and line detectors, in addition to the relatively narrowband spatial-frequency channels. Relatively narrowband channels alone, with probability summation among them, would be sufficient. The exact characteristics of these channels, however, remain to be determined.

FURTHER COMMENTS FOR INTERESTED READERS

Terminology

Channels. Rather than using a purely arbitrary word to name a concept, a person often chooses a word suggestive of the concept. Unfortunately, what the word suggests to one person may not be what it suggests to another. I have used the word *channel* to mean a two-dimensional array or, in terms of the physiological analogue, a collection of receptive fields that are identical except in position. I have heard at least two objections to this use of the word.

To some people, a "channel" should be something that produces only a single number as its output. These people might prefer to call each single neuron a channel. Or they might consider a channel to consist of the kind of array that I call a channel *plus* a "detector" whose output is either the height of peak response or perhaps a 0 or 1 depending on whether the peak response exceeds the criterion level. (The terminology I have used is consistent with that used in audition. The input for an auditory channel is an acoustic waveform whose amplitude varies with time. The output is also a waveform, filtered, whose amplitude varies with time. The output is a single number only for a single instant. When we draw the analogy between audition and vision, visual space takes the place of auditory time. So it is consistent with the usage in audition to consider both the input and output of a visual channel to be a waveform whose amplitude varies with spatial location.)

To some other people, a "channel" should be something that produces a distinctive perceptual effect—that is, the outputs of different channels should be kept quite separate and should make qualitatively different contributions to perception. Although my definition of "channels" does not exclude their having qualitatively different effects, the definition in no way requires it. And I do not want to require it, at least not in this context, since it is irrelevant for the kinds of experiments described here.

Detectors. There are several possible uses of terms like "line detector." If the bandwidth of the spatial frequency channels turns out to be wide enough, the weighting functions associated with the channels will be of the simple center-surround type (if symmetric). Each spatial frequency channel might then be called an array of "line detectors." These "line detectors," however, would *not* be the detectors deduced by Kulikowski and King-Smith from the experiments using combinations of lines and sine waves—that is, their weighting functions would not be the same, except by accident.

There is another possible use of the term "line detector." If it does turn out that the detection of lines is done by a subset of the spatial-frequency channels, that subset might be called a "line detector."

Modifications of the Model

Some slight modifications of the multiple-channels models described in this chapter will have little or no effect on these models' predictions. Three examples follow.

One peak detector or several? It was assumed here that each channel (each array of neurons having the same kind of receptive fields) has its own peak detector—that is, it was assumed that a pattern is above threshold for the visual system when it is above threshold for at least one channel, and that it is above threshold for a particular channel whenever the peak response in that channel (the response of the neuron that gives a bigger response than any other neuron in that particular channel) is above some criterion. However, without changing the predictions at all, one could instead assume that there is only one peak detector associated with the whole collection of channels—that is, it could be assumed that a pattern is above threshold whenever the peak response in the whole collection of channels (the response of the neuron that gives a bigger response than any other neuron in *any* channel) is above the criterion.

Peak or peak-trough detection? We could assume that the threshold is based on peak-trough detection (the difference between the highest and lowest points in a channel's response profile) instead of on peak detection (the difference between the highest point and the average across the profile). For very narrowband channels, the change in assumption would not affect predictions at all. For channels with slightly wider bandwidths (like the current idea of a spatial-frequency channel), the change will affect the predictions somewhat. (Assuming peak detection instead of peak-trough detection improves the approximation contained in Assumption 2 of the model summarized in Fig. 15.)

Retinal inhomogeneity. A third modification that might make little difference in the predictions of the multiple-channels model is based on retinal inhomogeneity. All sizes of receptive fields may not be present at all places in the retina. The small receptive fields subserving high-spatial-frequency channels may be located within and near the fovea, whereas the broader receptive fields subserving low-spatial-frequency channels may be located more peripherally. Whether or not retinal inhomogeneity makes a substantial difference in the

260   Norma Graham

predictions for aperiodic stimuli depends on several factors, including the bandwidth of the channels and the exact distribution of receptive field sizes. Retinal inhomogeneity remains a potentially important factor that has not been adequately explored.

Effect of Limited Extent of Gratings

Embodied in Assumption 2 of the model summarized in Fig. 15 is the assumption that the peak sensitivity of a channel is correctly estimated by the visual system's contrast sensitivity for that channel's center frequency. This assumption is, unfortunately, introducing an approximation that may vary systematically with spatial-frequency. The peak sensitivity of a channel in the model is the sensitivity for a grating containing only a single sinusoidal component. But in order to have only a single component, the grating would have to be infinite in extent. The contrast sensitivity of the visual system measured in an experiment is of course based on sinusoidal gratings that are limited in extent. In fact, changing the extent of gratings is known to change the shape of the contrast-sensitivity function. In other words, changing the extent changes the estimates of peak sensitivities by different factors for different channels.

There are good reasons, which should be incorporated into a more complete model of multiple channels, why varying the extent of gratings might have this experimentally observed effect. For one thing, a sine-wave grating that is limited in extent contains a band of frequencies in addition to the nominal frequency and thus stimulates a number of channels. For another, if the extent of a sine-wave grating is small enough, and the weighting functions are multilobed, the whole grating will be narrower than the weighting functions of the most sensitive channels, and then the peak response in these channels will be smaller than the peak in the channels' responses to an infinite grating. Further, the detection process in channels might depend on the extent of a grating in a way that would produce the observed effect of varying extent. (However, if the detection process is either simple peak detection or peak detection with probability summation across space, it would not depend on extent.) Finally, as mentioned above, the retina is not completely homogeneous, so the response may be different depending on how much of the retina is stimulated by the grating.

Reducing the Number of Free Parameters

If you fit the data for each test stimulus separately as was done in Fig. 16, you are using as many free parameters as there are test stimuli. (The original investigators used as many free parameters as there were data points.) It turns out that you can fit the data almost as well, and yet reduce the number of free parameters to *one*, by making an additional assumption. This assumption allows you to estimate a quantity that is proportional to the sum of all the channels' average responses to the test stimulus, regardless of what the test stimulus is. What you assume is that the channels are evenly spaced along the linear spatial-frequency axis (there is no evidence on this one way or another). Then the sum of the average responses of *all* the channels will be approximately proportional to the sum of the average responses of a *subset* of channels which have center frequencies evenly spaced along the linear spatial-frequency axis. (In my calculations I used a spacing of 1 cycle/degree.) You are then left with only one free constant (A times B divided by the constant of proportionality used in estimating the sum of the average responses), and that single constant can be adjusted to fit the data for all the test stimuli simultaneously.

The only difference between the predictions that are obtained if one free parameter is allowed and the predictions shown in Fig. 16 is that the vertical position of the predicted curve for the blurry bar is higher relative to the vertical positions of the predicted curves for other stimuli. This change in relative vertical position produces somewhat less impressive, although not bad, fits between data and predictions.

REFERENCES

(This list contains only those papers directly described in this chapter plus several recent papers to give the reader an entry into the current technical literature.)

Campbell, F. W., & Robson, J. G. Application of Fourier analysis to the visibility of gratings. *Journal of Physiology,* 1968, *197,* 551-566.

Graham, N. Visual detection of aperiodic spatial stimuli by probability summation among narrowband channels. *Vision Research,* 1977, *17,* 637-652.

Graham, N., & Nachmias, J. Detecting of grating patterns containing two spatial frequencies: A comparison of single and multiple channel models. *Vision Research,* 1971, *11,* 251-261.

Graham, N., Robson, J. G., & Nachmias, J. Visual detection of aperiodic spatial stimuli by probability summation among narrowband channels. *Vision Research,* 1978, *18,* 815-825.

Granger, E. An alternative model for grating detection. Paper presented at the meetings of the Association for Research in Vision and Ophthalmology, Sarasota, Florida, May, 1973.

Kulikowski, J. J., & King-Smith, P. E. Spatial arrangement of line, edge and grating detectors revealed by subthreshold summation. *Vision Research,* 1973, *13,* 1455-1478.

Lange, R. V., Sigel, C., & Stecher, S. Adapted and unadapted spatial frequency channels in human vision. *Vision Research,* 1973, *13,* 2139-2143.

Quick, R. F., Mullins, W. W., & Reichert, T. A. Spatial summation effects on two-component grating thresholds. *Journal of the Optical Society of America,* 1978, *68,* 116-121.

Sachs, M. B., Nachmias, J., & Robson, J. G. Spatial frequency channels in human vision. *Journal of the Optical Society of America,* 1971, *61,* 1176-1186.

Shapley, R. M., & Tolhurst, D. J.   Edge detectors in human vision.   *Journal of Physiology,*
1973, *229,* 165-183.
Thomas, J. P.   Model of the function of receptive fields in human vision.   *Psychological
Review,* 1970, *77,* 121-134.
Wilson, H., & Bergen, J.   A four mechanism model for spatial vision.   *Investigative
Ophthalmology and Visual Science, Supplement,* 1977 (April), 46.   (Abstract)

Spatial-Frequency Channels in One-, Two-, and Three-Dimensional Vision: Variations on an Auditory Theme by Bekesy

Bela Julesz

Bell Laboratories, Murray Hill, N.J.

> Nowhere in auditory theory or in acoustic psychophysiological practice is there anything more ubiquitous than the critical band....And likely, in one way or another, it will be part of our final understanding of how and why we perceive anything that reaches our ears. Students of vision have no such omnipresent entity to worry and console them. The other senses lack the mysteriousness of this unseen—perhaps nonexistent—but pervasive auditory filter [Tobias, 1970, p. 157].

In 1967 Ira Hirsch and I completed an assignment familiar to generations of graduate students: Compare and contrast visual and auditory perception. Ed David and Peter Denes were putting together a book on human communication (David & Denes, 1972) and thought that some crosstalk between a specialist in audition and one in visual perception might be illuminating. Our essay grew to a quite considerable length (Julesz & Hirsch, 1972), but I found the finished product somewhat less satisfying than I had hoped. Although we had found some interesting analogies between visual and auditory pattern perception, most of them represented rather complex processes at work. We had not been able to uncover any fundamental properties that the two modalities might actually share on a more basic level. In fact, we ended up speculating that vision and audition are basically very different sense modalities, perhaps because of their basically different functions earlier in evolution: Audition is used to detect distant things and events, as yet unrecognized but potentially dangerous; vision, to distinguish edible from poisonous, friend from foe, possible mate from rival.

By the time our galley proofs arrived, four years later, we knew that our essay had been just a bit premature. During the intervening years, physiological and psychophysical discoveries had revealed a fundamental, suggestive, and perhaps even "genuine" analogy between auditory and visual processing. Classic experiments and theories in audition had begun to gain precise counterparts in vision, and students of vision had begun to be "worried and consoled" by evidence for a pervasive visual filter that corresponds closely to the auditory critical band. Hirsch and I were able to insert only a brief mention of this breakthrough into our introduction. Here I will present the analogy in greater detail. I want to stress particularly the roundabout paths that some ideas in science have to follow before they reach full consciousness in certain creative minds, and the long, careful checking process that continues for years until these ideas are generally accepted.

FREQUENCY CHANNELS IN AUDITION

The idea that the ear can analyze complex sounds into their component frequencies is an old and intuitively plausible one. Ohm's Acoustic Law (Ohm, 1843) was inspired by the common experience that a good listener can hear each of the component tones that make up a musical chord. Since a pure tone has a sinusoidal waveform, hearing each of the frequencies in a chord is like performing a Fourier analysis: The chord's complex waveform is the sum of a set of simple sinusoidal components (Fig. 1).

We are so familiar with our ability to hear separate pitches within a chord that it is easy to make the mistake of thinking that this is an uninteresting ability. Because the chord is actually produced by combining separate frequencies, we tend to take it for granted that we can hear each of them. Yet one need only think about color mixtures to realize that sensory systems are *not* always able to isolate component frequencies from a mixture. An appropriate mixture of red and green lights looks yellow, and no amount of concentration or introspective analysis will enable us to see the red or green components. Even in hearing, casual listening does not always separate a waveform into its constituent frequencies. A pure vowel sound consists mainly of two pure tones, yet it is extremely difficult to hear it as such. Indeed, it is an amazing experience to hear two tuning forks, sounded together, say "aaahh"!

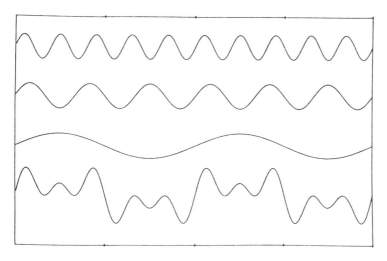

FIG. 1. A complex waveform as the sum of three sinusoids with frequencies f, 3f, and 5f.

Helmholtz's Resonator Theory

Helmholtz's Resonator (or Place) Theory of hearing (Helmholtz, 1863) is an anatomical model to explain Ohm's Acoustic Law. The theory likens the basilar membrane in the ear to a set of tuning forks or resonators. When a loud complex sound is produced near a bank of tuning forks, only those whose resonant frequencies match the complex sound's component frequencies are set into vibration. Helmholtz proposed that each small zone of the basilar membrane acts as a tuned resonator. A complex sound therefore activates patches of the basilar membrane that correspond to the constituent frequencies.

In Helmholtz's theory, a given frequency affects only an *extremely small part* of the basilar membrane. Conversely, a given region of the membrane would be stimulated by only a *narrow band* of adjacent frequencies. Helmholtz's theory, then, is that the basilar membrane is performing a very close approximation to a Fourier analysis. The profile of amounts of activity at each spot on the basilar membrane would be nearly the same as the Fourier magnitude spectrum, which shows how much of each frequency would be needed to duplicate the complex waveform. It should be noted that *any* sound would produce this result, not just chords that are generated by combining several pure tones; Fourier's Theorem states that any waveform that occurs in nature can be duplicated by combining sinusoidal components with appropriate frequencies, amplitudes and phases.

Although it is still generally believed that the major phenomena of hearing can be accounted for in terms of frequency analysis, we no longer think of the basilar membrane as made up of very narrowband analyzers such as Helmholtz had in mind. Instead, we think of a pure tone stimulating a somewhat more extensive region of the basilar membrane. Hence, each part of the membrane is affected by a limited, but not *extremely* limited, range of frequencies. This change in our thinking was prompted by a variety of psychoacoustical observations which only recently have turned out to have close parallels in vision, thereby strongly suggesting that the visual system operates in ways analogous to the auditory system's frequency analysis. Let us first consider a number of these auditory experiments and then go on to their visual counterparts.

Adaptation

In 1929 Georg von Bekesy observed that listening to a loud tone of 800 Hertz for two minutes reduces the perceived loudness of any subsequently heard tone that has a frequency near enough to 800 Hertz (Fig. 2). Bekesy used his data to rule out a number of alternative theories of hearing. In particular, he pointed out that since the loud 800 Hertz tone produces adaptation or fatigue for hearing tones of 600 or 1000 Hertz as well as 800 Hertz, Helmholtz's narrowly tuned resonator theory cannot hold. On Helmholtz's theory, the fatigue should have affected only very close neighbors of 800 Hertz.

For our purposes, it is the other aspect of Bekesy's data that is of more interest: the fact that adaptation produced by an 800 Hertz tone does *not* affect tones that are sufficiently different from 800 Hertz (300 or 2000 Hertz, for example). What this shows is that sufficiently different frequencies are responded to independently. In other words, auditory frequency analysis is not just a mathematical game (which Fourier's Theorem tells us can always be performed on any waveform). The auditory system must really possess some frequency-tuned analyzers that become fatigued by a sustained adapting tone. The bandwidth of the analyzers is not tiny, as Helmholtz supposed and as the Fourier Theorem would require, but it is limited. (A common measure of bandwidth is the width of a tuning curve at half its maximum height, if the height represents energy. For Fig. 2, this measure of bandwidth is somewhat less than ±1 octave.)

Perceived Frequency Shift

A more surprising finding by Bekesy (1929) is that adapting to an 800 Hertz tone affects not only the *loudness* of similar tones, but also their apparent *pitch*. Bekesy had found that if the loud adapting tone is heard by only one ear, only that ear is affected. This allowed him to measure the apparent pitch of a tone

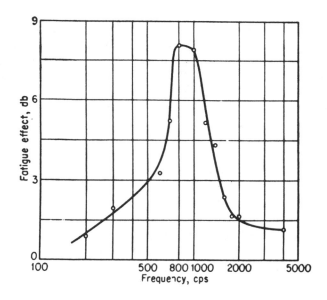

FIG. 2. Auditory adaptation produced by listening to a loud tone of 800 Hertz. (From Bekesy, 1929.)

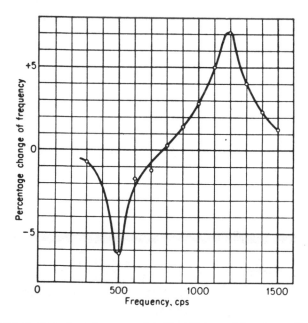

FIG. 3. Perceived frequency (pitch) shift in audition due to listening to a loud 800 Hertz tone. (From Bekesy,1929.)

267

in the fatigued ear by asking the subject to vary the frequency of a comparison tone in the other ear until the two tones sounded the same in pitch. After listening to a loud 800 Hertz tone, a typical listener said that a 1200 Hertz tone in the fatigued ear sounded higher than normal, and matched it with a 1260 Hertz tone in the other ear. A 500 Hertz tone sounded lower than normal, and was matched by a 470 Hertz tone in the unadapted ear. In general, test tones *higher* than the adapting tone sounded *higher still,* whereas *lower* tones sounded *lower still,* as shown in Fig. 3.

Bekesy's theory (now well-supported by the anatomical and psychophysical studies that earned him a Nobel Prize) is that a pure tone excites a considerable region of the basilar membrane, and the perceived pitch depends on the location of the maximum excitation. His explanation of the pitch-shift phenomenon is diagramed in Fig. 4. The x-axis represents location along the basilar membrane and the y-axis represents strength of excitation. The center curve shows the pattern of excitation produced by an 800 Hertz tone; the outer two show the patterns normally produced by a lower and a higher tone. Exposure to the 800 Hertz tone, says Bekesy, reduces the excitability of the whole region of basilar membrane that it stimulates, the whole region under the central curve. That means that the pattern of excitation produced by a tone lower than 800 Hertz will be less intense over the region where the leftmost and central curves overlap, as shown by the dotted line. The result is a leftward shift of the left curve's maximum. This shifted peak, in Bekesy's theory, corresponds to stimulation by a tone with a lower pitch. For a higher tone (the rightmost curve) the peak shifts in the opposite direction.

Again, for our purposes, it is important to note that if the test tone is *too* high or *too* low (in Fig. 3, less than 300 Hertz or more than 1500), its apparent pitch is unaffected by adaptation to 800 Hertz. This gives us another indication that a given analyzer responds only to a range of about 2 octaves (a bandwidth of about an octave).

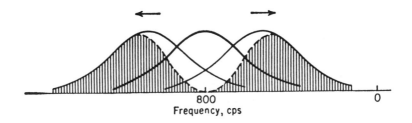

FIG. 4.   Diagram   of   Bekesy's   explanation   of   the   pitch-shift phenomenon. (From Bekesy, 1929.)

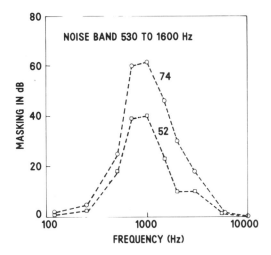

FIG. 5. Data from a typical critical-band masking paradigm: amount of masking of a signal tone (y-axis) in the presence of filtered masking noise at two intensity levels. (After Fletcher & Munson, 1937.)

Masking and Critical Bands

Masking is a phenomenon closely related to adaptation. Instead of presenting the loud tone first and noting that a subsequently presented tone sounds less loud, we present the two simultaneously, and find that the "signal" tone is harder to hear than when presented alone. Again, the signal tone is harder to hear *only* if it is *close enough* in frequency to the masking tone. Tones with very different frequencies do not mask one another.

One of my predecessors at Bell Laboratories, Harvey Fletcher, introduced the notion of "critical bands" to summarize observations on masking and relate them to perceived loudness of complex tones (Fletcher & Munson, 1937; Fletcher, 1940). If, instead of a single tone, our masking sound is a broadband noise containing a wide range of frequencies, only a relatively narrow range of frequencies around the signal tone contributes to masking it (Fig. 5). This limited range of effective masking frequencies he called a *critical band*. Fletcher observed that widening the noise band beyond this critical bandwidth did not produce greater masking.

A somewhat different version of the masking experiment is also revealing. One can use a white noise mask containing all frequencies, and then *remove* a band of frequencies in the masking noise, using a band-rejection filter centered on the signal tone. If this noise-free band is widened to a critical value, the masking noise loses its effect; the tone is detected just as well as when presented with no masking stimulus (Webster, Miller, Thompson, & Davenport, 1952).

As a final variation, one can use for masker a low-pass filtered noise and determine how far below the signal tone frequency the highest masking frequency must be in order to eliminate the masker's interference with the detection of the signal. Using a high-pass filter, one can determine the corresponding critical separation above the signal frequency.

In addition to these three methods, there are several others that can be used to define a critical band. Various methods yield slightly different estimates of the width of the critical band (Scharf, 1970). The main fact, however, is that all methods reveal the existence of some frequency band around any signal tone with the property that only masking noise components within this band have an effect on the audibility of the signal tone.

CRITICAL BANDS WITH ONE-DIMENSIONAL VISUAL STIMULI

It is surprising that after the publication of Ohm's law regarding frequency analysis in hearing, more than a century passed before analogous stimuli were tried in vision. Perhaps the visual experiments were delayed because spatial-frequency analysis in vision seems contrary to introspection. As already mentioned, a good musical ear can listen to a chord not only as a single entity, but can recognize separately the individual tones. However, no one can look at the Mona Lisa and recognize any sinusoidal gratings in it. The suggestion that the Mona Lisa can be duplicated by combining a number of sinusoidal gratings seems unbelievable and rather comical, despite the fact that it is true!

The Modulation Transfer Function

The first application of sinusoidal gratings to visual stimuli was made by engineers decades ago in order to describe the performance of optical lenses and television systems (see Schade, 1956, 1975). This technique, called the modulation transfer function (MTF) method, involves presenting sinusoidal gratings with various spatial frequencies as the input to a lens or television system and then determining the output contrast (modulation) of the resulting image. Only after an additional delay of many years was the MTF technique used to probe the human visual system (Lowry & DePalma, 1961; DePalma & Lowry, 1962; Bryngdahl, 1966). The test picture by Campbell and Robson that is reprinted in Fig. 6, permits direct observation of the reader's own MTF. Along the x-axis the spatial frequency of the vertical sinusoidal grating increases logarithmically, while along the y-axis the contrast decreases logarithmically. When Fig. 6 is held at arm's length, the spatial frequencies in the retinal image approximately correspond to those marked on the x-axis scale. The viewer will probably see an inverted-U shaped border separating a visibly striped region

FIG. 6. Pattern for observing one's own modulation transfer function. (After F. W. Campbell & J. G. Robson: photograph courtesy of J. G. Robson).

from an apparently homogeneous region. That border is a plot of the MTF, depicting the relative visibility (that is, the inverse of the contrast threshold) for each spatial frequency.

The peak is usually around 6 to 9 cycles/degree. As the viewing distance is changed, the location of the peak on the page changes, in agreement with the changing spatial frequencies of the retinal image. Let me note in passing that the contrast for visual stimuli (or modulation) is defined in terms of the maximum and minimum luminance values as $(L_{max} - L_{min})/(L_{max} + L_{min})$, where L_{max} and L_{min} are the maximum and minimum luminance, respectively. That is, the stimulus is treated as a sinusoidal grating with luminance amplitude $(L_{max} - L_{min})/2$ superimposed on a uniform background or "pedestal" with luminance $(L_{max} + L_{min})/2$; contrast is then the ratio of grating amplitude to pedestal luminance. In audition there is no corresponding notion of contrast. The human auditory system cannot perceive any sinusoidal stimulus below 20 Hertz, so no pedestal can be perceived. The visual system of course can perceive a uniform field of a given luminance, so visual contrast is a perceivable stimulus parameter. Therefore the auditory-visual analogy is between the MTF in vision and the audibility threshold as a function of temporal frequency (Hertz) and acoustical energy, as was first measured by Fletcher and Munson (1937) decades ago.

Adaptation and Threshold Elevation

In the kinds of studies mentioned so far, the use of *sinusoidal* visual stimuli is just a convenience. For linear systems (and most systems behave linearly when probed with signals that are near threshold) any other orthonormal functions (e.g. Bessel, Hankel, or prolate spheroidal functions) could equally well be used as analytic elements. The preference for sinusoids rests on the ease with which they can be generated and on most scientists' having greater familiarity with Fourier analysis than with other methods. In a sense, then, using sinusoidal stimuli in these studies is just a convenient mathematical game.

However, as discussed above, when Bekesy (1929) observed that a loud sustained tone can raise the audibility thresholds of a test tone of similar pitch, he demonstrated that frequency analysis is not just a mathematical game in audition. The auditory system must actually contain frequency-tuned analyzers that can be fatigued by a sustained adaptation tone.

It was not until 40 years later that the analogous adaptation experiment in vision was performed by Pantle and Sekuler (1968) and Blakemore and Campbell (1969). Gilinsky (1968) had found that after a high contrast grating is viewed for a few minutes, the threshold for detecting gratings of similar orientations is raised. Pantle and Sekuler, and Blakemore and Campbell, showed that spatial frequency is important too: The threshold is raised only for gratings with spatial frequencies similar to that of the high contrast grating (see Fig. 7 for a demonstration). One could almost take Bekesy's graph (Fig. 2) and simply relabel the axes to display the visual data (Fig. 8)! This finding indicates that in vision, too, frequency analysis is more than a mathematical convenience: It reflects the inherent operations of the visual system. Thus, these results constituted a different kind of support for Campbell and Robson's (1968) earlier proposal about the existence of spatial-frequency analysis in vision, based on their observation that a square-wave grating appears sinusoidal until the higher harmonics reach their own visibility thresholds.

With such a close correspondence between the auditory and visual adaptation experiments, why was there a forty-year lag between them? For one thing,

FIG. 7. Demonstration of adaptation to a grating. Observe the upper left grating for one minute, moving the gaze around the circle. Then look at the center pattern; the "rain" (a low-contrast grating) will temporarily be invisible. After observing any of the other gratings, which differ from the rain in either orientation or spatial frequency, the rain remains visible. (From Blakemore & Campbell, 1968.)

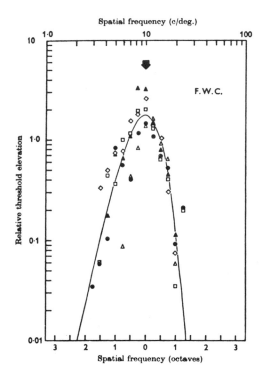

FIG. 8. Threshold elevation after viewing a 10 cycles/degree grating. Threshold elevation is measured as the difference between the thresholds before and after adaptation, for each test frequency. The results resemble those from Bekesy's 1929 auditory adaptation experiment. (From Blakemore & Campbell, 1969.)

visual stimuli are inherently two-dimensional, so even if one thinks of using sinusoidal stimuli, it is not self-evident *what* should be varied sinusoidally. The most obvious analog would be a sinusoidally wiggling line, as shown in Fig. 9 (Tyler, 1973) instead of a luminance profile that changes sinusoidally, as in Fig. 10. (It is interesting, as noted by Anstis, 1975, that Miller in 1916 used sinusoidally wiggling lines to analyze a woman's profile into its first 18 Fourier components!) Even if one decides on a sinusoidally changing luminance profile, it is not clear a priori that a one-dimensional sinusoidal grating is a proper candidate, rather than concentric circular bands or a two-dimensional grating.

Actually, as an eye-witness to these developments in vision, I can testify that the impetus for the visual spatial-frequency adaptation experiments did not come from the Bekesy experiments at all. Rather it emerged from ideas

FIG. 9.   One kind of sinusoidal visual stimulus.   (From Tyler, 1973.)

developed independently by Levinson (1959, 1960) and Kelly (1961) in successfully applying Fourier analysis to de Lange's (1958) flicker fusion experiments.   In the de Lange experiments the luminance of a spot was varied sinusoidally with *time* and the visibility threshold was determined as a function of contrast and rate of flicker.   Generalizing from a sinusoidal luminance variation with time to a sinusoidal luminance variation along one spatial dimension proved to be a conceptually easier step to take than finding directly a visual analog to the Bekesy experiments.

Perceived Frequency Shift

Once it was realized that the one-dimensional sinusoidal grating is the proper visual analog to sinusoidal temporal stimulation in audition, it should have been obvious how to test for visual analogs of other auditory phenomena. However, here again the early discoveries followed a different route.

In 1969 Blakemore and Sutton carried out experiments that exactly parallel Bekesy's on perceived frequency shift.   They showed that adaptation to a high contrast grating causes a shift of the apparent frequency of gratings of neighboring frequencies, away from the frequency of the adapting grating.   Figure 11 provides a demonstration of the apparent frequency shift.   As with the

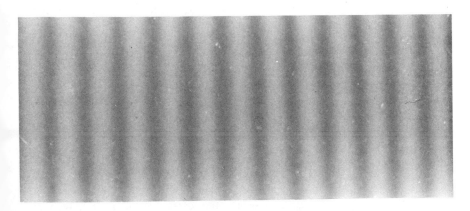

FIG. 10.   Visual stimulus with a luminance profile that changes sinusoidally.

FIG. 11. Demonstration of the visual perceived-frequency shift. Scan the horizontal fixation bar on the left for about two minutes, and then suddenly shift the gaze to the fixation mark on the right. The two identical gratings on the right will appear to have different spatial frequencies. The upper test grating, which falls on the area of the retina (and its cortical representation) that was previously adapted to a lower spatial frequency appears to have an increased frequency, while the lower test grating appears to have a lower frequency. (From Blakemore & Sutton, 1969.)

threshold-elevation data, one can almost use a relabeled version of Bekesy's graph (Fig. 3) to represent the visual frequency-shift findings in Fig. 12 (Blakemore & Sutton, 1969).

Despite the close parallels between the auditory and visual frequency-shift experiments, Blakemore and Sutton's discovery was not directly prompted by Bekesy's. Instead it arose as an incidental observation while they were attempting to repeat Harris' demonstration (Gibson & Harris, 1968; Harris, 1970) of spatial-frequency specificity in the McCollough color aftereffect (J. Nachmias, personal communication).

Masking and the Critical Band

Implications of adaptation studies. Although the threshold elevation and apparent frequency shift effects suggest the existence of fatiguable spatial-frequency-tuned analyzers, both effects are rather small ones. Furthermore, the implications of such adaptation effects are not completely clear. The human brain is such a powerful information processor that it will process almost any pattern; using *any* particular pattern might fatigue some "subroutines" that process it, creating the impression that there is something special about that pattern. Only if one systematically explored a gamut of pattern classes, from concentric circles to confocal hyperbolas, and found that *only* sinusoidal gratings produce adaptation phenomena, would one be justified in assigning special importance to sinusoidal spatial-frequency analyzers. To my knowledge, nobody has yet launched such a comprehensive program.

Masking. Because of these considerations, I was still skeptical in 1970 about the implications of these aftereffects. In my own research I prefer to pursue very robust phenomena, so I decided to look deliberately for other auditory-visual analogies that might lead to more powerful visual phenomena and stronger evidence for spatial-frequency-tuned channels in vision.

I suspected that a promising place to begin was the auditory masking experiments by Fletcher and his school (1937, 1940), in which it was shown that only noise components within the critical band will mask a tone in the center of the band. The visual analog I selected was the masking of a vertical grating by superimposed "dynamic visual noise": a rapidly changing pattern of stripes filtered to contain only certain ranges of spatial frequencies (Julesz, 1971a, 1971b). An example of filtered one-dimensional noise is shown in Fig. 13.

Stromeyer and I carried out such masking experiments in 1972. The filtered noise that was superimposed on the grating changed 60 times per second, with spatial frequencies always confined to a low frequency band (Fig. 14) or a high

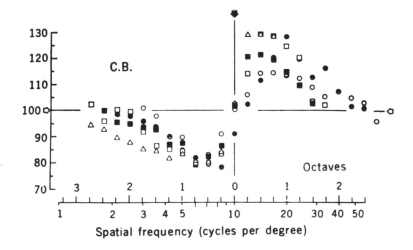

FIG. 12. Perceived spatial-frequency shift in vision. (From Blakemore & Sutton, 1969.)

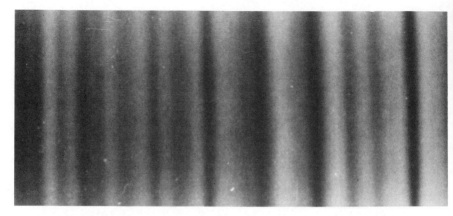

FIG. 13. One-dimensional noise used in visual masking. (From Stromeyer & Julesz, 1972.)

frequency band (Fig. 15). The sinusoidal grating whose threshold was measured was stationary, with a spatial frequency of either 2.5, 5 or 10 cycles/degree.

Each curve in Figs. 14 and 15 shows the relative threshold elevation for seeing a grating of a fixed frequency as we varied the upper bound (Fig. 14) or lower bound (Fig. 15) on the frequencies in the superimposed noise. (Relative threshold elevation is defined as the ratio of the contrast sensitivities of a grating viewed with and without noise, minus 1. Thus a value of 0 would indicate that the noise has no effect on visibility of the grating.) The curves that Stromeyer and I found proved to be identical to those that Blakemore and Campbell (1969) derived from threshold-elevation experiments.

As can be seen in Figs. 14 and 15, a masking noise that is 2 octaves away from the grating frequency has no effect on detection of the grating. By the usual definition of bandwidth—the separation between the points where the relative contrast threshold elevation has dropped by a ratio of $\sqrt{2}$ (3 decibels below its peak value)—the critical band is ± 0.5 octave wide. (Stromeyer and Julesz used a much more stringent criterion—the separation at which the masking noise has no measurable effect—resulting in a much wider, ± 2-octave critical band.)

Linearity. An unexpected aspect of our experiments was that the shape of the curves remained unchanged when we increased the average contrast of the noise by a factor of 10. Increasing the contrast by an order of magnitude—well above the inherent noise level of the visual system that is exploited by the usual threshold experiments—might have pushed the visual system into a nonlinear operating level, but apparently it did not. This finding considerably broadens the range of applicability of a linear-systems approach, since it implies

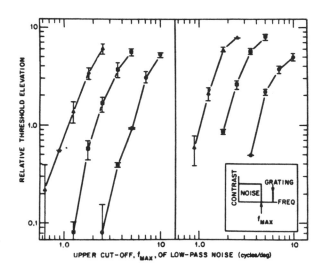

FIG. 14. Visual masking by low-pass filtered noise. (From Stromeyer & Julesz, 1972.)

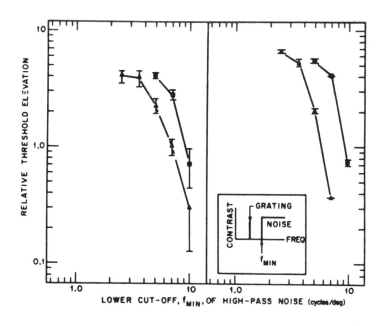

FIG. 15. Visual masking by high-pass filtered noise. (From Stromeyer & Julesz, 1972.)

279

that the visual system behaves linearly far above threshold. It is this fact that will later enable us to relate our findings directly to physiological data.

Neural analysis. Our findings with visual stimuli are remarkably similar in form to those with auditory stimuli (as in the experiment by Webster, Miller, Thompson, & Davenport, 1952), although the auditory critical bands are somewhat narrower. This visual-auditory parallel is all the more remarkable in view of the very different ways the two sensory systems implement their frequency analyses. In the ear, frequency analysis is largely the product of a mechanical filter (the basilar membrane of the cochlea), whereas spatial frequency analysis in vision must be entirely the result of neural processing (unless the packing of retinal receptors plays a significant role, as Kelly, 1975, has argued).

There *is* also some neural frequency analysis in the auditory system. As Schouten (1940) has pointed out, neural analysis is implied by the phenomenon of "residue (or periodicity) pitch"—hearing a pitch that corresponds to the rate of fluctuation of the envelope of a complex sound that has no energy at that frequency. I have speculated that if this neural component in auditory frequency analysis were assessed separately, by using residue pitches to measure critical bands, the estimated bandwidth might be as broad as for vision (Julesz, 1971b).

CRITICAL BANDS IN TWO-DIMENSIONAL PERCEPTION

Auditory stimuli are inherently one-dimensional: Pressure varies with time. But using one-dimensional stimuli for vision seems unduly restrictive, given that everything that we normally look at yields retinal images that vary in two spatial dimensions.

Masking by Distant Frequencies?

Can we extend the notion of a visual critical band from simple one-dimensional gratings to complex two-dimensional pictures? If you think a little about the rather unrecognizable portrait of Abraham Lincoln in Fig. 16, you might conclude that we cannot. Leon Harmon constructed Fig. 16 by dividing a photograph of Lincoln into 300 squares (15 × 20), calculating the average brightness within each square, and then filling the square uniformly with that average brightness instead of the original, varying brightness.

Why is Fig. 16 so hard to see as a real face rather than as an artificial, abstract assemblage of squares? Your first guess might be that the sharply defined edges of the squares are to blame, perhaps forcing the separateness of the squares to your attention at the expense of the more global pattern of lights and darks that represents the face. In spatial-frequency terms, it is the high frequencies that create the sharp edges (what engineers call "quantization noise"), just as it is the high frequencies that give a square-wave grating its sharp edges. The face, on the other hand, is conveyed only by low frequencies. Since the picture is only 20 squares high, it can represent at most 10 light-dark alternations in the vertical direction; thus the upper limit of the face's spectrum must be 10 cycles/degree (if the picture height is equal to 1°). It seems, then, that this picture contradicts our conclusions about one-dimensional masking: In the one-dimensional case, a low-frequency grating was made hard to see only by low-frequency components of overlaid visual noise, components that were within an octave or two of the grating's frequency. In the Lincoln picture, though, it seems as though high-frequency components—those that make the edges of the squares look sharp—are making the low-frequency components that represent the face hard to see.

Figure 17 might seem to give further support to the idea that it is high-frequency components that are responsible for impaired perception of the low-frequency face. Figure 17 is identical to Fig. 16 except that all frequencies higher than 10 cycles/degree have been removed by low-pass filtering. The result is similar to what you get by squinting at Fig. 16 and blurring it; blurring also removes high frequencies. In Fig. 17 Abraham Lincoln is unmasked. The picture looks blurred, of course, but it is unmistakably a blurred picture of a person rather than a flat collage of squares like Fig. 16. So, considered together, Figs. 16 and 17 might seem to rule out the possibility of critical bands in two-dimensional pattern recognition: It seems that even very high frequencies

FIG. 16. Block portrait, low-pass filtered before the average brightness value was quantized into 16 levels. (From Harmon & Julesz, 1973.)

FIG. 17. Low-pass filtered version of the portrait shown in Fig. 16. (From Harmon & Julesz, 1973.)

can mask a low-frequency two-dimensional pattern. And this would be consistent with the fact that the eye is especially sensitive to straight edges and regular geometric shapes (Harmon, Lesk, & Levinson, unpublished manuscript, 1971).

Masking Only by Adjacent Frequencies

However, when we investigated pictures like Figs. 16 and 17 more carefully, Leon Harmon and I discovered that two-dimensional masking is very much like one-dimensional masking after all (Harmon & Julesz, 1973). We found that it is spatial frequencies of the quantization noise that are *close* to the face's frequencies that are interfering most with perception of the face.

To show this, the low-pass filtering in Fig. 17 is not really appropriate. It cuts out not only high frequencies that are much higher than those of the face, but also frequencies that are only a little higher. Hence, although the frequencies that are much higher are the ones that make the edges of the squares prominent, we have to do some further experiments to find out if they are also the ones that are making Lincoln hard to see.

Accordingly, we made two more versions of the Lincoln portrait. Both contained exactly the same low-frequency representation of the face as in Figs. 16 and 17. One (Fig. 18) contains exactly the same high-frequency components as Fig. 16 above 40 cycles/degree, but *only* those above 40 cycles/degree—that is, more than 2 octaves away from the 10 cycles/degree upper limit of the face's spectrum. The intermediate frequencies, from a little more than 10 cycles/degree to a little less than 40 cycles/degree, have been eliminated. The consequence is that even with all the higher frequencies left in, and even with the resulting sharp edges clearly visible, the face is easily recognizable as a blurred face. The picture resembles Fig. 17 much more than it does Fig. 16. Although the sharp lines of Fig. 16 are present, they somehow appear not to be part of the picture, as if they were an overlaid grid through which we can see the blurred photograph. (Later we will see a very different example of a high-frequency pattern that is itself clearly perceptible yet does not interfere with perception of a low-frequency pattern.)

Figure 18, then, shows that just as with one-dimensional patterns, high frequencies do not make a low-frequency pattern harder to see *if* the frequency spectra of the two patterns are far enough apart.

Will frequencies that are *close* to those in the picture make it harder to see? Figure 19 gives the answer. Here we have filtered out all frequencies above 40 cycles/degree, but have left in the intermediate frequencies between about 10 cycles/degree and 40 cycles/degree, a 2-octave band above the face's spectrum. Now the boundaries of the squares aren't as sharp as in Fig. 16, but the overall impression is not much different: Figure 19 looks like a blurred mosaic of squares rather than a blurred portrait.

FIG. 18. Figure 16 and added masking noise with spectrum 2 octaves above the image spectrum. (From Harmon & Julesz, 1973.)

FIG. 19. Figure 16 and added masking noise with spectrum adjacent to image spectrum. (From Harmon & Julesz, 1973.)

Thus, the demonstrations in Figs. 16-19 establish clearly that the critical band notion applies to two dimensions as well as to one. The low-frequency channels that are used to recognize Lincoln's face respond only to frequencies within a limited range. Frequencies more than a couple of octaves above that range do not interfere with recognition of the low-frequency image.

Actually, this demonstration of the role of spatial-frequency channels in two-dimensional perception does more than simply extend the applicability of critical bands from one dimension to two. In the one-dimensional case, all that is needed in order to detect the grating is to see a few of its stripes standing in a fixed position amidst the continually varying noise stripes. The detection, and the masking, might be a relatively local affair. But seeing Lincoln in Fig. 18 is a much more global achievement. The judgment of how recognizable the portrait is must depend on a more extensive, unified perception than that of a couple of the small squares. Thus, these observations bring us much closer to everyday perception.

Filtering in the Two-Dimensional Fourier Domain

In the previous section, for didactic reasons, I did not specify the two-dimensional filtering in any detail. When I spoke about a 2-octave separation between image and noise spectra, I left it unclear what that notion meant.

Now I will introduce a detailed description of two-dimensional spatial-frequency analysis and the filtering applied in this domain. Two-dimensional spatial-frequency analysis is based on two-dimensional Fourier analysis. Here each frequency component (m,n) is a point in the real and imaginary two-dimensional Fourier domain and corresponds to an oriented one-dimensional sinusoidal grating $\cos[2\pi(mx+ny)]$ and $\sin[2\pi(mx+ny)]$, respectively. These oriented sinusoidal gratings have a spatial-frequency $f = (m^2 + n^2)^{1/2}$, and are at an angle θ to the x-axis, given by $\theta = \arctan(n/m)$. Such a two-dimensional Fourier transform method was applied for the first time by Mertz and Gray (1937) in studying television images.

To produce our experimental stimuli, we take a two-dimensional image, perform a two-dimensional Fourier analysis on it, carry out the desired filtering by removing certain frequency bands and/or adding noise, and then perform an inverse transformation back into the two-dimensional spatial domain. The resulting picture is therefore similar to the original one except for the removed spatial-frequency components and any added masking noise. (If the cutoff at the edge of the filter is sharp, the Fourier backtransform will include negative amplitudes for some components, making the filtering operation physically impossible. However, using somewhat more gradual transitions, as we actually did, makes those negative amplitudes negligible.)

In all the previous and following experiments involving two-dimensional images, we perform all the filtering operations in the two-dimensional spatial-frequency domain by limiting the signal and noise frequency components to areas confined in concentric circles or annuli around the origin, as shown in Figs. 20-23. With this limitation to concentric bands, the notion of two bands being separated by 2 octaves is easy to comprehend. It means that the inner radius of one annulus is four times as long as the outer radius of the concentric annulus which it surrounds. (One might generalize this notion to confocal ellipses to some extent, but it would require rather complex geometric definitions to specify the distance between two arbitrary spectral regions, particularly if they are nonconfocal.)

The Two-Dimensional Modulation Transfer Function

In this paradigm of masking, it is not adequate to show that a masking noise 2 octaves distant from the signal does not affect perception of the signal while noise that is adjacent to the signal does. We must also make sure that both noises have the same effective strength. If the human MTF were flat, we would not have to worry about the perceptual effectiveness of noises in various bands. However, the MTF is not flat and therefore we must compensate for the unequal attenuation of different frequencies. If we knew the shape of the two-dimensional MTF of the human visual system, we could simply read off the appropriate values. But we do not yet know it, and rotating the one-

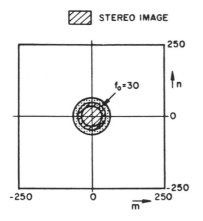

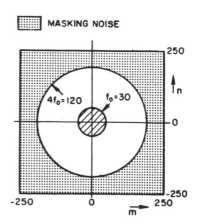

FIG. 20. Illustration in the two-dimensional Fourier domain of the masking paradigm used for low-pass filtered stereograms: The spectrum of the monocular image or of the left (or right) stereo image (lined disk) overlaps the spectrum of the masking noise (dotted annulus). (From Julesz & Miller, 1975.)

FIG. 21. Masking paradigm used for low-pass filtered stereograms, as in Fig. 20, except that in this case there is a separation of 2 octaves between the spectrum of the monocular image or of the left (or right) stereo image (lined disk) and the spectrum of the masking noise (dotted area). (From Julesz & Miller, 1975.)

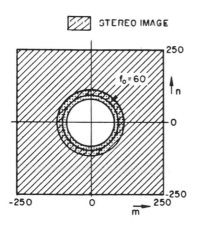

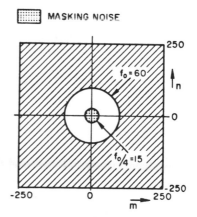

FIG. 22. Masking paradigm used for high-pass filtered stereograms: The spectrum of the monocular image or of the left (or right) stereo image (lined area) overlaps that of the masking noise (dotted annulus). (From Julesz & Miller, 1975.)

FIG. 23. Same as Fig. 22, except that the spectrum of the monocular image or the left (or right) stereo image (lined area) and the spectrum of the masking noise (dotted disk) are kept 2 octaves apart. (From Julesz & Miller, 1975.)

dimensional MTF curve into a surface does not yield a mathematically valid estimate of the two-dimensional MTF (Julesz, Slepian, & Sondhi, 1969).

A more direct psychophysical approach, similar to that used by Julesz and Miller (1975), would be to generate a pair of masking-noise patterns and vary the contrast of one until it appeared equal to the apparent contrast of the other. (Actually, in all of our two- and three-dimensional masking experiments, we selected our noise masks conservatively, making sure that the 2-octaves distant mask had *at least* as great apparent contrast as the mask with a spectrum adjacent to the target's.)

However, comparing the contrasts of two textures may be rather difficult if the textures have very different frequency spectra—like trying to match the brightnesses of two very different colors, such as red and blue. In colorimetry, the task is commonly made easier by matching a series of similar-color pairs that bridge the distance between the extremes. First red is matched with orange, then orange with yellow, etc., until green is matched with blue. The cumulative ratio of intensities required for these matches indicates the intensity ratio for equally bright red and blue.

Below we present an analogous procedure for noise textures, published here for the first time. The stimuli (generated with Jih-Jie Chang) have spatial-frequency spectra as diagrammed in Fig. 24, a two-dimensional spatial-frequency plot. This graph is divided into five concentric bands of successively higher spatial frequencies. The outer radius of each band corresponds to a spatial frequency which is $\sqrt[5]{2}$ times that represented by its inner radius. The width of each region gives the bandwidth of the spatial frequencies contained in a given stimulus. In Fig. 25A. the texture in the center has a spectrum

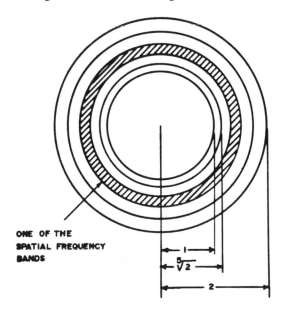

ONE OF THE
SPATIAL FREQUENCY
BANDS

FIG. 24.   The five concentric filter bands in the two-dimensional Fourier domain that yielded Figs. 25A, B, C, and D.

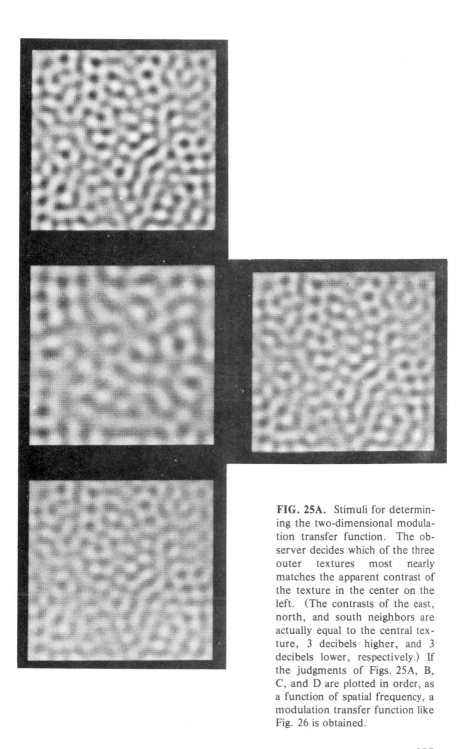

FIG. 25A. Stimuli for determining the two-dimensional modulation transfer function. The observer decides which of the three outer textures most nearly matches the apparent contrast of the texture in the center on the left. (The contrasts of the east, north, and south neighbors are actually equal to the central texture, 3 decibels higher, and 3 decibels lower, respectively.) If the judgments of Figs. 25A, B, C, and D are plotted in order, as a function of spatial frequency, a modulation transfer function like Fig. 26 is obtained.

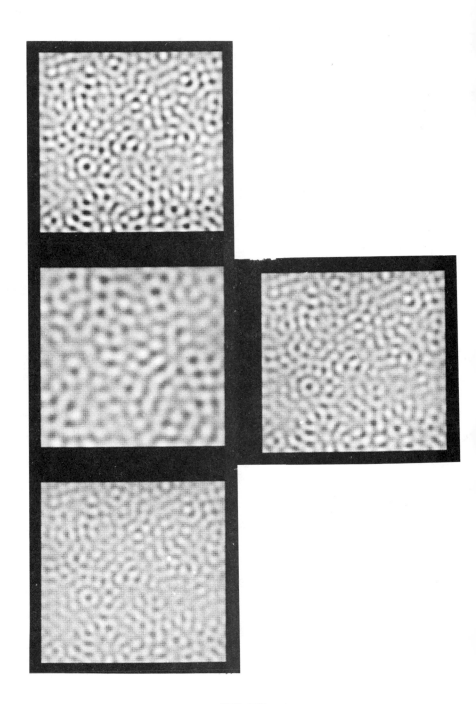

FIG. 25B.

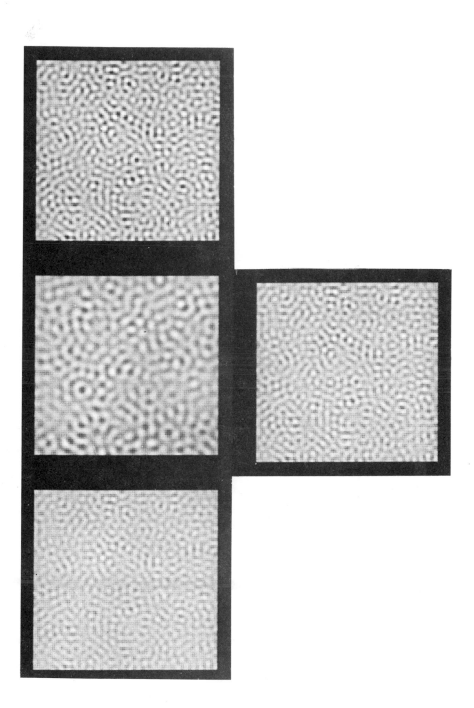

FIG. 25C.

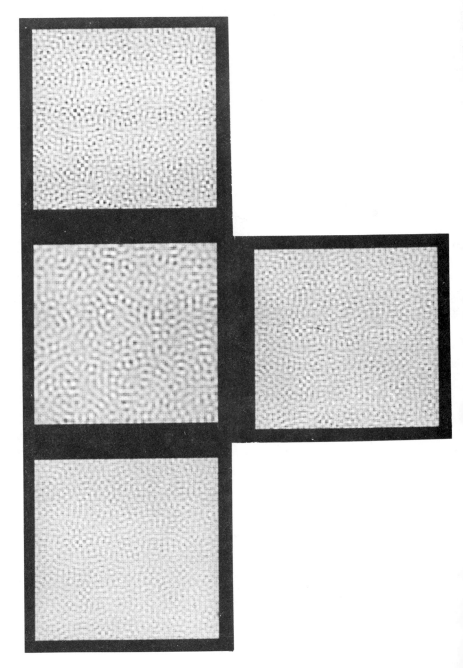

FIG. 25D.

corresponding to the innermost annulus in Fig. 24, while the three surrounding textures all have the same spectrum, corresponding to the next larger annulus. The center texture in Fig. 25B corresponds to that larger annulus, while its three neighbors correspond to the next larger one, and so on through Fig. 25D. The three surrounding samples on each page differ in contrast, with the east, north, and south neighbors being, respectively, equal to the center sample, 3 decibels higher, and 3 decibels lower. (Limited reproduction quality makes these ratios only approximate here.)

The observer decides which of the outer samples most nearly matches the apparent contrast of the center texture. The successive matches can be plotted by moving up 3 decibels, down 3, or remaining level, as appropriate, while moving along the spatial-frequency axis. A curve representing average results for 10 subjects (for nine pairwise comparisons) is shown in Fig. 26. This curve can be construed as a two-dimensional MTF.

Lower End of the Critical Band

Let us now apply the above principles to some new demonstrations. The demonstrations above with the Lincoln face tell only half the story of two-dimensional critical bands. Because the "signal" (the face) consisted of low frequencies in all cases, while the "noise" was composed of higher frequencies, only the upper limits of the critical band were studied. To explore the lower limit, we need a *high* frequency signal and *low* frequency noise. Such stimuli based on the Lincoln photograph are pictured by Harmon and Julesz (1973). Here I will instead use a different target pattern, a 4, as shown in Fig. 27. (Perhaps my choice of target was unconsciously influenced by the opening word of Lincoln's Gettysburg Address.)

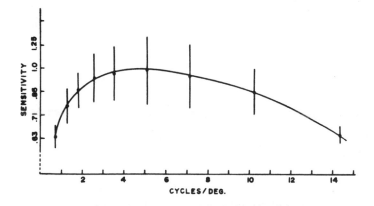

FIG. 26. The two-dimensional modulation transfer function as obtained by the method illustrated in Figs. 24A, B, C and D.

FIG. 27. The original image of a 4.

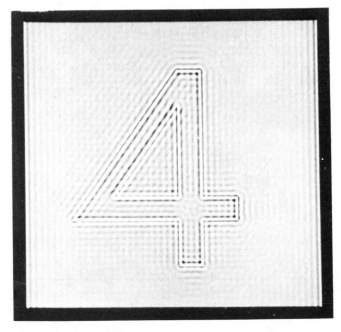

FIG. 28. High-pass filtered version of Fig. 27.

FIG. 29. Figure 28 with filtered masking-noise spectrum that overlaps the image spectrum.

The 4 in Fig. 28 has been filtered to remove all frequencies in a disk around the origin within a 10 cycles/degree radius (assuming the picture is viewed from a distance of five times its height). Thus the 4 is represented by only its higher-frequency components. In Fig. 29 two-dimensional random noise has been added to the high-frequency 4. This is the two-dimensional equivalent of the random-noise gratings used in the one-dimensional experiments described above. (In the Lincoln demonstrations, the noise is not random, but rather is the quantizing noise introduced by averaging brightness within squares, which is why it has straight contours rather than the irregular texture seen here.) The spatial-frequency spectrum of the noise overlaps that of the 4, in an annulus from 8 cycles/degree (inner radius) to 10 cycles/degree (outer radius), as diagramed in Fig. 22. As you can see, with the noise spectrum adjacent to the signal's spectrum, the 4 is not visible.

If, however, we filter the noise to remove all components closer than 2 octaves away from the spectrum of the 4 (as schematized in Fig. 23), limiting the noise spectrum to a disk around the origin with a 2.5 cycles/degree radius, Fig. 30 is produced. Here the high frequency 4 is clearly visible. With the

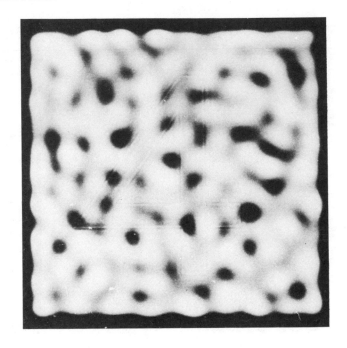

FIG. 30. Figure 28 with filtered masking-noise spectrum 2 octaves below image spectrum.

Lincoln pictures we showed that high-frequency noise masks a low-frequency image only if the noise spectrum falls within 2 octaves of the image's spectrum; with the 4, we see that the same is true when the *image* is composed of higher frequencies while the *noise* is low-frequency.

For comparison with the Lincoln pictures, Figs. 31-33 show stimuli comparable to those in Figs. 17-19 (schematized in Figs. 20 and 21). In all cases, the signal image is low-frequency while the noise is higher-frequency. In Fig. 20 the noise spectrum is adjacent to that of the signal and in the resulting Fig. 32 the 4 is difficult if not impossible to discern. In Fig. 33 the noise spectrum comes no closer than 2 octaves to that of the signal and the 4 is visible.

Once again we have confirmed the relevance of spatial-frequency channels in perception. And once again we have extended the range of applicability. In the Lincoln pictures, we might suppose that the naturalness of the portrait depends on the naturalness of the shading, which lends a three-dimensional appearance to the face and which is disrupted by chopping into squares. With the 4 we see that the same critical band notions also apply when there is no real-life object involved and when sharpness of the image, rather than smoothness and naturalness of shading, is fundamental to satisfactory perception.

FIG. 31. Low-pass filtered version of Fig. 27.

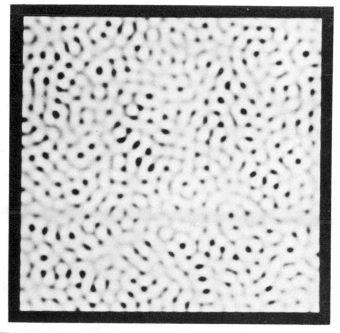

FIG. 32. Figure 31 with overlapping filtered masking-noise spectrum.

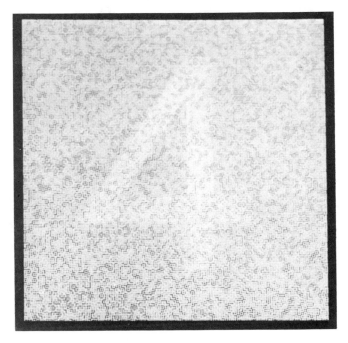

FIG. 33. Figure 31 with filtered masking noise 2 octaves above image spectrum.

CRITICAL BANDS IN THREE-DIMENSIONAL PERCEPTION

When we move from two-dimensional to three-dimensional perception, we find that some of the same principles of masking apply and some vivid new phenomena emerge.

Instead of Lincoln or a 4, we use as "signal" a stereoscopic image of a square standing out in depth in front of its background. In particular, we used random-dot stereograms (Julesz, 1960) like that shown in Fig. 34. The three-dimensional perception can be experienced by using a prism or crossing one's eyes to binocularly fuse Fig. 34. (Or go to the special stereo issue of the journal *Perception,* which contains red-green anaglyphs of Figs. 34-40 together with red-green glasses for viewing them [Julesz & Miller, 1975].) I call this a "cyclopean" perception (see Julesz, 1971a) because the square is visible only when the two eyes' views are combined. There is no such square in either half of Fig. 34, both of which are randomly speckled. Although the pattern of dots is random within each half, it is the same in one half as in the other, except that a square region in the left half is displaced two dot-widths to the right relative to the same region in the right half. When this disparity is detected by fusing the two patterns, the central square emerges in depth.

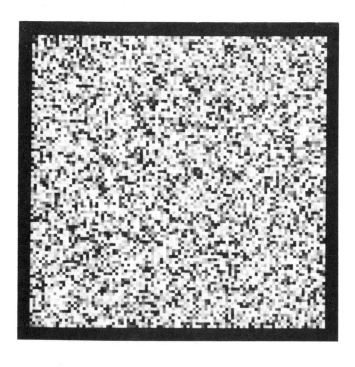

FIG. 34. Basic random-dot stereogram. (From Julesz, 1960.)

297

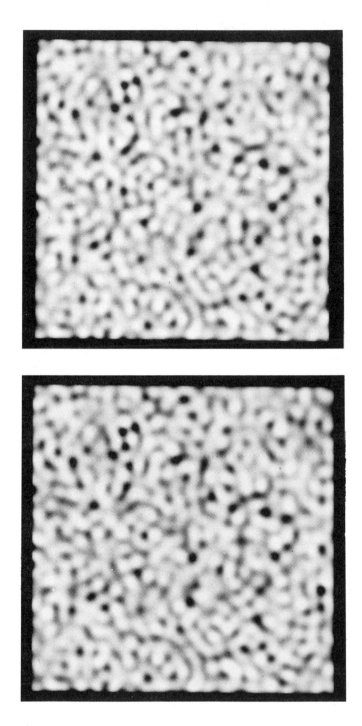

FIG. 35. Low-pass filtered version of Fig. 34. (From Julesz & Miller, 1975.)

If we filter out the high spatial frequencies from the stereogram in Fig. 34, we get the low-pass filtered stereogram shown in Fig. 35. Figure 35 is analogous to Figs. 17 and 31, with the central square taking the place of Lincoln or the 4 as the low-frequency signal. As can be easily verified, the filtering doesn't interfere at all with binocular perception of the central square standing out in depth.

In Fig. 36 (as in Figs. 19, 20 and 32) two-dimensional noise has been added to the right eye's picture, with the frequency range of the noise overlapping that of the random-dot stereogram. For most observers, the central square can no longer be seen. In fact, the two eyes' views cannot even be stably fused. Instead the experience is of binocular rivalry: First one eye's view predominates, then the other, and so on. As with Lincoln and the 4, nearby frequencies in the masking pattern effectively suppress perception of the signal.

In Fig. 37 the noise added to the right eye's picture contains only high frequencies, none nearer than 2 octaves away from the low-frequency stereogram (this corresponds to Figs. 18, 21 and 33). When one fuses the two images in Fig. 37, a novel and fascinating perceptual experience occurs. As in Fig. 36, there is binocular rivalry: The fine texture of the high-frequency noise fades in and out of view. But quite independently of this cyclic appearance and disappearance of the texture, the central square is seen persistently and stably standing out in depth! Evidently, with the low-frequency channels we are able to detect the correlation between the low-frequency images in the two eyes, achieving fusion and stable stereoscopic perception of the square. Simultaneously, with the high-frequency channels, we cannot find a correlation between the high-frequency images in the two eyes, and we can only alternate between the two disparate views (binocular rivalry).

For the sake of symmetry, Figs. 38-40 present stereograms analogous to Figs. 22-23 and 29-30. Figure 38 shows the stereogram from Fig. 34 filtered to remove all but the *high* frequencies. When high frequency noise is added to the right hand image, as in Fig. 39, stereopsis is blocked and the central square is not seen. If only low-frequency noise is added, as in Fig. 40, the square is easily seen in depth, persisting in spite of the fluctuations in visibility of the overlying low-frequency texture. Again, the low- and high-frequency channels function independently, this time with the high-frequency channels mediating stable stereoscopic perception while the low-frequency channels offer nothing but binocular rivalry.

Let us note again that in all the previous examples (including the Lincoln, 4, and stereoscopic demonstrations) the 2-octaves distant masking noise was equated for effectiveness, or made even more powerful, than the masking noise in adjacent bands. In spite of the preponderance of the more remote noise band, it did not affect perceiving the signal or fusing the stereogram, while the less-powerful adjacent noise did.

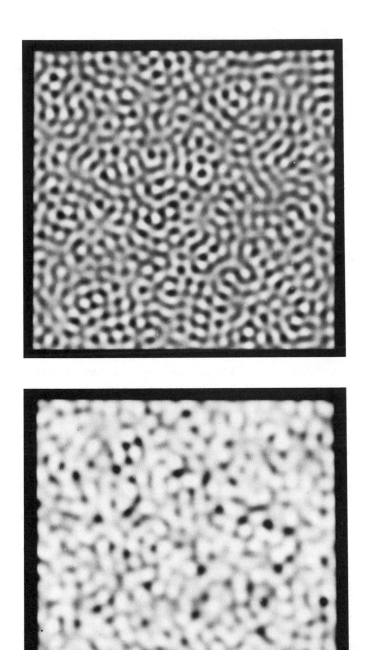

FIG. 36. Figure 34 to which masking noise is added to the right image with spectrum overlapping the spectrum of the stereogram. (From Julesz & Miller, 1975.)

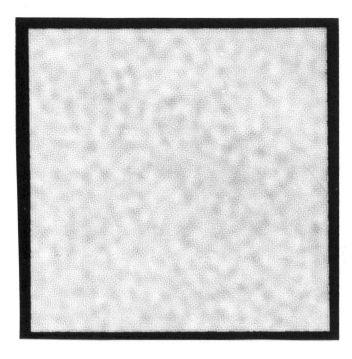

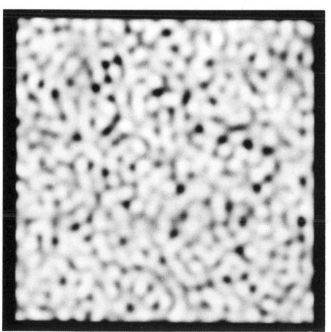

FIG. 37. Figure 34 to which masking noise is added to the right image with spectrum 2 octaves above the spectrum of the stereogram. (From Julesz & Miller, 1975.)

301

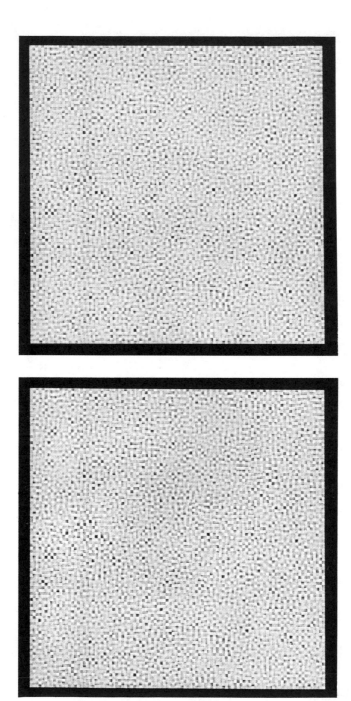

FIG. 38. High-pass filtered version of Fig. 34. (From Julesz & Miller, 1975.)

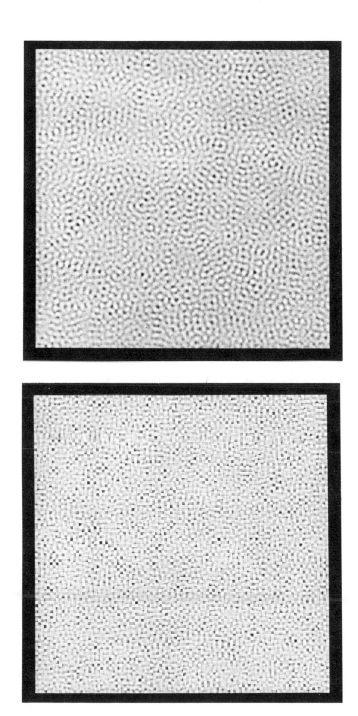

FIG. 39. Figure 38 to which masking noise is added to the right image with spectrum overlapping the spectrum of the stereogram. (From Julesz & Miller, 1975.)

303

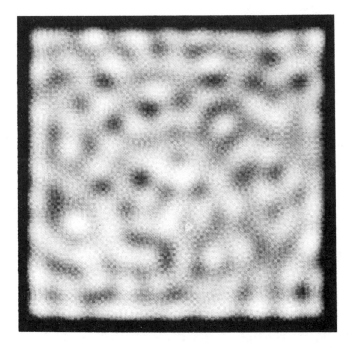

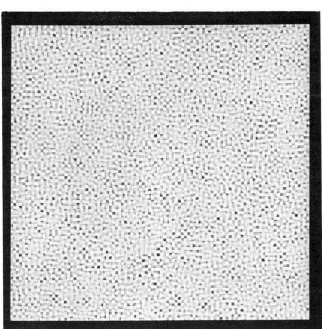

FIG. 40. Figure 38 to which masking noise is added to the right image with spectrum 2 octaves below the spectrum of the stereogram. (From Julesz & Miller, 1975.)

SPATIAL-FREQUENCY CHANNELS:
PHYSIOLOGICAL MECHANISMS

Up to this point, I have said nothing about what physiological mechanisms underlie the spatial-frequency channels that we have seen at work in our psychophysical experiments. This omission was a deliberate one, in line with my personal preference for the pursuit of "psychoanatomy" rather than neuroanatomy—deducing what is inside the "black box" of the visual system while remaining outside of it, rather than invading it with microelectrodes or the like. I think, though, that a few words are called for in order to dispel potential misunderstandings and to reassure the reader that our psychophysical findings, including those on two- and three-dimensional perception, are not at odds with established neurophysiological knowledge. In fact, in hindsight I am tempted to speculate that if, years ago, we had thought carefully about the known physiological mechanisms and applied the appropriate mathematical analysis, we would have reached many of the same conclusions that we instead reached by the psychoanatomical route! (My comments can be brief because Robson (1980) presents a detailed analysis of visual system physiology and its relation to spatial vision.)

One-Dimensional Stimuli

Many people, when they first saw block-sampled pictures like the one of Abraham Lincoln in Fig. 16, assumed that the difficulty in seeing it as a face stems from the prepotency of sharp, straight edges in visual perception. This intuition was bolstered not only by much psychological data, but also by Hubel and Wiesel's (1959) epochal discovery that cells in the visual cortex actually *are* specialized to respond to straight lines and edges. Our demonstration that edges do not in themselves hamper perception in such pictures may therefore seem out of line with our knowledge about the cortex. More generally, our findings of a critical band in vision, with masking dependent on proximity of spatial-frequency components, may seem quite unrelated to line and edge detectors.

However, looking back at Hubel and Wiesel's discoveries now, and thinking about the questions we should have asked and the reasoning we might have employed, one might almost assert that it was Hubel and Wiesel (or even Kuffler, 1953) who discovered visual critical bands! Consider an "on-center unit," a cell whose receptive field has a round excitatory region surrounded by a ring of inhibition (Fig. 41). A cross-section through such a receptive field would have a smoothly curved sensitivity profile something like Fig. 42, which we sometimes call a "Mexican-hat function." Looking at this curve, one can easily see that this receptive field is stimulated best by a stimulus with a *particular* width, equal to the base of the central peak. One can also surmise that the response would be minimal for a grating with stripes about double or half the optimal width (because both the positive and negative regions would be equally stimulated). Thus the bandwidth for the receptive field would be on the order of ±1 octave. One can also, in the light of the Stromeyer and Julesz (1972) evidence for linearity, go in the other direction, computing the Fourier transform of the channel's sensitivity function (spatial-frequency domain) to infer a sensitivity profile in the spatial domain. (Since many receptive field profiles are symmetric, one can assume zero phase response.) The result of transforming psychophysical data in this way to infer a receptive field profile is a Mexican-hat function like Fig. 42 (with perhaps a few periodic wrinkles on the brim). These additional domains of excitation and inhibition are much more attenuated than the center and two adjacent zones of antagonistic activity. Without going into details, such multiple-domain receptive fields were recently claimed by some neurophysiologists (Maffei & Fiorentini, 1973; Pollen & Ronner, 1975). Of course, Fourier analysis assumes infinitely long gratings or at least gratings of equal length, while receptive fields were found in a variety of lengths. Such and similar minor discrepancies, however, should be disregarded in this first-order model building.

    If only neurophysiologists had applied cross-correlation in the spatial domain between the image and the receptive field profiles, they might have predicted all the phenomena that were later obtained by the psychologists, who had to perform merely multiplication in the corresponding Fourier domain.

Two-Dimensional Stimuli

It is fairly easy to draw or visualize the Fourier spectrum of a one-dimensional grating, or of certain aperiodic stimuli such as a single bar. And it is easy to see how the structure of known receptive fields is suitable for detecting such one-dimensional patterns.

    Visualizing a two-dimensional Fourier analysis is more difficult, but in fact the same receptive fields that underlie one-dimensional critical bands can

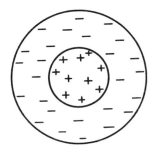

FIG. 41. On-center receptive field.

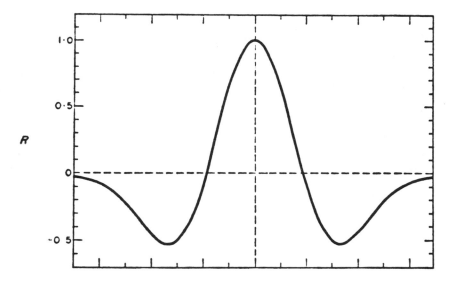

FIG. 42. A "Mexican hat" function: response as a function of distance of stimulus from center of receptive field.

produce critical bands with two-dimensional stimuli. As explained above, a two-dimensional Fourier analysis is fundamentally equivalent to a set of one-dimensional analyses into sinusoidal gratings, except that instead of being restricted to a single orientation, the gratings can take any possible orientation. Indeed, Hubel and Wiesel's bar detectors do have all possible orientations of receptive field and, as shown above, each different width of receptive field responds to a particular range of spatial frequencies. Thus the cell reacts to a two-dimensional pattern in the same way as to a one-dimensional grating, evincing the same critical band in either case.

Three-Dimensional Perception

To date we have only the beginnings of an understanding of the physiological mechanisms that produce stereoscopic vision. We know that there are cells in the visual cortex that receive inputs from both eyes (Hubel & Wiesel, 1968). Furthermore we know that for some of these cells the relative positions of the stimuli in the two eyes must be slightly mismatched laterally in order to produce an optimal response; the required amount of mismatch varies from cell to cell (Barlow, Blakemore, & Pettigrew, 1967; Pettigrew, Nikara, & Bishop, 1968; Hubel & Wiesel, 1970). Obviously such cells would respond to different binocular disparities and might be able to mediate stereoscopic vision with certain simple stimuli, where the pairing of parts of one eye's image with corresponding parts of the other eye's image could be done independently for each small region; that is, where stereopsis is purely local.

However, I have argued (Julesz, 1971a) that in the more general case, including typical random-dot stereograms, independent local detection of disparities cannot account for the coherent perceptions that are seen. There must be *global* mechanisms for stereopsis, which somehow take account simultaneously of disparities at many locations across the entire retinal image, reacting cooperatively to produce a "best solution" (usually, the densest possible surfaces). One model for such a global process is my spring-coupled magnetic dipole model (Julesz, 1971a). As yet, we have no physiological evidence for such a global mechanism and it is clear that it will be difficult indeed to obtain such evidence.

Nevertheless, our findings with filtered random-dot stereograms and masking noise do tell us a number of things about global stereopsis mechanisms. First, two-dimensional spatial-frequency-tuned channels with their characteristic critical bands play a role not only in two-dimensional perception, but in three-dimensional perception as well. Second, the functional site of these frequency-tuned channels must be prior to or at the level of the global stereopsis mechanism. And finally, for stimulus components that do not fall within the same critical band, the frequency-tuned channels operate independently of one another in two senses: in providing independent detection of stimuli (or, equivalently, absence of masking) and in permitting stereoscopic fusion and binocular rivalry to occur simultaneously.

THE ROLE OF SPATIAL-FREQUENCY CHANNELS

As in audition, the function of critical bands in vision remains somewhat mysterious. When the notion of spatial-frequency channels in vision first appeared, it seemed that this concept might lead to a radical new insight into the visual system. The possibility that the visual system performs a frequency analysis in turn held out the possibility that thinking of stimuli in terms of their Fourier spectra might solve long-standing riddles in visual pattern perception, such as our ability to recognize a shape when it appears in different sizes or places on the retina.

However, now that we know that the visual channels have bandwidths of 1 or 2 octaves, it is obvious that the visual system cannot be thought of as performing a Fourier analysis. Even the much more narrowly tuned frequency channels in audition are too broadly tuned for that. In order to perform a Fourier transform that preserves the information in the incoming stimulus, thereby allowing for an inverse Fourier transform that reconstructs the stimulus from its frequency components, the channels would have to have exceedingly narrow bandwidths (strictly speaking, infinitesimal). If each channel responds to frequencies over a range of an octave or two, then obviously it is providing an equivocal and unreliable report about the presence of any particular frequency.

Spatial-Frequency Channels and Attention

If spatial-frequency channels are too unselective to act as frequency analyzers for a Fourier analysis, what role *do* they play? My current guess is that their function has more to do with attention than with pattern recognition. Although there is not much point in asking what transformation such broad-band channels make from the retinal image (space domain) to a spatial-frequency mapping (Fourier domain), we can still ask what transformations such channels impose *within* the space domain. We can consider each channel as a spatial filter, producing a filtered version of the incoming stimulus, in some ways like the filtered pictures in Figs. 17, 28, 31, 35, and 38. One can already appreciate by looking at those figures that a low-frequency channel will discard fine details and thereby emphasize the overall layout of the entire picture. A high-frequency channel brings the local details into prominence, at the expense of the large-scale regions and structure.

Anyone who has ever listened to a dull lecture may recognize these as two extreme modes of looking at a visual scene. Most of the time, we probably concentrate on the lecturer's face, an intermediate stimulus in spatial-frequency terms. However, without moving from our seats, we can also adopt a broader view, seeing the whole layout of the lecture hall, with the lecturer as only one among many entities in it. Or we can direct our attention to fine details of the lecturer's complexion, hair style, and clothing.

We have something like a "perceptual zoom lens" that enables us to take a wide-angle, medium-range, or close-up view of a single visual array. My guess is that these three perceptual frames of reference are provided by the low, middle and high spatial-frequency-tuned channels. With optical and acuity factors limiting vision to the range from about 0.5 to 60 cycles/degree, a 2-octave-wide critical band would allow for about three such bands, perhaps running from 0.5 to 2, 2 to 8, and 8 to 32 cycles/degree or somewhat beyond. Each channel processes the visual input in its own characteristic way, attenuating frequencies beyond its critical band and constructing its filtered output from those within. Thus three or four different versions of the scene are available to be selectively attended to as the need or desire arises.

Ohm's Law in Vision

When I introduced the idea of frequency analysis in vision above, I noted that it seems contrary to introspection: No one can perceive the sinusoidal gratings that make up the Mona Lisa. Now, having recognized how broadly responsive each of the visual spatial-frequency channels is, it is easy to see why the introspective search for sinusoidal gratings fails. If we have only three or four independent channels (actually, a few times as many as that to cover all orientations, if orientation specificity as reported by Gilinsky [1968] also determines some separate critical bands), each channel responds to such a broad band of different spatial frequencies that there is no way for it to signal the presence of any particular spatial frequency. So, even though these independent visual channels *do*, in essence, constitute the visual analog of the auditory channels that underlie Ohm's Acoustic Law, stimulation of a narrowband auditory channel can lead to perception of a particular frequency whereas stimulation of a broadband visual channel cannot.

Thus, it is the coarseness of the visual critical bands that prevents us from introspecting the individual sinusoidal gratings of the Mona Lisa. However, any grain in the canvas, or smudge over the surface, whose spectral components lie 2 octaves above or below the spectrum of Mona Lisa herself can be perceptually ignored—or, alternatively, can be picked out as figure, while Mona Lisa becomes ground.

THE UBIQUITOUS CRITICAL BAND

The analogy between auditory and visual perception now appears to be rich and extensive. As we have seen, such auditory phenomena as threshold elevation by neighboring tones, apparent pitch shift, and various paradigms of masking all have close visual analogs. Indeed, the critical band in vision is beginning to appear as ubiquitous as in audition. The visual critical band manifests itself in studies using one- and two-dimensional stimuli, monocular and binocular vision, adaptation and masking. And the width of the critical band retains its value regardless of what stimuli and procedures are applied.

Restrictions on the Auditory-Visual Analogy

Of course, one has to realize that the analogy between auditory and visual perception is not perfect. I have already mentioned two important differences between the two modalities: First, there is no precise auditory counterpart for visual contrast. Second, frequency analysis in audition is largely the product of the basilar membrane's mechanical properties, whereas frequency analysis in vision is entirely neural.

Pitch. A third exception to the analogy is that there is no exact visual counterpart for auditory *pitch.* In audition, the pitch of a tone is a sensation in its own right, unaffected by phase. In fact, there is no direct perception of phase whatsoever. Even when *relative* phase has effects on hearing, as when a second tone is presented to the same or opposite ear, the result is a perception of something other than phase (i.e. beats, residue pitch, binaural localization, or release from binaural masking). In vision, on the other hand, there is no pure perception of spatial frequency apart from phase. One cannot even imagine seeing a grating without seeing it in a particular location (spatial phase).

An empirical illustration of the nonexistence of visual pitch is my failure to produce a visual analog to an experiment by Zwicker (1964). Zwicker adapted subjects to broadband auditory noise from which a narrow band had been removed; as an aftereffect, subjects heard a faint illusory sound—a sort of artificial tinnitus—corresponding in pitch to the removed frequency band. I have tried exposing subjects to one-dimensional dynamic visual noise with a narrow spatial-frequency band removed. Even after long durations of exposure, no visual aftereffect has been observed. I attribute this failure to the absence of phase-independent visual pitch. The visual system is unable, as it were, to provide an illusory spatial frequency without assigning it a phase, and the dynamic noise provides no basis for selecting any particular phase.

Further Auditory-Visual Analogies

Phase. Let us consider the question of phase further. In audition, while there are some subtle effects of phase, basically the ear is insensitive to phase. Therefore the multiple-channel hypothesis in audition (i.e. Ohm's Law) predicts a remarkable fact: If each of the independent auditory channels (critical bands) receives one sinusoidal signal much below its detection threshold, then there is no detection of the combined signal (even if the peaks of this signal would be very large for some phase relationships of the sinusoids).

Phase insensitivity holds too for detection thresholds in vision, as was shown by Graham and Nachmias (1971). They demonstrated that the visibility of the sum of two gratings having f and 3f spatial frequencies, respectively, did not depend on their relative phases, even though the intensity peaks were greatly different for different phase relationships. I will not dwell on this important experiment, since Graham (1980) gives a detailed account of this paradigm. Nevertheless, the multichannel hypothesis of vision inspired this thought: If nine years ago, when I believed the one-channel hypothesis held true for vision, I had stood in front of a radar screen and watched an aircraft vanish below my detection threshold, I would have been convinced that it approached the distance limit of the radar system. But today, I would not be quite so sure. What if the reflected signal from the airplane happened to be of such a shape that its radar image were the sum of, say, five sinusoidal gratings having f, 3f, 9f, 27f, and 81f spatial frequencies, respectively? Since these components would fall in five independent critical bands, the airplane could be much closer than the distance limit of the system and still remain invisible.

Texture. Since spatial position (phase) is obviously important in form perception (a slight alteration of the phase spectrum of a television picture distorts it beyond recognition), one might think that the phase independence found by Graham and Nachmias (1971) holds only for detection at threshold. However, my own research in visual texture discrimination indicates that phase insensitivity is typical even in suprathreshold vision, provided that detailed scrutiny of the image is avoided. This is the case in effortless texture discrimination, where two textures side-by-side are briefly presented and the observer has to report whether they appear as two distinct textures or form a single homogeneous texture.

The question of what statistical and geometrical properties underlie effortless texture discrimination has occupied me and my coworkers over 15 years (Julesz, 1962; Julesz, Gilbert, Shepp, & Frisch, 1973; Julesz, 1975; Caelli & Julesz, 1978). Since 1962 I became more and more convinced that in the discrimination of texture pairs their second-order (dipole) statistics play a fundamental role. Dipole statistics can be obtained by randomly throwing needles (dipoles) of all sizes and orientations on a texture and counting the frequencies that both ends of a dipole land on the same color (e.g. on black). Similarly, the probability of all n vertices of a randomly thrown n-gon of any given shape falling on certain color combinations determines the nth-order statistics.

We found several ways to generate two-dimensional black-and-white texture pairs such that their dipole statistics agreed, but their third- and higher-order statistics differed (Julesz, Gilbert, Shepp, & Frisch, 1973). Such texture pairs could generally not be immediately discriminated, even though the two kinds of texture elements that made up the two textures, respectively, appeared very different when viewed in isolation (Julesz, Gilbert, Shepp, & Frisch, 1973, Julesz, 1975). In the many texture pairs with identical dipole statistics that are not immediately discriminable (i.e. when presented in a brief flash), of course, with scrutiny, by scanning the textures element-by-element, one can slowly tell them apart. Also, recently we found some instances where textures with identical dipole statistics were discriminable, apparently because they contained some conspicuous structures, such as collinear chains of microelements, or chains that formed corners or closed loops (Caelli & Julesz, 1978).

Despite these few special cases, nevertheless the bulk of research attests that perceptual analyzers for differences in dipole statistics are the basic ones in texture perception. Now, for black and white textures, the dipole statistics are *identical* to the autocorrelation function, which in turn determines the power spectrum. Thus all of our nondiscriminable texture pairs with identical dipole statistics have identical power spectra but different phase spectra. In other words, in effortless texture discrimination phase has no immediate perceptual effect (perhaps except for a few properties such as "collinearity," "corner," and "closure"). Therefore visual *texture* perception *is* similar to audition, in which phase plays a minor role. (As a matter of fact, on a larger temporal scale, we generated long ago auditory "melodies" with identical second-order statistics but different third- and higher-order statistics [Julesz & Guttman, 1965] and found that these "auditory textures" could not be discriminated by trained musicians.)

In summary, careful scrutiny in vision corresponds to "figure" perception, in which the phase spectrum is important, while texture perception without scrutiny corresponds to "ground" perception, in which phase information is ignored. In many detection experiments with sinusoidal gratings, the observer was asked only to detect any change from uniformity, instead of identifying and reporting some specific feature of the gratings. In my opinion, this criterion difference leads not only to quantitative changes in the response, but to qualitative changes as well, since in the first case the gratings are treated as texture (ground), while in the second they are scrutinized and become figure.

AN AUTOBIOGRAPHICAL NOTE

Regardless what the real meaning of this extensive analogy between audition and vision might be, it is remarkable that it took almost a half century to find the visual counterparts of Bekesy's experiments. Was this lag due to poor communication between specialists of different disciplines? I think only partly. Partly it reflects the strange ways humans think, and I use myself as a case in point. Even throughout the several years I worked on this chapter, I did not realize the close connection with my own doctoral thesis, "The study of TV images by autocorrelation," which I wrote in 1956 in Hungary (by the way, at the same institute where Bekesy worked from 1924 to 1946).

In my thesis I studied real-life images (from single portraits to crowds), using incoherent optical methods to determine two-dimensional autocorrelation functions and thus power spectra. I became fascinated that real-life scenes approximated an exponential autocorrelation quite well, where the exponent alone described the power spectrum and thus the complexity of the images. This enabled me to use a variable preemphasis to make the power spectrum of television images always flat, a technique which has been used recently in cassette tape recorders and FM transmitters to combat auditory noise.

It took me two decades to realize that the dipole statistics in my texture discrimination work are actually the same autocorrelation method that I used in my first scientific paper! The only difference is that autocorrelation describes incompletely the real-life scenes in my thesis (because phase information is lost), while describing texture discrimination almost completely.

From the start of my scientific work in vision I was immersed in spatial-frequency spectra, modulation transfer functions, the enigmatic "human fidelity criterion" of information theory (Shannon, 1948), noise reduction, and the like. I was also amply acquainted with the receptive-field notions of the neurophysiologists in 1960. And yet, only after the notion of critical bands in vision emerged in the 1968-1971 period did all these diverse concepts coalesce for me into a single concept. Such sudden reorganization of many known facts into a unifying whole is the criterion of one kind of scientific paradigm (Kuhn, 1970). Although the critical-band paradigm of the visual psychologists did not emerge as a previously unsuspected, revolutionary idea—many of the component concepts were well known to communication engineers, visual neurophysiologists, and auditory psychologists for many years—it has brought closer within a novel framework workers in all these diverse disciplines.

CONCLUSION

The emergence of a far-ranging analogy between auditory and visual perception has been, for me, an exciting event to witness. Given the great differences in anatomy and physiology between the auditory and visual systems, it is amazing to what extent their perceptual functions share a deep-seated similarity. In spite of distinctions between audition and vision that might caution us, the extent of analogy already revealed between the two modalities is enough to make us wonder whether it may be more than just a happenstance. Perhaps it *is* more than a happenstance, and instead is a reflection of evolutionary pressures that have imposed similar modes of action on disparate sensory systems.

REFERENCES

Anstis, S. M. What does visual perception tell us about visual coding? In M. S. Gazzaniga & C. Blakemore (Eds.), *Handbook of psychobiology.* New York: Academic Press, 1975.

Barlow, H. B., Blakemore, C., & Pettigrew, J. D. The neural mechanism of binocular depth discrimination. *Journal of Physiology,* 1967, *193,* 327-342.

Bekesy, G. von. Zur Theorie des Hörens. *Physikalische Zeitschrift,* 1929, *30,* 115-125.

Blakemore, C., & Campbell, F. W. Adapation to spatial stimuli. *Journal of Physiology,* 1968, *200,* 11-13P.

Blakemore, C., & Campbell, F. W. On the existence of neurones in the visual system selectively sensitive to the orientation and size of retinal images. *Journal of Physiology,* 1969, *203,* 237-260.

Blakemore, C., & Sutton, P. Size adaptation: A new aftereffect. *Science,* 1969, *166,* 245-247.

Bryngdahl, O. Perceived contrast variation with eccentricity of spatial sine-wave stimuli: Size determination of receptive field centres. *Vision Research,* 1966, *6,* 553-565.

Caelli, T. M., & Julesz, B. On perceptual analyzers underlying visual texture discrimination: Part II. *Biological Cybernetics,* 1978, *29,* 201-214.

Campbell, F. W., & Robson, J. G. Application of Fourier analysis to the visibility of gratings. *Journal of Physiology,* 1968, *197,* 551-566.

David, E. E., Jr., & Denes, P. B. (Eds.) *Human communication: A unified view.* New

York: McGraw-Hill, 1972.

de Lange, H. Research into the dynamic nature of the human fovea-cortex systems with intermittent and modulated light: I. Attenuation characteristics with white and colored light. *Journal of the Optical Society of America*, 1958, *48*, 777-784.

DePalma, J. J., & Lowry, E. M. Sine-wave response of the visual system. II. Sine-wave and square-wave sensitivity. *Journal of the Optical Society of America*, 1962, *52*, 328-335.

Fletcher, H. Auditory patterns. *Review of Modern Physics*, 1940, *12*, 47-65.

Fletcher, H., & Munson, W. A. Relation between loudness and masking. *Journal of the Acoustical Society of America*, 1937, *9*, 1-10.

Gibson, A., & Harris, C. S. The McCollough effect: Color adaptation of edge-detectors or negative afterimages? Paper presented at Eastern Psychological Association, Washington, April 1968.

Gilinsky, A. S. Orientation-specific effects of patterns of adapting light on visual acuity. *Journal of the Optical Society of America*, 1968, *58*, 13-18.

Graham, N. Spatial-frequency channels in human vision: Detecting edges without edge detectors. In C. S. Harris (Ed.), *Visual coding and adaptability*. Hillsdale, New Jersey: Lawrence Erlbaum Associates, 1980.

Graham, N., & Nachmias, J. Detecting of grating patterns containing two spatial frequencies: A comparison of single and multiple channel models. *Vision Research*, 1971, *11*, 251-261.

Harmon, L. D., & Julesz, B. Masking in visual recognition: Effects of two-dimensional filtered noise. *Science*, 1973, *180*, 1194-1197.

Harris, C. S. Effect of viewing distance on a color aftereffect specific to spatial frequency. *Psychonomic Science*, 1970, *21*, 350. (Abstract)

Helmholtz, H. L. F. *Die Lehre von den Tonempfindungen als physiologische Grundlage für die Theorie der Musik*. Brunswick, Germany: Vieweg-Verlag, 1863.

Hubel, D. H., & Wiesel, T. N. Receptive fields of single neurones in the cat's striate cortex. *Journal of Physiology*, 1959, *148*, 574-591.

Hubel, D. H., & Wiesel, T. N. Receptive fields and functional architecture of monkey striate cortex. *Journal of Physiology*, 1968, *195*, 215-243.

Hubel, D. H., & Wiesel, T. N. Stereoscopic vision in macaque monkey. *Nature*, 1970, *225*, 41-42.

Julesz, B. Binocular depth perception of computer generated patterns. *Bell System Technical Journal*, 1960, *39*, 1125-1162.

Julesz, B. Visual pattern discrimination. *IRE Transactions on Information Theory*, 1962, *IT-8*, 84-92.

Julesz, B. *Foundations of cyclopean perception*. Chicago: University of Chicago Press, 1971a.

Julesz, B. Critical bands in vision and audition. *Proceedings of the Seventh International Congress of Acoustics (Akademiai Kiado, Budapest)*, 1971b, 445-448.

Julesz, B. Experiments in the visual perception of texture. *Scientific American*, 1975 (April), *232 (4)*, 34-43.

Julesz, B., Gilbert, E. N., Shepp, L. A., & Frisch, H. L. Inability of humans to discriminate between visual textures that agree in second-order statistics—revisited. *Perception*, 1973, *2*, 391-405.

Julesz, B., & Guttman, N. High-order statistics and short-term auditory memory. *Proceedings of the Fifth International Congress of Acoustics (Liege, Belgium)*, 1965, *1a*, Report B 15.

Julesz, B., & Hirsch, I. J. Visual and auditory perception—an essay of comparison. In E. E. David, Jr., & P. B. Denes (Eds.), *Human communication: A unified view*. New York: McGraw-Hill, 1972.

Julesz, B., & Miller, J. Independent spatial frequency tuned channels in binocular fusion and rivalry. *Perception*, 1975, *4*, 125-143.

Julesz, B., Slepian, D., & Sondhi, M. M. Correction for astigmatism by lens rotation and image processing. *Journal of the Optical Society of America*, 1969, *59*, 485.

Kelly, D. H. Flicker fusion and harmonic analysis. *Journal of the Optical Society of America*, 1961, *51*, 917-918.

Kelly, D. H. Spatial frequency selectivity in the retina. *Vision Research*, 1975, *15*, 665-672.

Kuffler, S. W. Discharge patterns and functional organization of mammalian retina. *Journal of Neurophysiology*, 1953, *16*, 37-68.

Kuhn, T. S. *The structure of scientific revolutions (2nd edition)*. Chicago: University of Chicago Press, 1970.

Levinson, J. Fusion of complex flicker. *Science*, 1959, *130*, 919-921.

Levinson, J. Fusion of complex flicker. Part II. *Science*, 1960, *131*, 1438-1440.

Lowry, E. M., & DePalma, J. J. Sine-wave response of the visual system. I. The Mach phenomenon. *Journal of the Optical Society of America*, 1961, *51*, 740-746.

Maffei, L., & Fiorentini, A. The visual cortex as a spatial frequency analyser. *Vision Research*, 1973, *13*, 1255-1267.

Mertz, P., & Gray, F. Theory of scanning and its relationship to the characteristics of the transmitted signal in telephotography and television. *Bell System Technical Journal*, 1937, *13*, 464-515.

Miller, D. C. *The science of musical sounds*. London: Macmillan, 1916.

Ohm, G. S. Über die Definition des Tones, nebst daran geknüpfter Theorie der Sirene und ähnlicher tonbildender Vorrichtungen. *Annalen der Physik und Chemie*, 1843, *59 (series 2)*, 513-565.

Pantle, A., & Sekuler, R. Size-detecting mechanisms in human vision. *Science*, 1968, *162*, 1146-48.

Pettigrew, J. D., Nikara, T., & Bishop, P. O. Binocular interaction in single units in cat striate cortex: Simultaneous stimulation by single moving slit with receptive fields in correspondence. *Experimental Brain Research*, 1968, *6*, 394-410.

Pollen, D. A., & Ronner, S. F. Periodic excitability changes across the receptive fields of complex cells in the striate and parastriate cortex of the cat. *Journal of Physiology*, 1975, *245*, 667-697.

Robson, J. Neural images: The physiological basis of spatial vision. In C. S. Harris (Ed.), *Visual coding and adaptability*. Hillsdale, New Jersey: Lawrence Erlbaum Associates, 1980.

Schade, O. H. Optical and photoelectric analog of the eye. *Journal of the Optical Society of America*, 1956, *46*, 721-739.

Schade, O. H. *Image quality: A comparison of photographic and television systems*. Princeton, New Jersey: RCA, 1975.

Scharf, B. Critical bands. In J. V. Tobias (Ed.), *Foundations of modern auditory theory*. Vol. 1. New York: Academic Press, 1970.

Schouten, J. F. The perception of pitch. *Philips Technical Review*, 1940, *5*, 286-294.

Shannon, C. E. A mathematical theory of communication. *Bell System Technical Journal*, 1948, *27*, 379-423, 623-656.

Stromeyer, C. F., III, & Julesz, B. Spatial-frequency masking in vision: Critical bands and spread of masking. *Journal of the Optical Society of America*, 1972, *62*, 1221-1232.

Tobias, J. V. (Ed.) *Foundations of modern auditory theory*. Vol. 1. New York: Academic Press, 1970.

Tyler, C. W. Periodic vernier acuity. *Journal of Physiology*, 1973, *220*, 637-647.

Webster, J. C., Miller, P. H., Thompson, P. O., & Davenport, E. W. The masking and pitch shifts of pure tones near abrupt changes in a thermal noise spectrum. *Journal of the Acoustical Society of America*, 1952, *24*, 147-152.

Zwicker, E. Negative afterimage in hearing. *Journal of the Acoustical Society of America*, 1964, *36*, 2413-2415.

Masking and the Unmasking of Distributed Representations in the Visual System

Naomi Weisstein

State University of New York at Buffalo

Charles S. Harris

Bell Laboratories, Murray Hill, N.J.

Welcome to our light show! Look over there: We've got 7,000,000 little light bulbs all wired up, flashing on and off, wires beeping and screeching, colors and rhythms! It boggles the mind!

Well, no. Usually it *doesn't* boggle the mind. Most of the time all we see is a rather stable, coherent tableau of meaningful objects—not a scintillating mosaic of 7,000,000 discrete, unrelated points, which is what the activity in our cones actually consists of. How do we do it? How do we turn what ought to be an incredible information overload into manageable—in fact invaluable—grist for our cognitive mills?

Theories of how we humans make sense out of a patterned visual input usually include two broad classes of operations, typically characterized by a sequence of the kind sketched in Fig. 1. *Encoding* is some kind of information extraction and compaction. The incoming flux is somehow encoded in terms of patterns more extensive than the activity of a single receptor, thereby providing much more information and stability than a single receptor can, packaged into a much smaller number of units. *Interpretation* somehow takes this simplified, coded version of the input and figures out what object or scene the pattern represents. It is by no means clear what specific suboperations are at

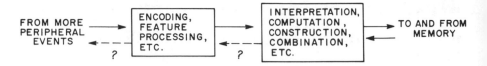

FIG. 1. Two classes of operations in human processing of visual inputs: "encoding" and "interpretation."

work in each of these two classes of operations, nor what physiological mechanisms could or do carry out such operations.

There's a provocative idea kicking around these days that the visual system may perform something like a crude Fourier or spatial-frequency analysis on patterns. We will start out by talking about why this idea cropped up and why a Fourier analysis would be such an interesting thing for the visual system to do. Indeed, even if the visual system isn't really doing a Fourier analysis but is doing something that shares *some* of a Fourier analysis' distinctive properties—if uncles, aunts, distant cousins, or fellow-travellers to a Fourier analysis are occurring—this still would offer us new ways to look at visual stimuli and perceptions. We will then discuss some experiments that suggest that *sometimes* the visual system may be doing *something* that is like a Fourier analysis in *some* ways—something that involves a distributed representation of stimuli and that seems to make more sense when we consider Fourier spectra of stimuli rather than the stimuli themselves. Along the way, we'll comment on how one might distinguish between a Fourier analysis (or some distant cousin) in the visual system, and extraction of local features such as width.

WHY FOURIER ANALYSIS?—EVIDENCE

Any visual pattern can be reproduced by appropriately superimposing a number of sine-wave gratings consisting of light and dark stripes whose luminance varies sinusoidally across the grating. The gratings can differ in orientation, spatial frequency (stripe width), amplitude (contrast), and phase (relative position of stripes). Fourier analysis is simply determining which orientations, spatial frequencies, amplitudes and phases the component sine-wave gratings must have in order to synthesize a given pattern. So if the visual system were doing a genuine Fourier analysis of a pattern, it would have a separate signal or response for each sine-wave component of a pattern. (For a more extensive introduction to some of the basic concepts of Fourier analysis, see Weisstein, 1980.)

Why did people begin to entertain the possibility that the visual system looks for sine-wave gratings in a pattern, rather than more obviously useful things like edges and corners and heights and widths? The motives stem from both data and theory (or, you might say, esthetics). The data come from neurophysiological studies of receptive fields and psychological studies of spatial-frequency channels.

Receptive Fields

What do studies of single cells in the mammalian visual cortex tell us? Do they point to anything like a Fourier analysis rather than to a simple feature-coding scheme that deals locally with the sizes and orientations, etc., of small parts of a pattern? The answer, at first glance, is no.

Units with single excitatory regions. Cortical "simple cells" (Hubel & Wiesel, 1962) respond optimally to a light/dark edge or to a dark or light bar with a certain width and orientation. Such units lend themselves to edge- or size-coding schemes much more readily than to Fourier analysis. A common variety of simple cell responds more strongly when more light falls on a certain narrow strip of the retina and more weakly when more light falls on two adjacent inhibitory areas that flank the excitatory strip. (Other simple cells do the opposite, responding more to light in the flanking areas. And others have only a single inhibitory area next to a single excitatory area.) Different cells have different widths and orientations of the center and flanking regions of their receptive fields. Each retinal point feeds into a variety of cells, meaning that by looking at which cells are firing most rapidly, one can deduce the orientation and separation of contours within each small region of the retinal image. The "complex cells" are much like the simple cells except they are not tied so precisely to retinal location: A bar of the right width and orientation can fire a complex cell when it falls anywhere within a limited region—up to about a degree or two wide for regions near the primate fovea (Hubel & Wiesel, 1968)— whereas the simple cell demands that the bar be in a specific location.

Although cells with these types of receptive fields would give their maximal response when a light bar just matches the width of the central strip, they will also give sizable responses for bars somewhat wider or narrower than that. In fact, if the excitatory and inhibitory regions are balanced so as to give no net response when the whole receptive field is illuminated, then a bar would have to be something like three times as wide as optimal in order to give no response at all—or even wider if the inhibitory flanks are wider than the center strip. So this kind of cell wouldn't be a very useful device for extracting the information we need for a Fourier analysis. Instead of telling us the amplitude of a sine-wave component with a given spatial frequency, it would tell us some sort of average amplitude for a broad *range* of spatial frequencies. This center-plus-flanks receptive field would have a rather broad *bandwidth*.

Units with multiple excitatory and inhibitory regions. There is now evidence that some cortical cells may respond optimally not to a *single* bar, but to *several* parallel bars—three, five, or even more. The receptive field apparently has several excitatory strips. This changes things. Although a cell with a multiple-region receptive field will respond to a single bar over as big a range of widths as a center-plus-two-flanks one will, it will respond to a much more restricted range of *spatial frequencies* when a grating instead of a single bar is used. This is illustrated in Fig. 2. Figures 2a, 2b and 2c show three receptive-field profiles that plot a unit's response to illumination at each retinal location (let's assume that each profile stretches in the horizontal direction across a vertically oriented receptive field). Figure 2c is a highly hypothetical profile with *many* strong excitatory and inhibitory sidebands. Figure 2d is an input pattern, a sine-wave grating with bars slightly narrower than the excitatory centers in the three receptive fields. Because the peaks are lined up, stimulus 2d will evoke a large response from receptive field 2a. But the response from receptive field 2c will be much smaller, because as one travels away from the central peak, the stimulus peaks get farther out of step with receptive field 2c's sensitivity peaks. Thus, unlike 2a, 2c's response decreases drastically when spatial frequency departs slightly from the optimum; it has a narrow bandwidth. Figure 2b is an intermediate case, because it has fewer (and weaker) sidebands than 2c to get out of step with.

In fact, the more sidebands a receptive field has, the more frequency-specific it becomes and the more suitable to serve as an element in a Fourier analyzing system. If the receptive field had ripples extending out indefinitely, the cell would respond to only a single spatial frequency: Unless the spatial frequencies of grating and profile matched *exactly*, *any* grating (also extending indefinitely) would get out of step with the profile an indefinite number of times, making the amount of inhibition equal the amount of excitation.

It's worth mentioning that receptive fields with many sidebands really *ought* to exist if the connectivity in successively higher stages of the visual system follows the simple scheme that it typically follows in the lower stages. Assume that each unit at a given stage is excited by some units in the preceding stage and inhibited by neighboring units in that stage. This is the same antagonistic center-flanks connectivity we've been discussing, but generalized to inputs from a layer of neurons instead of directly from retinal receptors.

However, even though receptive fields with many sidebands ought to exist, so far they haven't actually been found much; that is, very few cells have been shown to have more than a few sidebands in their receptive fields. On the other hand, when certain kinds of stimulation are applied (such as motion in a particular direction [Frost, 1979]), receptive fields are found to be much more extensive than typically estimated. In fact, strong effects of stimuli can often

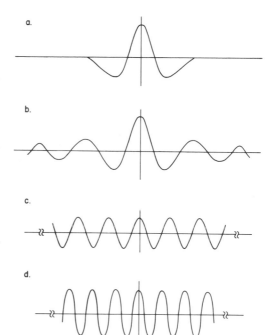

FIG. 2. Some hypothetical receptive fields (a, b, c) and a sine-wave input (d). The x-axis represents horizontal spatial position across the retina. The y-axis represents frequency of firing for the receptive fields, and luminance for the sine-wave input.

be observed when the *entire* classically measured receptive field is shielded from stimulation (Nelson & Frost, 1978; Nelson & Mitchell, in preparation).

Summing up the physiological data, we can say that *most* cells studied so far are best considered as bar detectors rather than spatial-frequency analyzers. A few, with multiple sidebands in their receptive fields, would do a better job of spatial-frequency analysis, and an argument from typical neural connectivity suggests there may be units higher up in the visual system that would do a still better job. Notice that the better the frequency analysis (the narrower the bandwidth), the wider the region of retina from which the unit receives inputs. We'll be coming back to this intriguing happenstance later.

Psychophysical Channels

The second line of evidence pertinent to visual Fourier analysis also presents an equivocal picture, qualitatively hinting at a Fourier analysis while, on the whole, quantitatively denying it.

A variety of psychophysical techniques have indicated that there are a number of independent mechanisms in the visual system, each responsive to only a limited range of spatial frequencies. These "channels" detect different

322 Naomi Weisstein and Charles S. Harris

spatial-frequency components of compound stimuli independently, can be adapted or masked separately, can contribute independently to binocular fusion or rivalry, and can separately influence the perception of color, motion and orientation (Campbell & Robson, 1968; for reviews and references, see Anstis, 1975; Graham, 1980; Harris, 1980; Julesz, 1980).

Some of the early findings were striking and counterintuitive, and could be derived precisely by calculating Fourier transforms of the stimuli. For example, Campbell and Robson (1968) found that a square-wave grating (sharp-contoured homogeneous stripes) was just detectable when the amplitude of its fundamental sine-wave component was exactly the same as in a just-detectable sine-wave grating. In fact the square-wave grating looked just like a sine-wave grating until its contrast was raised enough to bring its third-harmonic component (three times the fundamental frequency) to an amplitude that allows it to be detected when presented in isolation.

Spatial-frequency selectivity: bandwidth. More to the point, some calculations based on detection of two-component gratings seemed to show that individual spatial-frequency channels have very narrow bandwidths, with a change of only 12% in spatial frequency reducing the response magnitude by half (Sachs, Nachmias, & Robson, 1971; Kulikowski & King-Smith, 1973). Channels with bandwidths this narrow might actually be able to serve as elements in a crude Fourier analyzing system, reporting on the presence and amplitude of quite narrow ranges of spatial frequencies. However, subsequent evaluation indicates that these early estimates were misleadingly narrow (see Graham, 1980). Although there is some newer psychophysical evidence that may point indirectly toward very narrow bandwidths (Kelly, 1975), on the whole estimates derived from psychophysical data hover around one to four octaves (i.c. a change in spatial frequency by a factor of two to eight) for half-amplitude response—a lot broader than one would like for a reasonable approximation to a Fourier analysis.

Another approach: spatial distribution. In the discussion of receptive fields above, we noted that spatial-frequency selectivity or bandwidth is inversely related to the number of receptive-field sidebands or, correspondingly, to total spatial extent. That suggests another sort of psychophysical measure—spatial extent of interaction between stimuli—that could be used to assess the plausibility of visual Fourier analysis. This measure might be applicable when estimations of bandwidth are difficult, or it might permit experiments that tap in on visual system operations at some level different from that delineated by bandwidth-type experiments.

We won't comment further on spatial distribution here, except to mention that the psychophysical data that we have obtained on spatial extent of interactions, data discussed in the last half of this chapter, *are* very much in line with what you might expect from a visual Fourier analysis.

WHY FOURIER ANALYSIS?—ESTHETIC APPEAL

Quite apart from the data, applying Fourier analysis to the visual system has a certain esthetic, and pragmatic, appeal. This appeal shows up from two different points of view: outside looking in, and inside looking out.

Outside Looking In

Even if the visual system doesn't do anything that is uniquely identifiable as a Fourier analysis, we as scientists may find that Fourier analysis is a helpful tool for exploring and comprehending what the visual system is doing.

Linear systems analysis. Fourier transform techniques are useful tools in performing certain algebraic operations that would require more complicated procedures in the space domain (the ordinary, untransformed spatial geometry) and in investigating the properties of linear systems in general. For that reason, long before people wondered whether the visual system is itself performing Fourier transformations, the techniques of Fourier analysis were used to explore the properties of the visual system (Schade, 1956; and see Cornsweet, 1970, for an excellent exposition).

One can use Fourier transform techniques to explore the properties of a system without making any assumptions about the system itself, except that it's linear. In most cases, this is a trivial assumption, since almost any system can approximate linearity over a small range. If one assumes that the visual system is linear enough, one can use frequency techniques to determine the impulse response of the system. At one level of analysis, the impulse response of a (linear) system is all one needs to know about that system. The impulse response can be thought of as the way the system responds to something that has no width—an infinitely narrow, infinitely bright stimulus. Presenting such a stimulus (which can't be done, although there are frequency-domain techniques available to obtain the same answer—another reason why frequency analysis is so useful) allows one to observe the "pure" system response—the response of the system unencumbered by any spatially extended characteristics of the input. Then, given any stimulus, one can completely describe the output by calculating the impulse response of the system at each successive point in space where there is input.

Suggestive analogies. Under the heading "The Ubiquitous Fourier Transform," Brigham (1974, p. 7) remarked: "The term ubiquitous means to be everywhere at the same time. Because of the great variety of seemingly unrelated topics that can be dealt with effectively using the Fourier transform, the modifier "ubiquitous" is certainly appropriate. One can easily carry over the Fourier analysis techniques developed in one field to many diverse areas." He then listed such areas as optics, antennas, quantum physics, probability, and random processes. To this list we can add audition; Julesz (1980) gives examples of how analogies between temporal-frequency analysis in audition and spatial-frequency analysis in vision can suggest new experiments and stimuli. Brigham went on to note (1974, p. 7) "...it is stimulating to find a theory and technique which enables one to invade an unfamiliar field with familiar tools." We would add that it can be even more stimulating to reattack a familiar field with unfamiliar but powerful and versatile tools.

Alternative representation of stimuli. Subjects' numerical judgments of the apparent strengths of sensations such as brightness, loudness, etc., typically are related by a power function to the pertinent physical variable (Stevens, 1962). Psychophysicists who gather such magnitude-estimation data often plot it on log-log graph paper. The logarithmic transformation of the two axes neither adds nor subtracts any information from the data, but it does make it easier for the scientist to assess, comprehend and remember the relations among the data points. This is because all power functions, which produce an infinite variety of different curves on ordinary linear-linear plots, show up as straight lines on a log-log plot. So a log-log plot provides a useful way to look at this kind of psychophysical data, without any implication that the subjects' sensory systems are actually applying a logarithmic transform to the incoming stimulus and a corresponding transform to convert their sensations into numbers to be output.

Similarly, the Fourier transform gives us a new way of thinking about the representation of spatial information—a way that is detailed, specific, compact, and well-defined. (In fact, it is so well-defined that we can easily discover the ways in which it is inadequate as a description of what the visual system is doing.)

The Fourier representation preserves all the information in the original pattern, but in an entirely new form. The new form makes it easier to perform certain operations. To give just one example, cross-correlation in the space domain can be quite a chore. One has to multiply, integrate, translate, and so forth. In the Fourier domain, cross-correlation requires one simple multiplication. There are a number of models of how patterns are detected or recognized which are based either on autocorrelation (Uttal, 1975) or cross-correlation (McLachlan, 1962). Similarly, convolution is performed by a simple multiplication in the frequency domain.

New stimuli. Each new approach to visual perception brings with it an emphasis on some class of stimuli that are easiest to relate to the new approach. Think of the Gestalt psychologists' outline, dotted, and hidden figures, Hebb's lines and angles, information theorists' dot matrices, psychophysicists' disks or disks plus rings, cognitive-hypothesis theorists' illusions and impossible figures (Fig. 3). Fourier analysis, too, encourages us to use new stimuli, some (such as sine-wave gratings) that we would otherwise never have dreamed of using,

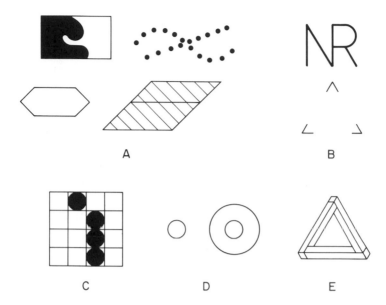

FIG. 3. Types of stimuli emphasized by various approaches to understanding visual perception: A. Gestalt psychology; B. Hebb's theory;
C. information theory; D. psychophysics; E. cognitive-hypothesis theory.

others that we might have liked to use but had no convenient way to describe,
order, generate, and vary (such as texture gradients [Rosinski, 1976] and
filtered stimuli and noise patterns [Julesz, 1980]). Such stimuli have often
prompted observations that have outlived the theories that instigated them, revealing aspects of visual functioning that would have been discerned laborious-
ly if at all using other forms of stimuli.

Inside Looking Out

If *we* find Fourier analysis so useful for so many tasks, maybe the visual system does too. Maybe in addition to the overall, tautologous correspondence
between visual system performance and a precise Fourier analytic description
of that performance, the visual system actually carries out suboperations or
codings that correspond to particular suboperations that could form parts of a
Fourier analysis. Maybe some aspects of visual processing relate more directly
to the Fourier transforms of stimuli than to the stimuli themselves. This
doesn't have to be all or nothing. What the visual system is doing might bear
some resemblances to a Fourier analysis or to some suboperations of one
without there being an extensive enough correspondence to say that the visual
system really is doing a Fourier analysis. Indeed, that's what we'd guess is
probably going on; maybe if we try pretending for a while that the visual sys-

326   Naomi Weisstein and Charles S. Harris

tem is doing a Fourier analysis, we will discover and be able to think about some novel aspects of what it's really doing.

So for a while we'll play "Let's Pretend" and consider what doing a Fourier transform would buy for the visual system.

What Fourier would buy. There are those who argue that the Fourier transform actually would buy very little for the visual system, because the Fourier transform of a pattern is mathematically precisely equivalent (or iso-morphic) to the pattern. *All* the information in the original pattern is also in the Fourier transform and *only* the information in the original is in the transform. The Fourier transform, so the argument goes, is useful only as a tool for scientists on the outside looking in. Their uses of Fourier analysis in describing and testing the visual system say nothing about the nature of the system except perhaps that it is linear.

However, if one asserts that the system *itself* is operating as a Fourier analyzer, this is a more sweeping claim, testable and falsifiable. The Fourier transform of a pattern may contain the same information as the input pattern, but it's in a very different format. What we will argue is that this kind of format—the Fourier transform or some related form of distributed representation—would be an enormously powerful way for the visual system to code information; indeed, some such representation almost seems to be *re-quired* by our pattern recognition capabilities.

Simplified calculations. Just as working with Fourier transforms simplifies many calculations for the scientist, Fourier analysis could serve as a preproces-sor in the visual system to simplify other operations that would be useful for pattern recognition, such as the already-mentioned auto- and cross-correlation (Uttal 1973; McLachlan, 1962). Simple neural circuits that are known to per-form simple operations like subtraction and multiplication could thus carry out complex calculations that we might otherwise hesitate to relate to known physi-ological mechanisms.

Coded representation of stimuli. A log-log plot of data can help a psychophysi-cist pick up similarities among seemingly different curves, notice deviations from expectation, summarize data easily and compactly, and deal appropriately with variability. Likewise, performing a Fourier transform may enable (or compel) the visual system to recognize in the frequency domain similarities, simplicities and regularities that are not nearly so obvious in the space domain.

Some of our perceptual abilities that are quite mysterious when we look at the retinal image point by point or in terms of local features follow almost au-tomatically from a Fourier transform of the stimuli. Rosinski (1976) has re-cently shown that certain simple properties of the Fourier transforms of images of slanted textures show variation and invariances that correspond with their *perceived* slants in depth; similar correspondences are not found if the visual system is assumed to act as a "projective geometer," looking only at contours, orientations and widths.

DISTRIBUTION

There is one important attribute of a genuine Fourier transform that is so interesting, and potentially so useful to the visual system, that it deserves treatment in a section all its own: *distribution*. Saying that a representation is distributed means that all (or most) points in the input pattern contribute to determining each point in the representation of that pattern. Conversely, information about each point or region in the input pattern is generally located over all (or much) of the representation, rather than being restricted to a point or small region in the representation. That is, in the general case, each part (or most parts) of the representation contains information about all parts of the input pattern; therefore each point in the distributed representation in some sense contains information about the entire input pattern.

Some kinds of representation or transformation of input patterns meet these defining criteria, but not in a very interesting way. For example, if each point in a visual "representation" consists of an unweighted sum of all input points (that is, with all input points contributing equally), we would indeed have every input point contributing to every point in the representation. And every point in the representation would carry the same information about the input pattern. But that information would tell nothing but overall intensity; it would say nothing at all about the spatial structure of the input pattern.

However, there are more interesting kinds of distribution. The Fourier transform, for instance, is a distributed representation in that, in general, each point in the original input pattern contributes to determining all points in its Fourier transform. But, unlike a simple summing mechanism, the Fourier transform preserves all of the information about the original pattern, including its overall structure and local details. How does it do this?

For many of us, the idea of a distributed representation is unfamiliar, making it hard to see how something that combines information from all over the input pattern could preserve the details of that pattern's layout and elements. One virtue of Fourier analysis is that it offers a precise way to think about one kind of structured distributed representation and facilitates the use of other physical models that may be easier to deal with.

We have found that analogies from optics help us visualize many of the intriguing properties that distributed representations can have. (If you find such analogies more confusing than helpful, skip ahead to the section headed "Memory.")

Optics

Interference. Take two point sources of red light (we say "red" to insure that the light waves from both sources have the same temporal frequency; green or blue would be just as suitable). Shine them on a screen, using collimating lenses to make their rays parallel and their wavefronts flat (Fig. 4). On the screen you'll see an interference pattern—a grating consisting of alternating black and red bars. This grating fits our definition of a distributed representation: Each of the two input point sources contributes to determining the illumination of each point on the screen.

Moreover, the interference grating is an interesting form of distributed representation in that it contains all the information needed to retrieve the original two-points input pattern. All you have to do is make a photographic transparency and then illuminate it with one of the original point sources. Each bar in the grating acts like a tiny slit, producing its own family of cylindrical waves (Fig. 5). The crests of these cylindrical waves line up to create a new flat wavefront. It turns out that this planar wave is a replica of the original input wave. If you put it back through the same kind of collimating lens that you used for the input, you get back your original red point source.

Now, in this example it's obvious that no one spot on the grating has any special claim to representing the two input points. In fact, it's obvious that you can cut the grating into little pieces and (as long as they're not *too* little) you can use the procedure shown in Fig. 5 to reconstruct the input points from any one of the pieces.

Transforming two red points into a grating and then back again may seem like pretentious busy-work, but what we've been describing is actually none

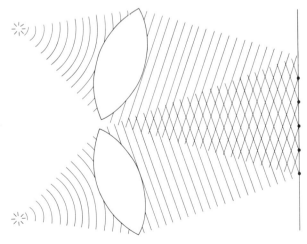

FIG. 4. Grating pattern produced by interference between two beams of light.

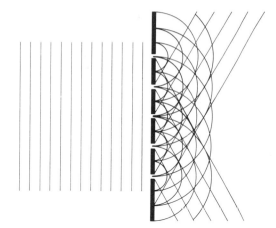

FIG. 5. Flat wavefronts reconstructed by shining light through a photograph of the interference grating in Fig. 4.

other than one form of hologram. The transparency of the grating was a hologram of two point sources. Not a very exciting hologram, but a hologram nonetheless.

Holograms. Now imagine substituting for one of the red point sources an object—a silver dollar, say. Let's use a mirror to shine some of the light from the remaining point source onto the silver dollar (Fig. 6). That insures a stable relation between the temporal phases of the light that hits the screen directly from the point source (the "reference beam") and the light that hits it after bouncing off any point on the silver dollar. Just as in the example with the two point sources, the light from the point source will form a set of interference fringes with the light from any one point on the silver dollar. Because the silver dollar is rather close to the screen, the fringes won't be evenly spaced; the spacing will depend on the angle between the screen and the impinging spherical wavefront (Fig. 6).

When you bounce light off it, the silver dollar becomes a collection of point sources. Thus there will now be a whole host of interference patterns on the screen, each one produced by a pair of points (one the dollar, one the red point source). The spacing of the black and red bars produced by each pair of points will depend on how far apart those two points are (the farther apart the points, the closer spaced the bars). You might think the result would be a hodge-podge. It is, but it's a *structured* hodge-podge, which retains all of the information about each interference pattern. Because light combines linearly, the patterns don't destroy one another, they summate. Like the waves made by tossing several pebbles into a puddle, each pattern proceeds on its own independent way.

If you make a hologram, by photographing the complex conglomerate pattern on the screen, you can get back an image of the silver dollar the same way as you recreated the two point sources in Fig. 6. You illuminate the transpar-

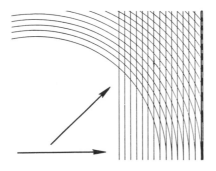

FIG. 6. Nonuniformly spaced fringes produced by interference between direct light beam and reflection from a point on an object.

ency with the original red point source and thereby create a set of wavefronts that duplicate those produced by the silver dollar itself.

The hologram as Fourier transform. Believe it or not, holograms have something to do with Fourier transforms. In fact, if the conditions are changed slightly, the kind of hologram we've been talking about (there are other kinds) *is* a Fourier transform! If you look at the different interference patterns that appear on the screen when you use various simple patterns in place of the silver dollar, you find that the input pattern and the result on the screen form Fourier transform pairs; two points yield a sinusoidal grating; a narrow slit (pulse) yields a $\sin x / x$ grating; a point (delta function or impulse) yields homogeneous illumination; and so on. (To get simple interference patterns, though, the inputs have to be extremely small and very close together.)

Memory

Holograms have a number of amazing properties, which stem in large part from the fact that they are distributed representations of the input pattern. Other kinds of distributed representation share some or all of these properties and, even more amazing, so does human memory.

Consider the simple case (actually, it's an incredibly complex one, but that's all to the good) of running into and recognizing someone you haven't seen for years. True, we often fail to recognize the old acquaintance, but sometimes we succeed and sometimes the recognition seems immediate and effortless. What kind of a memory system could allow such a feat of recognition?

First, the memory would have to have *tremendous capacity.* How many faces have you seen in your lifetime, each one a complex stimulus sharing many features with many other faces? How many of them would you recognize? Experiments like Shepard's (1972) on memory for pictures suggest you would recognize a huge number, knowing immediately that you had seen them before. Second, the memory must be *content addressable* and offer *parallel access.* There just isn't enough time to check, serially, all the faces you've stored, in order to find one that matches the one you're now looking at. The current perception must somehow go straight to similar stored ones. Third, the memory must be *associative*. Recognition of a face usually brings with it a wealth of other information about the person.

Memory Models and Holograms

Faced with accounting for such properties of human memory. many investigators have come up with models that make use of distributed representations. The most vivid examples are models based on analogies to holograms (Julesz & Pennington, 1965; Longuet-Higgins, 1968; Pribram, 1971).

Like human memory, holograms have a *tremendous capacity* for stored information. By varying the angle and/or wavelength of the reference beam, one can record an indefinite number of different images, each of which can be retrieved separately by using the appropriate reference beam. The images are all stored in exactly the same storage space, without interfering with one another.

A given image can be retrieved not only by the appropriate reference beam, but by illuminating the hologram with any small portion of the original scene. Retrieval is *associative*. The stored images are *content addressable* and can be *accessed in parallel*, instantaneously, with no time-consuming search through irrelevant items. A final property that memory seems to share with holograms is directly related to distribution: *redundancy*. As Lashley (1950) demonstrated years ago, a given memory seems not to be stored at any particular single place in the brain, but can be retrieved from many different places. Extensive chunks of the cortex can be destroyed in an animal without, by and large, obliterating any particular memory. Similarly, one can throw away most of a hologram and still reconstruct from the remaining fragment all of the stored images (with less detail, but with overall structure intact).

One can gain some understanding of the storage system by considering the hypothetical receptive fields with several excitatory strips, discussed earlier. In some sense, one cycle width in those fields contains all the information about what the pattern looks like; the additional cycles merely repeat that information. But it is the repetition of information that allows differentiation between two patterns that have almost the same frequencies. The sum of the local responses to the similar but not optimal frequencies would cancel out if there were a sufficient number of sidebands; only the response to the optimal frequency would cumulate. In a rough way, parallel access, large storage capacity, and content-addressability follow from distributed, overwritten storage. You could think of it as an enormously efficient template system, with all the templates in the same place but with none of them interfering with each other. Then retrieval is something like simultaneous cancellation of all stored templates other than the one that matches the image that's coming in.

Of course, distribution of retinal information (as in the Fourier model we've been discussing) does not necessarily imply distribution higher up. That is, one can easily imagine channels whose input comes from an extensively distributed area of the visual field, but whose output is a single signal in a single location. So, even if retinal signals pass through a distributed coding mechanism, this would not necessarily imply that distributed representations are stored in memory. On the other hand, if memory does rely on distributed representations, distribution of retinal signals might be a useful first step.

Summary: Distribution, Perception, and Memory

To summarize: There is some evidence, both psychophysical and neurophysiological, that some level of the visual system responds to incoming stimuli in terms of limited bands of spatial frequencies. A representation in terms of spatial frequencies (an approximation to a Fourier analysis) would be useful in many ways, in the process of forming perceptions. Current models of the visual system, and some physiological data, suggest that analysis into spatial-frequency components entails forming a more or less distributed representation of stimuli. Distributed representations, in turn, could serve as an extremely powerful basis for memory storage and retrieval. Holograms, which are distributed representations of input images, share with human memory such amazing properties as tremendous capacity, associative recall, content-addressability, parallel access, and redundancy. Thus, mechanisms that accomplish feats of both perception and memory may rely on a single kind of format for information, one that involves distributed representations (Fourier transforms are one form, but by no means the only possible one).

SPREAD OF MASKING

Under normal viewing conditions, steady-state conditions, we don't see sine-wave gratings in a complex scene, no matter how convinced we may be that the scene *has* to be equivalent to a set of such gratings. So, even if the visual system is doing a Fourier analysis somewhere along the way, we can't examine that analysis by simple introspection.

But perhaps we can somehow catch the visual system during those transient stages which comprise the *process* of forming the steady-state picture. Perhaps there are ways to test whether, in some of these transient stages, the visual system codes stimuli in a distributed fashion that shares some attributes with a Fourier transform of incoming stimuli.

Masking

Our strategy for catching the visual system in the act of forming a picture was to use a forward-masking procedure. In forward masking, a visual pattern is presented for a relatively short duration, and then immediately or a short time afterward another pattern is flashed. The idea is to measure how much, and in what ways, exposure to the first stimulus (the "mask") interferes with perception of the second stimulus (the "target"). (The procedure is basically the same as in experiments on "adaptation," except that in adaptation studies the first pattern is viewed for many seconds or minutes.) Given certain assumptions, such interference may provide a measure of what the two stimuli have in common, according to the visual system. The visual system may notice that the two stimuli have Fourier components in common, or it may pick up some other similarities, such as locally defined features. The response to the second stimulus would depend on what definition of similarity the visual system uses.

What are the assumptions behind this strategy? We assume that: (1) certain visual mechanisms lose sensitivity to patterns to which they are exposed; (2) the decrease in sensitivity to a subsequent pattern will be greater the more similar (in "pertinent" ways) the second pattern is to the original one; (3) the decrease in sensitivity will be reflected in a decrease in the apparent contrast of the subsequent pattern. Given these assumptions, if the visual system is doing something like a Fourier analysis at some stage and if we can find the right conditions to produce masking at that stage, then the reduction in apparent contrast of the subsequent pattern should depend on how similar the Fourier transforms of the two patterns are. More specifically, the amount of masking (contrast reduction) should depend more on overlap of the Fourier spectra of the stimuli than on spatial overlap of the stimuli themselves.

General Procedure

The procedure was similar in all of the masking studies described below. On each trial the mask was presented first, for a short duration such as 10 milliseconds or a longer duration, 10 seconds. Next came a short interval (20-30 milliseconds) during which only a dim background field and a tiny fixation point were visible. Then a brief (10-30 milliseconds) but clearly visible target pattern was presented.

Subjects had to report two things about the appearance of the target: how great its contrast appeared, and whether or not the contrast appeared uniform over the entire pattern. To describe the target's apparent contrast, subjects made magnitude estimations, assigning numbers proportional to how great the contrast between the target's black portions and white portions appeared to them. These estimations were made with reference to a standard, called "10": the same target pattern flashed for 10 milliseconds against the dim background, with no preceding mask. To indicate whether masking was affecting the whole target or only some parts of it, subjects reported on the apparent uniformity of the target. If target contrast appeared greater in some parts of the target than in others, subjects were to call it "nonuniform," while if all parts of the target seemed to have equal contrast they called it "uniform."

Note that the target stimuli were always well above threshold. This was deliberate: The aim was to find out what these target stimuli *looked* like after exposure to a mask, not just whether a barely visible target was rendered invisible by a mask. It should also be emphasized that in each experiment, one mask duration was short enough (100 milliseconds or less) to insure that the whole presentation—the mask, the short delay, the target—was essentially projected onto a fixed retinal area. Thus any spatial spread of masking that was found could not be attributed to eye movements.

Each masking experiment investigated the effects of particular types of patterned mask—a bar, a grating, and so forth—on subsequent patterned targets. A blank field, with the same outside dimensions (aperture) and mean luminance as the patterned masks, was also presented in each experiment. This blank-field control made it possible to assess components of masking that are due to the change in the overall luminance of the field and to transient effects of turning any mask on and off. Such components, which don't depend on the particular stimulus pattern, are not of primary concern here. What is of interest is *pattern specific masking*: effects that are greater than those obtained with the blank field alone. Thus, the measure of pattern-specific masking is the difference between the judged target contrasts with a pattern mask and with a blank field of the same mean luminance.

A Bar Masks a Grating—All Over

Earlier adaptation and masking studies had shown that a grating can reduce the visibility of a subsequently viewed grating if their stripes have similar orientations and widths. The same is true for a single bar and a subsequently viewed bar.

But such grating-grating or bar-bar masking or adaptation can be interpreted in two different ways. It could be the result of *local* feature mechanisms, each responding to a fairly restricted portion of the retinal image. On the other hand, it could just as well be produced by mechanisms that are picking up periodicities over a much wider area of the retina. To get any indication of which is the more appropriate description—width or spatial frequency—we have to use target and masking patterns that are different from each other.

Suppose we use a single bar as mask and follow it with a many-stripe grating as target. If masking depends on having the same retinal receptors stimulated by both mask and target, then the bar ought to mask just *one* of the grating's bars, the one that it overlaps on the retina. If masking depends on mechanisms that extract local features, such as bar width, then the bar might mask the grating's central bar plus perhaps one or two on either side. That kind of result—masking dependent on local-feature similarity, and extending only a degree or so beyond the masking stimulus contours—would be in line with the usual expectation among visual scientists, based on a number of previous studies.

But that's not at all what was found when a single dark bar was used as mask and a grating as target (Weisstein & Bisaha, 1972). The subjects all reported that the bar reduced the apparent contrast of the grating (Fig. 7) and they insisted that the reduction in contrast was not confined to the central stripe or central 1° region, but extended *uniformly* across the entire 6.7° wide grating. The same result appeared with three different bar widths, paired with gratings with matching stripe width (3, 10, and 15 cycles/degree), and with several mask durations. The lone bar masked the whole grating on 95% of all trials. The bar was having effects not just over a degree or two, but over a distance of more than 3°.

Remember that whenever we talk about masking here we mean pattern-specific masking: a reduction in apparent contrast that goes beyond that produced by a homogeneous blank-field mask. The blank field, of course, reduces the apparent contrast of the entire grating. What is being measured, when judgments that follow the blank field are subtracted from those that follow the dark bar, is the *additional* masking attributable to the bar.

What the subjects were saying was that the masking due to the bar was affecting parts of the grating several degrees away. If we accept the usual assumption that masking indicates that the mask is affecting (desensitizing, adapting, inhibiting, interfering with, occupying) some mechanism that's used to perceive the target, then these results indicate that the bar was stimulating some mechanism that keeps tabs on a fairly large chunk of the visual field, rather than just a local bar detector. This fits in with the kind of multiple-sideband receptive fields that, as explained above, would be needed to implement a good Fourier analysis. More generally, it fits in with the idea that interactions are occurring between distributed representations of stimuli, instead of being confined to identical or adjacent receptors or local feature detectors.

Another, related aspect of this experiment also fits in better with expectations based on Fourier analysis than with those based on local feature detection. For an array of independent bar detectors, a single bar is very different from a grating: The bar would stimulate only a few bar detectors, whereas the grating would stimulate many, over a wide region. In terms of Fourier transforms, a bar and a grating are different too, but in a different way. Fig-

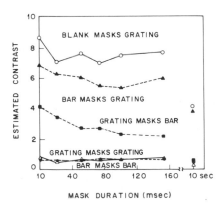

FIG. 7. Masking of a grating by a single dark bar (▲). The data shown are for a bar 3 minutes of arc wide, and a grating with the same width stripes (10 cycles/degree). Data for other combinations of target and mask are also shown, for comparison. (From Weisstein & Bisaha, 1972.)

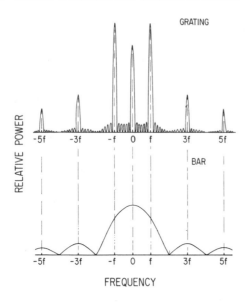

FIG. 8. Fourier power spectra for a square-wave grating (top) and a single bar from that grating (bottom). The y-axis scale in the lower graph is greatly expanded relative to that in the upper one. (From Weisstein, Harris, Berbaum, Tangney, & A. Williams, 1977.)

ure 8 shows Fourier power spectra for a single bar (bottom) and a square-wave grating (top). Although the peaks are much broader for the bar, the two spectra have a basic similarity. If the two graphs were overlapped, each of the bar's peaks would coincide with one of the grating's peaks. In other words, the bar stimulates all of the spatial-frequency-specific mechanisms that respond strongly to the grating. Just as overlap of a grating and a similar grating on the retina (space-domain) makes intuitive sense out of grating-grating masking, so overlap of bar and grating power spectra (Fourier domain) could make sense out of bar-grating masking.

Thus we have some support for two predictions that might be made if we thought the visual system were carrying out a reasonable counterpart of a Fourier analysis: (1) stimuli should interact, even though they are quite dissimilar geometrically, if they share Fourier components (i.e. if their power spectra overlap); (2) the interactions should extend across large distances in the visual field. Another way to summarize this is to say that if masking occurs when two stimuli affect a common mechanism, then spatial spread of masking demonstrates that a bar and a grating affect mechanisms in common and that those mechanisms take in information from a wide retinal region.

A Dot as Mask: Two-Dimensional Stimuli

So far we have considered evidence that a small stimulus (a narrow bar) can reduce the perceived contrast of a larger stimulus (a grating) with which it shares Fourier components, even though the masking stimulus covers only a small part of the target stimulus and even if most of the target stimulus is quite a distance away from the masking stimulus.

We can go further in restricting the retinal region covered by the masking stimulus, by using a single *tiny dot*, just 0.17° in diameter, as the masking stimulus. We can find out whether this miniscule entity can mask a full 8° × 5° grating and also what it does to a circularly symmetrical counterpart of a grating: a bullseye pattern composed of concentric bands with the same 15-cycle/degree spacing as the grating. For purposes of comparison, we included a bar 2 minutes wide as mask, as in the previous experiment but oriented diagonally this time, and we displayed the target grating in three different orientations (vertical, horizontal, and diagonal). That yielded eight combinations of the two masks and four targets (Weisstein, Harris, Berbaum, Tangney, & A. Williams, 1977).

Figure 9 shows the amounts of pattern-specific masking that we found for each target-mask combination. First, notice that there *is* some pattern-specific masking for most of the combinations; that is, the little dot or bar masked the bullseye or grating more than a blank field did. Second, note that the amount of masking *differed* for different combinations; for some combinations there was a lot, for some there was a middling amount, and for some (the bar plus the bullseye, vertical grating, or horizontal grating) there was no significant pattern-specific masking (contrast reduction by the bar was not significantly different from that by the blank field). And finally, note that our subjects reported that the reduced contrast of the gratings appeared uniform throughout the entire 8° × 5° field 92% of the time, whether preceded by the dot or the bar. The contrast of the bullseye was judged uniform 77% of the time.

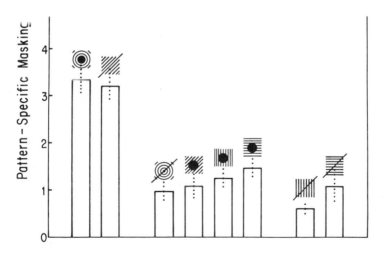

FIG. 9. Pattern-specific masking for various combinations of masking stimulus (dot or bar) and target (bullseye or grating). The y-axis represents the mean difference between magnitude estimations of the apparent contrast of a target when preceded by a given mask and when preceded by a blank flash. (From Weisstein, Harris, Berbaum, Tangney, & A. Williams, 1977.)

These findings are something of a mystery if we look only at the stimuli themselves. The bullseye and gratings cover a large stretch of retina, stimulating many retinal receptors and many cortical "edge detectors," "bar detectors," "dot detectors" and "curve detectors" (if there are any). The image of the dot or bar falls on only a tiny bit of retina, stimulating only a small fraction of the receptors or detectors that the bullseye or grating targets stimulate. Why should there be *any* masking to speak of? And since the small amount of spatial overlap is roughly the same for all target-mask pairs, why should there be differences in the amounts of masking? Finally, if masking depends on mechanisms that respond to local features, why does the masking appear uniform over such a wide area? In other words, if we stay within the space domain, looking at the untransformed stimuli, we don't find much basis for predicting or understanding these results.

In the Fourier domain, though, things look very different. Because the dot and bullseye vary in two dimensions instead of just one, we have to look at their Fourier power spectra as two-dimensional polar plots, in which distance from the center represents spatial frequency of a sine-wave component, and direction from the center represents its orientation (the sine-wave grating's orientation is perpendicular to that of the line between a plotted point and the center). There's no universally adequate way to represent the power of each component; we've chosen to give a qualitative picture, adequate for present purposes, by letting density of stippling stand for power (Fig. 10).

In the space domain, you would look at the retinal overlap of the target and mask, or at proximity of similar features, to get an idea of how much masking to expect. That didn't work for our data. So let's look at overlap in the Fourier domain, as an indication of the extent to which the mask contains sinusoidal components with the same orientations and spatial frequencies as the target. If you imagine superimposing the dot or the bar's spectrum on that of each target, you'll find there are three categories of overlap. The dot's spectrum blankets the bullseye's (the bullseye's outer ring at 45 cycles/degree doesn't contribute much to visibility) and the diagonal bar does the same to the diagonal grating. For those two pairs, spectrum overlap is *maximal*. And those are the two for which we found the most masking (Fig. 9). The diagonal bar's spectrum crosses that of the vertical or horizontal grating at only one place, at the center. Spectrum overlap is *minimal*. For those two pairs we found no significant pattern-specific masking.

The situation is less clearcut for the four remaining pairs, bar with bullseye and dot with each of the three grating orientations. Their spectra overlap along a single radius. By that criterion, spectrum overlap is *intermediate*. However, one radius is all there is to the gratings' spectra, whereas it's only a small fraction of the bullseye's spectrum. So it might be more reasonable to call the bar-bullseye overlap minimal; and indeed pattern-specific masking was not significant for that pair. The dot's spectrum blankets the entire spectrum of any grating, so one might expect masking to be maximal, as with the bar mask.

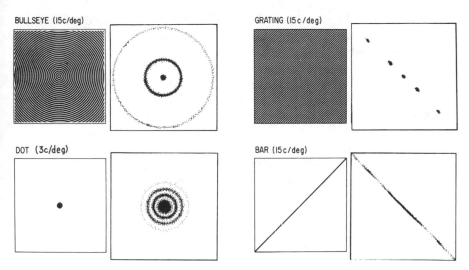

FIG. 10. Two masking stimuli (dot and bar) and two targets (bullseye and diagonal grating), with their two-dimensional Fourier power spectra. The pictures represent small parts of the 8.4° × 5.1° stimuli. The spectra are polar plots in which spatial frequency is represented by distance from the center, orientation by angle about the center, and power by density of stippling (not to scale). (From Weisstein, Harris, Berbaum, Tangney, & A. Williams, 1977.)

But whereas all of the power in the bar mask is concentrated along the diagonal in its spectrum, the same total power is spread out around the dot spectrum's rings, leaving much less of it in the part that overlaps a grating's spectrum. Thus we'd expect the grating to be masked much more strongly by an appropriately oriented bar than by a dot, and that's what we found.

Thus, when we look at Fourier transforms rather than at the stimuli themselves, our findings fall into place. When Fourier spectra overlap maximally, we get a lot of masking; when they overlap minimally, we get no significant pattern-specific masking; and when overlap is substantial but less than optimal, we generally get an intermediate degree of masking. And even though the mask is a tiny dot or a skinny line, whatever masking there is usually extends uniformly across the entire target pattern, just as we'd expect from mechanisms that integrate information from large regions of the retina.

Dots and Lines Depart from the Center of the Field

We had some hesitation about drawing conclusions from these experiments. The dot or bar mask was always right at the point of fixation, where vision is much better than a few degrees to the side. Maybe the masking really was local; maybe it was affecting judgments of our big target patterns only because we were masking the part of the retinal image that counts the most, the foveal part. What would happen if we gave subjects a better chance to detect nonuniformities in masking and a better look at unmasked parts of the field?

We moved the bar and dot masks off the fovea, 2° to the right or left of the fixation point, while leaving the gratings and bullseye targets centered. This meant that the maximum distance from the masking stimulus to the edge of the grating or bullseye target could be 6° (instead of 4° with the centered masks in the preceding experiment) while all of the target was still within 4° of fixation.

Figure 11 plots the amounts of pattern-specific masking by the off-fixation bar and dot and by an on-fixation bar that were randomly intermixed with other masks in this experiment, together with data on the on-fixation dot from the preceding experiment. Figure 11 shows that moving the masking dot or bar off the fixation point made hardly any difference. The amount of masking was nearly the same whether the mask was centered on the fovea or 2° away. If masking were a local phenomenon, and if foveal stimulation plays the dominant role in judgments of contrast (which is what we'd have to assume to explain our earlier findings), then we would have found marked differences: much masking when the masking stimulus fell right where the subject was looking, none at all when it fell 2° away, allowing an unobstructed view of the grating in the crucial foveal region. Similarly, if masking were local, and the off-fixation stimuli produced appreciable masking, the subjects should now have no trouble reporting the resultant nonuniformities in apparent contrast. They could compare the region right around the off-fixation mask either with a precisely comparable region symmetrically located 2° on the opposite side of fixation, or with the region at fixation, or with the far edge of the target, 6° away from the mask. Masking *wasn't* local, though: Our subjects said the tar-

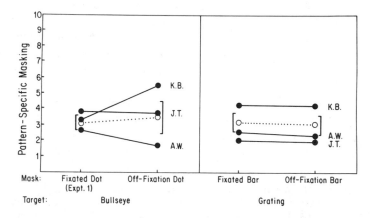

FIG. 11. Masking of a bullseye or grating by a fixated or off-fixation dot or bar. The open circles represent the means across the three subjects, with S.E.'s given by the brackets. (From Weisstein, Harris, Berbaum, Tangney, & A. Williams, 1977.)

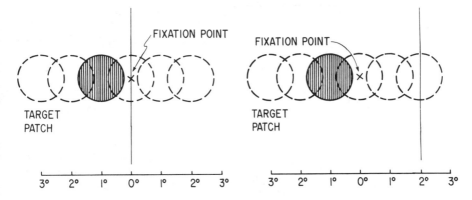

FIG. 12. Fixated bar mask (left), off-fixation bar mask (right), and possible locations of grating patch. On each trial, the circular patch of grating appeared in only one location. (From Weisstein, Harris, Berbaum, Tangney, & A. Williams, 1977.)

get contrast appeared uniform between 87% and 100% of the time for the various combinations of target and masks.

Peripatetic Patches

Mike Matthews suggested an even more radical way to test the difference between a distributed representation and one that represents patterns in terms of local features. Previously, we've been asking the subjects to judge an entire grating to see whether apparent contrast is depressed by different amounts in parts that are different distances from the masking bar. Now we simplify the task and let the subject see only a little piece of the grating each time. We flash the bar mask and follow it with a 1.5° circular patch of grating in some location or other (Fig. 12). All the subject has to tell us is the apparent contrast of that little patch. By placing the patch at different distances from the masking bar, we can use it as a probe to map out the spatial spread of the masking. We don't have to worry any more about how good subjects are at reporting nonuniformities of contrast.

Figure 12 shows the two possible locations for the bar mask and the six possible locations for the target patch. The x-axis lists the center-to-center distances between target and mask (the measure traditionally given in studies of spread of masking).

Figure 13 shows the amount of pattern-specific masking for each separation between target and mask, averaged across three subjects. (The x-axis here is labelled with a more conservative measure of separation: the minimum distance between the masking bar and the nearest edge of the target patch—0.75° less than the center-to-center distance. There does appear to be a little more

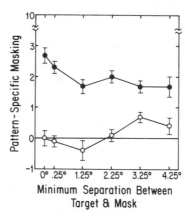

FIG. 13. Masking of patches of vertical and horizontal grating by a vertical bar. (From Weisstein, Harris, Berbaum, Tangney, & A. Williams, 1977.)

masking when the bar is centered on the target patch (0°) or is right alongside it (0.25° minimum separation), but what's noteworthy is that the masking persists out to separations as great as 4.25°. The masking is both pattern-specific (greater than that produced by a blank field) and orientation-specific: The vertical bar masked the vertically-striped patch but not, by and large, the horizontally-striped patch. So now we're getting reliable masking with *no* spatial overlap of mask and target, in fact with a hefty open space between them.

We also analyzed these data in a different way, translating the magnitude estimation data into "equivalent physical contrasts" by finding out, in a separate experiment, the correspondence between our subjects' magnitude estimations and the physically measured contrast of an unmasked grating. In effect, this converts the numerical estimates of apparent contrast into a matching procedure, telling us what physical contrast of an unmasked grating has the same apparent contrast as a masked grating patch. The results of this simulated matching procedure were not much different from those shown in Fig. 13. If anything, the spatial spread of masking appeared a little more uniform, less peaked at 0°.

CONTEXT-DEPENDENT PERCEPTION

It would be rash to claim that this section follows logically from the one above. It would be rash even to assert that there is any substantive connection at all. Nevertheless, we suspect that the connection is more than merely verbal or metaphorical, though it will take a lot more research to establish whether it is or isn't.

All of the experiments in this section deal with relatively simple perceptual judgments, which in principle could be determined by stimulation confined to a small region of the retina (and which might therefore be mediated by feature detectors that deal with only a small retinal region). However, in all of these experiments, we find instead that perceptions are influenced by what is present over a considerable area of the retina—by "contextual" stimuli that wouldn't impinge at all on the presumably pertinent feature detectors. At that level of description, these experiments therefore fall into the same category as the masking studies described above. One might venture the guess that these experiments too depend on some sort of distributed representation, which brings together, somewhere in the nervous system, information about stimulus structures over a wide retinal expanse.

In the experiments summarized in this section, as in those discussed previously, the results obtained usually depend on the values chosen for temporal parameters such as durations of various parts of the stimulus presentation and of delays between them. This is to be expected, since different visual processes at different processing stages are likely to have different time courses for build-up of response, transmission, adaptation, and recovery. Indeed, it is our hope that we can capitalize on distinctive temporal characteristics in order to gain information about where and how particular operations take place. In general, then, "catching" the visual system in the act of performing some operation requires particular conditions of timing, and in the summaries below we mention only those conditions that manifest the effects described. Readers interested in the experimental details, including those that cast doubt on alternative less-interesting interpretations of the findings, should consult the original papers.

Cube in Front of Grating

If the patterns shown in Fig. 14a or 14b are used as masking stimuli, and subjects are asked to judge the apparent contrast of a subsequently presented tar-

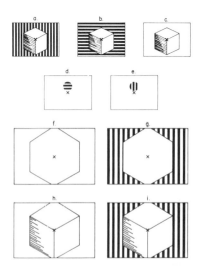

FIG. 14. Stimuli used to assess masking by part of a grating that is hidden by a drawing of a cube (a and b). (From Weisstein, Montalvo, & Ozog, 1972.)

get patch like Fig. 14d or 14e, the results (Weisstein, 1970) are much like those described above under the heading "Peripatetic Patches." As in the earlier experiment, the masking stimulus (a grating here, instead of a single line) does not fall on the same retinal area as the target patch, yet there is significant masking when the orientations of mask and target match (Fig. 15). There is some masking when orientations do not match, but considerably less than when they do. Thus we again have evidence of orientation-specific masking occurring across an appreciable retinal separation. (To subtract out the kinds of generalized masking that are not of interest here, the masking produced by Fig. 14c, identical to Figs. 14a and 14b except for the missing grating, was used as baseline; hence the masking in Fig. 15 is labeled "grating-specific masking.")

However, by using Fig. 14g as mask (with Fig. 14f as the appropriate baseline comparison), it is possible to go beyond the previous findings (Weisstein, Montalvo, & Ozog, 1972). Here too the grating is separated from a target, in fact separated in just the same way as with masks 14a and 14b. Yet, for certain conditions (masks exposed for 20-40 seconds, followed by a 20-50 millisecond delay before the target patch appears), mask 14g is a significantly less effective mask than 14i (essentially the same pattern as 14 a), as shown in Fig. 16.

Why the difference? The difference may be related to the obvious perceptual difference between the two types of mask. Figures 14a and 14b obviously portray a cube in front of a grating. The grating stripes appear to extend continuously behind the cube; one would be taken aback if removing the cube revealed a hexagonal hole in the grating! The perception of Figs. 14f and 14g is more variable: Sometimes to some subjects it looks like an opaque white hex-

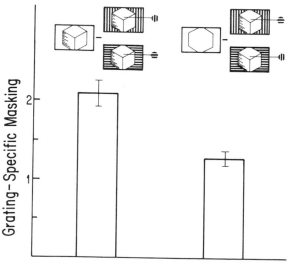

FIG. 15. Masking obtained when part of a grating is hidden by a drawing of a cube. The amount of masking is greater when the small test patch is oriented the same way as the large grating (left) than when they are perpendicular (right). The y-axis represents the difference between magnitude estimations of the test patch's contrast when preceded by the cube-plus-grating and by the cube alone. (Redrawn from Weisstein, Montalvo, & Ozog, 1972.)

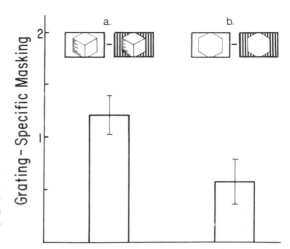

FIG. 16. Masking obtained when part of a grating is hidden either by a drawing of a cube (left) or by a blank hexagon (right). (Redrawn from Weisstein, Montalvo, & Ozog, 1972.)

agon resting against the grating; occasionally like a cube with the some of the edges hard to see; and most often like a hole in the grating. In any case, the perception of an object standing out in depth in front of the grating is much less compelling in Fig. 14f than in 14a and 14b.

The hypothesis is that just as *we* react to the cube as if the grating is continuous behind it, so does some neural mechanism that is capable of producing masking. Given suitable depth cues, such a mechanism could be adapted by a grating that is subjectively present but retinally absent at the place where the target patch is viewed. It may be, then, that distributed masking effects are pointing toward mechanisms that are involved in the perception of objects, separation in depth, and the versatile "filling-in" processes in perception.

Illusory Gratings

There are other configurations that yield more vivid perceptions of contours that are not actually present in the retinal image. Figure 17 gives some illus-

FIG. 17. Examples of illusory contours. Sharp contours bounding the central figures are visible where there is no corresponding physical discontinuity. In addition, the central figures appear brighter than the surrounding paper. (From, left to right, Ehrenstein, 1954; Weisstein & Maguire, 1978; Kanizsa, 1955.)

trations. It has been suggested that such subjective or illusory contours are related to depth cues (Coren, 1972; Gregory, 1972).

What happens if we construct a grating out of illusory contours, as in Fig. 18? It turns out (Fig. 19) that an illusory grating of this sort can mask, and be masked by, a real grating with the same orientation (Weisstein, Matthews, & Berbaum, 1974). Control experiments show that it is the illusory contours, not the tiny black figures that produce them, that are responsible for the masking.

Thus it appears that illusory contours and real contours affect some common visual mechanism. A further intriguing aspect of these findings is that masking of illusory contours by real ones is greatest when the masking spatial frequency is three times the illusory target frequency rather than when the frequencies are equal. This suggests that the mechanisms responsible for illusory contours may be particularly concerned with sharp contours (normally specified by high spatial-frequency components) rather than differences in luminance over wider areas (low spatial frequencies).

Phantom Contours

A somewhat different way to induce perception of contours where none are present retinally was described by Tynan and Sekuler (1975). If a horizontal strip of opaque black tape is used to cover up part of a moving vertical grating, the contours are perceived to continue through the taped-over region—clearly, but with lower contrast, as if the tape were partially transparent. With this configuration (Fig. 20b), unlike those illustrated above, no subjective contours are seen if the grating is stationary; for that reason, Tynan and Sekuler coined a new name for them, "moving phantoms."

Even when the grating is moving, phantoms are not seen if the opaque tape is oriented vertically as in Fig. 20c, instead of horizontally. We don't yet know why the orientation of the blank region matters, but as with other illusory contours there appears to be a connection with perceived depth, whether as cause or effect. The horizontal blank strip appears to lie practically in the same plane as the moving grating and to be somewhat transparent; the vertical blank strip typically seems to stand out an inch or more in front of the grating and looks

FIG. 18.   An illusory grating (top) and a real grating (bottom). (From Weisstein, Matthews, & Berbaum, 1974.)

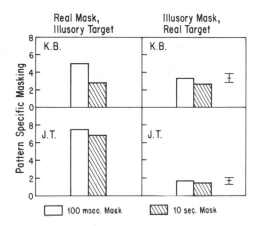

FIG. 19. Masking of an illusory grating by a real grating (left) and vice versa (right). For the illusory target (left), the y-axis represents the difference between magnitude estimations of apparent contrast of the illusory grating when preceded by the real grating and by a blank field with the same mean luminance. For the real target (right), the comparison is between the illusory grating and a pattern containing only the small half-disks from Fig. 18a, which does not produce illusory contours. Data from two observers, with each of two mask durations. (From Weisstein, Matthews, & Berbaum, 1974.)

opaque (Weisstein, Maguire, & Berbaum, 1977). If the blank region is trapezoidal (Fig. 21), phantoms are seen whenever the trapezoid appears to be in the same plane as or in back of the stripes, but not when it appears to stand out in front of the stripes.

The moving contours that give rise to the phantom contours need not be physically present—moving illusory contours will do just as well (Fig. 22). In fact, this kind of stimulus yields a startling observation: One sees not only phantom contours crossing the blank region, but also—dimly but unmistakably—columns of ×'s!

Phantom-Motion Aftereffect

Moving phantom contours have been found to produce a strong motion aftereffect (Weisstein, Maguire, & Berbaum, 1977). After two minutes' observation of the moving phantoms while fixating on a luminous point within the horizontal blank region, a small stationary patch of grating that fell entirely within that region (Fig. 20, bottom) appeared to move in the opposite direction (Fig. 23). The aftereffect depended on the perceived phantom contours rather than on the physically present moving contours: With the blank strip vertical (Fig. 20c) phantoms were not seen and there was little aftereffect.

What makes this phantom-motion aftereffect so interesting is that virtually all of the voluminous literature on motion aftereffects has indicated that such

FIG. 20. Phantom contours (Tynan & Sekuler, 1975). If a strip of opaque black tape is placed over a set of moving stripes like (a), producing a display like (b), illusory moving contours are seen crossing the taped-over region. Phantom contours are not seen if the tape is oriented vertically (c). (From Weisstein, Maguire, & Berbaum, 1977.)

FIG. 21. Phantom contours dependent on perceived depth. Phantom contours are seen within the empty trapezoidal region when it is perceived as lying in the same plane as the moving stripes or behind them, but not when it appears to stand out in front of them. (From Weisstein & Maguire, 1978.)

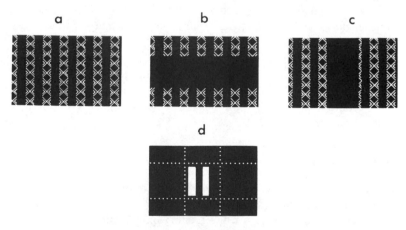

FIG. 22. Phantom contours induced by moving illusory contours. If moving illusory vertical contours (a) are covered with an opaque strip of tape (b), phantom contours with dimly visible ×'s are seen crossing the tape. With the tape oriented vertically (c), phantom contours are not seen. A small test patch (d) can be used to assess motion aftereffects within a retinal region that has not been directly stimulated by moving contours. (From Weisstein, Maguire, & Berbaum, 1977.)

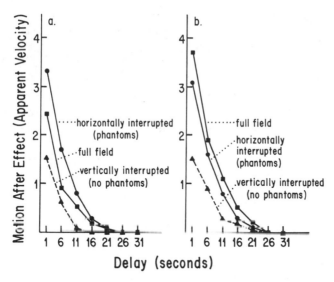

FIG. 23.   Phantom-motion aftereffects.   Strength of the motion aftereffect seen with a small test patch (Fig. 20, bottom) at various delays after observing moving contours ("full-field"), moving phantom contours ("horizontally interrupted"), or no perceived contours ("vertically interrupted").   The stimuli were (left) square wave gratings as in Fig. 20 or (right) illusory gratings as in Fig. 22.   Judged velocity of a small patch of grating is plotted as a function of the delay after the end of adaptation.   (From Weisstein, Maguire, & Berbaum, 1977.)

aftereffects are confined to retinal regions that have actually been stimulated by moving contours (Wohlgemuth, 1911; Anstis & Gregory, 1965; Masland, 1965).   Perceived motion without retinal displacement (as when following a moving stimulus with the eyes) has been shown to be insufficient for a motion aftereffect (Anstis & Gregory, 1965).

'Such strict dependence on local retinal stimulation made local motion-detecting mechanisms seem the logical candidate for explaining the aftereffect (Barlow & Hill, 1963).   So compelling was the connection that even when an exception was found—aftereffects produced within a stationary region that was made to appear to move by motion in the surrounding area—relatively local relative-motion detectors were invoked in explanation (Anstis & Rinehart-Rutland, 1976).   The phantom-motion aftereffect, though, is different from Anstis and Rinehart-Rutland's: ours goes in the opposite direction, and cannot be explained by detectors that straddle moving and stationary regions.

Object Superiority

Up to this point, the experiments we've been summarizing show perceptual effects occurring within retinal regions that have not been subjected to the presumably pertinent stimulation. In the following experiments, adequate stimulus information *is* present, confined to a small retinal region, but perception is found to be crucially affected by the configuration of stimuli falling on a much more extensive region.

In our basic experiment, the task seems ideally suited to detectors that specialize in signalling the presence of contours with a certain orientation at a certain retinal location. Our subjects had to report which one of four diagonal line segments, differing in orientation and location, had been briefly flashed (Fig. 24, a-d). What we found was that other lines, vertical and horizontal, influenced accuracy in identifying the diagonal line, depending on the total configuration (Weisstein & Harris, 1974). Certain configurations of these context lines, such as the overlapping squares in Fig. 24e, combine with each diagonal line to yield a distinctive perception of a unified, three-dimensional object (Fig. 24f-i), whereas other arrangements of the same lines don't (Fig. 25c-f and 26b-e).

We found that accuracy in identifying the diagonal lines was greater when they were accompanied by these overlapping squares than with any other arrangement of these context lines that has been tried (Figs. 25-28), even when the extra lines in the immediate neighborhood of the diagonal line were arranged identically (Fig. 27). We have labelled this basic finding (greater accuracy with an object-like pattern) the *object-superiority effect*. Under certain conditions, accuracy on the diagonal lines is actually greater when they are part of the object-like pictures than when presented all alone, even though extra lines normally *decrease* accuracy in detecting a target (because of simultaneous masking, reduced signal-to-noise ratio, etc.). This comparison is called the *object-line effect*. Both phenomena have now been replicated in a number of la-

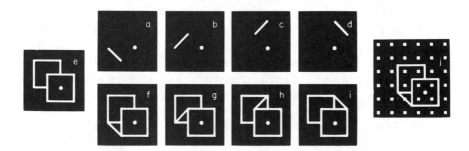

FIG. 24. Stimuli for demonstrating object superiority. Subjects report which one of four diagonal lines (a-d) is flashed on each trial. When additional lines accompany the target line, the combinations may look like three-dimensional objects (f-i). Because the context pattern (e) is the same for all four target lines, it provides no clue about which line is present. In some experiments, a dotted masking pattern (j) follows each stimulus flash. (From Weisstein & Harris, 1974.)

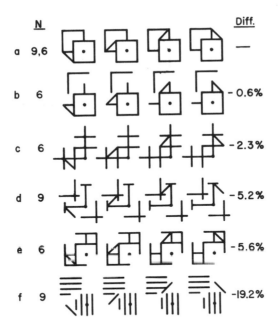

FIG. 25. Object superiority. Relative accuracy in identifying diagonal line segments when briefly flashed with various context patterns. *Diff* is the mean deficit in accuracy with each context as compared to the overlapping squares (row a). (From Weisstein & Harris, 1974.)

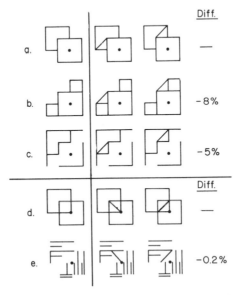

FIG. 26. Object superiority. As in Fig. 25, but with only two target lines. When context a was modified slightly to produce a flatter appearance (d), accuracy was the same as with e. (a-c from A. Williams & Weisstein, 1977; d and e from Womersley, 1977.)

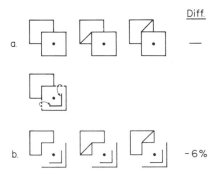

Diff.

FIG. 27. Object superiority with identical surroundings for the target lines. Two line segments are moved, leaving the local neighborhoods of the target line segments identical; nevertheless, accuracy is better by 6% for the more connected, apparently three-dimensional drawing. (From A. Williams & Weisstein, 1977.)

boratories, with a number of different procedures and stimuli (Spoehr, 1975; Womersley, 1977; Klein, 1978; McClelland, 1978; A. Williams & Weisstein, 1978; Earhard & Armitage, 1979).

Word superiority. These "object-superiority" and "object-line" effects are closely analogous to the much-studied "word-superiority" and "word-letter" effects: A letter is typically detected better when flashed as part of a pronounceable word than in an unpronounceable string of letters or alone (for a review, see Baron, 1978). In both cases, a constituent element (letter or line segment) is perceived better when the context creates a well-formed unit, even if the context provides no clues about the correct choice on a given trial (as in Fig. 24).

Since the identity of the whole unit depends on the identity of the critical constituent, it seems paradoxical that the overall configuration can aid perception of the constituent. In particular, such findings create difficulties for hierarchical pattern-recognition models which assume that elementary features must reach some perceptually available threshold value before overall structure can be ascertained from the identified features. In fact, even with a masking stimulus that reduced identification all the way to a chance level for a single letter in isolation (or in a nonsense string), the same letter could be identified quite reliably as part of a word (with words chosen to supply no information about which target letter was present; Matthews, Weisstein, & A. Williams, 1974).

Three-dimensionality and coherence. The early evidence suggested that both perceived coherence and perceived depth contribute to the object-superiority effect. The rank ordering of accuracies with our patterns and with a different set used by Greg Ozog in an unpublished experiment seems to fit well with this idea. So does Womersley's finding (1977) that the accuracy advantage with overlapping squares disappeared when they were modified slightly, so that they yielded much flatter perceptions (Fig. 26d). Additional evidence comes from a pilot study in which we asked subjects not only to identify the diagonal line but also to indicate, on each trial, whether the figure appeared unitary and three-dimensional. Subjects were *more* accurate in identifying the diagonal line on trials when they *incorrectly* perceived Fig. 25b as a unitary object.

The most direct evidence for the contribution of three-dimensionality to target enhancement comes from recent experiments using the patterns shown in Fig. 28 (Weisstein, M. C. Williams, & Harris, 1979). In addition to testing subjects' accuracy in identifying the target lines, we had other subjects rate the apparent depth of each pattern on a scale from 1 to 10. As Fig. 29 shows, mean accuracy in detecting the diagonal target lines corresponded very closely with mean depth rating. The correlation between accuracy and judged connectedness was much lower.

Time course. In one popular masking procedure, known as "metacontrast," a target is flashed first and an adjacent masking pattern follows. By varying the delay between target and mask, and measuring accuracy of target detection at each delay, we can map out the temporal metacontrast function. The function typically found is U-shaped. Accuracy at first decreases and then recovers as the masking pattern is delayed by longer amounts, presumably as a result of the interaction between a fast inhibitory response to the masking pattern and a slower excitatory response to the target (Weisstein, 1968, 1972; Weisstein, Ozog, & Szoc, 1975; Matin, 1975; Breitmeyer & Ganz, 1976). When the metacontrast paradigm is employed with our patterns, presenting the context lines at various times after the diagonal target lines are flashed, it turns out that accuracy with three-dimensional patterns has a different time course from

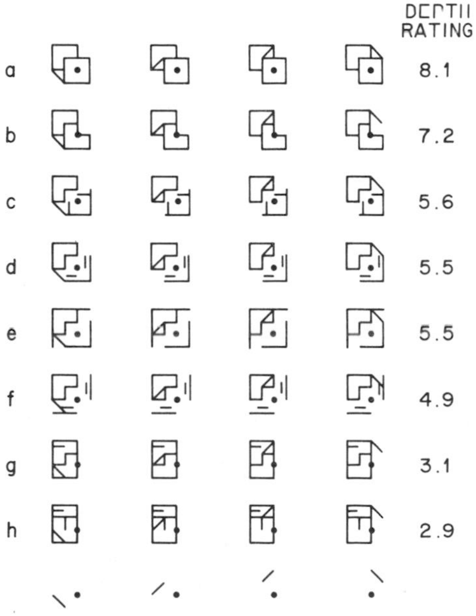

FIG. 28. Patterns for assessing the relation of object superiority to apparent depth. Ten subjects' mean ratings (on a 10-point scale) of the apparent three-dimensionality of each pattern are given to the right of each set. (From Weisstein, M. C. Williams, & Harris, 1979.)

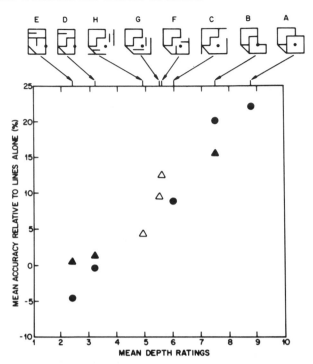

FIG. 29. Object superiority and apparent depth. The y-axis represents relative accuracy in identifying briefly flashed diagonal line segments in the eight contexts shown in Fig. 28. Percentage correct when the lines were flashed alone was subtracted from percentage correct with each context to yield the relative advantages given on the y-axis. ●: 4 experienced observers; △: 8 naive observers; ▲: 10 naive observers. The x-axis represents 10 other observers' mean ratings of the apparent depth of each set of patterns. (From Weisstein, M. C. Williams, & Harris, 1979.)

that with flatter patterns (A. Williams & Weisstein, 1977; Weisstein, M. C. Williams, & A. Williams, 1979).

Each context pattern produces a different characteristic temporal function, and the function changes in systematic ways as the perceived depth of the pattern decreases (Fig. 30). These differences suggest that visual rise time and latency for flat patterns and three-dimensional ones are different. There are also characteristic differences between the temporal functions for connected patterns and for fragmented ones. Thus, both visual rise time and latency appear to differ for classes of patterns that differ in certain global ways.

Vertices.

We have also looked for effects analogous to object superiority with simpler patterns of lines that could represent vertices of three-dimensional objects

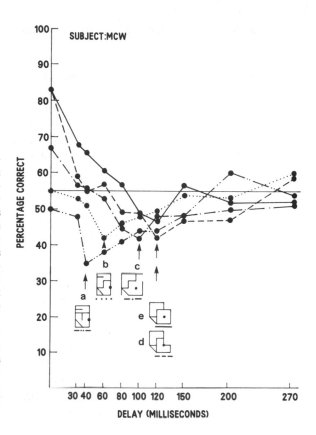

FIG. 30. The time course of object superiority: accuracy in detecting briefly flashed line segments as a function of the delay between the line and various context patterns. The baseline (horizontal line) is accuracy when a diagonal line alone is flashed. As apparent three-dimensionality increases, from pattern a to e, the lowest point in the masking curve moves to the right. Also note that patterns c, d, and e show higher accuracy than for lines alone at zero and short delays, whereas the flattest patterns, a and b, do not. (From Weisstein, M. C. Williams, & A. Williams, 1979.)

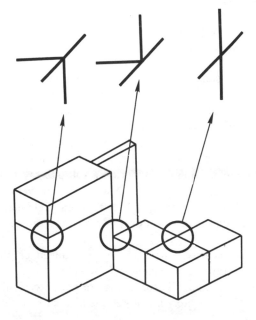

FIG. 31. Line patterns that can represent vertices of objects. Although the patterns do not look particularly three-dimensional, subjects' accuracy in detecting diagonal target lines corresponded to each pattern's reliability in indicating a single solid object according to Guzman's (1968) computer scene-analysis programs. (From Berbaum, 1978.)

355

(Fig. 31). When presented in isolation, such configurations do not reliably lead to the perception of depth. But we thought that perception of three-dimensionality might not be essential if the configuration is one that normally plays an important role in object perception. With the same task as in the object-superiority experiments, but with the diagonal target line forming part of one or another vertex configuration, we found that accuracy corresponded to the reliability with which each vertex would indicate a single solid object according to Guzman's (1968) computer scene-analysis programs (Berbaum, Weisstein, & Harris, 1975).

However, we should note that vertex effects do not appear to account for object superiority, at least not in any simple, additive way. In the patterns we used (Figs. 25-28), neither the presence or absence of particular vertices nor the total number of vertices gives good predictions of performance. For example, Fig. 25e contains as many vertices as Fig. 25a, and all of the same types of vertex, yet accuracy is lower for the flatter-looking figure.

Similar comparisons among our patterns rule out other potential, relatively local, explanations of object superiority. The number, orientation, total length, and proximity of lines near the target line or fixation point may influence accuracy through masking or the creation of "emergent features" such as triangles (Mezrich, 1975; Pomerantz, Sager, & Stoever, 1977). But such emergent features are found in both high and low-accuracy patterns, and the number of lines that touch the fixation point (Earhard & Armitage, 1979) also appears to be unrelated to accuracy in these patterns.

Illusory Pauses

We described above conditions for producing a perception of motion within a retinal region that is not being stimulated by moving contours. During the course of experiments with computer-generated movies of rotating randomly dotted spheres (Lappin, Doner, Kottas, & Harris, 1978), a complementary illusion unexpectedly emerged: a perception of *no* motion with a stimulus that actually *is* moving. (A similar illusion was mentioned by Mace, 1971.)

More specifically, under certain conditions stimuli that are actually moving at a constant speed appear to hesitate briefly before resuming their steady velocity. These illusory pauses can be produced by having two identical arrays (for example, luminous spots on a cathode ray tube, or black squares on overlapping transparencies) move with uniform velocity in opposite directions. When the arrays match up—that is, when their elements simultaneously coincide—they appear to slow down or even stop momentarily (Harris, Schwartz, Patashnik, & Lappin, 1978).

The apparent pausing can be reduced or eliminated by briefly speeding up the arrays in the vicinity of the coincidence point. (Of course, there is still an illusion, since the speed-ups are not perceived.) So far, it appears that as long as the oppositely moving items in each pair have the same shape and all of the pairs overlap at the same time, the illusory pauses persist despite many variations of the stimulus—with one exception.

The one procedure that markedly reduces the prominence of illusory pauses is easiest to understand if one pictures the dots as they would appear on a strip of movie film. A typical pair of dots, moving in opposite directions, is shown in Fig. 32A. (Although the pauses can easily be observed with stimuli that are moving smoothly and continuously, most of the observations have in fact been made with the equivalent of movies: successive 20- or 40-millisecond still "frames" displayed on a cathode ray tube.) Suppose that each frame of the movie lasts for 20 milliseconds. If we black out the frame before and the one after the frame in which the corresponding pairs of dots coincide (Fig. 32B), the dots generally appear to sail past one another smoothly, instead of seeming to hesitate as they cross.

Now, certain classes of motion detectors, which respond to sequential stimulation of adjacent retinal points, might behave similarly—signalling "no motion" when stimulated simultaneously by two adjacent dots, and signalling "motion" if the pairs of dots disappear whenever they would be close enough together to stimulate the same detector. But a further modification of the movie yields a surprising result. In addition to the two frames adjacent to the coincidence frame, we black out every second frame throughout the sequence,

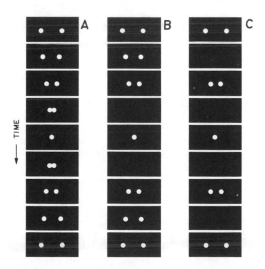

FIG. 32. Illusory pauses of moving dots. Successive frames from movies of oppositely moving arrays of dots; only one dot from each array is shown. The dots appear to pause when they coincide (A), even though the distance traveled is constant from frame to frame. If the dots are eliminated from the frames before and after the coincidence frame (B), smooth motion is perceived. If the dots are eliminated from alternate frames throughout the movie (C), the illusory pauses return. (From Schwartz, Harris, & Patashnik, 1979.)

as in Fig. 32C (Schwartz, Harris, & Patashnik, 1979). The illusory pause returns!

It is difficult to devise any strictly local motion detector—one that looks at stimuli only over a very restricted region of time and space—that would respond as human observers do in all three cases. It seems that a local motion detector would either report pauses in both A and B, or smooth motion in both B and C. Indeed, Harris, Schwartz, Patashnik, and Lappin (1978) considered a wide variety of possible kinds of explanation—from optical (intensity transients) to sensory (vector addition or averaging) to perceptual (motion ambiguity) to cognitive (expectations about collisions)—without finding any one that could deal with all of the observations on illusory pauses.

There is a tantalizing parallel between illusory pauses and object superiority. In both cases we are dealing with a perception that could be based on very local stimulus information—either the location and orientation of a line segment or the motion of points. And in both cases we find that the potentially local perception is decisively influenced by stimuli that are situated some distance away—the context patterns for object superiority, and the alternating blank frames for illusory pauses.

Summary

In all of the experiments outlined in this section, we have found perceptual effects that depend critically on configurations of stimuli over large retinal regions, including regions distant from those where the effect is measured, even though there previously seemed to be strong theoretical and/or empirical reasons for supposing that these perceptual performances should depend exclusively on stimulation within very restricted regions, making local feature detectors adequate explanatory mechanisms.

The connection with distributed representations is at present tenuous, but a distributed representation might be one way to bring together, for further processing, information about configurations over large retinal regions. Information about the entire input pattern is present at each point or small region in a distributed representation. Analogously, in these experiments, it is as if, at whatever stage in the visual system these effects occur, information about the entire input pattern is having an effect at each point in the representation, including those where (if the representation were a topographical map) there is no pertinent input stimulation. Indeed it seems likely that a distributed representation's *function* would be more than simply combining activity from a wide area (as in the masking studies); rather it could contribute to establishing the overall *structure* that allows us to perceive a coherent, meaningful world of objects and spatial relations.

CONCLUSIONS

Why Fourier? (Reprise)

We started out by discussing why there has been so much excitement over the idea that the visual system may perform something like a Fourier analysis, dealing with complex visual stimuli in terms of their spatial-frequency components. There are two main reasons: (1) a considerable amount of data, both physiological and psychophysical, pointed to the existence of channels that respond only to restricted bands of spatial frequency; and (2) such an analysis would be a very interesting and powerful way to code visual information for further processing. In particular, much of the novelty and utility of the code would derive from an important accompaniment of precise spatial-frequency coding: distributed representation, meaning that each point in the input stimulus contributes to a wide region of the neural representation and, conversely, that each point or unit in the neural representation contains, in some sense, information about an extensive portion of the the original stimulus pattern.

We then summarized some research that was inspired by two predictions that might be derived if the visual system were doing a reasonable approximation to a Fourier analysis. Other evidence relating to Fourier analysis in the visual system has been pouring out of many laboratories recently, some of it consistent with the idea (for example, Kelly, 1975), some inconsistent (for example, Greenwood, 1973; Limb & Rubinstein, 1977). The data described here add to the variety of evidence consistent with the idea. First, we have found that pattern-specific masking generally adheres more closely to overlap of the *transforms* of stimuli in the Fourier domain than to retinal overlap of the stimuli themselves, in the space domain. Second, we have found a variety of evidence that stimuli interact across much greater retinal distances than would be expected in terms of purely local features. Since these interactions are dependent on spatial-pattern relationships, their extensive spread suggests that, at some stage in visual processing, there are distributed representations of stimuli.

Why Not Fourier?

We certainly wouldn't want to conclude from these data that the visual system really *is* Fourier analyzing visual patterns. There are a number of serious obstacles to that heady conclusion. For one thing, Fourier analysis requires linearity, and linearity is violated again and again in the visual system. There are compressive transformations on luminance and, apparently, on contrast as well (e.g. Blakemore, Muncey, & Ridley, 1973). In a linear system, each component must contribute independently to the sum, yet sometimes individual spatial-frequency components don't add up; they seem instead to inhibit each other (Tolhurst, 1972). Furthermore, a true Fourier analysis calls for highly selective spatial-frequency channels, yet even the most extreme estimates so far yield channel bandwidths that are too broad for a precise, reversible Fourier transform or for the extent of spatial distribution seen in our experiments.

Fourier's Cousins

Yet even if the visual system doesn't carry out a true Fourier analysis, there are a number of related things it may be doing that might be extremely useful. A Fourier *series*, adequate for representing any pattern within a delimited interval, does not have to use trigonometric functions as its elementary components; any set of orthogonal functions will do. If visual analysis rests on nontrigonometric functions, then channel bandwidth estimates that are based on sine-wave stimuli might give little idea of the relevant selectivity of the analyzers. In addition, with some other functions one wouldn't have to make the awkward assumption that spatial distribution would have to span most of the retina to allow good pattern discrimination; a few degrees might be sufficient for a serviceable analysis.

Some of these alternative transforms would share many of the processing advantages mentioned above for the Fourier transform; some would have other or additional advantages. Undoubtedly some would share enough with the Fourier transform to give as good or better fits to the available data. Any such scheme of analysis, however, would share the property of extracting patterns from more than a very restricted patch of the retinal image.

Distributed Representations

What if we find out some day that in fact these data have nothing at all to do with Fourier, not even with the most general form of Fourier's theorem? Would all the brouhaha over Fourier analysis in the visual system then have been a total waste of time? We don't think so. Whatever the visual system *is* doing, looking at it as if it were doing a Fourier analysis has already proven to be a useful heuristic, leading us to experiments and insights that we otherwise would not have come to. Many of the observations made and the methods devised will become a lasting part of visual science. Distribution and spread of masking; masking related to global transforms rather than local similarity— these findings emerge easily and understandably from a Fourier rationale. If a Fourier scheme leads to such otherwise counterintuitive data, this in itself may justify at least figuring out what the Fourier predictions would be and seeing how closely predictions are matched by empirical data.

We would go further than that. Our guess is that the idea of distribution, which was fostered and clarified by Fourier analysis, will (in some yet-to-beelaborated form) outlive the notion of Fourier analysis in the visual system. The idea of distribution extends well beyond the particular mathematics of Fourier analysis. As discussed above, it has implications for a much larger portion of the pattern-recognition process: for speed of processing, for the basic nature of processing, for context effects in perception, for memory. The fact that you can identify a line segment better when it is part of a three-dimensional pattern than when it is presented in a less meaningful flat design, and that you can recognize an object better in a coherent picture than in a jumbled one (Biederman, 1974), may hint at extensively distributed representations of all local aspects of a pattern, to facilitate rapid calculations of what the scene is about. Similarly, masking by a part of a grating that is not actually present on the retina—either because the grating consists entirely of illusory contours or because it is mostly hidden behind an opaque cube may hint that the visual system is *using* distributed mechanisms to figure out what constitutes an object and what extends behind it as background.

To sum up, thinking about Fourier analysis gives us new ways to think about representations of visual stimuli. Ultimately we may find—the empirical hints are already turning up—that distribution serves diverse and versatile functions in the process of transforming the meaningless mosaic of light energy on our retinas into the pictures in our heads.

ACKNOWLEDGMENTS

Some of the research described here was supported in part by grants 5 R01 EY 01330 from the National Eye Institute and BNS76-02059 from the National Science Foundation to N. W.

REFERENCES

Anstis, S. M. What does visual perception tell us about visual coding? In M. S. Gazzaniga & C. Blakemore (Eds.), *Handbook of psychobiology.* New York: Academic Press, 1975.

Anstis, S. M., & Gregory, R. L. The aftereffect of seen motion: The role of retinal stimulation and eye movements. *Quarterly Journal of Experimental Psychology,* 1965, *17,* 173-175.

Anstis, S. M., & Reinhardt-Rutland, A. H. Interactions between motion aftereffects and induced movement. *Vision Research,* 1976, *16,* 1391-1394.

Barlow, H. B., & Hill, R. M. Evidence for a physiological explanation of the waterfall illusion and figural aftereffects. *Nature,* 1963, *200,* 1434-1435.

Baron, J. The word-superiority effect: Perceptual learning from reading. In W. K. Estes (Ed.), *Handbook of learning and cognitive processes.* Vol. 6. Hillsdale, New Jersey: Lawrence Erlbaum Associates, 1978.

Berbaum, K. *Investigations of the psychological reality of certain visual syntactic predictions derived from contemporary computer algorithms for scene parsing and analysis.* Doctoral dissertation, State University of New York at Buffalo, 1978.

Berbaum, K., Weisstein, N., & Harris, C. S. Certain types of vertices aid line detection. *Bulletin of the Psychonomic Society,* 1975, *6,* 418. (Abstract)

362   Naomi Weisstein and Charles S. Harris

Biederman, I. Perceiving real-world scenes. *Science*, 1972, *177*, 77-79.

Blakemore, C., Muncey, J. P. J., & Ridley, R. M. Stimulus specificity in the human visual system. *Vision Research*, 1973, *13*, 1915-1931.

Breitmeyer, B. G., & Ganz, L. Implications of sustained and transient channels for theories of visual pattern masking, saccadic suppression, and information processing. *Psychological Review*, 1976, *83*, 1-36.

Brigham, E. O. *The fast Fourier transform*. Englewood Cliffs, New Jersey: Prentice-Hall, 1974.

Campbell, F. W., & Robson, J. G. Application of Fourier analysis to the visibility of gratings. *Journal of Physiology*, 1968, *197*, 551-556.

Coren, S. Subjective contours and apparent depth. *Psychological Review*, 1972, *79*, 359-367.

Cornsweet, T. N. *Visual perception*. New York: Academic Press, 1970.

Earhard, B., & Armitage, R. The object-line superiority effect: Is it an object or a more general perceptual context effect? Paper presented at Eastern Psychological Association, Philadelphia, April 1979.

Ehrenstein, W. *Probleme der ganzheitspsychologischen Wahrnehmungslehre*. Leipzig: Barth, 1954.

Frost, B. J. Contextual influences on the specificity of visual neurons. Paper presented at Lake Ontario Visionary Establishment, Niagara Falls, Ontario, February 1979.

Graham, N. Spatial-frequency channels in human vision: Detecting edges without edge detectors. In C. S. Harris (Ed.), *Visual coding and adaptability*. Hillsdale, New Jersey: Lawrence Erlbaum Associates, 1980.

Greenwood, R. E. Visibility of structured and unstructured images. *Journal of the Optical Society of America*, 1973, *63*, 226-231.

Gregory, R. L. Cognitive contours. *Nature*, 1972, *238*, 51-52.

Guzman, A. Computer recognition of three-dimensional objects in a visual scene. *Project MAC Technical Report 59*. Cambridge, Massachusetts: MIT Artificial Intelligence Laboratory, 1968.

Harris, C. S. Insight or out of sight?: Two examples of perceptual plasticity in the human adult. In C. S. Harris (Ed.), *Visual coding and adaptability*. Hillsdale, New Jersey: Lawrence Erlbaum Associates, 1980.

Harris, C. S., Schwartz, B. J., Patashnik, O., & Lappin, J. S. Illusory pauses of moving dots. *Bulletin of the Psychonomic Society*, 1978, *12*, 257. (Abstract)

Hubel, D. H., & Wiesel, T. N. Receptive fields, binocular interaction, and functional architecture in the cat's visual cortex. *Journal of Physiology*, 1962, *160*, 106-154.

Hubel, D. H., & Wiesel, T. N. Receptive fields and functional architecture of monkey striate cortex. *Journal of Physiology*, 1968, *195*, 215-243.

Julesz, B. Spatial-frequency channels in one-, two-, and three-dimensional vision: Variations on an auditory theme by Bekesy. In C. S. Harris (Ed.), *Visual coding and adaptability*. Hillsdale, New Jersey: Lawrence Erlbaum Associates, 1980.

Julesz, B., & Pennington, K. S. Equidistributed information mapping: An analogy to holograms and memory. *Journal of the Optical Society of America*, 1965, *55*, 604.

Kanizsa, G. Marzini quazi-percettive in campi con stimolazione omogenea. *Rivista di Psicologia*, 1955, *49*, 7-30.

Kelly, D. H. Spatial frequency selectivity in the retina. *Vision Research*, 1975, *15*, 665-672.

Klein, R. Visual detection of line segments: Two exceptions to the object superiority effect. *Perception & Psychophysics*, 1978, *24*, 237-242.

Kulikowski, J. J., & King-Smith, P. E. Spatial arrangement of line, edge and grating detectors revealed by subthreshold summation. *Vision Research*, 1973, *13*, 1455-1478.

Lappin, J. S., Doner, J., Kottas, B. L., & Harris, C. S. Sufficient conditions for detection of structure and motion in three dimensions. *Bulletin of the Psychonomic Society*, 1978,

12, 257. (Abstract)

Lashley, K. S. In search of the engram. In *Symposia of the Society for Experimental Biology,* No. 4, 454-482. New York: Cambridge University Press, 1950.

Limb, J. O., & Rubinstein, C. B. A model of threshold vision incorporating inhomogeneity of the visual field. *Vision Research,* 1977, *17,* 571-584.

Longuet-Higgins, H. C. The non-local storage and associative retrieval of spatio-temporal patterns. In K. N. Leibovic (Ed.), *Information processing in the nervous system.* Heidelberg: Springer-Verlag, 1968.

Mace, W. *An investigation of spatial and kinetic information for separation in depth using computer generated dot patterns.* Doctoral dissertation, University of Minnesota, 1971.

Maffei, L., & Fiorentini, A. The unresponsive regions of visual cortical receptive fields. *Vision Research,* 1976, *16,* 1131-1140.

Masland, R. H. Visual motion perception: Experimental modification. *Science,* 1969, *165,* 819-821.

Matin, E. The two transient (masking) paradigm. *Psychological Review,* 1975, *82,* 451-461.

Matthews, M , Weisstein, N., & Williams, A. Masking of letter features does not remove the word-superiority effect. *Bulletin of the Psychonomic Society,* 1974, *4,* 262. (Abstract)

McClelland, J. L. Perception and masking of wholes and parts. *Journal of Experimental Psychology: Human Perception and Performance,* 1978, *4,* 210-223.

McLachlan, D. The role of optics in applying correlation functions to pattern recognition. *Journal of the Optical Society of America,* 1962, *52,* 454-459.

Mezrich, J. J. Pattern meaningfulness and pattern detectability. *RCA Review,* 1975, *36,* 621-631.

Nelson, J. I., & Frost, B. J. Orientation-selective inhibition from beyond the classic visual receptive field. *Brain Research,* 1978, *139,* 359-365.

Nelson, J. I., & Mitchell, D. E. Response to visual stimuli presented beyond the limits of topographically mapped cortical receptive fields. II. Properties. In preparation.

Pomerantz, J. R., Sager, L. C., & Stoever, R. G. Perception of wholes and their component parts: Some configural superiority effects. *Journal of Experimental Psychology: Human Perception and Performance,* 1977, *3,* 422-435.

Pribram, K. H. *Languages of the brain.* Englewood Cliffs, New Jersey: Prentice-Hall, 1971.

Rosinski, R. R. Spatial frequency analysis and monocular space perception. Paper presented at Association for Research in Vision and Ophthalmology, Sarasota, April 1976.

Sachs, M., Nachmias, J., & Robson, J. G. Spatial frequency channels in human vision. *Journal of the Optical Society of America,* 1971, *61,* 1176-1186.

Schade, O. H. Optical and photoelectric analog of the eye. *Journal of the Optical Society of America,* 1956, *46,* 721-739.

Schwartz, B. J., Harris, C. S., & Patashnik, O. Illusory departures from uniform motion. *Investigative Ophthalmology and Visual Science,* 1979, *18 (Supplement),* 2-3. (Abstract)

Shepard, R. N. Recognition memory for words, sentences, and pictures. *Journal of Verbal Learning and Verbal Behavior,* 1967, *6,* 156-163.

Spoehr, K. Personal communication, 1975.

Stevens, S. S. The surprising simplicity of sensory metrics. *American Psychologist,* 1962, *17,* 29-39.

Tolhurst, D. J. Adaptation to square-wave gratings: Inhibition between spatial frequency channels in human visual system. *Journal of Physiology,* 1972, *226,* 797-804.

Tynan, P., & Sekuler, R. Moving visual phantoms: A new contour completion effect. *Science,* 1975,

Uttal, W. R. The effect of deviations from linearity on the detection of dotted line pat-

terns. *Vision Research,* 1973, *13,* 2155-2164.
Uttal, W. R. *An autocorrelation theory of form detection.* Hillsdale, New Jersey: Lawrence Erlbaum Associates, 1975.
Weisstein, N. A Rashevsky-Landahl neural net: Simulation of metacontrast. *Psychological Review,* 1968, *75,* 494-521.
Weisstein, N. Neural symbolic activity: A psychophysical measure. *Science,* 1970, *168,* 1489-1491.
Weisstein, N. Metacontrast. In D. Jameson & L. Hurvich (Eds.), *Handbook of sensory physiology* (Vol. 7, Part 4): *Visual psychophysics.* Heidelberg: Springer-Verlag, 1972.
Weisstein, N. Beyond the yellow-Volkswagen detector and the grandmother cell: A general strategy for the exploration of operations in human pattern recognition. In R. Solso (Ed.) *Contemporary issues in cognitive psychology: The Loyola Symposium.* Washington, D. C.: Winston, 1973.
Weisstein, N. The joy of Fourier analysis. In C. S. Harris (Ed.), *Visual coding and adaptability.* Hillsdale, New Jersey: Lawrence Erlbaum Associates, 1980.
Weisstein, N., & Bisaha, J. Gratings mask bars and bars mask gratings: Visual frequency response to aperiodic stimuli. *Science,* 1972, *176,* 1047-1049.
Weisstein, N., & Harris, C. S. Visual detection of line segments: An object-superiority effect. *Science,* 1974, *186,* 752-755.
Weisstein, N., Harris, C. S., Berbaum, K., Tangney, J., & Williams, A. Contrast reduction by small localized stimuli: Extensive spatial spread of above-threshold orientation-selective masking. *Vision Research,* 1977, *17,* 341-350.
Weisstein, N., & Maguire, W. Computing the next step: Psychophysical measures of representation and interpretation. In E. Riseman & A. Hanson (Eds.), *Computer vision systems.* New York: Academic Press, 1978.
Weisstein, N., Maguire, W., & Berbaum, K. Visual phantoms produced by moving subjective contours generate a motion aftereffect. *Bulletin of the Psychonomic Society,* 1976, *8,* 240. (Abstract)
Weisstein, N., Maguire, W., & Williams, M. C. Moving phantom contours and the phantom-motion aftereffect vary with perceived depth. *Bulletin of the Psychonomic Society,* 1978, *12,* 248. (Abstract)
Weisstein, N., Matthews, M., & Berbaum, K. Illusory contours can mask real contours. *Bulletin of the Psychonomic Society,* 1974, *4,* 266. (Abstract)
Weisstein, N., Montalvo, F. S., & Ozog, G. Differential adaptation to gratings blocked by cubes and gratings blocked by hexagons: A test of the neural symbolic activity hypothesis. *Psychonomic Science,* 1972, *27,* 89-91.
Weisstein, N., Ozog, G., & Szoc, G. A comparison and elaboration of two models of metacontrast. *Psychological Review,* 1975, *82,* 321-328.
Weisstein, N., Williams, M. C., & Harris, C. S. Line segments are harder to see in flatter patterns: The role of three-dimensionality in "object-line" and "object-superiority" effects. Paper submitted to Psychonomic Society, Phoenix, November 1979.
Weisstein, N., Williams, M. C., & Williams, A. Connectedness and three-dimensionality affect different aspects of the metacontrast function. *Investigative Ophthalmology and Visual Science,* 1979, *18 (Supplement),* 1. (Abstract)
Williams, A., & Weisstein, N. The time course of object superiority with contexts whose local environments are similar. *Bulletin of the Psychonomic Society,* 1977, *10,* 243. (Abstract)
Williams, A., & Weisstein, N. Line segments are perceived better in a coherent context than alone: An object-line effect. *Memory and Cognition,* 1978, *6,* 85-90.
Wohlgemuth, A. On the aftereffect of seen movement. *British Journal of Psychology (Monograph Supplement), No. 1,* 1911.
Womersley, M. A contextual effect in feature detection with application of signal detection methodology. *Perception & Psychophysics,* 1977, *21,* 88-92.

TUTORIAL

The Joy of Fourier Analysis

Naomi Weisstein

State University of New York at Buffalo

.

Maybe you're a person who cringes at the sight of an integral sign and who can never remember whether the abscissa is the tall one, the wide one, or the one that needs to be watered every day. If so, do not despair: You can skip the formulas that lurk here and still pick up a basic familiarity with the language of Fourier analysis. If, on the other hand, you are unruffled by integrals and the like, you may still find what follows to be a useful introduction to (or reminder of) the material in the books listed below and the current literature on vision.

FOURIER ANALYSIS AND FOURIER SYNTHESIS

At the outset, let's distinguish between a Fourier analysis and a Fourier synthesis. When we juggle sine waves, claiming that a pattern can be built up as a sum of sinusoidal gratings of various frequencies, amplitudes and orientations, we are talking about a Fourier *synthesis*. That is, we are talking about components that, when all added up together, will give you the pattern you want. In order to find out what the components of a given pattern are, you do a Fourier *analysis*.

Putting the concept of synthesis in the old cringe-inducing terms, the "general" Fourier synthesis theorem says that any function can be represented over some interval as the sum of a set of other functions, providing that these other functions are *orthogonal* with respect to each other. Orthogonal means that if

365

you take any two functions in the set, multiply them together, and "integrate," you get zero. In other words, after you multiply each point on one function by the corresponding point on the other function, you add up all the products. If the result is zero, the functions are orthogonal. Getting zero at the end of such labor seems like a lot of work for nothing, and that's exactly what it is: Orthogonal functions let you do a lot of work and end up with nothing.

The Trigonometric Fourier Series

Although the generalized Fourier theorem does not call for any special kind of functions, the particular Fourier theorems that vision researchers have been working with use the trigonometric functions. With trigonometric functions, one can rephrase the Fourier synthesis theorem this way: Any function can be described as a sum of sine waves of different frequencies, with each frequency having a particular amplitude and a particular phase. Frequency tells you how often the sine wave repeats per unit something (generally space or time). Phase tells you where in its cycle it starts out. (A peak? That would be a 90° phase angle, sometimes known as π radians. A trough? That would be $-90°$, or $-\pi$, or 270°. And so on.) Amplitude tells you how high it goes.

If the function we want to make is a *periodic* function—that is, one that repeats itself at regular intervals—it can be synthesized from a Fourier series. A *Fourier series* is a set of sine waves that are integral multiples of the lowest, or "fundamental," frequency. So if the function repeats itself p times per unit time or space, the members of the series might have frequencies p, 3p, 5p, and so on.

Periodic Stimuli

Let's translate this into what vision researchers mean when they talk about spatial frequencies. First consider a pattern of black and white stripes of equal width, as shown in Fig. 1a. We can make a graph of this pattern (Fig. 1b) by letting the horizontal axis represent spatial position across the pattern (measured in degrees or minutes of visual angle) and letting the vertical axis represent the relative intensity of the stimulus (for example, from black to gray to white) along a horizontal slice such as the line across Fig. 1a. This is a square repeating function, a *square wave* in the horizontal direction. (The vertical direction doesn't count because one assumes that the bars go on indefinitely in the up and down dimension. So we're looking now at a one-dimensional function.) The bar width is inversely related to the spatial frequency: A black bar and a white bar comprise one cycle, and the frequency is the reciprocal of this cycle width, usually measured in degrees of visual angle (a different kind of angle from the angle that tells you where the sine wave is

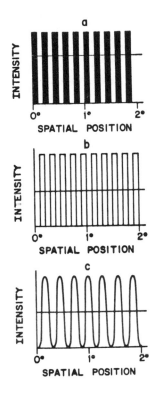

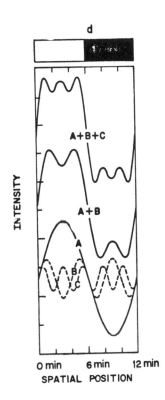

FIG. 1. A square wave grating, and how to make one from sine wave gratings. (a) A square wave grating; (b) luminance distribution of the grating; (c) luminance distribution of a sine wave grating; (d) the addition of sine waves to synthesize a square wave (from Cornsweet, 1970). One cycle of the square wave is shown.

in its cycle). If you have a bar that is 6 minutes wide in visual angle (0.1°), the cycle is 12 minutes wide and there are five cycles per degree of visual angle.

Let's construct this square wave pattern from a sum of sine waves. The sine waves themselves, in the visual version, are sets of light and dark stripes (Fig. 1c). They differ from the square wave in that they change gradually from light to dark, so they look like a blurred version of the square wave grating. To sharpen up the edges of the sine wave so that it looks more like a square wave, one adds sine waves of higher frequencies; these pull the edges of the fundamental sine wave up, as shown in Fig. 1d. Each successive sine wave smooths out the lumps left by its lower-frequency predecessor. If you add up enough of them, each an odd multiple of the original sine wave's frequency — 3p, 5p, 7p,...—you will finally get a nice, square, square wave back.

Aperiodic Stimuli

It is also important to see how one can add up sine waves and get a *single bar* back. This is harder to imagine: How does one get a single bar from a collection of repeating bars? Let's start with the narrowest, brightest single stimulus you can have: a really narrow bar that is also really bright—actually, infinitely narrow and infinitely bright. The procedure for getting it is fairly easy (or at least is easily stated). You add up an infinite number of sine waves all of the same amplitude, and all beginning at the same place in their cycle—that is, all of the same *phase*. The sine waves now vary *continuously* in their frequency, unlike the periodic functions discussed above, where the sine waves that make up the function were integral multiples of the fundamental frequency.

A start at adding up all the sine waves of all the different frequencies but of the same amplitude and phase is shown in Fig. 2a. In most places, all the different sine waves cancel each other out, because some are at their peaks

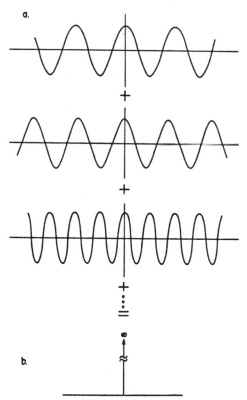

FIG. 2. A narrow bright bar, and how to make it from sine wave gratings. (a) Some of the continuously varying frequencies of the same amplitude needed to make (b) an infinitely narrow, infinitely bright bar.

while others are at their troughs. But at the origin, instead of cancelling, all of the sine waves add up. The sum just increases and increases, as one adds more sine waves. If one went on adding sine waves forever (there are worse things one could do), finally the origin would be the only place where a signal remained—every other place would be cancelled out. Hence you get a narrow bright bar (Fig. 2b) from a sum of different sinusoidal gratings.

In this account, each sinusoidal grating on the continuum is one *Fourier component*. The *Fourier spectra* are the functions that give the respective *Fourier magnitudes* and *phase angles* (discussed below) for each different sinusoid or Fourier component.

For a narrow bright bar at the origin, the Fourier spectra are very simple. All the different sine waves have the same amplitude, so the Fourier magnitude spectrum, which plots amplitude against frequency, is just a horizontal line of constant amplitude. All the sine waves start out at the same phase, 90° (the sine of 90° is 1, its maximum value before it's multiplied by an amplitude), so the phase spectrum, which plots phase against frequency, is also just a horizontal line—the phase is constant. The *Fourier transform* is the function which includes both magnitude and phase information. For a narrow bright bar at the origin, the Fourier transform is a constant. In general, the Fourier transform is a recipe for producing the pattern you want. Also, it's the equation you get when you do a Fourier analysis.

Periodic vs. Aperiodic Stimuli

Now let's consider the Fourier magnitude spectrum of a single bar that is a little less bright and a little less narrow than the infinitely bright, infinitely narrow bar we've just been looking at. The Fourier magnitude spectrum won't be constant any more, because we don't want the sine waves to cancel out everywhere—the bar has a width to it. But the magnitude spectrum won't really change much—a few sine waves will be omitted here and there, and others will be lowered in amplitude by various amounts, so that not everything cancels (Fig. 3, bottom).

Let's compare the bar's magnitude spectrum with that of a grating made up of such bars. In space, they look very much alike: The bar is just a grating that has lost the rest of its bars. But their Fourier transforms are not very much alike. The bar has a continuous magnitude spectrum: Continually varying frequencies have to be added up to synthesize a bar from a number of sine waves. The grating has a discrete Fourier magnitude spectrum: Sine waves must be added up only at odd multiples of the fundamental frequency (Fig. 3, top). Periodic patterns, like the grating, have discrete Fourier components and are described by a Fourier series. Aperiodic patterns, like the single bar, have continuously varying Fourier components and are described by a Fourier integral.

Two-Dimensional Patterns

If a pattern varies in two dimensions (a bullseye instead of a grating, for instance), or if you want to compare two one-dimensional patterns that differ in orientation (a vertical and a diagonal grating, for instance), you need to visualize the transforms in two dimensions. There are various ways to represent Fourier spectra in two dimensions; each way entails certain distortions. Figure 4, though simplified and distorted in several respects, will give you an idea of how to interpret such two-dimensional plots.

Figure 4 shows Fourier transforms for three different fields of the same size. The first field (top) is blank; the second (bottom left) contains a grating made up of bars 2 minutes wide, 15 cycles/degree; and the third (bottom right) contains a single 2-minute bar. Each graph is a polar plot. The farther you go in any direction from the center of the graph, the higher the spatial frequency. The areas of the black regions represent the Fourier amplitudes at those frequencies. (Actually, area represents *power*, the square of the amplitude, and using blobs with different areas necessarily obscures some local details about frequency and orientation.) If you want to look at the frequency spectrum for a particular orientation, you travel along a line drawn from the center and perpendicular to that orientation. Since we are considering vertical bars and gratings, we look at power along the horizontal axis.

Start with the lower right part of Fig. 4, the transform of a vertical bar. It's basically the same as the bottom part of Fig. 3. In Fig. 3, height above the baseline represents power; in Fig. 4, width about the horizontal axis does. The vertical bar has a continuous smear of energy except at the even multiples of

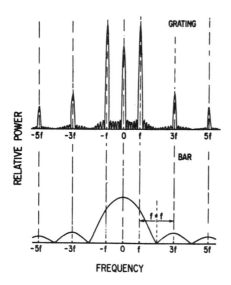

FIG. 3. The Fourier transforms of a grating and a bar. (From Weisstein, Harris, Berbaum, Tangney, & A. Williams, 1977.)

BLANK FIELD (APERTURE)

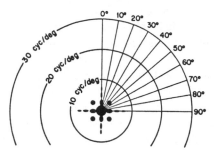

VERTICAL GRATING (5 cycles/degrees)   VERTICAL BAR (0.1° WIDE)

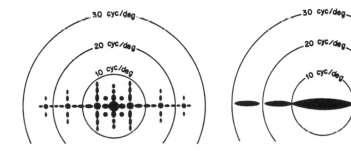

FIG. 4. The Fourier transforms of a blank field, a grating, and a bar, in polar-coordinate graphs. (Details in text.)

the reciprocal of the bar width. (These zero-crossing points are the sine waves you have to get rid of completely from the constant-amplitude magnitude spectrum of an infinitely narrow bright bar in order to change it to one that has some...well, flesh on it.)

The transform of the vertical grating shown in the lower left of Fig. 4 is also very much like the one shown in the top of Fig. 3, though the similarity is a little harder to see with the sharp peaks of Fig. 3 flattened down into circles. In both plots, the points of highest energy are at 0 and at the odd multiples of the grating's fundamental frequency (5, 15, 25, ... cycles/degree). What about the extra little blobs in Fig. 4 (and the little ripples in Fig. 3)? The top plot in Fig. 4 shows where they come from. A blank field—for instance, a bright, square region in an otherwise dark room—has Fourier components too. The Fourier transform of a blank field is called an *aperture function*. Since a square is just a short, fat vertical bar, the portion of its transform that falls along the horizontal axis is just a miniature (low-frequency) version of the bar's spectrum. And since a square is just a short, fat *horizontal* bar, the transform is the same along the vertical axis as along the horizontal. The square also has width when measured in other directions, such as along a diagonal, so it also has

Fourier components at other orientations, a few of which are indicated by the stray dots here. If a grating appears within an aperture, instead of stretching out to infinity, each component is accompanied by a replica of the aperture function. So in addition to a small number of big, widely spaced dots, we have a lot of little ones (which, in a more realistic graph, would be even littler). The transform of the vertical bar should also reflect the aperture function, but that would turn this kind of plot into a rather nondescript blur.

Figure 5 contains four plots that are similar to those in Fig. 4, except that here power is represented by density of stippling instead of by area. (The aperture functions are omitted.) The diagonal bar and grating have transforms that are just like those for the vertical bar and grating, but oriented diagonally. The transforms of the dot and bullseye look quite different from any of the preceding plots, because they have Fourier components at all orientations. The bullseye, like the grating, has widely separated components; the dot, like the bar, has a more or less continuous smear, except for the zero-crossings.

In summary, you can think of the two-dimensional functions as standing perpendicular to the plane of the paper, with wider (or darker) areas farther away from the paper. A Fourier series, such as the grating's, shows up as discrete spots of black; a Fourier integral, such as the bar's, appears as a nearly continuous line.

Phase

I have been talking about different magnitude spectra. Now consider phase, and consider again the example of the small, bright bar. Suppose we wanted to Fourier synthesize this bar—that is, suppose we wanted to produce this bar by

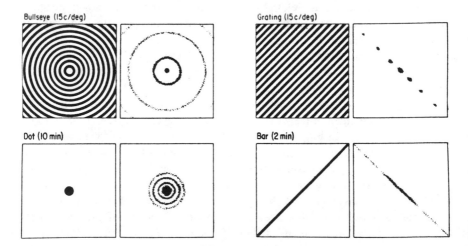

FIG. 5. A bullseye, dot, diagonal grating, and diagonal bar, together with their Fourier transforms. (From Weisstein, Harris, Berbaum, Tangney, & A. Williams, 1977.)

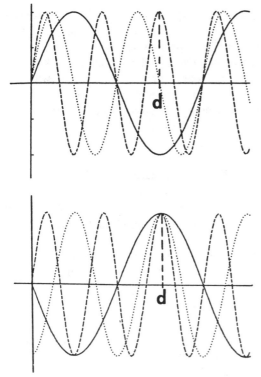

FIG. 6. How to adjust phases in order to synthesize a narrow, bright bar at a distance d from the middle of the visual field.

adding up the infinite number of sine waves it contains, but we didn't want the bar to be in the middle of the field. Rather, we wanted it to be a certain distance d from the middle of the field. In this case, we would do the same thing we did for the bar in the middle of the field, but we would center the sine waves so that each had a maximum at d. Centering the sine wave maxima at d is equivalent to specifying for each frequency a new phase angle at the origin so that they all have peaks lined up at d. This is shown in Fig. 6. Instead of starting the sine waves rolling out at 90°, we set them rolling at whatever place in their cycle (whatever phase angle) insures that all of them will reach a maximum at d. So if a stimulus is shifted some distance d along the x-axis, then its magnitude spectrum remains the same but its phase spectrum changes.

The notion that two stimuli may be far apart and still affect each other follows from this Fourier legerdemain of transforming space into phase angle. The two bright bars at 0 and at d have an identical Fourier magnitude spectrum. We take the same Fourier components, the same set of sine waves. We start out in the same place. We simply shift the phases, so that the sine waves are at different points in their cycles at the start. What this implies is that the sine waves themselves extend a sufficient distance so that we can construct a bar at 0, or at d, or at 2d. In other words, our sine waves overlap; the synthesis, the summation of all the sine waves to produce things like bars, does not result in overlapping stimuli.

This brings us to the concepts of space-domain and frequency-domain representations. The bar itself is a space-domain representation. The frequency-domain representation of the bar is its Fourier magnitude spectrum. In a space-domain representation, stimuli have to look alike to look alike. In a frequency-domain representation, stimuli don't have to look at all alike (in space) to share Fourier components in common. For example, a bar of a certain width has more in common with a field of random squares of that width than with a grating made up of bars of that width.

FOURIER ANALYSIS BY NEURAL MECHANISMS

Earlier I said that the functions that result from a Fourier analysis have to be orthogonal with respect to each other, so that if you multiply two of them together and integrate you get zero. Let's take two of these functions—two *different* functions—and call them F_n and F_m. Because they are functions of x we write them $F_n(x)$ and $F_m(x)$. If you let x vary from a to b, then

$$\int_a^b F_n(x) \cdot F_m(x)\, dx = 0 \qquad (m \neq n; \ a \leqslant x \leqslant b).$$

This expression, cleverly disguised as an integral, exactly describes how a receptive field can behave as a Fourier component.

Suppose we have a receptive field like the one in Fig. 7a, and we give it an input pattern like Fig. 7b—a pattern with the "wrong" frequency. We'll call the receptive field $F_n(x)$ and the input pattern $F_m(x)$. The receptive field is a mechanism that, at every location, looks at the corresponding location of the input function and weights each point by the sensitivity to input at that location. Wherever the peaks of the input function coincide with the peaks of the receptive field, there will be a big positive response. There will also be a big positive response when the troughs of the two functions coincide. But wherever a peak coincides with a trough there will be *inhibition*—a response *below* the spontaneous firing level of the visual system.

Since the functions in 7a and 7b are mismatched, in the long run there will be as much inhibition as excitation. And since the mechanism totals up all the excitation and inhibition, the sum will be zero, or what is effectively zero (spontaneous firing) for the visual system. What this means is that each point of the input function is multiplied by a corresponding point on the receptive-field sensitivity function, and then the products are added. But that's just what the integral in Equation 1 does. The integral sign is just a summation sign, put there for compulsives who want to add up the narrowest possible slices.

The reason you can do a Fourier analysis in the first place is because the functions you choose are orthogonal to each other. When you do a Fourier

a. RECEPTIVE FIELD F$_n$ (X)

b. INPUT PATTERN F$_m$ (X)

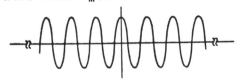

c. COMPLICATED INPUT PATTERN

d. RECEPTIVE FIELD

FIG. 7. Some hypothetical receptive fields and input functions. For the receptive fields, the y-axis is frequency of firing and the x-axis is space; for the input functions, the y-axis is luminance and the x-axis is, again, space.

analysis you tabulate how much of each orthogonal function is present in an input function. Generally, the input function would not be a sinusoid, as in Fig. 7b, but would consist of some more complicated-looking thing, f(x), as in Fig. 7c. But here's the nice part: Since one of Fourier's theorems says that any (reasonable) function can be described as a sum of orthogonal functions—sinusoids, in the example at hand—the receptive field of Fig. 7a behaves the same for *any* input as it does for the input illustrated in Fig. 7b. That is, in any arbitrary function f(x), each component sinusoid that does not match the sinusoid of Fig. 7a will result in an overall firing change of zero. But if there is some component of f(x) that *does* match the sinusoid in Fig. 7a, this will be the only component that won't result in a firing change of zero. So the receptive field in Fig. 7a behaves as a detector of one Fourier component, a point in the Fourier transform: It tells how much of its function, and only its function, is present in the input.

Consider the form of the Fourier integral that gives the Fourier components—this is the Fourier *analysis* integral:

$$F(\omega) = \int_{-\infty}^{+\infty} f(x) \cdot cos(\omega x) \, dx.$$

In this equation ω represents frequency and we now have to add up everything from minus infinity to plus infinity ("I can't believe I integrated the whole thing!"). The cosine here is really just a sine wave that got a late start; it's shifted 90° in phase, so that it has a peak at the origin instead of a zero-crossing. The $\cos(\omega x)$ term for any frequency ω behaves just like the receptive field of a frequency ω, extracting that portion of $f(x)$ which contains frequency ω. For that frequency, the multiplication and integration will result in some non-zero number, whereas for all other components of $f(x)$ we will get zero. Since ω is a continuous variable, the integral tells us how much of *every* frequency is in $f(x)$; to do this in the visual system, we would need receptive fields like the one in Fig. 7a at every frequency.

Another form of the Fourier integral is the one that allows us to do a Fourier *synthesis*:

$$f(x) = \frac{1}{2\pi} \int_{-\infty}^{+\infty} F(\omega) \cdot \cos(\omega x)\, dx.$$

This integral can be translated, more or less directly, into the original statement that you can represent a function by a sum of sinusoidal functions of varying frequencies and amplitudes. You can think of either integral as saying this, or as saying that the sinusoidal part of the integral takes its matching sinusoid out of the function and cancels the rest. It's just two ways of looking at the same thing.

I want to stress that, although in vision research we have been thinking mainly about trigonometric functions, the generalized Fourier series does not have to consist of a set of trigonometric functions. What this means is that if a particular input is represented in the visual system by a set of other functions, this set does not have to be sine or cosine functions. So we should keep in mind that the visual system *might* compute a Fourier representation of a stimulus by encoding it as a set of functions that do not resemble the space-domain representation of the stimulus, but that are not sine waves either.

There is one important assumption that has not yet been stated explicitly, but that underlies the whole concept of Fourier analysis. That assumption is *linearity*. Linearity implies, first, that there is no threshold and no upper limit. If a mechanism responds to a particular input, it will respond to it whether it's very, very weak or very, very intense—and the response will be proportional to the input. Linearity also means additivity: A unit of stimulus energy at a given place makes the same contribution to the overall response, regardless of what is happening at other locations and regardless of the absolute level of stimulation. This is what makes it possible to add functions together and then take them apart again, as in Fourier synthesis and analysis. You can think of a sum of linear functions as a plate of spaghetti. It's always possible to separate each strand and examine it individually (although you might get pretty hungry in the process). The Fourier way of separating strands (functions) is to multiply by individual sine waves. This also makes some people hungry.

Real Receptive Fields

It is clear that a receptive field like the one in Fig. 7a would produce a frequency-domain representation. But that is theory. How would we climb up to the theory from the evidence at hand? Are there grounds for believing that receptive fields actually have the kind of organization that would lead to a frequency-domain representation?

It is highly unlikely that receptive fields such as those illustrated in Fig. 7a will be found in the visual system. But it is not unlikely that receptive fields something like Fig. 7d could be found. Whether these would be good candidates for Fourier analyzers would depend on a lot of things; but the prior question of whether such receptive fields would be likely to occur in the visual system can be answered. Yes. Relatives to these receptive fields have been found already; moreover, from our understanding of visual system organization, receptive fields with a number of side bands seem a very reasonable out come of the several levels of spatially overlapping units in the visual pathway.

Neural Images

To see how this would happen, let's follow a signal through successive levels in the visual system. Suppose we start out with our old aperiodic Fourier friend, the single, infinitely narrow, infinitely bright bar, as in Fig. 8. Let's jump to the ganglion cell layer, and see what could happen to the representation of this bar. Consider only the horizontal direction. Let's assume that all units have the familiar "Mexican hat" receptive-field sensitivity profile in the horizontal direction (shown in Fig. 8, dashed lines), and let's assume extensive spatial overlap. That is, let's assume that every unit has an identical receptive-field sensitivity profile, and that every unit's receptive field—the area of the retina that, if appropriately stimulated, can produce a response in that unit—partially overlaps with its immediate neighbors. (There should also be different receptive-field sizes or sensitivity profiles, but for now let's just consider one single size.)

Overlap is shown in Fig. 8 on the left. The bright bar falls in the center of one receptive field, and to various sides of the other receptive fields. The responses of all units that respond to this bright bar can be thought of as the *neural image* of the bar.

What will this neural image look like? When a receptive field is centered on the bright bar, the unit will fire a lot. As each unit's receptive-field location shifts to either side of the bar, the unit will fire less and less, because the bar will fall on areas of its receptive field that are less sensitive. Finally, the bar will fall on the inhibitory flanks of a unit, and that unit will fire below its spontaneous level.

Figure 8 represents the neural image in two ways. First, the height of each vertical line represents the frequency of firing from a receptive field whose center is at the location of that vertical line. Second, an envelope—the solid black line—is drawn around these vertical lines, to give a clearer picture of the shape of the neural image.

Figure 8 also shows the sensitivity profile of a unit whose receptive field is centered at x_1 (dashed lines). The frequency of firing of this unit is represented, as for the other units, by a vertical line. Since the maximum sensitivity of the inhibitory flank of the unit's receptive field falls directly on the bar, at 0, the frequency of firing of this unit will be suppressed below its spontaneous level. Thus, the vertical line extends *below* the axis.

The neural image that emerges from this first layer when a single narrow bright bar is input is simply a copy of the receptive-field sensitivity profile of the units we are considering. (Because the input is a single narrow bright bar, a mere "impulse" in space, this particular neural image is also called an "impulse response.")

This neural image, or output at layer 1, is now input to the next layer, layer 2. What happens at layer 2? Let's look at a unit whose receptive field is centered this time at x_2. Again, the dashed line around x_2 shows the sensitivity profile for that unit. Now, the main thing to notice about a unit at this particular location is that it will fire *above* its spontaneous level, producing an excitatory side band in the neural image. This happens because the unit's inhibitory flank will not receive its customary input—a spontaneous level of firing from the preceding afferent layer—but will receive less than that. That is, the units which normally fire in the inhibitory portion of this receptive field will have been suppressed, and so there won't be as much inhibition on this unit as there usually is. But, since there will be as much excitatory input as usual, there will be an increase in firing. This will also be true of receptive fields nearby. The neural image has thus acquired an excitatory side band, as shown. It also acquires an excitatory side band on the other side, by the same reasoning. Layer 2, then, will have two excitatory side bands in its neural image, one on each side.

You can go on indefinitely in this fashion. Since the neural image of the second layer now contains two excitatory side bands, at the third afferent layer two additional inhibitory side bands will be produced (Fig. 8, layer 3). The outside inhibitory side bands of the neural image from layer 3 will produce two additional excitatory side bands in layer 4, and so on. In general, there will be 2n side bands for n afferent layers.

Note that side bands appear even though it is assumed that *all* units have the *same* connections. That is, no matter what layer it is in, each unit receives immediate input simply from two inhibitory flanks and an excitatory center. But these flanks and center are affected by stimuli over a considerable retinal distance, once the neural image spreads out far enough. Since each successive

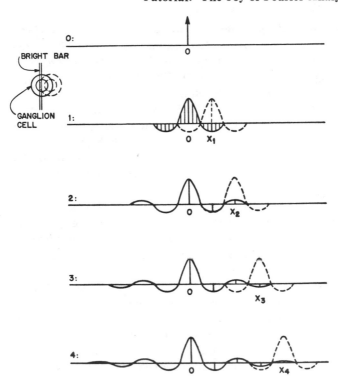

FIG. 8. The appearance of side bands at successive afferent orders. Left: overlapping ganglion-unit receptive fields, with a bright bar falling in the middle of one of them. Row numbers: afferent layers, with ganglion cell layer = 1. 0: A narrow bright bar. 1: The neural image produced at layer 1 by such a stimulus. Each vertical line represents the frequency of firing of a single unit. The solid line is the envelope around these, the "neural image." The dashed line shows the sensitivity profile of a unit centered at x_1. 2, 3, and 4: Neural images at layers 2, 3, and 4. Each pair of side bands is produced as a function of the neural image input from the previous layer.

afferent order spreads the signal out a little more, at each successive afferent order the unit can be influenced by stimuli farther and farther away from the center of the receptive field.

Single Receptive Fields

I have been talking about neural images—the response of all the receptive fields in a particular afferent layer. What does this have to do with a single receptive field? Although this may not seem obvious, the neural image is identical with a single receptive field. Just as the impulse function produced a neural image at layer 1 that imitated the sensitivity of a unit at layer 1, the neural image at successive afferent orders will imitate the sensitivity profiles of units at these orders. In other words, if the neural image has side bands, so will the receptive fields. Think about it this way: If a unit at x_2 fires to a bar at 0, then its receptive field must include 0. This is true by definition: A unit's receptive field is that area of the retina which, if appropriately stimulated, can produce a response in the unit. A unit in layer 4 will respond to a bar at 0; hence, included in this unit's receptive field is the location 0. The unit will also respond to a bar at x_1, x_2, x_3, and x_4: Moving the bar to these locations is equivalent to sliding the center of the neural image over to these locations. As the image center gets closer to the unit, the unit will respond in greater and greater strength.

So far, we have talked only about one size. But this scheme can easily be extended to a number of different sizes. A picture emerges, then, plausible from the data at hand, and possible as a frequency-domain representation: receptive fields that overlap in size and space, and respond to stimulation from a considerably broad retinal area.

As I mentioned before, receptive fields like the one pictured in Fig. 7d have been found, and these are the kind of fields one would expect from the process I've described. Whether the number of side bands so far found is all we're going to find, or whether more looking will uncover more side bands, is not yet clear. Nor is it clear whether units like these will do as frequency coders. But this last is a different question: In many respects it is a psychophysical question (Weisstein & Harris, 1980).

ACKNOWLEDGMENTS

I thank Judith R. Harris for her skillful editing.

REFERENCES

Bracewell, R. *The Fourier transform and its applications.* New York: McGraw-Hill, 1965.

Brigham, E. O. *The fast Fourier transform.* Englewood Cliffs, New Jersey: Prentice-Hall, 1974.

Cornsweet, T. N. *Visual perception.* New York: Academic Press, 1970.

Goodman, J. W. *Introduction to Fourier optics.* New York: McGraw-Hill, 1968.

Pearson, D. E. *Transmission and display of pictorial information.* New York: Halsted (Wiley), 1975.

Weisstein, N., & Harris, C. S. Masking and the unmasking of distributed representations in the visual system. In C. S. Harris (Ed.), *Visual coding and adaptability.* Hillsdale, New Jersey: Lawrence Erlbaum Associates, 1980.

Weisstein, N., Harris, C. S., Berbaum, K., Tangney, J., & Williams, A. Contrast reduction by small localized stimuli: Extensive spatial spread of above-threshold orientation-selective masking. *Vision Research,* 1977, *17,* 341-350.

Author Index

Numbers in *italics* refer to pages on which the complete references are listed.

Davenport, E. W., 269, 280, *316*
David, E. E., 263, *314*
Dawson, B. W., 124, *149*
de Lange, H., 275, *315*
DeMott, D. W., 185, *213*
Denes, P. B. 263, *314*
DePalma, J. J., 270, *315-316*
De Valois, R. L., 127, *145*, 204, 213
Dews, P. B., 18, *47*
Diamond, R. M., 62-63, 65, *66-67*
Dodwell, P. C., 102, 139, *145*
Doner, J., 356, *362*
Dowling, J. E., 3, 18, *50*
Dreher, B., 204, 206, 214
Dubin, M. W., 193, *213*
Duke-Elder, W. S., 23, 29, 34, *47*
Dupuy, O., 183-185, *213*

Earhard, B., 352, 356, *362*
Ebenholtz, S. M., 138, *145*
Efstathiou, A., 104
Ehrenstein, W., 345, *362*
Eimas, P. D., 130, *148*
Ellis, S. R., 128, 133, *145*
Emery, D., 73, *94*
Emsley, H. H., 20, 25, *47*
Enroth-Cugell, C., 184-185, 187, 191-193, 195-196, 198-200, 202-203, *213-214*
Epstein, W., 1, *47*

Ferguson, D. C., 3, 18, *50*
Festinger, L., 138, *145*
Fidell, L. S., 128, 134, *145*
Finke, R. A., 141, *145*
Fiorentini, A., 38, *47*, 196, 202, 206, *214*, 306, *316*
Fischer, B., 201, *213*
Fitch, M., 18, *48*
Fletcher, H., 269, 272, 277, *315*
Flom, M. C., 42, *47*
Flood, D. G., 9, *48*
Frégnac, Y., 12, *48*
Freedman, S. J., 107, 140-141, *145*, *147*
Freeman, R. D., 9-10, 20-24, 26-28, 30, 32, 34, 36, 38, *48-50*
French, J., 44, *48*
Frisch, H. L., 312, *315*
Frome, F., 130-131, 144, *145*
Frost, B. J., 38, *46*, 320-321, *362-363*

Ganz, L., 18, *48*, 353, *362*
Garcia, J., 134-135

Garrett, J. B., 141, *149*
Gentry, T. A., 115, 129-130, *148*
Gibson, A. R., 117, 121, 123-126, 128, *145*, *146*, 276, *315*
Gibson, E. J., 105, *145*
Gibson, J. J., 69, 73-74, *93*, 131, 139, 141, *145*
Giffin, F., 17, 18, *48-49*
Gilbert, E. N., 312, *315*
Gilchrist, A., 142-143, *146*
Gilinsky, A. S., 41, *48*, 272, 310, *315*
Glezer, V. D., 212, *213*
Goodman, J. W., *380*
Gordon, B., 9, *48*
Gower, E., 57-58, *67*
Graham, N., 130, *145*, 190, 205, 207, *214*, 215-261, *261*, 311-312, *315*, 322, *362*
Granger, E., 237, *261*
Gray, F., 284, *316*
Graybiel, A. M., 65, *66*
Green, D. G., 20, 31, 45, *47*, 183, 187, *213*
Greenwood, R. E., 359, *362*
Gregory, R. L., 346, 349, *361-362*
Grigg, P., 3, *46*
Guttman, N., 313, *315*
Guzman, A., 355-356, *362*
Gwiazda, J., 44, *49*

Haegerstrom, G., 21-24, 26-28, 32, 34, 36, *49*
Hager, J. L., 135, *148*
Hajos, A., 76, *93*
Hall, S. B., 141, *145*
Hamilton, C. R., 104, 106, 138, *145*
Hansel, C. E. M., 131, *145*
Hardt, M. E., 72, *93*, 104, 137, *146*
Harmon, L. D., 280-283, *315*
Harris, C. S., 72, 75, *93*, 95-144, *145-146*, *148*, 207, 276, *315*, 317-361, *361-364*, 370, 372, 380, *380*
Harris, J. R., 107-109, 141, 143-144, *146*, *148*, 380
Hay, J. C., 104, 106, 129, *146*
Hebb, D. O., 114, *146*, 324-325
Hein, A. V., 1, 5, 10, *47-48*, 51-66, *66-67*, 72, *93*, 97-98, 138, *146*
Held, R., 1, 5, 39, 44, *48-49*, 52-55, 57-58, 60-61, 63, 65, *66*, *67*, 69-93, *93-94*, 96-98, 104, 106, 137, 141, *144*, *146-147*
Helmholtz, H. von, 2, *48*, 72, *94*, 98-100, 106, 138, *147*, 265-266, *315*
Henry, G. H., 207, *213*

Subject Index

Numbers in *italics* refer to pages that include a definition or other explanation of the entry.

Retinal eccentricity, 201
Retinal ganglion cells, 165-166, 188-203, 218
  ganglion cell image, 200-201
Retinal image, 118, 119, 178-185
Retinal inhomogeneity, 259-260
Retino-cortical pathway, 177, 193
Reversed vision, see Adaptation to reversal
Risley prism, see Prism, variable

Sampling, 186-188, 200, 202, 208
Scattered light, 184-185
Scene perception, 317, 356, 358, 360
Scotopic vision, 65
Self-produced movement, see Movement, active
Sensitivity, *241*
Sensitivity profile, 377-379, see also Receptive field, Weighting function
Sensitization, 151-152, 157-174
Sensorimotor, *136-137*
Shape perception, 74, see also Face and Object perception, Pattern recognition
Sidebands, see Receptive field, multilobed
Simple cells, 117, 203-206, 212, 218, 319
Sine wave (sinusoid), 216, 225, 264-265, 275, 366
  component, see Sinusoidal component
  grating, 216-257, 260, 318, 320-322, 332, 367, see also Sinusoidal grating
Single-channel model, 215-228, 233, 239, 311
Sinusoidal component, 181, 216, 218, 223, 226, 230, 251, 260, 264-265, 318-319, 336, 338, 365, 369, 374-376, see also Spatial-frequency component, Spectrum
Sinusoidal grating, 178, 181-*182*, 192, 197, 270, 272, 274, 277-278, 284, 307, 310, 313, 365, 369-372, see also Sine-wave grating
Size, 216, 319
  aftereffect, 73, 130, 131, see also Frequency shift
Size constancy, 119, 134
Space domain, 284, 306, 309, *323*, 326, 336, 338, 359, *374*
Spaghetti, 376
Spatial frequency, *15*, 73, 76, 134, 216-*217*, *318*, *366*
  analysis, 270, 273, 280, 284, 318, see also Fourier analysis
  channels, 207, 209, 217, 226, 228-261, 277, 283, 294, 305-311, *321*-322, 359
  component, 186, 212, 322, 360, see also

Sinusoidal component
  cutoff, *25*-36, *182*
  domain, 284, 306, 309, 326, 336, 338, 359, *374*, 380 see also Spectrum
  perceived vs. retinal, 118-119
  selectivity (tuning), 118-121, 199, 204-208, 210-212, 272, 276, 320-321, see also Bandwidth
  shift, 275-276
  vs. width, 119
Spatial-frequency-specific adaptation, 118-120, see also Size aftereffect, Threshold elevation
Spatial sensitization effect, 151-152, 157-174
Spectrum, *253*, *265*, 282-285, 312, 336, 338, 369, 373, see also Fourier domain, Sinusoidal component
Spontaneous level, 374, 377
Spread function, 185-187
Spread of masking, 322, 332, 335, 360
Square wave, *366*, 368
Square-wave grating, 273, *322*, 336, 367
Stereoblindness, 40-43
Stereopsis, 2, 40, 45, 76, 78, 296-304, 307
  global, 308
Stereoscopy, chromatic, 88
Stiles-Crawford effect, 185
Strabismus, 5, 40, 43
Straight ahead
  judgments, 106-107, 142-144
  pointing, 103-104, 142-143
Straight-ahead shift, 141-144
Summation, subthreshold, 235, 239-257
Summation within a channel, 231, 234, 237
Superposition, *180*
Sustained cells, 193
Symmetry
  even, 208, 306
  odd, *193*, 208

Temporal factors, 343, 353-355
Test-stimulus detector, *240*-245, 252, 254-255, 257
Texture, 212, 286, 291, 293, 299, 312-313, 325, 327
Third harmonic, *322*
Three-dimensionality, see Depth
Threshold, 158-160, 164, 167-169, 190, 225-226, 228-230, 233-234, 236, 240, 242, 246-247, 249, 256, 259, 272, 275, 311, see also Contrast sensitivity, Contrast threshold, Detection, Sensitization
  auditory, 272